THE FULLNESS OF FREE TIME

Selected Titles from the Moral Traditions Series
David Cloutier, Andrea Vicini, SJ, and Darlene Weaver, Editors

The Vice of Luxury: Economic Excess in a Consumer Age
David Cloutier

Diverse Voices in Modern US Moral Theology
Charles E. Curran

The Structures of Virtue and Vice
Daniel J. Daly

Consumer Ethics in a Global Economy: How Buying Here Causes Injustice There
Daniel K. Finn

Kinship across Borders: A Christian Ethic of Immigration
Kristin E. Heyer

Radical Sufficiency: Work, Livelihood, and a US Catholic Economic Ethic
Christine Firer Hinze

Keeping Faith with Human Rights
Linda Hogan

Humanity in Crisis: Ethical and Religious Response to Refugees
David Hollenbach, SJ

Reimagining Human Rights: Religion and the Common Good
William O'Neill, SJ

Hope for Common Ground: Mediating the Personal and the Political in a Divided Church
Julie Hanlon Rubio

Love and Christian Ethics: Tradition, Theory, and Society
Frederick V. Simmons, Editor

All God's Animals: A Catholic Theological Framework for Animal Ethics
Christopher Steck, SJ

THE FULLNESS OF FREE TIME

A Theological Account of Leisure *and* Recreation *in the* Moral Life

CONOR M. KELLY

GEORGETOWN UNIVERSITY PRESS
WASHINGTON, DC

© 2020 Georgetown University Press. All rights reserved. No part of this book may be reproduced or utilized in any form or by any means, electronic or mechanical, including photocopying and recording, or by any information storage and retrieval system, without permission in writing from the publisher.

The publisher is not responsible for third-party websites or their content. URL links were active at time of publication.

Library of Congress Cataloging-in-Publication Data
Names: Kelly, Conor M., author.
Title: The fullness of free time : a theological account of leisure and recreation in the moral life / Conor M. Kelly.
Other titles: Moral traditions series.
Description: Washington, DC : Georgetown University Press, 2020. | Series: Moral traditions series | Includes bibliographical references and index.
Identifiers: LCCN 2020003727 (print) | LCCN 2020003728 (ebook) | ISBN 9781647120139 (hardcover) | ISBN 9781647120146 (paperback) | ISBN 9781647120153 (ebook)
Subjects: LCSH: Leisure—Religious aspects—Christianity. | Recreation—Religious aspects—Christianity. | Leisure—Religious aspects—Catholic Church. | Recreation—Religious aspects—Catholic Church.
Classification: LCC BV4597.55 .K45 2020 (print) | LCC BV4597.55 (ebook) | DDC 241/.65—dc23
LC record available at https://lccn.loc.gov/2020003727
LC ebook record available at https://lccn.loc.gov/2020003728

21 20   9 8 7 6 5 4 3 2   First printing

Cover design by Erin Kirk.

Chapter 2 is a revised version of "Everyday Solidarity: A Framework for Integrating Theological Ethics and Ordinary Life," by Conor M. Kelly, in *Theological Studies* (published ahead of print). The author gratefully acknowledges SAGE Publishing for granting permission to reprint this work.

*For my wife, Kate,
and my children, Clare and Ryan,
in whose company I have come to
know the fullness of free time.*

CONTENTS

Acknowledgments ix

Introduction xiii

PART I: PRECONDITIONS

1 The Necessary Distinction between Leisure and Recreation 3

2 An Ethical Framework for Everyday Solidarity 31

PART II: APPLICATIONS TO LEISURE

3 Leisure and the Principle of Everyday Solidarity 63

4 Leisure and the Virtue of Everyday Solidarity 83

PART III: APPLICATIONS TO RECREATION

5 Television 111

6 Digital Media Use 133

7 Spectator Sports 157

8 Travel 181

Conclusion 205

Bibliography 219

Index 243

About the Author 249

ACKNOWLEDGMENTS

Every book has a history all its own, and I am struck by how the narrative of this book's genesis is inextricably linked to the people who have been influencing its development—and my own—along the way. I would like to take stock of these relational connections that have led to this book in its present form and to express my gratitude to each of the people who has made this work possible.

First, I want to acknowledge Caitlin Booth Smith, a friend from my undergraduate days whose questions of conscience prompted me to reevaluate free time as an ethical concern. From a dorm-room conversation about how a group of friends ought to spend their fall break, years of research and (finally) hundreds of pages of finished text have emerged. This book is, in so many ways, the explanation I wish I could have given to her thoughtful challenges all those years ago, only I could not do so because I needed all this time and study to realize what was at stake for myself.

Next, I have a number of faculty from my time at Notre Dame whose support and encouragement were integral to my decision to pursue graduate studies in theology, and thus to the realization of this project. I want particularly to thank Daniel Graff, a history professor who first introduced me to the delicate art of crafting a research argument and situating it in relation to existing scholarship. I am also indebted to Margie Pfeil, who—as a teacher, scholar, and Catholic worker—has modeled for me the life of genuine discernment in all things that I want this book to encourage. Finally, David Clairmont has been a most generous mentor, teaching the first moral theology class I ever took, directing the senior thesis that emerged from an offhanded comment in that class, and demystifying the world of graduate studies in theology at exactly the time when I needed it most. It is one of my great pleasures to be coworkers in the same vineyard with this inspiring Catholic man, and I appreciate the ways I still continue to learn from him.

After my time at Notre Dame I pursued doctoral studies at Boston College, where faculty and other colleagues indelibly shaped not only this book project but also my work as a whole. Jim Keenan was the most astute of dissertation directors, prodding me in just the right ways to help me develop my own voice as a scholar. Through conversations with Jim, I was finally able to articulate the concerns for discernment in ordinary life that have become the centerpiece of my work as a theologian and an ethicist, and I can only hope that in this endeavor I will one day live up to the lofty standards set by others who share the luxury of being identified simply and glowingly as "one of Jim's students." I am also grateful for the opportunity to have worked with Lisa Sowle Cahill, whose challenging and provoking assessments of my work in classes, in my dissertation, and beyond have made me a better theologian who is always attentive to the features that make theological ethics distinctly theological. Ken Himes has been an outstanding friend, instilling an ethos of compassion in my teaching and a spark of originality in my scholarship. Beyond the faculty, I benefited immensely from my colleagues in the doctoral program, especially those studying ethics. I want to explicitly thank Dan DiLeo, Chris Jones, and Megan McCabe for their commitment to wrestling through theological quandaries with me as well as their kind friendship during our time in Boston and since. I know I needed both to finish the book now in front of you.

Since completing my PhD, I have had the great privilege of joining the Department of Theology at Marquette University, where the university in general and the department in particular have been exceptionally supportive of my work as a teacher and scholar starting out on the tenure track. For this institutional support, I want to thank the three fine department chairs under whom I have served: Bob Masson, who brought me on board and fought as tirelessly for my protections as a junior scholar as he fought for the well-being of our department as a whole; Susan Wood, who made me feel at home as an officemate and then as a chair championed me; and Danielle Nussberger, who epitomized the combination of leadership and service that we purport to idealize. Among my many excellent colleagues I want especially to thank my fellow junior scholars in the ethics section—Kate Ward, Drew Kim, and Alex Martins—who have helped me shepherd the area. I also would like to acknowledge the late Lúcás Chan, whose encouragement and support set the preconditions for my job offer and whose friendship I anticipated while planning the move. The sudden passing of this gentle soul has left a void that continues to be felt in our department and beyond. I am also keenly aware of the fact that my ability to write this book was due in large part to the ways others have helped me carry my teaching load or lightened it altogether. The former include the graduate students who have served as part of the team-taught introductory course during the time I have been at Marquette, as well as Steve Calme, who was a phenomenal teaching assistant during my first year (and later a member of the team-taught course). The latter include those colleagues who have accepted the contingent status of visiting assistant professors during the last five years, taking on a much more demanding teaching schedule than those of us on the tenure track. I know I am able to do what I do only because of what they do, so I want to offer special thanks to Gretchen Baumgardt, Mark Chapman, Nick Elder, Chris Gooding, Jen Henery, Matt Neujahr, Karen Ross, Krista Stevens, Lee Sytsma, and Kate Ward (who assumed this role for a year).

As this project slowly moved toward publication, I had helpful conversations with the editors at Georgetown University Press—first, Richard Brown; then, Hope LeGro; and ultimately, Al Bertrand. Similarly, the editors of the Moral Traditions Series were consistently encouraging as I went through the growing pains of producing my first monograph, so I want to thank Kristin Heyer (whose term has since ended) for her kind words of encouragement and advice on numerous occasions, David Cloutier for his enthusiasm and reassurance, and Andrea Vicini for his invaluable guidance and untiring patience. Although I have not worked directly with Darlene Fozard Weaver in this context, I have still benefited from the work she is doing to bring great scholarship to press, so I want to thank her too for that service. In the production phase, I have greatly benefited from the work of Hannah Greco and Elizabeth Crowley Webber, and I am particularly indebted to Alfred Imhoff for his exceptional copyediting. Many thanks are also due to Erin Kirk for the fantastic cover design, which so faithfully captures the spirit of this book.

Of course, the people who have the most profound impact on all the work that I do and whose support has made every word in this book not simply possible but also worthwhile are the ones whose connections to me completely eclipse this project. I am therefore honored to be able to close these acknowledgments with a word of gratitude to my parents, Peter and Geraldine, and my brother, Colm, who have all, in their own ways, given me their full support as I embarked on the foolhardy yet rewarding path of pursuing a career built around the life of the mind. My in-laws have also supported this path and this project in ways for which I cannot begin to account, so I offer heartfelt thanks to Jeff Crecelius and express the hope that I can in some small way honor the memory of Pat Crecelius with this published text. Finally, my wife, Kate, has put up with much in support of my studies and work, including the anxieties of a husband who seems set on subjecting his own mundane decisions (and by extension, hers as well) to an agonizing degree of scrutiny. She has borne the burden with mercy and with grace, and for that I am grateful. I am also grateful for the ways our two young children, Clare and Ryan, have tolerated my work on this project at odd hours and in odd ways. As I say in the dedication, they, along with their mother, have made the fullness of free time a reality for me.

INTRODUCTION

Caring about Free Time

In the early 1950s, the legendary broadcaster Edward R. Murrow hosted a new radio series called *This I Believe*, which asked interviewees from all walks of life to explain in a few hundred words one of their core, driving beliefs. The result was a nearly five-year run that provided a window into the convictions that shaped everyday life for people in the United States. Among those interviews was a statement of belief from Oscar Hammerstein II, the famed Broadway musical librettist, who titled his contribution to the series "Happy Talk." His overriding point was that even in the midst of an obviously imperfect world, there remains much goodness to celebrate, as long as one refuses to fixate on the darkness.[1] This is a claim that resonates well with Christian theologians, including major figures like Augustine and Aquinas, who noted that if God is the source of all that exists and God is good, then anything that exists has at least some goodness insofar as it exists.[2] Apart from Hammerstein's theological instincts, however, what stands out the most from his response is the opening assertion that his belief in happiness sets him apart. It is far easier, and thus more typical, he argued, to focus on the things that go wrong, and far less common to recognize the goodness that remains. "It is a modern tragedy," he proclaimed, "that *despair* has so many spokesmen, and *hope* so few" (emphasis in the original).[3]

This book is premised on something of an analogical claim, namely, that free time—defined as "time free from work, obligation, or any other necessary activity"—is one example of the goodness that can be celebrated as a source of happiness, if only people are primed to see it that way.[4] At the moment, however, there is not a robust sense of the goodness of free time. In the public consciousness, leisure and recreation more readily align with binge watching Netflix and laziness than with the sense of something genuinely worthwhile. This view, of course, creates a stark contrast with the sphere of work, the flipside of free time, wherein healthy virtues like productivity and industriousness reign supreme. As a result, there is much greater support for the latter than the former; yet this is not a fair comparison. In fact, it does a disservice to both spheres of life. For instance, the contrast reinforces the assumption that work has an almost absolute value because of its utility, strengthening the culture of overwork that already permeates life in the United States—to the detriment of workers and their families. At the same time, the juxtaposition undermines the very resource that could counteract this fallacy, denigrating free time for its lack of utility instead of allowing its inherent goodness to challenge the prevailing value system. To paraphrase Hammerstein, then, one might say there is a modern tragedy in the fact that busyness has so many champions and free time so few.

Of course, this is not to say that work deserves no support nor to claim that the benefits of free time have been entirely ignored. Work, in the Catholic theological tradition, has an inherent dignity that emerges from its humanity, and this theological vision provides the means to defend the value of work without conflating it with busyness.[5] Furthermore, some theologians have criticized the current US work ethic on its own terms.[6] Other scholars, meanwhile, have produced at least a few apologia for free time, ranging from Brian O'Connor's *Idleness: A Philosophical Essay* to Graham Neville's *Free Time: Toward a Theology of Leisure* and Josef Pieper's classic, *Leisure: The Basis of Culture*.[7]

Such critiques are the exception, not the norm, however, and in the case of the books defending free time, they still leave questions unanswered. The general sense of what free time is and how it can be regarded as a genuine good is still missing from the popular imagination. Just as significantly, there is little indication of how people might turn these criticisms into action in their lives. There needs to be both a higher vision for what free time can become, so that people will assess it in light of its potential rather than its nadir, and a clearer sense of the practical path that ordinary people can follow to achieve this end, so that this lofty potential is not relegated to the fate of dismissiveness that befalls all quixotic proposals. These two concerns serve as the rationale for this book, which seeks to provide a deeply theological vision for the fullness of free time and then explores how the resources of theological ethics, especially the Catholic understanding of solidarity, can help moral agents transform leisure and recreation for themselves and in their communities in order to make this goodness of free time more apparent and more appealing.

Before delving into the specifics of how the book unfolds in pursuit of this transformation, it seems appropriate, and even necessary, to address a basic question that can easily serve as a stumbling block to embarking on this project: Why bother with free time at all? This is hardly a surprising question, especially in the current cultural environment of the United States, given the idolization of busyness just discussed. Behind the question lurk two assumptions. First, there is a sense that free time is insignificant, at least from a moral or theological perspective. Thus, one might readily affirm the need to find more goodness in the world, as Hammerstein suggested, but resist the idea that leisure or recreation provides the best place to look. According to this perspective, there are other forms of goodness that deserve our attention more. Furthermore, if one is already inclined to recognize the darkness (as Hammerstein suggests most are), then an insufficient attention to the value of free time likely appears to be a minor concern. There are ample injustices in the world with more immediate and more obvious detrimental effects on human well-being, so dedicating an entire book to the ethical analysis of free time seems, at best, like a waste of time and, at worst, a distraction calculated to preserve the status quo. The second assumption is linked to this concern, for beyond fears about the insignificance of free time there is also a worry that the ethics of leisure is a patently bourgeois project. Not everyone has access to free time in a meaningful way, so why exert so much energy to analyze something that has a real impact only for the privileged few?

These two concerns, and the larger question they undergird, are quite legitimate, but they are not definitively damning. In fact, much of this book goes on to show that these fears are based on false premises. First, the presumed insignificance of leisure is partly a result of the broader elevation of the totalizing US work ethic, which leaves people ill equipped to evaluate the significance of something that serves no immediately useful end. A central premise of the Christian faith, however, is that value is not confined to utility; otherwise, there would be no way to appreciate the significance of God's grace in creation, nor the miracle of life itself. Free time is therefore important for the way it can contribute to the revitalization of this alternative view of value, strengthening a Christian outlook while challenging a damaging cultural assumption. Assumptions about free time's insignificance are not confined to the prioritization of an unrealistic work ethic alone, however. This view is also supported by the tendency to view free time in isolation from other areas of life. As a discrete topic, free time is fairly limited in its implications for a person's well-being, but a strictly compartmentalized view of ordinary life fails to account for the fact that there is a common agent behind the disparate activities who is shaped by all that they do throughout the day. When the focus shifts from the activity to its effects on the person doing the activity, the significance of something like free time begins to look a little different. With this broader perspective, free time takes on a new moral weight, because it can either reinforce a person's internalization of the values that they theoretically profess to ascribe or undermine that entire process of integration. Far from being insignificant, free time can have a vital part to play in the ongoing development of a person's moral character, and for that reason alone it merits further ethical analysis.

The notion that evaluating free time from an ethical perspective is a bourgeois project is similarly tied to premises that need not be the case. Certainly, access to free time is not distributed universally or equally in the United States today, as chapter 4 discusses in more detail. Yet assessing how one ought to use one's free time only becomes an exclusivist task to the extent that one is unwilling to recognize and address this reality. If, however, one is ready to directly challenge the structural underpinnings of this situation, then an ethics of free time can become more than merely a form of bourgeois navel gazing; it can become a tool for combating the very inequalities of leisure that lead to this objection in the first place. This kind of structural analysis is a consistent thread woven throughout the book, serving as a constant reminder of the need to see the value of free time as a human good and to resist the tendency to treat it as an unnecessary luxury.

For the moment, these comments should provide a sufficient response to the challenges that free time is morally insignificant and too tied to economic privilege to be worthy of analysis. By taking the contrary position that free time has moral significance and can be relevant to all, this book seeks to accomplish two things. First, motivated by the assertion that there should be greater integration of theological ethics, and especially moral discernment, into ordinary life, the book evaluates free time in order to create a practical pathway for connecting faith commitments and everyday concerns. In this sense, free time provides a test case of sorts for a larger proposal about the proper way to move from ethical abstractions to concrete decisions. Chapter 2, which develops a new species of solidarity dubbed "everyday solidarity," constitutes the essence of this methodological proposal, and the chapters in parts II and III, which consider the ethical implications of free time in light of everyday solidarity, illustrate how to apply this framework to ordinary life in practice. Read in this way, the latter parts of the book invite the reader to pose an implicit question about whether similar applications of everyday solidarity could be made to other areas of ordinary life. Ultimately, the conclusion explicitly takes up this consideration, exploring the general implications for theological ethics and everyday life that emerge from treating the evaluation of free time as a test case.

Of course, the book is not just accidentally about free time. Although free time facilitates larger claims about the integration of theological ethics and ordinary life, it is also a theological and ethical concern in its own right. Consequently, the book advances substantive arguments about the proper evaluation of free time from a theological and ethical perspective, contributing new insights to a topic that has received scant attention in the academic literature. Chapter 1, which articulates a distinction between leisure and recreation that carries through the entire book, is particularly significant in this regard, because it presents a robustly theological interpretation of the nature and purpose of both leisure and recreation, establishing the parameters for evaluating how free time ought to fit into the moral life. From this perspective, the chapters in parts II and III illustrate the practical steps that people of faith might take to incarnate these theological claims in their own free time choices, paving the way for a greater realization of the fullness of free time. Like the general claims about the integration of theological ethics and ordinary life, these particular claims about the ethical transformation of free time also address a significant need, because they speak to anyone who wants to improve the quality of their free time—a matter that is of increasing concern as technologies push the boundaries between work and home, creating fewer opportunities for free time and stronger desires for better leisure.[8]

Given the two intertwined aims of this book, readers may choose to approach the text differently based on their specific interests. Specialists, of course, will benefit from the book as a whole, but other readers may find one of two paths through the book more productive. Those who are drawn to the larger question of integrating faith and life will gain the most from reading chapter 2, which lays out the framework of everyday solidarity, and then choosing chapters in parts II and III that appeal to their specific interests, because each one illustrates effective ways to apply this framework to a concrete context in ordinary life. Readers who are more concerned with the specific question of how to evaluate free time ought to read all of parts I and II in order to understand not just the ethical framework of everyday solidarity (from chapter 2) but also the distinction between leisure and recreation and some of its overarching implications. These readers can then select the chapters in part III that address particular forms of recreation about which they would like to think more deeply. Notably, readers in these last two categories can even begin their selection processes now, as the next two sections of this introduction delve more deeply into the rationale for the aims of this book, a concern that speaks most directly to scholars in the field. Though these discussions will provide helpful context for anyone trying to make sense of the book, it is possible that some readers will prefer to stay out of the weeds of these academic debates. In that case, they might find it more helpful to skip to the last two paragraphs of the penultimate section of this introduction, where the unique features of this book are identified, and then to read the final section, which provides additional detail about the book's structure. They can then move on to their chosen pathway through the rest of the text from there.

THE GENERAL GOAL OF ATTENDING TO FREE TIME

At the general level, the rationale for a book about theological ethics and free time is similar to the point made in response to claims that free time is an insignificant sphere of moral concern. That is, free time is not simply a minor activity that has no bearing on the rest of a person's existence. It is, rather, one piece of ordinary life as a whole, and it deserves attention as part of that larger picture. At the general level, then, the rationale for evaluating free time in light of theological ethics comes down to the assertion that theological ethics should attend to ordinary life overall, so it can justifiably attend to free time as part of that broader goal.

The challenge, however, is that the value of that broader goal is not self-evident. Although there have recently been some efforts to bring theological ethics into closer contact with ordinary life—for instance, Julie Hanlon Rubio's finely researched and challenging *Family Ethics*—this is not the norm for the field.[9] The closest one sees to a broad-based acceptance of this idea is in the work of virtue ethicists, whose approach emphasizes the importance of attending to the ways that habits can form moral agents, which in turn highlights the cumulative impact of smaller, ordinary moral choices.[10] Because virtue ethics holds an increasingly larger share of the field in theological ethics, especially in Catholic theological ethics, this view is beginning to have a greater impact; but at this point, the effects of this insight remain in their infancy. More needs to be done to extend theological ethics into ordinary life, and a sustained analysis of free time offers one way to do just this.

Additionally, there is a strong argument to be made that more *should* be done to further integrate theological ethics and ordinary life. This assertion is based on the idea that one's faith convictions ought to have an impact on the entirety of a person's life, ordinary life included. Recall again the *This I Believe* radio series hosted by Murrow. Part of what made the series so successful was the chance to listen to people articulate the fundamental beliefs that they thought served as the core of their identities and shaped everything that they tried to do. Ostensibly, people of faith have religious convictions that serve this function in their lives, but how often do they actually make decisions with these values at the forefront of their minds? Almost certainly not as often as they would like, and arguably not as often as they should. The religious person is, after all, supposed to be characterized by the primary influence of their faith—at least, that is how the influential scholar of religion Mircea Eliade framed the distinction when he insisted that the religious individual is differentiated from nonreligious individuals by a readiness to identify the sacred and transcendent in every aspect of life.[11] If this is true, ethics certainly cannot be immune to this vantage point. On the contrary, ethics must be a decidedly theological task for the person of faith; otherwise, the believer's disposition to the transcendent would be unacceptably compartmentalized. The challenge, however, is that this requires a robust process of moral discernment, and few people are readily equipped to navigate the nuances of their concrete moral choices with a direct connection to their faith.

This should not be seen as a criticism of the faithful but rather as an indictment of theologians and religious leaders, who, particularly in the Catholic tradition, have not regularly viewed support for discernment as the crux of their task, choosing instead to prioritize the provision of clear-cut responses to discrete moral problems.[12] Consequently, most people are left with a sense of how their faith matters for morality in a few distinct areas— for example, sexual ethics and health care ethics—but not much vision for what difference it might make in other areas of life. For most, then, faith has little effect on decisions outside the narrow list of issues that regularly get cast as religious concerns, leading them to appeal to other values in these arenas. The most common values, unsurprisingly, are the ones that are already prevalent in the broader culture, whether these are consistent with a person's faith or not. Thus, in the United States, many Catholics make decisions about work, schools, neighborhoods, money, and free time with the same materialistic standard of well-being and the same individualistic vision of success that characterize the American Dream, despite the fact that the Catholic notion of the common good and the Catholic understanding of human flourishing significantly challenge these narratives. If a person's Catholic faith truly influenced the totality of his or her life, then a Catholic theological anthropology that affirms both the importance of relationality and participation in the common good as constitutive elements of the good life ought to figure more prominently in their decisions. For this to occur, the everyday Catholic would need additional resources to see how these convictions could guide moral discernment in all matters and not just in stereotypically Catholic ones. They would need, in essence, the tools to cultivate a habit of theologically informed moral discernment during ordinary life.

The best way to develop these tools is to help people examine the choices they are already making on a daily basis with more sustained ethical scrutiny. This is a different task than the one so far undertaken by theological ethicists, even those who are attuned to the importance of ordinary life. Take, for instance, Michael Banner, who has explicitly lamented the fact that "moral theology itself... is disinclined to take up the construction of an everyday ethics" and has offered a vision for how it might manage to do so.[13] His focus, however, is on framing everyday life as a whole—that is to say, the entirety of a human life as it moves through the milestones of conception, birth, suffering, death, and burial mentioned in the Christian creedal pronouncements of the life of Christ—rather than on the daily decisions of moral agents. His goal is to produce "an everyday ethics which would sustain and support the Christian imagination of the human" that could be understood in relation to other, non-Christian interpretations of a good human life and thereby guide moral thinking generally.[14] In pursuit of this goal, Banner champions a connection between moral theology and social anthropology, so that the latter can help the former understand how people normally make weighty moral decisions and then realistically develop strategies for shaping these significant choices in a manner that is more consistent with the above-mentioned Christian imagination of the human.[15]

Banner's critiques of moral theology are similar to the ones described here, but his solution goes in a different direction. In part because of his appeal to social anthropology, he advances the development of an everyday ethics built on what one might call liminal moments in a human person's natural existence. These are the major life events that societies already imbue with meaning, and Banner's work seeks to help Christians identify ways that their faith might have an alternative meaning in mind. This is a valuable task, but it still only gets part of the way toward the end of a close and consistent link between faith and ordinary life. Banner's Christian imagination of the human can help provide a distinctly Christian account of the human "life course," and this broader vision can then inform moral agents' thinking about the socially significant, liminal moments they encounter as they move through that life course, but it does not target discernment as a practice per se.[16] This larger meta-ethics question still needs a complementary application process, and one important way to achieve this goal is to address how the same sorts of foundational faith commitments that constitute a Christian imagination of the human can shape daily decisions and not just the ones that arise from facing the "paradigmatically human" experiences of conception, birth, suffering, death, and burial.[17] In fact, one premise of this book is that Christians will not be able to effectively face these weightier choices unless they have already internalized a discernment process that puts faith and morality into regular contact during the more mundane elements of their ordinary lives.

Hence, one can see the general rationale for this book emerge. Evaluating free time from the perspective of theological ethics is justified insofar as it can create a new practice for regularly making decisions in light of faith, thereby contributing to the larger goal of strengthening moral discernment during ordinary life. Within this general rationale, however, there is also a further, specific argument explaining why free time, which is obviously only one aspect of ordinary life, deserves attention when the goal is to transform discernment more broadly. This argument hinges on both the proportion of ordinary life occupied by free time and the relative inattention given to it from the perspective of theological ethics. As a result of both these factors, free time is especially ripe for a more critical evaluation when the end goal is a closer connection between faith and ordinary life.

THE SPECIFIC AIM OF ATTENDING TO FREE TIME

To the extent that ordinary life can be categorized by general activities, free time is unquestionably one of the most significant. Free time occupies the largest chunk of ordinary life after work, yet it is one of the least studied areas of life, especially from a theological perspective. As such, free time is a particularly poignant candidate for incorporation into the larger project of transforming moral discernment during ordinary life because it provides a daily testing ground for any model of ethical evaluation. Also, because free time is not regularly categorized as a place of theological or moral significance, it represents something of a blank slate for the contributions of theological ethics. Because people do not have a host of preconceived notions about how their faith should inform their free time, those who are willing to subject their choices to closer scrutiny will have an easier time cultivating a new form of moral discernment that can be more nuanced than the methods to which they might default in other areas of life. More resources for discernment during free time can therefore have a profound impact on the effort to strengthen moral discernment as a practice for all of ordinary life.

The challenge is to provide resources for discernment in this area of life. There are, as mentioned above, some works that examine free time from a theological or an ethical perspective, but none of these yet do so in a way that can sustain an effective, theologically rooted approach to moral discernment throughout ordinary life. For instance, two scholars have discussed the relationship between leisure and spirituality, providing a theological lens for free time, but unfortunately in a way that limits the links to ethics. Thus,

Paul Heintzman's *Leisure and Spirituality* and his two coedited volumes titled *Christianity and Leisure* present an almost sociological account of how religion does shape leisure rather than a normative assessment of how theology should transform free time.[18] His main normative claim, that leisure should be a spiritual attitude that transforms how one views both work and free time, leads only to a narrow ethical evaluation of leisure that is "limit[ed] . . . to the implications of the Golden Rule for leisure activity."[19] This, of course, is not a bad way for Christians to think about leisure, but Heintzman's discussion of the ethics of leisure does not reveal how this perspective might be applied with any specificity, leaving the movement from this vision to an ordinary practice of discernment underdeveloped.

Similarly, Leonard Doohan's *Leisure: A Spiritual Need* insists that free time serves a necessary function in the spiritual life and suggests a normative vision for leisure as akin to a prayer experience. He leaves readers with some practical advice, but like Heintzman's, it is limited in its application, mainly distilled into a few attitudes and activities that would allow one to enrich one's spirituality during free time.[20] To be clear, there is nothing wrong with either of these approaches in themselves. They both serve an important function in the broader assessment of the links between theology and free time, but they are not sufficient bases on which to develop a robust practice of ethical discernment for this sphere of life, let alone ordinary life more broadly. Largely, this is because the shift to ethics is an ancillary concern for both Heintzman and Doohan, which means that a different approach is still necessary to articulate a detailed vision for the impact of theological ethics on free time.

One essential step in this alternative approach is to connect free time with broader theological convictions, not simply with the sphere of spirituality. Both Leland Ryken and Ben Witherington have done this to a certain extent, but their works still have limits when the aim is to produce a process of ethical discernment that can both yield thorough scrutiny of free time decisions and extend into ordinary life as a whole. Thus, Ryken's *Redeeming the Time* is almost exclusively biblical in its sources, which generates a richly theological interpretation of leisure, but chiefly in a way that points to the most explicit overlaps with the idea of leisure—for instance, the notion of rest or Sabbath.[21] As a result, there is a good sense of how leisure might be understood in the Bible but not much sense of how other aspects of life might be similarly informed by Scripture. Without links to more general theological claims, like the role of grace in the world or the proper understanding of the human person that emerges from theological anthropology, there is a limited basis for connecting theology with other aspects of ordinary life beyond free time. A theological vision built exclusively on biblical claims about rest has the potential to lose sight of the forest for the trees.

Witherington, meanwhile, includes an evaluation of leisure that situates its ethical significance in relation to a larger vision for ordinary life. Drawing on the "kingdom perspective" that he first developed during an assessment of the theology of work, he treats "play" as one aspect of ordinary life that can be transformed by a Christian's desire to embrace the values of the reign of God that were at the heart of Jesus's earthly ministry.[22] In this way, his treatment of free time is part of a much larger claim about the ways that Christian faith should inform the totality of life, but it is still not a sufficient basis for the transformation of moral discernment sought here. First, play constitutes a small portion of his evaluation.[23] As a starting point, this is useful; but of necessity, a short treatment means that many ethical implications of free time remain unaddressed. A more detailed account and a more sustained engagement with the impact of theological ethics on various free time activities are still needed if one wishes to generate a practice of discernment that can reshape ordinary life. After all, moral discernment must occur in one's conscience, where a moral decision is made in light of distinct circumstances and with reference to concrete concerns. Some way of evaluating the details, even if one cannot cover all the eventualities, is essential if moral agents are going to be conscientiously formed for this complex task. Thus, there is a reasonable argument for a longer, more detailed, book-length analysis of free time.

Second, and more important, Witherington's larger vision for connecting faith and ordinary life has a restricted emphasis on personal responsibility, at the expense of an agent's complementary responsibilities to address structural injustices. The proper theological vision for rest, he asserts, amounts to a peaceful confidence in God's providence and in one's salvation in Christ—a sense that only emerges from a personal relationship with Jesus.[24] Also, he explains how "play" can prefigure elements of eternal life in the Kingdom of God, amounting to "an escape *from* reality ... [and] *an escape into the future reality that God intend[s] for us all*" (emphasis in the original).[25] Though both these claims parallel arguments made in this present book about the theological purpose of leisure, they do so in the service of a broader vision that has the effect of forestalling a complete analysis of one's moral obligations. Specifically, the sense that play is a form of escape can quickly turn this part of free time into a message of political quietism that tells the oppressed to suffer through injustices now because they have access to "an eschatological better day when things go right."[26] Although Witherington does not explicitly argue for this position, there is not an evident sense of attention to the ways that structural sin might be behind the sufferings people otherwise use play to escape, and as a result there is an implicit sense that free time fits into a kingdom perspective for ordinary life as a whole chiefly through a form of personal conversion that shifts the way one sees the world individually without necessarily requiring an effort to challenge the imperfections of that world along the way. Though personal conversion is absolutely essential for any truly Christian ethic of ordinary life, so too is an attention to structural concerns, because the effects of social structures are an unavoidable part of everyday life, and one's complicity in sinful social structures is a question that conscience cannot ignore.[27] This is especially true in the sphere of free time, where an inattentiveness to the structural forces shaping access to free time has the potential to turn the ethics of free time into the bourgeois project described above. At the moment, this is precisely what is missing from the efforts to link ethics with free time, in Witherington's work and beyond.[28]

The last major work to assess free time theologically, Neville's *Free Time*, is more comprehensive in the aspects of leisure that it explores, but it still proceeds in something of a piecemeal fashion as it captures boredom, play, imagination, and other elements of free time. As a result, it is not as easy to move from Neville's theological vision to a plan for a consistent form of ethical discernment throughout ordinary life. The challenge is amplified by Neville's willingness to treat leisure as "an area of human life which is beyond morality."[29] Notably, he does not mean that leisure has no ethical importance; in fact, he explicitly notes that one's free time choices are socially conditioned, and for this reason he encourages attention to "the framework within which the individual enjoys freedom of choice—a framework which includes structures of employment for those who provide the facilities necessary for each particular leisure activity or even its equipment."[30]

In this way, Neville shows some deference to the structural dimensions shaping free time, and he indicates that free time does indeed have ethical significance. Nevertheless, he still insists that leisure is beyond morality insofar as it serves as an end in itself, which leads him to assert that it should not be subject to the same kind of scrutiny that one would apply to more instrumental choices, which have moral value in relation to the legitimacy of the ends they are chosen to serve. For Neville, the moral value of leisure comes from its inherent goodness, not from its place in a larger teleological chain.[31] Although affirming the intrinsic value of at least some elements of free time is essential (as discussed in more detail in chapter 1 below), Neville's model for doing so creates an artificial separation between the way one ought to think morally about free time and the way one ought to approach moral choices in other areas of life. Such a division obviously frustrates the desire to use ethical discernment in free time as a training ground for revitalizing ethical discernment in the rest of life. There needs to be a different approach.

In light of these limits in existing assessments of free time, this book seeks to advance the conversation about the value and significance of free time from the perspective of theological ethics. Because the intent is both to enrich free time so that it can reach its full potential and to strengthen moral discernment more broadly, this book offers several new dimensions that extend the results of existing work. First, it takes care to distinguish between two major categories of free time activities, allowing for a more nuanced account of the theological purposes free time can serve.[32] This makes the analysis more realistic and more relatable, which paves the way for a greater impact on the practice of moral discernment. Second, the theological vision for free time is complemented by an ethical framework for ordinary life as a whole that is rooted in a robustly theological anthropology. This creates a theological standard by which to assess the moral value of various free time pursuits while also guaranteeing that the skills cultivated in this process can have relevance beyond the sphere of free time. Third, the application of this standard facilitates a deep analysis of specific free time activities, a task that is especially prominent in the book's last four chapters. This depth helpfully illustrates how discernment in conscience can actually shape practical decisions about free time and how it can proceed in the concrete circumstances of ordinary life more generally. Fourth, this book is explicitly attentive to the structural dimensions of morality in free time, directly highlighting the moral agent's responsibility to attend to the structural injustices undermining people's access to high-quality free time and to the structures of sin that negatively constrain specific free time pursuits. This emphasis prevents the ethics of leisure from devolving into a bourgeois project, ensuring that the theological vision for fuller human flourishing through the proper enjoyment of free time is accessible to all.

These four characteristics set the contributions of this book apart and direct its efforts toward the revitalization of moral discernment as a practice for ordinary life. They thus represent the specific argument for crafting a book about the theological ethics of free time. At the same time, these four dimensions also point to a fifth one that speaks both to the distinctiveness of this book in relation to other works on the theological or ethical significance of free time and to its specific justification. This dimension is an intentionally Catholic thrust to the theological and ethical evaluation of free time. To date, no other work has explored the theological importance of free time with explicit reference to the contributions of the Catholic theological tradition, although many have incorporated elements of Catholic theology as part of a broader discussion of the impact of Christian claims on leisure. Catholic sources are therefore brought to bear on the theology of free time in this book as a way of addressing this lacuna, and the Catholic moral tradition clearly informs the ethical framework of everyday solidarity and the vision of moral discernment that shape the analysis of specific free time pursuits.

Although intentional, this appeal to Catholic resources is not designed to be parochial. Instead, the tradition of Catholic social teaching and Catholic insights into theological anthropology are used in a way that also incorporates ecumenical interlocutors, so this project should have relevance beyond the lives of committed Catholics. Indeed, insofar as these claims reflect an account of what it means to flourish as a human being, the arguments developed in this book should be both accessible and applicable to the proverbial category of "all people of goodwill."[33] Nevertheless, this book represents a work of Catholic theological ethics, so it will discuss how the vision for ethical discernment during free time, and by extension throughout the remainder of ordinary life, can serve as a resource for Catholics seeking to live out their religious commitments more faithfully in everyday ways. The hope is that by expressing this task in relation to one particular tradition, it can remain accountable to a consistent theological vision while still yielding benefits to those outside the tradition who would like to use these claims to subject their own interpretations to more critical scrutiny.

THE STRUCTURE OF THIS BOOK

With this account of both the general and specific rationales behind the analysis of free time in place, it is useful to finally provide more details about the structure of this book as it serves these two ends. The book has three parts. Part I, which has two chapters, provides the broader theological and ethical claims that allow the analysis of free time to generate a meaningful connection between theology, ethics, and ordinary life. Thus, chapter 1 defines leisure and recreation as two distinct terms and then develops an appropriate theological vision for each one. Noting that these theological visions are not going to be sufficient, on their own, to guide every moral choice in the sphere of free time—let alone to shape ethical discernment in ordinary life more broadly—chapter 2 develops an ethical framework for connecting Catholic theological anthropology with everyday moral choices. Based on the Catholic understanding of solidarity, this framework orients moral discernment to the human person's full flourishing as a relational creature made in the image and likeness of a relational God, proposing a twofold standard of "everyday solidarity" as a principle that can guide personal moral discernment and a virtue that will prompt work for social transformation. With these two pieces, part I provides the theological and ethical basis for scrutinizing free time more carefully.

Part II applies the theological and ethical resources developed in part I to the sphere of leisure. Chapter 3 discusses how moral agents might make choices about various leisure pursuits when they have both the theological vision for leisure and their relational identity in mind. This analysis results in the suggestion to prioritize leisure over recreation by means of an ordering of leisure that is based on an analogical application of the traditional Christian ordering of love. Chapter 4 then addresses the structural constraints affecting people's access to free time in general and to high-quality leisure pursuits in particular, elucidating practical reforms that agents can champion in the sphere of work to ensure that neither free time nor the ideal of leisure become luxury goods.

Part III of the book turns to the ethics of recreation, addressing television, digital media, spectator sports, and travel with their own chapters. In each case the principle of everyday solidarity serves as a tool to highlight the morally relevant factors one ought to consider in conscience when assessing these pursuits with relational flourishing in mind. The virtue of everyday solidarity then outlines how these personal concerns must also extend to structural reforms so that the kind of flourishing one ideally seeks in recreation is not only an exclusive good designed to honor one's responsibilities for self-care but also a more broadly accessible good that accords with one's obligations for justice.

The brief conclusion summarizes these arguments and then reconnects the specific discussions about ethical discernment during free time to the larger aim of cultivating a new practice of theologically informed ethical discernment throughout ordinary life. This argument, unsurprisingly, emphasizes the ways in which the skills developed to apply the framework of everyday solidarity during one's free time transfer into other areas of ordinary life like work and health. In the end, then, this book should leave the reader with two takeaways. First, by offering a positive vision for the full potential of free time alongside a detailed account of the process of ethical discernment that will lead people to that end, this book should correct some of the contemporary imbalance between busyness and free time. Second, by linking its process of ethical discernment to the broader concerns of ordinary life, this book should also generate the resources for a closer connection between the goodness of faith and the challenges of ordinary life. Both these contributions, hopefully, will help the reader see the many ways in which God's grace is already breaking into ordinary life—so that, like Hammerstein, she or he will find it easier to see the goodness and to celebrate it, in free time and beyond, than to dwell on the obvious imperfections that nonetheless persist. May this be a pathway to that fuller vision.

NOTES

1. Hammerstein, "Happy Talk," 106–8.
2. Augustine, *Confessions*, VII.xii.18; Aquinas, *Summa Theologiae*, I-II.18.1.c (hereafter *ST*).
3. Hammerstein, "Happy Talk," 106.
4. Goodale and Cooper, "Philosophical Perspectives," 33.
5. John Paul II, *Laborem exercens*, 6.
6. The writings of Jonathan Malesic on this point stand out, for both their precision and their theological substance. See, e.g., Malesic, "When Work and Meaning Part Ways"; and Malesic, "Taming the Demon."
7. O'Connor, *Idleness*; Neville, *Free Time*; Pieper, *Leisure*.
8. Commercial Café, "Work-Life Balance Survey."
9. Rubio, *Family Ethics*.
10. See Kotva, *Christian Case*, 37; Keenan, *Virtues*; and Austin and Geivett, *Being Good*.
11. Eliade, *Sacred and the Profane*, 11–16.
12. Kelly, "Role of the Moral Theologian," 934–40.
13. Banner, *Ethics*, 6.
14. Banner, 23.
15. Banner, 24.
16. Banner, 5.
17. Banner, 2.
18. Heintzman, *Leisure and Spirituality*; Heintzman, Van Andel, and Visker, *Christianity and Leisure, Volume 1*; Heintzman and Van Andel, *Christianity and Leisure, Volume 2*.
19. Heintzman, *Leisure and Spirituality*, 209–13, at 211.
20. Doohan, *Leisure*, 87–95.
21. Ryken, *Redeeming the Time*, 165–69, 177.
22. See Witherington, *Work*.
23. Witherington, *Rest of Life*, chaps. 1 and 2.
24. Witherington, 29–30.
25. Witherington, 56.
26. Witherington, 57; see also 62.
27. On the Catholic Church's recognition of the importance of incorporating a structural analysis into ethics and conversion, see Baum, "Structures of Sin," 111–12. For more details on the influence of these structural forces see Finn, "What Is a Sinful Social Structure?" On the importance of thinking about both personal conversion and structural transformation together in the moral life, see Sievernich, "Social Sin," 60–61.
28. For instance, one reviewer of O'Connor's defense of idleness critiqued his work for its failure to "address the reality of structural inequality under capitalism, which most determines who can afford to be idle and who is forced to be idle." Shippen, "Review of *Idleness*."

29. Neville, *Free Time*, 25.
30. Neville, 79.
31. Neville, 27–28, 30–31; more broadly, see also 25–43.
32. This is not to say that other works have no distinctions. Witherington, for example, distinguishes "rest" from "play" in a way that mirrors the differences between leisure and recreation advocated here. Nevertheless, the basis for the distinction and the significance of it is different in this book. Witherington, *Rest of Life*, 41–43.
33. This is a common formulation in Catholic social teaching documents. See Himes, "Introduction," 5.

PART I
Preconditions

CHAPTER 1

The Necessary Distinction between Leisure and Recreation

At the heart of free time lies a simple distinction: leisure and recreation are not the same thing. Certainly, they both fit within the larger category of free time, which again encompasses "time free from work, obligation, or any other necessary activity."[1] Within this larger genus, however, leisure and recreation are two distinct species. This division is quite common in academic analyses, where leisure and recreation are regularly distinguished from each other, using a split between means and ends. The terminology is not always uniform (e.g., leisure is sometimes collapsed into "play") and the divisions are not absolute (e.g., one person's leisure pursuit might be another person's recreational activity), but scholars of leisure studies generally define leisure as those free time activities that serve valuable ends in themselves and then equate recreation with free time pursuits that provide means to more worthwhile ends.[2] From a theological perspective, this distinction is quite informative. Indeed, as this chapter explains, the distinction between leisure and recreation is a necessary one, for it creates the conditions for a more nuanced analysis of free time, yielding a more comprehensive account of the theological and ethical significance of free time as a whole. In particular, the traditional alignment of leisure with ends and recreation with means indicates that the two types of free time activity have different theological values and therefore different ethical consequences. The point of this chapter is to develop this distinction and explore these differences so that a fuller appreciation of the theological significance and ethical potential of free time can be developed in the rest of the book.

In effect, this chapter defines the terms that recur throughout the book, establishing the two major categories that are analyzed during the practical evaluation of free time in parts II and III. Although the definitions of leisure and recreation developed here are shaped by existing scholarship in leisure studies and philosophy, this chapter does not adopt any of the current descriptions of leisure or recreation in isolation but instead constructs a distinct definition of leisure by appealing to the psychological conception of "flow" before identifying recreation as the mirror image of this free time category. Though not developed arbitrarily or in isolation from the work of others, the definitions of leisure and recreation presented in this chapter and used throughout the book are nonetheless novel, so readers should pay particular attention to the substance of the constructive definition of leisure and the corollary definition of recreation articulated in the first section of this chapter. With those definitions in mind, the second section of this chapter delves into the theological implications of these definitions, building on a parallel with Augustine's famous distinction between using and enjoying to establish two different theological values for leisure and recreation that fittingly reflect their complementary definitions. The fundamental takeaway from chapter 1 is therefore unique definitions of leisure and recreation that highlight not just a theoretical distinction but also a theological one, creating the parameters for the subsequent analyses of leisure's and recreation's ethical significance in parts II and III of this book.

THE THEORETICAL DISTINCTION BETWEEN LEISURE AND RECREATION

Although a distinction between leisure and recreation is not uncommon, unfortunately, there are no standard definitions of these terms. Consequently, one cannot appropriate a textbook definition for leisure or for recreation from an existing field of study.[3] This is not to suggest, however, that existing scholarship has nothing to say about the distinction between leisure and recreation. On the contrary, as this chapter shows, there is much to be gained from the work others have done reflecting on the nature and purpose of leisure and its relation to recreation. Nevertheless, that work does not answer all the questions.

In the context of this book, the lack of agreed-on definitions is not entirely a liability, because it creates the opportunity to develop an understanding of leisure and recreation that better serves the task at hand. From this perspective, leisure and recreation do not need to be identified definitively, because heuristic definitions will work just as well for the purpose of analyzing these categories of free time in light of theological ethics. Hence, one need not parse out minutely detailed definitions of leisure and recreation that account for every possible application of the two. Instead, leisure and recreation can be defined in relation to each other. The best way to do this is to treat leisure and recreation as the two general categories that together constitute the whole of free time. Then, within the confines of free time, leisure and recreation become mirror images of one another: that which is not leisure is recreation, and vice versa. Effectively, this strategy means that only one of these two categories needs a concrete definition, for the other can be specified as a remainder concept. This is an especially appropriate strategy when one is concerned with a theological and ethical evaluation of free time as a whole, for a part/remainder distinction ensures that no piece of free time escapes that evaluation. For these reasons, this book defines the distinction between leisure and recreation using the idea of a direct definition for one and a remainder concept for the other.

Theoretically, both leisure and recreation are viable candidates for delineation. Analyzing each is equally important for a full assessment of free time, so there is no preexisting rationale for making one the remainder concept over the other. Practically, however, leisure is easier to define because so much of the existing literature has focused on analyzing some element of free time under this category heading. As a result, this chapter spells out a concrete definition for leisure and then introduces recreation as the concept that captures all other free time activities.

Existing Definitions of Leisure

Simply focusing on the term "leisure," there are still various potential definitions to consider, but some hold more promise than others. For instance, the psychologist and leisure studies scholar Seppo Iso-Ahola explains that typical definitions of leisure fall into one of two categories: those that seek to describe leisure "objectively" and those that seek to interpret the phenomenon "subjectively." Although one might hope for an objective definition of leisure that would apply universally and therefore help to differentiate leisure and recreation consistently, Iso-Ahola indicates that the objective approach reduces leisure to "time left over after work."[4] This description too quickly elides leisure and free time more generally, which means that the objective approach is inappropriate for the present project, because the whole purpose of defining leisure in relation to recreation is to add nuance to the understanding of free time.

Unlike attempts to describe leisure objectively, the efforts to articulate a subjective definition of leisure are much more fruitful for the present purposes. In Iso-Ahola's typology, the subjective understanding of leisure hinges on "a person's own perception and inference of quality and quantity of activities."[5] To develop this point, Iso-Ahola appeals to John Neulinger's pioneering work on the social psychology of leisure, which asserted that leisure activities could be defined subjectively with specific reference to a person's perception of freedom and their sense of intrinsic motivation.[6] In this view, leisure depends on the individual agent's sense that they freely choose to engage in an activity and that the activity is pursued for its own sake, as an end in itself. Both these criteria have roots in more traditional interpretations of leisure. For instance, the importance of freedom aligns with the etymology of "leisure" in English, which "seems to have been more directly related to the Latin *licere*, meaning 'to be permitted' or 'to be free.'"[7] Originally, the freedom or license referred to the liberty of the upper classes, whose wealth and social status freed them from the need to work set schedules and permitted them to pursue less strictly utilitarian activities.[8] Obviously, this more objective account of freedom is hard to transpose into a modern context, where "the leisure class" is not as distinct as it once was and where leisure remains a possibility for people with more limited freedoms.[9] Neulinger's appeal to *perceived* freedom nevertheless offers a caveat that allows one of the original elements of leisure to apply today. His qualification is essential, for there are numerous ways in which a person's "free" choices about how to spend their free time are influenced, if not outright constrained, by the forces of cultural habit and social expectation.[10] By interpreting freedom more subjectively, Neulinger preserves the place of freedom in the definition of leisure without having to presume a type of absolute freedom that is unrealistic in the face of contemporary social and cultural pressures.

Just as the notion of perceived freedom is an obvious extension of earlier understandings of leisure, so the criterion of intrinsic motivation also has parallels with classical interpretations. Indeed, Aristotle's examination of leisure in his *Politics* stressed its intrinsic value, contrasting leisure with business on the grounds that "leisure seems itself to contain pleasure and happiness and felicity of life" and therefore "is more desirable and more fully an end than business."[11] Hence, Sebastian de Grazia concluded that the "distinguishing mark" of leisure in the classical Aristotelian sense is its intrinsic value. "Leisure," he argued, "is a state of being in which activity is performed for its own sake or as its own end."[12] Other scholars regularly note that this sense of intrinsic motivation is the hallmark of leisure in the classical (Greek) interpretation.[13] Neulinger's emphasis on intrinsic motivation thus links his definition of leisure to a much larger tradition, helpfully opening up a trove of potential resources for the analysis of leisure.

Overall, Neulinger's two criteria for leisure present a viable definition of the concept that faithfully captures the essential elements that are traditionally ascribed to leisure. Despite these advantages, Neulinger's subjective approach still does not yield a truly discrete account of leisure. Certainly, the criteria of perceived freedom and intrinsic motivation create boundaries, allowing one at least to assert that certain free time pursuits are not forms of leisure. This is not an insignificant development, especially when one aims to delineate leisure from recreation, but the mere establishment of a boundary leaves a lot of open space within the concept of leisure. Neulinger acknowledges this when he uses his two criteria to create a "paradigm of leisure" that includes six categories. Although three of the categories fall into "nonleisure" because they encompass activities done under the experience of perceived constraint, the sphere of leisure still covers three distinct categories defined by whether a person's motivation is fully intrinsic, fully extrinsic, or some combination of the two.[14] As a result of this taxonomy, "pure leisure" is restricted to activities that are freely chosen and intrinsically motivated, which amounts to "an ideal to be striven for, but hardly ever attained."[15] This is the closest one comes to a succinct definition of leisure using Neulinger's criteria, but it is, in Neulinger's own assessment, a rather unrealistic goal. But this type of idealization is not unique to Neulinger's criteria. Instead, idealization can be understood as a feature of the subjective approach to leisure more broadly.

To understand the tendency toward idealization, consider another significant attempt to assess leisure subjectively, Josef Pieper's *Leisure: The Basis of Culture*. Pieper's work included a resolute rejection of the objective interpretation of leisure and a bold defense of the subjective approach, proclaiming, "Leisure, it must be clearly understood, is a mental and spiritual attitude—it is not simply the result of external factors, it is not the inevitable result of spare time, a holiday, a week-end or a vacation."[16] Pieper built on this assumption to describe leisure in emphatically idealistic terms. "Leisure is only possible when a man is at one with himself," he asserted, "when he acquiesces in his own being."[17] He aligned leisure with contemplation, but in a fashion that envisioned the contemplative prowess of an ascetic, insisting that leisure "is not only the occasion but also the capacity for steeping oneself in the whole of creation" and being right with God.[18] In essence, he argued, the point of leisure is to allow the person simply to be, making the experience of leisure both human and superhuman.[19] Certainly, Pieper did not think leisure in this sense was unattainable—after all, he described it as the wellspring from which all culture has come. Nevertheless, there is something of the ideal in his vision, especially for a contemporary context where the skills for contemplation, and indeed for simply being, have eroded as a result of the fast-paced world of constant technological contact.[20] Perhaps the clearest illustration of this challenge is a 2014 study that asked participants to sit with their thoughts for fifteen minutes in a room that had no stimuli except the possibility of self-administering an electric shock. Everyone participating in the study experienced the shock in advance, and most of the participants (forty-two out of fifty-five) indicated that the experience was so unpleasant that they would pay money to not be subjected to the shock a second time. Nonetheless, when left alone with their thoughts, one-quarter of the women and two-thirds of the men still chose to shock themselves again. In other words, "simply being alone with their thoughts for 15 min[utes] was apparently so aversive that it drove many participants to self-administer an electric shock that they had earlier said they would pay to avoid."[21] Given this sort of empirical data, the spirit of contemplation and the aim of simply being that Pieper envisioned for leisure undoubtedly represent more of an idealistic than a realistic goal.

As Neulinger and Pieper show, subjective definitions of leisure tend toward the ideal. To some extent, this is an asset rather than a liability for assessing the theological and ethical significance of leisure. After all, one of the reasons for bringing theology into contact with this sphere of life is to allow free time to achieve its fullest potential. An idealistic understanding of leisure serves this goal quite well, setting a high standard by which one's existing free time pursuits can be examined more critically. Furthermore, an idealistic vision for leisure is more tolerable when one recognizes that leisure is not meant to capture the whole of free time. By pairing leisure with recreation, one can combat the assumption that every free time pursuit has to rise to the level of the ideal. Thus, insofar as recreation has its own distinct value and can therefore affirm the worthwhile nature of those free time pursuits that fall short of the ideal, leisure can serve as the loftier goal for which people continue to strive.

Nevertheless, there are limitations. This strategy can still be undone by an excessively idealistic understanding of leisure. A balance must be struck, for if the leisure ideal is too far removed from the experience of ordinary life, it can no longer serve as an adequate guide for free time. In all likelihood, people will dismiss the ideal of leisure as unattainable and settle for recreation instead, which would undermine the larger goal of subjecting free time to critical scrutiny so that it might better live up to its true potential. The challenge, then, is to define leisure not just as an ideal but also as a realistic ideal. The subjective approach found in the existing literature provides the resources needed for this task, but not the specificity. Consequently, the theological and ethical analysis of free time demands a more constructive definition of leisure, which will need to move beyond existing scholarship without ignoring it.

A Constructive Definition of Leisure

Given the benefits and the shortcomings of existing definitions of leisure, a new constructive definition needs to serve two purposes. First, the new definition needs to preserve the useful insights from existing definitions. Chiefly, this means adopting the ideal nature of leisure found in subjective approaches. In order to do this, the constructive definition must maintain the link between leisure and intrinsic motivation, because this connection is the source of leisure's idealistic value in the subjective definitions. Second, the constructive definition must move beyond the limitations of the existing understandings of leisure by closing the gap between the idealization of leisure and the practical possibilities of ordinary life. The best way to do this is to add specificity to the notion of leisure's intrinsic motivation in order to turn this essential element of leisure into something discrete and identifiable, thereby making the ideal more attainable.

Within these parameters, leisure can be defined in a more productive way by linking its ideal elements with the psychological concept of "flow." First identified by the psychologist Mihaly Csikszentmihalyi in the 1970s and then refined throughout the 1980s, the idea of flow refers to "optimal experience," when a person achieves a complete—if fleeting—state of psychological fulfillment. In effect, flow is a way of analyzing and describing the experience of happiness in psychological terms.[22] It was identified during Csikszentmihalyi's research into the psychological states of ordinary life, which revealed that despite vast cultural differences, almost all participants in his studies described their happiest moments in nearly identical terms.[23] Specifically, people reported being so caught up in the experience that they felt what they typically described as a sensation of being carried away by the experience at hand. Hence, Csikszentmihalyi referred to "this state [as] the *flow experience*, because this is the term many of the people we interviewed had used in their descriptions of how it felt to be in top form: 'It was like floating,' 'I was carried on by the flow'" (emphasis in the original).[24] As it turns out, this state of optimal experience has a great affinity with the understanding of leisure that emerges from more subjective definitions, especially in their emphasis on intrinsic motivation. Through these parallels, the notion of flow can add specificity to the description of leisure, facilitating the development of a new constructive definition that transforms leisure into an attainable ideal.

In order to understand how Csikszentmihalyi's concept of flow can yield this substantive, usable definition of leisure, the notion of flow first needs to be described in more detail, particularly because this notion is used throughout the book to differentiate leisure and recreation in a fashion that identifies the intrinsic value of leisure. In practical terms, flow represents a distinct state of being "in which people are so involved in an activity that nothing else seems to matter."[25] According to Csikszentmihalyi, flow allows individuals to completely control their consciousness so that all of their "psychic energy" is directed at achieving a particular goal.[26] The result is an experience of true enjoyment, which Csikszentmihalyi contrasts with mere pleasure because the psychological rewards come from fulfilling more than just basic biological needs and instead stem from the achievement of freely determined goals.[27]

Assessing the commonalities between different people's encounters with this optimal experience, Csikszentmihalyi determined that enjoyment—and thus flow—could be further specified in relation to its distinct characteristics. First, the flow state results from a close alignment between an individual's perceived skills and the perceived challenges of the activity, which allows the agent to avoid both boredom (when skill exceeds challenge) and anxiety (when challenge exceeds skill).[28] This perfect balance facilitates complete focus on the activity, making it seem like success is effortless, even though the activity requires a substantial amount of energy. In fact, it is precisely because the activity requires so much psychic energy that the experience of being carried along is possible, because one needs to be completely focused on the task at hand in order to succeed and therefore cannot waste any time thinking about other concerns.[29] This creates an experience not unlike the unity of consciousness sought in contemplation, because there is a sense of self-transcendence in the ability to limit the distractions of self-doubt and to attend exclusively to the immediate experience.[30] The end result, according to Csikszentmihalyi, is an expansion or development of the self.[31]

The experience of flow, especially as Csikszentmihalyi has come to describe it, has significant parallels with the subjective experience of leisure. Other scholars have noted this connection, but only in passing.[32] Here, the connections are used to establish flow as the defining characteristic of leisure, particularly in its contrasts with recreation. First, at a general level, flow aligns well with the notion of leisure as an activity pursued out of intrinsic motivation. According to Csikszentmihalyi, the effect of flow is "so enjoyable that people will do it even at great cost, for the sheer sake of doing it."[33] In light of this observation, Csikszentmihalyi identifies flow as an "autotelic experience"—meaning that, much like leisure, it is sought as an end in itself. Notably, Csikszentmihalyi cautions that flow's autotelic nature does not mean that the motivation for seeking flow is exclusively intrinsic, because he recognizes a possible mixing of motives.[34] This caveat makes flow an even more apt basis for a new constructive definition of leisure, because it allows one to underscore the centrality of intrinsic motivation without assuming that it must always be realized to absolute perfection. Indeed, Csikszentmihalyi's work on flow demonstrates that additional sources of motivation can be present without undermining the claim that an experience is still properly defined in relation to its intrinsic motivation. As Csikszentmihalyi explains, one can begin an activity with a variety of motivations in mind before eventually arriving at the point where one can appreciate the activity as an end in itself. Because flow is properly an autotelic experience, though, one must arrive at this new stage of appreciation before an otherwise pleasurable activity can transform into the enjoyment of the flow state.[35] By analogy, one can say the same thing about leisure, namely, that although one might initially choose a particular free time activity with a mix of motivations, it only properly transforms into leisure when it is enjoyed for its own sake.

Beyond the parallels related to intrinsic motivation, flow also aligns with other emphases found in the subjective definitions of leisure, especially Pieper's. Recall again that Pieper's interpretation of leisure as the basis of culture emphasized an idealistic interpretation of leisure as a form of contemplation that allowed persons simply to be, and also to be aware of their place in relation to creation and to God. The state of flow amounts to a very similar experience, at least insofar as flow is about "order in consciousness," as Csikszentmihalyi maintains.[36] As a full engagement of a person's psychic energy, flow opposes "psychic entropy," or distraction, and allows a form of concentration on the present experience that is consistent with Pieper's account of contemplation as the aim of leisure.[37] Furthermore, the sense of self-transcendence found in flow, which allows one to forget about one's own self-conscious concerns, and the experience of transcending time to just live in the moment both speak to Pieper's notion of leisure as "the power of stepping beyond the workaday world."[38] In addition, Pieper also described his vision for the fullness of leisure in exceptionally flow-like terms. "The soul of leisure," he insisted, "lies in 'celebration.' Celebration is the point at which the three key elements of leisure emerge together: effortlessness, calm and relaxation, and its superiority to all and every function."[39] These three key elements all correspond closely to central features of the experience of flow: the perception of effortlessness that makes one feel as though he or she is going along with the flow of things, the enjoyment that stems from achieving self-determined goals and dismissing worries, and the optimal nature of this experience that prompts people to pursue it so vigorously.[40]

All these links ultimately point to the crucial alignment that makes leisure and flow so eminently compatible: the curious blending of rest with activity. Pieper's account of contemplation as leisure's ideal describes an experience of being that nonetheless emerges from doing something. Flow similarly requires an activity, but it ultimately refers to the experience of being united with that activity. As such, flow is also about a state of being that arises from doing. In this way, both Pieper's leisure and Csikszentmihalyi's flow capture a distinctive human experience that combines being and doing, and rest and activity, in a meaningful way. As discussed below, this unique feature makes leisure particularly valuable from a theological perspective. For the moment, however, it is sufficient to identify this combination as a distinguishing feature of leisure that can be underscored and specified through its parallels in flow.

Notably, specificity was not the only rationale for developing a new definition of leisure. The other main motivation was to reconceptualize the ideal nature of leisure in a way that made it more attainable. Fortunately, flow serves this end effectively as well. To begin, the ideal nature of leisure is not sacrificed with the introduction of flow. Flow is, after all, an optimal experience, and it is therefore associated not with easy achievement but with the moments "when a person's body or mind is stretched to its limits."[41] Hence, it is hard to imagine that everyone reaches the level of optimal experience continuously, or perhaps even regularly. Csikszentmihalyi indicates that people's capacity for the attainment of flow will vary, and although he admits the existence of some people with "autotelic personalities" who are capable of transforming almost any activity into the experience of flow, he indicates that this results from a unique combination of nature and nurture that makes it the exception rather than the rule.[42] The more common experience, he suggests, is the latent capacity for flow—a skill set that is present but not yet fully developed.[43] There is a certain logic to this assertion, because flow requires that the challenges of an activity align with a person's skill level for that activity, a difficult sweet spot to find. The proper balance of skill and challenge may be difficult to find, but it is certainly not impossible; and as Csikszentmihalyi's research indicates, there are precise steps one can take to make the attainment of flow more common.[44] Consequently, using flow to define leisure not only adds specificity to the idea of leisure's intrinsic motivation but also does so in a way that makes leisure a realistically attainable ideal. Flow is thus a useful basis for a constructive definition of leisure.

In light of these connections, a new constructive definition emerges, with leisure defined as those free time pursuits that generate the experience of flow. Significantly, this preserves both of Neulinger's criteria, for the nature of flow captures the criterion of intrinsic motivation, and the restriction that this flow must occur within the confines of free time limits leisure to those activities chosen under the auspices of perceived freedom. This, as it turns out, is an important piece of the definition, for though Csikszentmihalyi allows that leisure activities are often well suited to the attainment of flow, he does not limit flow to leisure alone. In fact, he relays specific stories of people experiencing flow at work.[45] By stressing free time as a precondition for leisure, then, one limits the type of flow experiences that will be properly covered by this term.

In practice, all leisure experiences will be experiences of flow, but not all flow experiences will be experiences of leisure. Importantly, the confinement of leisure to free time is at odds with Neulinger's paradigm, where the subjective and objective definitions of leisure are so opposed that an empirical criterion like "free time" is something of a category error. Nevertheless, this decision is not without precedent, because other leisure studies scholars similarly adapt Neulinger's subjective definition to incorporate free time precisely as a "prerequisite for leisure," even when they emphasize its subjective dimensions.[46] Furthermore, in the context of this project, the decision to link leisure with free time has an additional rationale, for this parameter adds specificity to what constitutes leisure, allowing one to identify leisure more concretely in practice, which ultimately serves to make leisure more attainable, just as the constructive definition is designed to do. The idea of flow, then, generates a coherent definition of leisure, establishing an ideal to orient people's free time pursuits. This, in turn, points to a new definition for recreation as well.

A Corollary Definition of Recreation

Insofar as recreation is the flipside of leisure in the categorization of free time advocated here, the constructive definition of leisure yields a corollary definition of recreation. Specifically, recreation can be defined as nonflow free time activities. This corollary description obviously makes recreation the more encompassing category, because flow represents an ideal that can be difficult to attain. Yet precisely for this reason, recreation ought to be a fluid and encompassing category, because there needs to be some way to account for the breadth of free time experiences that cannot and will not fit within the narrower category of leisure. This is not to say that the corollary definition of recreation is so broad that it offers no resources for the critical evaluation of this subset of free time. Quite the contrary, because the definition of recreation is a corollary of the definition of leisure, the constitutive elements of leisure can be used to refine the nature and purpose of recreation in a way that adds new dimensions opening recreation to further theological analysis.

The central implication of defining recreation as the nonflow corollary of leisure is that the value of recreational activities becomes extrinsic rather than intrinsic. As discussed above, one of the chief elements of leisure is its intrinsic motivation. In the constructive definition, the concept of flow serves to highlight this distinctive feature. The absence of flow in recreation therefore suggests that intrinsic motivation is not a hallmark of recreational experiences. Granted, one could theoretically imagine some element other than flow that might be sought for its own end in recreation, but in order to remain faithful to the notion that recreation is a remainder concept defined in relation to leisure, it is appropriate to treat intrinsic motivation as a dividing line between the two. This is a reasonable extension of the division between flow and nonflow activities during free time, and it helpfully aligns recreation with some of its existing interpretations.

Before making the comparison with existing definitions, it is important to note that there is no single definition of recreation, not even in the field of leisure studies. Nevertheless, recreation, like leisure, has traditional roots, and the idea of extrinsic motivation is a common feature. "Historically," one leisure studies scholar explains, "the term 'recreation' stems from the Latin word *recreatio*, meaning that which refreshes or restores. In its traditional sense, recreation has been a period of light and restful activity, voluntarily chosen, which restores one for heavy, obligatory activity, or work."[47] This etymological history points toward an extrinsic motivation for recreation, specifically in its ability to help a worker restore his or her strength for work. The purpose of recreation is thus re-creation, or personal recovery and recuperation. Recreational activities are thus used for the sake of some other goal; they are a means to some other valued end. As Charles Sylvester has pointed out, this understanding of recreation as a means has classical roots in the work of Aristotle.[48] Significantly, the Aristotelian parallels underscore the value of separating leisure and recreation on the basis of intrinsic and extrinsic motivation respectively; for, though Aristotle insisted that "we do business [i.e., we work] in order that we may have leisure," he simultaneously commended the maxim "play in order that you may work" as an antidote to excessive "amusement," which other scholars point to as his term for recreation.[49] Hence, Aristotle's account gives credence to both a definition of leisure that emphasizes its value as an end and a definition of recreation that insists upon its value as a means. The corollary definition of recreation as those free time activities that do not produce flow—and that are therefore sought for extrinsic purposes—preserves these Aristotelian impulses.

Although the corollary definition thus aligns with Aristotle's approach to those free time pursuits that fell short of his leisure ideal, this account does not align with every scholarly use of the term "recreation." Despite Aristotle's suggestion that something like recreation is properly a means and not an end, some twentieth-century leisure studies scholars preferred to apply the language of recreation to free time activities with more intrinsic value. For instance, Martin Neumeyer and Esther Neumeyer, early pioneers in the field of leisure studies, opted for a definition of recreation borrowed from the *Dictionary of Sociology*, which defined recreation as "any activity pursued during leisure, either individual or collective, that is free and pleasureful, having its own immediate appeal, not impelled by a delayed reward beyond itself or by any immediate necessity."[50] This view obviously links recreation with more intrinsic motivations, and the Neumeyers even insisted that, in their view, recreation "has an intrinsic value."[51] Other scholars have similarly championed a closer connection between recreation and intrinsic motivation, with Richard Kraus criticizing the Aristotelian tendency to value recreation for its restorative functions, arguing instead that "recreation must be perceived as valuable in its own right, not simply because it makes it possible for one to engage in more work."[52] Both these insights are important, but neither one precludes the corollary definition of recreation proposed here, because the broader context behind each of these assertions shows that these scholars' concerns about the intrinsic value of recreation are not as restrictive as they might initially appear.

First, the Neumeyers' preferred description of recreation essentially equates recreation with free time. They openly acknowledge that the dictionary definition they borrow "makes recreation synonymous with leisure," but they nuance the alignment to insist that "the emphasis in leisure is on the time element, whereas recreation refers to the way leisure is spent."[53] By describing leisure this way, they are referring to the broader category of free time and suggesting that recreation is simply the name for what one does with one's free time. Given the freedom that free time presumes, it is natural that they would describe the value of recreation in intrinsic terms, because there is a fine line between choosing an activity for a type of extrinsic reward and ceding to a form of perceived obligation. Nevertheless, there is a line, and as long as one preserves the distinction between external obligation and external reward, one can intelligibly identify free time activities that serve external ends while still remaining free. To the extent that this is possible, there ought to be language to distinguish those free time activities that are thus sought for external ends from those that are sought for more intrinsic purposes. If leisure is the latter, then recreation can become the former. Although this is not the way that the Neumeyers use the term, it is still a functional possibility and, in the context of this project, a necessary distinction. One must simply recognize that this particular usage of recreation cannot be universally assumed.

Second, the definition of recreation via external reward requires some nuance. Part of Kraus's objection to this more traditional interpretation is found in his observation that "the idea that recreation is primarily intended to restore one for work has no meaning for such groups as aging persons who have *no* work but who certainly need recreation to make their life meaningful" (emphasis in the original).[54] Certainly, this is a fair point; but turning recreation into an intrinsic good is not the only way to address this concern. Another way to fix this problem is to expand the understanding of that for which recreation is supposed to restore the human person. Kraus assumes that recreation is meant to restore a person for his or her work, but he presumes a narrow definition of work, as evidenced by the fact that he imagines some people—specifically the elderly—who have no work to do. If work is merely paid employment, this is a legitimate objection; but work hardly needs to be confined to activities that receive economic remuneration. In the Catholic theological tradition, for example, work is understood to include not only paid labor done in the context of the market economy but also unpaid labor done as a result of one's domestic duties to one's family.[55] More important, Catholic social teaching advances "a vision of work as 'transformative vocation.' That is, work is a way men and women collaborate in the ongoing creation and re-creation of the self, the workplace, and the world."[56] From this vantage point, there is never a time when someone is without work entirely, for there is always the possibility of contributing to the work of God in the world. This is especially evident when one recognizes the close connection between the transformative vocation of work and the Second Vatican Council's account of the "universal call to holiness."[57] Insofar as the human person's pursuit of holiness is the overarching vocation that work is designed to serve, there is always "work" to be done, no matter one's stage in life.[58] If one adopts a more expansive definition of work like this one, then the concern that recreation's restorative function could serve no purpose for some individuals or for entire populations begins to diminish. As long as the human person has vocational responsibilities to address, there will always be ample reason to pursue recreation for its extrinsic rewards.

Finally, any disconnect between the corollary definition of recreation proposed here and existing accounts of recreation found in the field of leisure studies is not inherently problematic, because these two descriptions are designed to serve different purposes. The corollary definition is intended to facilitate a theological and ethical project; thus, it is entirely appropriate that this definition would be refined in light of existing theological resources like the theology of work found in Catholic social teaching. Furthermore, the corollary definition needs to establish a clear connection between recreation and leisure. When the field of leisure studies discusses recreation and leisure, it is not always done with this end in mind. Therefore, the corollary definition of recreation can and should depart from specific definitions of recreation in the field of leisure studies, insofar as these departures facilitate a clearer account of the distinctions between leisure and recreation. Together, these two concessions justify the corollary definition of recreation as nonflow free time pursuits that are sought for the extrinsic benefit of restoring the human person for his or her vocational responsibilities.

A Summary Account of Leisure and Recreation

When combined with the vision of leisure as flow-inducing free time pursuits sought for their own end, the corollary definition of recreation yields a comprehensive categorization of free time as a whole. The dividing line is, of course, intrinsic versus extrinsic motivation, which matches the emphasis on flow in the definition of leisure and the role of restoration in the Aristotelian understanding of recreation. This distinction sets the stage for a more comprehensive ethical analysis of free time because the difference between goods that have intrinsic value and those that have extrinsic value implies an ethical ordering. It also raises important theological questions, however, because the assertion that something has an intrinsic value rightly elicits concerns about the dangers of idolatry. These concerns must be addressed before one can consider the ethical implications of the definitions just proposed.

THE THEOLOGICAL DISTINCTION BETWEEN LEISURE AND RECREATION

From a theological perspective, the main issue at stake in the theoretical distinction between leisure and recreation is the rationale for identifying an intrinsic value in the former and insisting upon an extrinsic value for the latter. More specifically, the question is whether the experience of flow can rightly be described as an intrinsic good and, similarly, whether the pursuit of restoration is a legitimate instrumental end. Unfortunately, there is not a lengthy tradition of theological reflection on free time, so it is difficult to resolve this matter with substantive references to the theological value of leisure and of recreation per se. There are, however, ample resources to help assess the more general distinction between intrinsic and extrinsic value. The most influential of these is Saint Augustine's famed distinction between goods that are to be enjoyed and those that are to be used. Although Augustine never considered leisure or recreation within this typology, his insights go to the heart of the issues involved in the proposed definitions of leisure and recreation developed here. With a little bit of analogical application, his categories can be used to develop a robustly theological account of the proper distinction between leisure and recreation, so that the ethical evaluation of free time can become an opportunity to more fully integrate faith and life.

Adapting the Augustinian Insight about Enjoying and Using

Augustine's fundamental distinction between use and enjoyment is a fairly straightforward concept. In *De doctrina Christiana*, where he explained the idea most fully, he presented the division as though it were an obvious fact. "There are some things which are meant to be enjoyed, others which are meant to be used," he stated bluntly.[59] Further detailing the difference, he explained, "Enjoyment, after all, consists in clinging to something lovingly *for its own sake*, while use consists *in referring what has come your way to what your love aims at obtaining*" (emphasis added).[60] Fundamentally, Augustine's classic distinction between enjoyment and use is a contrast between intrinsic and instrumental value.[61] This, of course, creates parallels with the distinction between leisure and recreation, providing a theological rationale for the enjoyment of one and the use of the other. Such a claim, however, requires considerable nuance, because there is neither a simple nor direct correlation between Augustine's categories of enjoyment and use and the distinctions between leisure and recreation. In fact, there is a major complication that needs to be addressed before one can rightly talk about enjoying leisure or even using recreation in an Augustinian sense.

The major complication is that Augustine was exceptionally protective of the category of enjoyment. "The things therefore that are to be enjoyed," he allowed, "are the Father and the Son and the Holy Spirit."[62] Nothing apart from God was to be enjoyed—at least not enjoyed in the purest sense. Everything else was to be used, including humans.[63] Naturally, this poses problems for the idea that something like leisure might be enjoyed, but the objections are not insurmountable, because contemporary Augustinian scholars have contextualized Augustine's account of enjoyment and use in a way that opens the door for a slightly more expansive account of enjoyment's applications.

At the heart of this expansion is an effort to translate Augustine's vision of enjoyment and use for a contemporary audience that, steeped in the legacy of Immanuel Kant's categorical imperative, bristles at the suggestion that human beings ought to be used. In response, many contemporary Augustinians have sought to soften Augustine's language by noting that he does not (nor could he) presume a Kantian account of use, and that he instead had a more defensible vision of use as a form of love.[64] Furthermore, building on

Augustine's suggestion that in heaven "all of us who enjoy [God] should also enjoy one another in [God],"[65] contemporary scholars argue that there is a way in which humans might be enjoyed, at least insofar as they are made in the image and likeness of God, which would allow one to enjoy not so much the other person *in se* but God in that person.[66] As Sarah Stewart-Kroeker explains, when this understanding is combined with the doctrine of the Incarnation, it becomes possible to talk of enjoying a range of finite goods in which God's presence is mediated sacramentally—provided, of course, that one is careful to note that it is the presence or experience of God in the thing that is enjoyed rather than the thing itself.[67]

By taking these developments seriously, it becomes easier to employ Augustine's categories of enjoyment and use to justify a theological distinction between leisure and recreation. Specifically, one finds a theological argument for the intrinsic value of leisure to the extent that leisure offers an opportunity to encounter God, because this element of leisure could therefore be enjoyed for its own sake. Recreation, meanwhile, remains an instrumental good insofar as it falls short of the leisure ideal and is therefore properly used as a means to some other worthy end. Such an interpretation depends, of course, on the argument that leisure does indeed facilitate an encounter with the divine, and that recreation's restorative potential serves a higher good. Fortunately, both these claims can be supported as a result of the definitions of leisure and recreation developed above.

Flow as a Prefiguration of Heavenly Rest

The central element of leisure as defined in this book is not merely its intrinsic motivation but also the fact that the experience of flow is the source of that intrinsic motivation. To the extent that leisure is to be enjoyed, it must be through the experience of flow. This is not an untenable claim, because the particular features of the flow state create profound parallels with theological descriptions of eternal life in the presence of God, allowing leisure to become a temporal prefiguration of heavenly rest. The parallel emerges because flow affords access to a form of rest that occurs simultaneously with activity. Recall that according to Csikszentmihalyi, people in flow states feel united with their environment and their chosen activity as a result of the ordering of consciousness that pushes all other mundane thoughts into the background. This creates a sense of effortlessness that allows someone in the state of flow to be at rest in the middle of their activity. This sense of rest as peace or contentment, not as inactivity, is precisely the type of rest associated with Christians' eschatological expectations.

To focus merely on two luminaries, Augustine and Thomas Aquinas offer two separate but complementary explanations of eschatological rest that accentuate the correlation with flow. First, Augustine embraced the scriptural notion of rest as humanity's ultimate telos, arguing that God put "a desire for rest" in the human person at the beginning of creation, which ensures that "our hearts are restless until they rest in you."[68] Augustine stated that this longing could only be fulfilled in the "perpetual Sabbath" of eternal life,[69] and he described this future as "the peace of quietness, the peace of the Sabbath, a peace with no evening."[70] Significantly, however, Augustine maintained that this kind of rest as peace did not emerge from inactivity. Instead, he argued, this eschatological rest was properly a sharing in the rest of God, who rested on the seventh day in a way that somehow allowed Jesus nonetheless to declare, "My Father is still working [now]" (John 5:17). Augustine concluded that God must have rested in a way that made rest compatible with activity, suggesting that humanity's eschatological rest would similarly be defined as the peaceful experience of completion and satisfaction and not the cessation of activity altogether.[71]

Aquinas affirmed this insight, but in a different fashion. Similarly identifying God as "the last end" of humanity and all created things, he explained that the human person would attain this end "by knowing and loving God."[72] This description entailed a form of rest, because Aquinas's account of love hinged on a union between the lover and the beloved that would produce a "complacency" of the lover in the beloved.[73] This complacency was restful, but not inactive, for it required the act of love, which had two operations for Aquinas, such that "in one role love is passive, quiescent, complacent; in the other it is active, striving, tending to an object."[74] Thus, when Aquinas discussed charity—or the love of God—as humanity's last end, he alluded to the twofold operation of love, insisting that charity (actively) "attains God himself *that it may rest in Him*" (emphasis added).[75] Yet at the same time, Aquinas identified peace as an essential effect of charity, and he defined peace as not just the absence of conflict between individuals but also as "the union of appetites even in one man."[76] Peace for Aquinas therefore required a peace of mind that nicely complements the ordering of consciousness that defines flow. Consequently, Aquinas described rest in God as an active form of loving that still produced an internal sense of peace. He, like Augustine, presented heavenly rest in conjunction with, rather than in opposition to, activity.

As the ideas of Augustine and Aquinas illustrate, the notion of rest in the midst of activity is not foreign to the Christian tradition. Rather, it is a central aspect of the Christian description of eschatological rest. From a Christian perspective, then, human existence is teleologically ordered to an experience that very much correlates with flow. As a result, flow itself affords a unique opportunity, providing Christians with a literal foretaste of what they hope to attain in the next life. Such a glimpse, however fleeting, of what eschatological union with God will be like is fairly considered an intrinsic good. It can be sought and even enjoyed for its own sake, because it allows access—albeit in a limited way—to God.[77] Insofar as leisure is the experience of flow during free time, it is reasonable to talk about the enjoyment of leisure, and thus to affirm the theological potential of leisure as an intrinsic good.

This understanding obviously ascribes a high value to leisure. Although this is quite consistent with the notion that leisure represents something of free time's ideal potential, the loftiness of this vision nevertheless raises two problems. First, there is a danger of idolatry if one begins to assume that leisure is the only good worthy of enjoyment, or if one forgets that it is the glimpse of God and not the leisure activity itself that is supposed to be enjoyed. Second, there is the risk of elevating leisure at the expense of recreation, suggesting that free time should always and only be oriented to the enjoyment of leisure rather than the mere use of free time. Although both these problems are real, they can be adequately mitigated by remembering that the enjoyment of leisure stems from and fits within the parameters of Augustine's categorization. Above all else, Augustine's typology of enjoyment and use served as an argument for the proper ordering of goods. Augustine's assessment certainly recognized that not everything could be the human person's summum bonum, but his categories still acknowledged that those things that fall short of the final end have genuine value in relation to this end.[78] Instead of disparaging those things assigned to the category of use, then, Augustine's distinction shows how things that are used have a role to play in the good life.[79] Similarly, as an argument for the proper ordering of goods, Augustine's enjoyment/use distinction reiterates that no finite good can suffice as the human being's final end. As a result, the overarching categorization itself serves as a hedge against idolatry.[80]

The hedge against idolatry is a particularly important feature to remember in the analogical application of Augustine's categories to leisure, because the description of flow as an intrinsic good must not be misinterpreted to suggest that it is an absolute good. God is the only absolute good in the Christian understanding, and although the parallels with Augustine's category of enjoyment allow one to talk about enjoying God in leisure, this is still only a partial experience of God that remains bound up with a finite, material good. The mere existence of flow is therefore not determinative of the moral significance of leisure alone, because the finite conditions surrounding a particular leisure activity also need to be assessed to ensure that the experience of flow emerges from actions that are in fact compatible with the values Christians ascribe to life with God in heaven. Hence, for example, if a flow experience were to rely on a morally questionable activity, then its value as an experience of rest in activity would not be enough to assert that it ought to be enjoyed in the Augustinian sense. Instead, this activity would not be countenanced as a proper form of leisure but would actually be condemned as an illegitimate misuse of free time. In other words, flow is a necessary but not sufficient condition to create a form of leisure that Christians can enjoy as a glimpse of heavenly rest. Ancillary conditions must be evaluated as well, which means that the moral assessment of leisure will often require a nuanced analysis because of the distinction between an intrinsic and an absolute good. In this book, the clearest example of this nuance is in chapter 6, where the prospect of finding flow in video games is discussed as part of the ethical evaluation of digital media use as a form of recreation, which indicates that the significance of leisure can shift when the intrinsic good of flow as a prefiguration of heavenly rest stands in tension with other higher goods.

Although this cautionary reminder to combat the elision of intrinsic and absolute goods helps to guard against the dangers of idolatry in the assertion that leisure can be enjoyed, the other half of the application of Augustine's typology to free time—the insistence that recreation is to be used—still introduces other unresolved problems. Specifically, the ordering of goods at the heart of Augustine's distinctions between enjoyment and use at least implies that leisure ought to be prioritized above recreation, because enjoyment represents a relatively higher good than use. As a result, the analogical application of Augustine's categories might lead to an unintended denigration of recreation. In order to counteract this danger, one must recognize that recreation is still a good, however instrumental. This recognition, in turn, requires a clearer account of the value of recreation and its use.

Restoration as a Creaturely Necessity

Recreation, again, is set apart from leisure by both the absence of flow and the centrality of extrinsic motivation. Each of these features points toward the use of recreation rather than its enjoyment, for it is flow that allows leisure to be enjoyed as a prefiguration of heavenly rest, and it is extrinsic rewards that make use a functional category in the first place. There is therefore a logical consistency in the assertion that recreation is to be used; but this claim is insufficient alone. One still needs to explain how to use recreation properly as an instrumental good, and this requires identifying the purpose that recreation is meant to serve. From a theological perspective, the best way to answer this question is to appeal to one of the most essential elements of Christian theological anthropology: creatureliness.

Creatureliness highlights the finite nature of human beings, who are creatures of an infinite Creator, and therefore are not limitless but rather "radically dependent on God."[81] As Reinhold Niebuhr stressed, failure to appreciate this feature of the human condition easily leads to sin, because a denial of finitude facilitates the misuse of freedom in rebellion against God.[82] A recognition of creatureliness, however, accepts that human beings are finite and therefore have temporal needs that must be met. Among these is a legitimate need for a break from the physical and mental demands of one's central vocational responsibilities. From this point of view, recreation is properly counted among the many goods of human life because it serves the rejuvenation of the body and the soul. In fact, recreation has an important theological value because it militates against the temptations of idolatry by reaffirming the creatureliness of the human person and, by extension, the uniqueness of the divine Creator.

Such an assessment of recreation is entirely consistent with the witness of the Christian tradition. Aquinas, for example, acknowledged both the value of recreation for finite creatures and the necessity of recreation as a hedge against idolatry. Each person, he explained, must take breaks "for the body's refreshment, because he cannot always be at work, since his power is finite and equal to a certain fixed amount of labor." Furthermore, he added that human finitude required relaxation not only for the body but also for the soul, "whose power is also finite and equal to a fixed amount of work." He thus affirmed that "the remedy for weariness of soul must needs consist in the application of some pleasure," and he proposed "playful or humorous" words, deeds, and games as appropriate remedies.[83] Naturally, he envisioned some limits, arguing that playfulness must not result from crude or immoral endeavors, and critiquing those who made "inordinate use of fun, especially by... mak[ing] the pleasure of games their end."[84] Ultimately, however, he insisted, "play is necessary for the intercourse of human life," and, in a testimony to recreation's theological contributions, he even identified a lack of playful enjoyment as a sin.[85]

The tradition of Catholic social teaching has similarly defended the value of recreation as an appropriate reaction to human finitude. The first papal encyclical in this tradition, *Rerum novarum*, asserted that "man's powers, like his general nature, are limited, and beyond these limits he cannot go."[86] As a consequence, the encyclical proposed a "general principle" dictating that workers ought to be given a reasonable amount of daily rest and adequate weekly free time to recuperate from the "wear and tear" of their jobs.

Strikingly, the letter emphasized that this was a matter of self-care, insisting that workers could not actually consent to working without any guaranteed breaks because this would require abdicating their duties not only to God but also to themselves.[87] Subsequent reflections in the magisterial tradition have preserved and strengthened these claims, to the point that the United States' bishops would ultimately describe both weekly days off from work and "periodic holidays for recreation and leisure" as demands of justice.[88]

Finally, the example of Jesus's own life provides a theological defense of rest for the sake of recuperation. Although his moments of prayer might seem best suited to a parallel with the category of leisure—because temporal communion with God is appropriately described as a prefiguration of eternal life—his private retreats also served as a form of recreation. This is most apparent in the Gospel of Mark (6:31), where, in one instance, the overwhelming crowds prompt Jesus to invite his disciples to "come away to a deserted place all by yourselves and rest a while." This may be a paradigmatic example, but it is not an isolated incident. Consequently, commentators interpret Jesus's retreat as both a testament to the taxing nature of his work and evidence of his efforts to find creaturely rejuvenation in the midst of his ministry.[89] Meanwhile, the depictions of Jesus at prayer in the other gospels suggest that prayer played a multifaceted role in his life, allowing for this one activity to serve as a form of leisure in some cases and as a manifestation of recreation in others.[90] Finally, Jesus's years in active ministry were not restricted to work and leisure alone. The gospels and other sources depict an image of "Jesus the bon vivant," who had a "well-known—and, to some, notorious—practice of regularly engaging in feasting and wine-drinking, especially with the social and religious lowlife of the day."[91] Given that feasts and banquets in Jesus's culture were elaborate affairs, involving "a formal meal in a luxurious setting with the best food and wine that the host and his family could offer," alongside various forms of entertainment, Jesus's reputation as a partier reveals a ready acceptance of recreation.[92]

In light of these examples, one can rightly affirm recreation as a theologically legitimate acknowledgment of human finitude. In fact, one might say that an honest recognition of humanity's creatureliness requires a defense of rest for the sake of personal renewal, thereby making recreation, no less than leisure, an integral part of the divine plan.[93] Yet even from this more positive perspective, one must remember that recreation remains an instrumental good. The real theological value of recreation therefore lies in the service of higher goods. Work can be one of these goods, especially when understood as part of the human person's larger vocation to holiness; but even more fundamentally, the human person's relational capacity is perhaps the most important good that recreation serves. Catholic theological anthropology insists that all human persons are called to self-gift in order to achieve their fullest flourishing, but even this task has its natural limits because there must be a self left to give.[94] Feminist theologians have made this abundantly clear, from at least the time of Valerie Saiving Goldstein's watershed article critiquing the exclusive emphasis on pride as the quintessential form of sin.[95] Adopting this insight, recreation becomes an instrumental but no less essential good that helps to restore a person's relational capacity for self-gift, thus facilitating the pursuit of each person's full flourishing.

To put this assessment in Augustinian terms, recreation's service to creatureliness means that recreation is rightly considered a thing to be used rather than enjoyed. In this way, recreation can be recognized as an instrumental good that serves the human person's pursuit of a life ever more in union with God—that is, an instrumental good that supports a person's attainment of those goods that are to be enjoyed. Because leisure can be enjoyed but recreation should only be used, leisure stands higher in the relative ordering of goods. Importantly, this observation does not mean that all free time should be dedicated to leisure, because the significant instrumental value of recreation means that it is a legitimate free time pursuit as well. Of course, the specifics of this relative ordering need to be parsed out in more detail, but that is a task for subsequent sections of this book. At the moment, the fundamental conclusion is that the theoretical distinction between leisure and recreation can be theologically justified.

CONCLUSION

The main point of this chapter has been to clarify the distinction between leisure and recreation in order to lay the foundation for a more critical analysis of free time. This has led to three key observations. First, according to the constructive definition of leisure developed here, leisure can be described as those free time activities or experiences that allow one to experience flow and that are therefore sought for their own sake. Second, the identification of recreation as a remainder concept yields the corollary definition of recreation as nonflow free time activities that restore the human person for his or her vocational responsibilities. Third, these theoretical definitions can be connected to Augustine's distinction between enjoying and using to produce a theological evaluation of the nature and purpose of both leisure and recreation. Specifically, leisure can be enjoyed as an intrinsic good that offers a prefiguration of heavenly rest, and recreation can be used as an instrumental good that addresses the human person's creaturely needs for recovery and restoration. These theological claims already imply ethical responsibilities, not merely in the relative ordering of leisure and recreation but also in the suggestion that leisure and recreation each has a proper telos that should be respected. These respective tele can and should inform the ethical evaluation of leisure and recreation, but however necessary, they are not sufficient for a full assessment of one's ethical responsibilities during free time. In order to achieve this goal, the ends of leisure and recreation need to be further situated within a broader theological and ethical vision that is capable of integrating faith into ordinary life as a whole. Chapter 2 addresses this issue.

NOTES

1. Goodale and Cooper, "Philosophical Perspectives," 33.
2. Sylvester, "Ethics of Play," 181; cf. Gray, *Philosophy of Man*, 47–50.
3. Best, *Leisure Studies*, 3.
4. Iso-Ahola, *Social Psychology of Leisure*, 7.
5. Iso-Ahola, 7–8, quoting Iso-Ahola, "On the Theoretical Link," 4.
6. Neulinger, *Psychology of Leisure*, 16.
7. Kraus, *Recreation and Leisure*, 253.
8. Kraus, 253.
9. See Veblen, *Theory of the Leisure Class*.
10. The degree to which cultural and structural forces like this constrain freedom in leisure is the subject of debate in the field of leisure studies, but the mere existence of that debate reveals that freedom is not so neatly delineated in leisure pursuits. Spracklen, *Meaning and Purpose of Leisure*, 13–30.
11. Aristotle, *Politics*, 1338a, 1337b.
12. de Grazia, *Of Time, Work, and Leisure*, 15.
13. See Kraus, *Recreation and Leisure*, 254; Heintzman, *Leisure and Spirituality*, 57–68; cf. Stebbins, *Idea of Leisure*, 24–26. Stebbins asserts that freedom is the distinguishing mark in the classical Greek understanding, not the intrinsic motivation per se.
14. Neulinger, *Psychology of Leisure*, 17–18.
15. Neulinger, 18.
16. Pieper, *Leisure*, 51–52.
17. Pieper, 51.
18. Pieper, 52.
19. Pieper, 57, 58.
20. Turkle, *Alone Together*, 202–3, 272, 288–89.
21. Wilson et al., "Just Think," 76. See also "Supplementary Materials for Just Think," *Science*, July 4, 2014, 7–10, esp. 9–10, http://science.sciencemag.org/content/sci/suppl/2014/07/02/345.6192.75.DC1/Wilson.SM.pdf.
22. Csikszentmihalyi, *Flow*, 3.
23. Csikszentmihalyi, 4; see also 48–49. For more on Csikszentmihalyi's research methods, see Csikszentmihalyi and Larson, "Validity and Reliability."

24. Csikszentmihalyi, *Flow*, 40.
25. Csikszentmihalyi, 4.
26. Csikszentmihalyi, 39–40; see also 21–31.
27. Csikszentmihalyi, 46.
28. Csikszentmihalyi, 74–75.
29. Csikszentmihalyi, 53–54, 58–59.
30. Csikszentmihalyi, 59, 62–64.
31. Csikszentmihalyi, 65, 74.
32. Best, *Leisure Studies*, 9–11; Heintzman, *Leisure and Spirituality*, 16–17.
33. Csikszentmihalyi, *Flow*, 4.
34. Csikszentmihalyi, 67–68.
35. Csikszentmihalyi, 67–68. This recalls Alasdair MacIntyre's description of virtue in relation to the pursuit of "those goods which are internal to [specific] practices." As part of this account, he outlines a particular definition of practices and refers to the example of enticing a young child to learn to play chess by bribing the child with candy. This obviously involves an extrinsic motivation, but MacIntyre suggests that if he does this often enough, the child might eventually enjoy playing chess so much that she or he will no longer need the extrinsic reward of candy in order to start a game and will instead seek to play chess for its intrinsic rewards. MacIntyre, *After Virtue*, 187–88, at 191.
36. Csikszentmihalyi, *Flow*, 6.
37. Csikszentmihalyi, 31–33, 36–39, 59.
38. Csikszentmihalyi, 62–67; Pieper, *Leisure*, 56–58, at 57.
39. Pieper, *Leisure*, 71.
40. See, again, Csikszentmihalyi, *Flow*, 4, 46, 53–54, 58.
41. Csikszentmihalyi, 3.
42. Csikszentmihalyi, 90–93.
43. Csikszentmihalyi, 83.
44. Csikszentmihalyi has even published multiple books offering advice for this purpose. See Csikszentmihalyi, *Finding Flow*; Csikszentmihalyi, *Beyond Boredom*; and, more specifically, Csikszentmihalyi, Latter, and Duranso, *Running Flow*.
45. Csikszentmihalyi, *Flow*, 50–51, 143–63; see also Csikszentmihalyi and Kleiber, "Leisure," 94, 96.
46. Iso-Ahola, *Social Psychology of Leisure*, 8.
47. Kraus, *Recreation and Leisure*, 260.
48. Sylvester, "Ethics of Play," 181.
49. Aristotle, *Nicomachean Ethics*, 1177b, 1177a. On the interpretation of Aristotle's "play" and "amusement" as recreation, see Heintzman, *Leisure and Spirituality*, 60–61.
50. Neumeyer and Neumeyer, *Leisure and Recreation*, 17.
51. In fact, the Neumeyers go on to acknowledge that, in their view, recreation "has an intrinsic value." Neumeyer and Neumeyer, 18.
52. Kraus, *Recreation and Leisure*, 261.
53. Neumeyer and Neumeyer, *Leisure and Recreation*, 17.
54. Kraus, *Recreation and Leisure*, 261.
55. For a succinct, and critical, explanation of this broader view of work, see Hinze, "Women, Families, and the Legacy of *Laborem exercens*."
56. Lamoureux, "Commentary on *Laborem exercens*," 408.
57. *Lumen gentium*, 39.

58. For more on these links, see May, "Work," esp. 997–1000.
59. Augustine, *De doctrina Christiana*, I.3.3.
60. Augustine, I.4.4.
61. It is worth noting that at least one observer has suggested that transient versus final, and not instrumental versus intrinsic, is the primary axis of the split between use and enjoyment. Even this scholar, however, admits that a split between intrinsic and instrumental values is evident in Augustine's division, calling this the starting point of the divide between enjoyment and use. Baer, "Fruit of Charity," 52; cf. 51.
62. Augustine, *De doctrina Christiana*, I.5.5.
63. Augustine, I.22.20–I.23.22, I.31.34.
64. See Baer, "Fruit of Charity," 47–49; O'Connor, "*Uti/Frui* Distinction," 45; Hannam, "*Ad illud ubi permanendum est*," 169–70; Dupont, "To Use or Enjoy Humans?" 89.
65. Augustine, *De doctrina Christiana*, I.32.35; see also I.23.22.
66. Dupont, "To Use or Enjoy Humans?" 92–93; Hannam, "*Ad illud ubi permanendum est*," 171–73. Augustine seems to grant something like this when he allows that the use of a human is properly "a closely related sense of 'enjoy' meaning 'to use with delight.'" Augustine, *De doctrina Christiana*, I.33.37.
67. Stewart-Kroeker, "Resisting Idolatry," 214–17.
68. Augustine, *Literal Meaning of Genesis*, IV.14.25; Augustine, *Confessions*, I.1.1. For an explanation of the scriptural understanding of rest as humanity's final end, see Hasel, "Sabbath in the Pentateuch," 23; and Barth, *Church Dogmatics*, III.1.218.
69. Augustine, *Literal Meaning of Genesis*, IV.13.24, 8.15.
70. Augustine, *Confessions*, XIII.35.50.
71. Augustine, *Literal Meaning of Genesis*, IV.9.16–12.22. This description is not unlike Augustine's account of human work before the Fall, which he argued was free from the "stress of wearisome toil" and therefore best understood as a form of leisure. Augustine, *Literal Meaning of Genesis*, VIII.15, 10.22.
72. Aquinas, *ST*, I-II.1.8 c.
73. Aquinas, *ST*, I-II.26.2 c, ad 2; I-II.28.1 c.
74. Crowe, "Complacency and Concern [1]," 3; see also Crowe, "Complacency and Concern [3]," 349.
75. Aquinas, *ST*, II-II.23. 6 c. See also, Crowe, "Complacency and Concern [1]," 13, 25.
76. Aquinas, *ST*, II-II.29.1 c; II-II.29.3 c.
77. Christian theology often defends the value of the liturgy in these terms. Although the liturgy provides a number of ancillary goods for a community, one of its most essential benefits is its ability to make the eschatological hopes of Christians present in their midst, which makes the celebration of the liturgy valuable for its own sake, quite apart from any utility that might occur after the fact. Saliers, *Worship as Theology*, 56–60.
78. See McGowan, "To Use and to Enjoy," 97; Hannam, "*Ad illud ubi permanendum est*," 170–71.
79. Cf. O'Donovan, "*Usus* and *Fruitio*," esp. 363, 381–83.
80. See Stewart-Kroeker, "Resisting Idolatry," 209–11.
81. Rahner, *Foundations*, 78.
82. Niebuhr, *Nature and Destiny of Man*, 17, 167–68, 182–86.
83. Aquinas, *ST*, II-II.168.2 c.
84. Aquinas, *ST*, II-II.168.2 ad 2; see also II-II.168.3 c.
85. Aquinas, *ST*, II-II.168.3 ad 3; see also II-II.168.4 c.

86. Leo XIII, *Rerum novarum*, 42.
87. Leo XIII.
88. US Conference of Catholic Bishops, *Economic Justice for All*, 103. See also John XXIII, *Pacem in terris*, 11, 63, 64; *Gaudium et spes*, 67; John Paul II, *Laborem excercens*, 19; John Paul II, *Centesimus annus*, 7.
89. Donahue and Harrington, *Gospel of Mark*, 204; Black, *Mark*, 158; France, *Gospel of Mark*, 260–61.
90. See Goergen, *Theology of Jesus, Volume 1*, 143–44.
91. Meier, *Marginal Jew*, 627, 626.
92. Neel and Pugh, *Food and Feasts of Jesus*, 98, 101.
93. See Ryken, *Redeeming the Time*, 207. Ryken defends the appropriateness of "leisure" in these terms, but he does not distinguish between leisure and recreation, so his argument can apply to both.
94. *Gaudium et spes*, 24.
95. Goldstein, "Human Situation."

CHAPTER 2

An Ethical Framework for Everyday Solidarity

Although it may be tempting to dive into an ethical assessment of leisure and recreation directly, the reality is that this is not a particularly feasible task. As noted in the introduction, free time typically escapes sustained ethical scrutiny, and it has seldom received this attention in a theological context. As a result, there are limited resources for a direct ethical analysis of leisure and recreation as discrete topics. There are, however, more resources from the Catholic theological tradition to sustain an indirect assessment when leisure and recreation are situated in a broader context. Given the nature of free time, the category of ordinary life provides the most appropriate context for analyzing leisure and recreation, although this broader area too has received only limited theological attention. The point of this chapter, then, is to develop an ethical framework for an intentional approach to ordinary life that allows Catholic theological convictions to inform everyday decisions. Once established, this framework can guide the critical assessment of otherwise underanalyzed experiences in ordinary life, like leisure and recreation, so that the ethical evaluation of these everyday issues can proceed in a unified fashion that promotes moral integrity rather than fragmentation. Significantly, although the focus of this book remains free time, the framework has the potential to also apply to other areas of ordinary life, so its effectiveness as a tool for analyzing leisure and recreation is also a sign of its usefulness as a tool for the larger task of integrating theological ethics and ordinary life—a point to which the conclusion of this book will return.

In more specific terms, this chapter proposes "everyday solidarity" as the foundation for a theological approach to ordinary life. This proposal is rooted in the idea of solidarity found and developed in the tradition of Catholic social teaching, but it moves beyond this notion in order to adapt it to the context of personal moral discernment in ordinary life, creating what amounts to a new species of solidarity. The end result is a twofold account that understands everyday solidarity as both a principle, which guides ethical discernment, and a virtue, which prompts a commitment to structural change so that the principle can be employed more realistically by more people in their ordinary lives. Together, these two elements of everyday solidarity provide the groundwork for a holistic approach to ordinary life that allows the fundamental convictions of Catholic theological anthropology to shape distinct topics, like leisure and recreation, in a consistent fashion.

Notably, the account of everyday solidarity developed here serves as an essential resource for the ethical evaluation of leisure and recreation that occurs in parts II and III of this book. As the foundation for this moral analysis, everyday solidarity obviously reappears throughout the book, so readers will want to attend to the nuances of this term as it is developed here in this chapter. To highlight these nuances, much of this chapter engages the existing understanding of solidarity found in Catholic social teaching, chiefly to parse out the distinctive features of a new form of everyday solidarity that, though properly a species of the larger genus, is not coterminous with its generic type. Thus, the first section of this chapter distills three key features of solidarity as it is presented in Catholic social teaching, establishing the traits that everyday solidarity can bring to the evaluation of ordinary life. The chapter's second section then clarifies several ambiguities in Catholic social teaching's current presentation of solidarity before detailing the way everyday solidarity functions as a principle and as a virtue. Although these functions are related to existing interpretations of principles and virtues in the moral life, these terms are used in a very particular way when applied to the specific form of everyday solidarity, creating a distinct interpretation that is preserved throughout the remainder of this book. By attending to the nuances of solidarity discussed in this chapter, then, one will be prepared to interpret the specific ethical interpretations of leisure and recreation that form the heart of this book in parts II and III.

INSIGHTS FROM CATHOLIC SOCIAL TEACHING ABOUT SOLIDARITY

In its most basic usage, solidarity refers to a sense of interconnectedness between individuals, like the spirit of shared commitment that prompts a group of otherwise independent actors to see themselves as part of a common cause.[1] In a Catholic context, solidarity has taken on significant theological meaning as a result of its prominence in the papal tradition of Catholic social teaching. Based on this interpretation, solidarity has three key advantages that allow it to serve as the ideal basis for a richly theological approach to ordinary life. First, solidarity highlights the relational and social account of the human person that is at the heart of Catholic theological anthropology and illustrates the ethical implications of this view. This connection makes solidarity a helpful resource for ethical discernment in ordinary life because it creates an inherent link between the practical concerns of moral discernment and the theological presuppositions of moral theology that often go overlooked. Second, solidarity provides a deliberate alternative to individualism, both critiquing and correcting this problematic trend. Because a unique form of atomistic individualism pervades ordinary life in the United States today, relying on solidarity as the basis for everyday ethical discernment helpfully provides the guidance to reprioritize Catholic commitments over the default assumptions of a powerful US culture. Third, solidarity insists that moral change requires converting not only personal agents but also social structures. Consequently, solidarity indicates that an ethical approach to ordinary life cannot succeed by appealing to the formation of individual moral agents in isolation but must also encourage moral actors to take responsibility for the challenges and limitations of the social context that surrounds them. By focusing on these three key features, the essence of solidarity emerges from its multifaceted, and sometimes convoluted, presentation in Catholic social teaching, which generates a clearer description of the idea that can then inform the creation of a narrower species for everyday ethical decisions.

Notably, though solidarity has these three key features that allow it to address some of the most significant aspects of ethics in ordinary life, it should not be interpreted as a perfect resource in isolation. The notion of everyday solidarity developed in this chapter does indeed provide a reasonably comprehensive framework for assessing moral decisions in ordinary life, for all the reasons just articulated, but it would be foolhardy to suggest that it could capture the entirety of the moral life, which the Catholic tradition identifies as a dynamic response of the personal moral agent to the call to follow Christ in the world.[2] Everyday solidarity provides a way of developing that dynamic response in ordinary life, and, as explained below, it highlights the essential features that distinguish a Catholic form of this response because of solidarity's close connections to Catholic theological anthropology and to the Catholic account of the call to conversion. Everyday solidarity can only function in this fashion, however, only because it presumes larger theological claims, perhaps most especially the Catholic assertion that charity is the form of the moral life, which is another way of interpreting the priority of love of God and love of neighbor in the Christian tradition.[3]

In essence, everyday solidarity is effective as an overarching ethical framework because it serves to distill these kinds of fundamental convictions into a practical tool that can illustrate how to live out the quintessential aspects of Christian discipleship in ordinary life. Precisely because it presumes and distills these major features, however, everyday solidarity cannot be understood apart from the larger moral tradition that it captures and that it is designed to serve. Consequently, everyday solidarity will only be effective as a reasonably comprehensive tool for the ethical analysis of ordinary life when it is understood within the broader Catholic vision for the moral life, meaning that this overarching framework should be read as an extension of, not as a replacement for, the call to discipleship that is rooted in Jesus's multifaceted love command. Ultimately, it is in light of this background that the three advantages of using solidarity as the basis for a new overarching framework come into focus.

Solidarity as the Moral Extension of Catholic Theological Anthropology

According to the magisterial tradition of Catholic social teaching, solidarity is both a descriptive reality and a prescriptive force. More precisely, solidarity underscores the reality of human interconnectedness (i.e., the sense of a shared humanity that unites all human beings into one human family), while it simultaneously reveals that ethical obligations unavoidably follow from this fact of life. This twofold balance of the "fact" of solidarity and its moral consequences has its roots in the thought of two Jesuits, Heinrich Pesch and Oswald von Nell-Breuning, whose defense of "solidarism" in the early twentieth century influenced Pope Pius XII.[4] It is hardly surprising, then, that both aspects of solidarity appeared in Pius XII's 1939 encyclical *Summi pontificatus*, which was the first papal document to mention the term.[5] Specifically, Pius XII aligned "world-wide Catholic solidarity" with the "supernatural brotherhood of peoples around their Common Father," showing that as a descriptive concept, solidarity points to human interconnectedness as an incontestable fact.[6] At the same time, he also appealed to "the law of human solidarity and charity which is dictated and imposed by our common origin and by the equality of rational nature in all men, to whatever people they belong, and by the redeeming Sacrifice offered by Jesus Christ... on behalf of [all] sinful mankind."[7] By thus emphasizing solidarity as a *law* that emerges from humanity's shared history of creation and salvation, Pius XII pointed to a prescriptive interpretation as well, revealing that normative obligations accompany the descriptive reality of humanity's interconnectedness.

Subsequent interpretations of solidarity in Catholic theology have never forgotten these two emphases, and in many ways the entire magisterial evolution of solidarity amounts to a specification of each element.[8]

To give merely two examples, Pope John XXIII's *Mater et magistra* spoke descriptively of "the solidarity which binds all men together as members of a common family" before noting, prescriptively, that this solidarity required national and international efforts to eliminate hunger, poverty, and the general disparities in access to resources and well-being that define the opposing fates of what are now referred to as the Global North and Global South.[9] Subsequently, the Second Vatican Council emphasized the Christological dimensions of this interpretation, insisting in its decree on the laity that through the Incarnation, Christ "bound the whole human race to Himself as a family through a certain supernatural solidarity," and adding in its Pastoral Constitution, *Gaudium et spes*, that the Paschal Mystery also united humans in a bond of solidarity as mutual members of the one Body of Christ.[10] These interpretations help to show a distinctively Catholic understanding of solidarity that presumes descriptive theological convictions behind the prescriptive ethical implications.

Significantly, the true nexus of solidarity's descriptive and prescriptive elements in Catholic social teaching is the theological account of the human person found in the Catholic tradition. Building on the scriptural belief that human beings were created in the image and likeness of a trinitarian God, Catholic theological anthropology asserts that the human person is by nature a relational creature, whose full flourishing can only be realized in a relational context.[11] The ethical significance of this relational nature is then amplified by faith in the Incarnation, for the conviction that Jesus Christ is both fully human and fully divine entails the corollary conclusion that Jesus's life reveals the fullness of human flourishing.[12] This fullness of flourishing, as exemplified in the cross, points toward selflessness, prompting the Second Vatican Council to declare, in one of the most succinct and authoritative accounts of Catholic theological anthropology, that the human person "who is the only creature on earth which God willed for itself, cannot fully find himself [or herself] except through a sincere gift of [self]."[13] The prescriptive features of solidarity are rooted in this descriptive background, calling all moral agents to see themselves in others' shoes so that they might make moral decisions in a spirit of selflessness instead of self-interest. In this way, solidarity requires a greater awareness of the inherently relational nature of the human person, allowing the basic convictions of Catholic theological anthropology to shape ethical discernment.

In the concrete context of ordinary life, a spirit of solidarity ensures that the personal moral agent has the proper perspective in mind. By emphasizing the relational nature of the human person, solidarity reorients specific moral choices to what Catholic theology understands to be the most fundamental aspect of the human condition: creatureliness before a trinitarian God. This underlying theological conviction may seem somewhat basic, but that is an asset rather than a liability, because the best way for faith to inform something as broad as ordinary life is through the general and universal rather than the narrow and particular. At the same time, the prescriptive dimensions of solidarity reveal that this general belief still has specific moral implications. By deriving moral responsibility from Catholicism's relational anthropology, solidarity insists that even seemingly individual choices have social consequences, because human beings are innately social creatures. In the context of free time, this reminder is essential because one of the reasons free time often escapes ethical analysis is that people assume this area of life is simply a matter of personal preference and therefore is beyond moral scrutiny. The message of solidarity, however, is that there is no such thing as a personal choice that has no effect on other people. Relational beings always exist in a relational context, and if one takes this theological anthropology seriously, then one must consider the relational ramifications of even the most mundane decisions.

Solidarity as an Antidote to Individualism

The second major benefit of using solidarity as the primary lens for ethics in ordinary life is that Catholic social teaching presents solidarity as an antidote to individualism. In some respects, this is an obvious extension of solidarity's roots in Catholicism's relational anthropology, for this conviction naturally leads to a more communitarian vision for social life.[14] In the papal tradition of Catholic social teaching, however, there is also a more precise account of how solidarity responds to individualism, and the particular features of this vision make solidarity an especially useful tool for connecting Catholic theological commitments and ordinary life in a place like the United States, where a distinctive brand of individualism is one prominent feature of the broader cultural landscape.

Rather than simply decrying individualism and paving the way for deficiencies in the other direction, the Catholic notion of solidarity specifies the insufficiency of this ideology and points toward a more nuanced alternative. The nuance emerges from *Gaudium et spes*'s promotion of solidarity, which appealed to the unifying image of the Body of Christ to assert that "everyone, as members one of the other, would render mutual service according to the different gifts bestowed on each."[15] *Gaudium et spes* thus rejected the unencumbered assertions of individualistic ideologies, but the Pastoral Constitution also developed this point further by insisting that the orientation to mutual service did not eliminate personal autonomy but instead assumed and preserved the compatibility of "personal initiative with the solidarity of the whole social organism."[16] In this way, the Second Vatican Council offered a vision of solidarity as a sense of mutual concern that still respected the dignity and difference of each individual. Hence, Meghan Clark has presented solidarity in Catholic social teaching as the virtuous mean between excessive individualism and "any form of collectivism in which persons are subsumed by the whole or subverted to it."[17] The notion of solidarity presented in *Gaudium et spes* therefore responds to the pitfalls of an overly individualistic interpretation of the human person in a way that avoids swinging the pendulum to the opposite extreme. Consequently, the Catholic view of solidarity is a genuinely helpful response to individualism and not simply a reactionary rejection of it.

Subsequent accounts of solidarity in magisterial sources have only made the nuanced contrast with individualism more pronounced. Pope Paul VI's *Populorum progressio*, for instance, encouraged public officials to overcome "distrust and selfishness among nations" with "a stronger desire for mutual collaboration and a heightened sense of solidarity."[18] Although he was concerned mainly with national actors, Paul VI's opposition between self-interest and solidarity shows how the latter can challenge one of the basic assumptions underlying troubling forms of individualism. Pope John Paul II explicitly extended this claim to personal moral agents, arguing in *Centesimus annus* that "in order to overcome today's widespread individualistic mentality, what is required is *a concrete commitment to solidarity and charity*" (emphasis in the original).[19] Pope Benedict XVI, meanwhile, made a similar point in *Caritas in veritate* when he defended solidarity as a moral force capable of refuting those who "would claim that they owe nothing to anyone, except themselves" by highlighting "how *rights presuppose duties*" (emphasis in the original).[20] This latter claim, in particular, underscores solidarity's contrast with individualism because individualism, especially in the form that is most common in the United States, prefers to use rights as a buffer against responsibility, maximizing license and minimizing accountability. In contrast, Catholic social teaching presents solidarity as a reminder of the human person's relational nature, and thus her or his relational responsibilities, promoting a mind-set and a way of proceeding that assumes mutual moral obligations and looks for ways to fulfill them. Significantly, because solidarity emphasizes the unity of the entire human family and not just the connections of those who look alike or think alike, solidarity broadens the range of these relational responsibilities not only beyond the narrow strictures of individualism but also beyond the confines of in-group bias.

Solidarity's nuanced corrective to excessive forms of individualism is another important asset for the creation of an overarching framework for moral discernment because, at least in the United States, a skewed form of individualism holds a prominent influence in ordinary life today. Over the years, US culture has often been associated with some form of individualism,[21] but what is truly significant is not that the United States is a more individualistic nation than its peers but that it is home to a qualitatively different brand of *atomistic* individualism that makes the force of solidarity so essential for ordinary life in a US context. As a distinct species of individualism, this atomistic form appeals to the scientific notion of the atom as the basic building block of the material world, building on the Greek metaphysical assumption that the atom was "indivisible" to assert the inherent completeness of the individual on their own.[22]

This approach does not prohibit links between individuals; it simply qualifies their conditions and minimizes their necessity. Just as atomic theory imagines the possibility of molecular bonding but still insists that every atom can exist on its own, so atomistic individualism argues that the individual can create bonds but that he or she does not need to, because each individual is sufficient alone. As the philosopher Charles Taylor explains, this is not a claim that every human person can survive on their own out in the wilderness, like the titular character in the television series *Survivorman*. Instead, atomistic individualism's assertions of self-sufficiency are best understood as a contrast to Aristotle's description of the human person as a social animal. The latter insists that a truly human life is impossible alone because interactions and social responsibilities are constitutive of a *human* life.[23] According to atomistic individualism, however, "our obligation to belong to or sustain a society, or to obey its authorities, is seen as derivative, as laid on us conditionally, through our consent, or through its being to our advantage."[24] The real defining characteristic of atomistic individualism, then, is the conviction that every human person is an individual who is capable of fulfillment on their own and thus "unencumbered" by all external responsibilities, except for the responsibilities the individual has freely chosen to create through voluntary consent.[25]

Over time, an atomistic form of individualism has been on the rise in the United States, and today it functions as a pervasive cultural force.[26] In this environment, the atomistic conception of the individual serves as a kind of shared language, both framing the issues that need to be addressed and constraining the options presumed to be available to address those issues. Thus,

Taylor notes that "the starting point in individual rights has an undeniable prima facie force for us" and can be taken for granted in public discourse rather than demonstrated.[27] Likewise, the seminal sociological account of contemporary mores, *Habits of the Heart*, identified individualism as the common "first language" of people in the United States.[28] More to the point, Robert Bellah and his coauthors argued that this first language reflected not just a generic individualism but an individualism in which "the entire social world is made up of individuals, each endowed with the right to be free of others' demands."[29] In other words, Bellah and his colleagues described a specifically atomistic form of individualism as the first language of US culture.[30]

Practical illustrations bear out this trend. As Francis Fukuyama explained, the growing influence of atomistic individualism can be seen in the fact that "involuntary ties and obligations based on inherited social class, religion, gender, race, ethnicity, and the like [have been] replaced by ties undertaken voluntarily, . . . [so people] connect only with those with whom they choose to associate."[31] Consequently, people are able to personalize more aspects of their everyday lives, increasingly shaping these interactions to conform to their own image. The journalist Paul Roberts describes this trend well when he notes that "it is now completely normal to demand a personally customized lifestyle. . . . We can choose a vehicle to express our hipness or hostility. We can move to a neighborhood that matches our social values, find a news outlet that mirrors our politics, create a social network that 'likes' everything we say or post."[32] This preference for customization through strictly voluntary association has resulted in what Bill Bishop calls "the Big Sort." According to Bishop, communities in the United States have become more homogeneous since the 1980s, creating starker contrasts between communities and making individuals more likely to self-select where they live in an effort to find neighbors who match their education levels, economic status, political leanings, and even personal tastes.[33] This trend, more than any other, reveals the influence of atomistic individualism because such calculated self-sorting means that what was formerly one of the most unavoidable "encumbrances" of ordinary life in the United States—the local community—has become simply the by-product of unencumbered individuals' voluntaristic choices. The assumption is therefore that individuals are free to disengage from their local community whenever they want, which limits the demands the community can place on its members and reinforces an atomistic notion of the individual as self-sufficient and independent.

Unsurprisingly, this vision of the individual has begun to affect specific elements of ordinary life. Free time is certainly not immune, and recreational choices in particular have begun to reinforce this broader culture of atomistic individualism. Subsequent chapters will delve into these developments in more detail, but suffice it to note that the sociologist Robert Putnam's famous study of declining social capital (and thus, in a way, rising individualism) built its central metaphor, *Bowling Alone*, around changing free time habits.[34] Solidarity's alternative to individualism—especially its excesses in forms like atomistic individualism—makes it a valuable resource for a more critical analysis of both ordinary life as a whole and the specific sphere of free time. Indeed, in a context like the United States, it is impossible to experience free time or any other element of ordinary life apart from the influence of atomistic individualism. Therefore, from a Catholic perspective, it is impossible to conceive of an ethical approach to free time, or any other element of ordinary life, apart from solidarity, which directly challenges the insufficient assumptions of atomistic individualism and presents a nuanced alternative.

Solidarity as the Summons to Both Conversion and Structural Change

If the first two advantages of using solidarity to construct an ethical framework for ordinary life speak to its potential as a necessary and useful critic, the third advantage stems from solidarity's prospects as a solution to the very problems it identifies. This advantage emerges most directly from the work of John Paul II, "who develop[ed] a much more vigorous usage of the term [solidarity]" than any of his predecessors had done.[35] Specifically, he gave sustained attention to the way solidarity's descriptive reality translates into concrete ethical demands, ultimately arguing that earlier treatments of solidarity as a principle needed to be complemented by a new understanding of solidarity as a virtue.[36] In the process, he expanded the application of solidarity to the realm of social structures, articulating an essential third feature of solidarity that adds to its potential as an ethical guide for ordinary life.

The most thorough resource for understanding John Paul II's reinterpretation of solidarity as a virtue is his 1987 encyclical *Sollicitudo rei socialis*. A new feature of this encyclical was its overt treatment of "structures of sin," which created a new connection between solidarity's prescriptive role as a virtue with the moral agent's responsibility to transform social structures. First developed in the work of Latin American theologians after the Second Vatican Council, the notion of structures of sin (or sometimes structural sin) called attention to the unjust institutions and practices that ordered societies in ways that benefited a wealthy subset of the population at the expense of the poorer majorities.[37] Although the idea initially sparked controversy at the Vatican, where some feared that structural sin eradicated personal responsibility, John Paul II showed sympathy for the notion early in his pontificate.[38] In *Sollicitudo rei socialis*, he explicitly argued that the language of structures of sin provided a necessary diagnostic tool for the complex forms of "selfishness" and "shortsightedness" that keep individuals and nations focused on their own exclusive interest rather than the well-being of others.[39] Significantly, John Paul II also argued that the path away from this structural form of sin lay in "the growing awareness of interdependence among individuals and nations ... sensed as a system determining relationships in the contemporary world ... and accepted as a moral category."[40] In effect, he was advancing solidarity's descriptive and prescriptive functions as the appropriate counterweight to structural sin.

Remarkably, when John Paul II described solidarity as an antidote to structures of sin, he also chose to shift the categorization of solidarity's normative function, identifying solidarity as a virtue rather than as a principle. Thus, John Paul II explained the role of solidarity in combating the structures of sin by arguing that "when interdependence becomes recognized in this way, the correlative response as a moral and social attitude, as a 'virtue,' is solidarity." Underscoring the application of this virtue to structural concerns, he further explained, "This then is not a feeling of vague compassion or shallow distress at the misfortunes of so many people, both near and far. On the contrary, it is a firm and persevering determination to commit oneself to the common good; that is to say to the good of all and of each individual, because we are all really responsible for all."[41] In addition, he also avowed that structures of sin "are *only* conquered" by the "commitment to the good of one's neighbor with the readiness, in the gospel sense, to 'lose oneself' for the sake of the other" that defines the virtue of solidarity (emphasis added).[42] John Paul II's description of solidarity as a virtue therefore further highlighted the role of solidarity in structural reform. This was not, however, the only innovation of the encyclical.

In the process of promoting solidarity as a remedy to structural sin, John Paul II also aligned the magisterial interpretation of solidarity with another prominent concept in liberation theology: the preferential option for the poor. To an extent, he did this by encouraging solidarity among the poor, indicating that a close collaboration among the poor themselves could lessen some of the consequences of structural sin.[43] He also argued more broadly that the "option or love of preference for the poor" should be fully incorporated into Catholic social teaching, and then connected this idea with his own explanation of solidarity as a virtue, insisting that solidarity's orientation to the common good and pursuit of structural change was to be manifest "in the love and service of neighbor, *especially of the poorest*" (emphasis added).[44] Consequently, *Sollicitudo rei socialis*'s presentation of solidarity as a virtue became not simply a commitment to the common good but also a commitment to interpreting that common good in light of the experiences of the poor. This distinct perspective further refines the way solidarity can work as a virtue to combat structural sin, ultimately strengthening its status as the appropriate bridge between theological ethics and ordinary life.

Ultimately, John Paul II's vision of solidarity as a virtue adds an essential dimension to ethical discernment in ordinary life because the influence of social structures is unavoidable in this realm. Moral agents therefore need to evaluate not only personal moral responsibility but also social concern when discerning in conscience. The necessity of both of these questions is especially apparent when one understands the function of social structures, especially sinful ones, in more detail. Daniel Finn has proposed a compelling account of how social structures function in ordinary life, drawing on critical realist sociology to add precision to what is often a vague idea in Catholic theology.[45] Although critical realists have multiple ways of describing social structures, Dave Elder-Vass has offered one pithy definition, asserting that "social structure is best understood as the causal power of social groups."[46] Finn follows another critical realist, Margaret Archer, to identify the mechanism of this causal power in "the restrictions, enablements, and incentives which are built into the relationships among social positions."[47] In other words, social structures are the means whereby collective entities affect personal choices, chiefly by ascribing benefits (i.e., enablements and incentives) to the actions they want to encourage and by attaching costs (i.e., restrictions) to the things they want to discourage. As Finn repeatedly stresses, this is not a deterministic effect, because personal agents are always free to ignore the incentives and restrictions accompanying their social positions. Yet the pressures are real nonetheless, and if a social group truly desired a particular outcome, it could make the benefits so strong or the costs so steep as to minimize resistance.[48] When the outcomes that are enforced in this way are morally problematic, they begin to look like structures of sin.

The power of these sinful social structures can be quite significant, for moral psychology has suggested that human beings are evolutionarily preconditioned to adopt the ethical judgments of their immediate social group as a way to facilitate social bonding, which improves the group's ability to protect itself and its members from threats.[49] When structures of sin validate dangerous moral judgments with incentives or other enablements, they effectively encourage personal moral agents to adopt this same perspective, skewing consciences and normalizing sin. As a result, doing the right thing often becomes more difficult (but notably not impossible) in an environment of structural sin.⁵⁰ Unfortunately, such structures really are unavoidable, especially in today's complex, globalized world. The everyday challenges of ordinary life are thus colored by structures of sin, and so solidarity is especially appropriate as an ethical resource in this context because, as both a principle and a virtue, it simultaneously calls attention to personal moral responsibility, which preserves agency in the face of structural sin, and structural accountability, which demands awareness of the corrosive effects of structural sin and a commitment to do something about them. Just as important, by orienting action to the common good and defining the common good in light of the preferential option for the poor, the Catholic notion of solidarity has the ability to shift one's perspective, allowing one to see some of the morally significant features of an ordinary decision that are easy to miss when immersed in the influence of various structures of sin.⁵¹

Solidarity in Sum

Taken together, the three key advantages of solidarity that arise from the magisterial tradition of Catholic social teaching reveal why solidarity is the proper foundation on which to construct an ethical framework for ordinary life—and thus, by extension, the proper tool to shape the ethical evaluation of leisure and recreation. First, the basic presupposition that solidarity is both descriptive and prescriptive attaches the ethics of solidarity to the fundamental convictions of Catholic theological anthropology, ensuring that any prescriptive practices for ordinary life are tied to central faith convictions, thereby creating a robustly theological approach to the ethics of ordinary life. Second, the description of solidarity as an antidote to individualism establishes clear direction for the normative applications of solidarity in a cultural context defined by atomistic individualism, adding specificity to this distinctively Catholic approach. Finally, the presentation of solidarity as both a principle and a virtue gives further guidance for the incorporation of solidarity into ordinary life, indicating that solidarity's commitment to the common good must be defined in reference to the perspective of the poor and pursued through both personal change and structural reform. In essence, then, solidarity provides the framework for empowering theology to inform a whole new way of life and not just a new way of thinking. The major challenge, however, is to figure out how solidarity can be put into practice in the concrete reality of ordinary life. The solution requires adapting the traditional understanding of solidarity in Catholic social teaching, with all three of its advantages for ordinary life intact, into a distinct new form of everyday solidarity that has direct relevance in quotidian situations.

EVERYDAY SOLIDARITY

In order to move from solidarity as it appears in the magisterial tradition of Catholic social teaching to a more immediately practical form of everyday solidarity, two obstacles need to be addressed, one superficial and one substantive. The superficial obstacle is that magisterial documents have traditionally aligned solidarity with collective agents, like nation-states, rather than personal moral actors. This problem is relatively easy to surmount, because there have been recent revisions to the traditional alignment. Nevertheless, the historical roots of solidarity as a resource for international actors mean that the appropriateness of using solidarity as a guide for personal agents still needs some defense. The substantive obstacle, which demands a more critical response, is that the exact nature of solidarity's prescriptive function remains ambiguous in magisterial accounts. One scholar notes that it is variously referred to as a "duty," a "principle," an "attitude," and a "virtue," each of which connotes a different interpretation of solidarity's function as a normative force.[52] In order to explain solidarity's implications for ethics in ordinary life, then, the disconnect between national actors and personal moral agents needs to be addressed; but even more important, the ambiguity surrounding solidarity's normative status needs to be untangled.

Solidarity and the Personal Moral Agent

To begin with the superficial objection, it is a fact that Catholic social teaching has not always envisioned solidarity as a guide for personal action. The most common appeal to solidarity in papal documents has been in the context of international relations, where the primary actor is assumed to be the state rather than the person. This was certainly the case in *Mater et magistra* and *Populorum Progressio*, but it was also true in *Sollicitudo rei socialis*, where John Paul II discussed solidarity in more personal terms but nevertheless identified groups of people as the referents for the moral actions solidarity envisioned.[53] The notion of solidarity as a guide for collective agents thus has the most explicit support in the magisterial tradition of Catholic social teaching, whereas the understanding of solidarity as a tool for personal moral discernment has emerged more implicitly. As a result, there is a degree to which the Catholic notion of solidarity needs to be adapted to serve as a framework for personal discernment in ordinary life. Fortunately, much of the work for such an adaptation has already occurred at both the magisterial level and in the broader body of Catholic social thought.

First, the magisterial account of solidarity has slowly evolved to create more space for a personal form, particularly in the aftermath of *Sollicitudo rei socialis*. Thus, Pope Benedict XVI gave support to a personal interpretation, calling solidarity "first and foremost a sense of responsibility on the part of everyone with regard to everyone" and explicitly insisting that "it cannot therefore be merely delegated to the State."[54] Although his account left room for the more common notion of solidarity as a force governing intergroup relations, it gave more priority to the personal form. Pope Francis, meanwhile, has reinforced this priority, to the point of promoting the cultivation of solidarity in everyday activities like saying grace before meals.[55] His subsequent efforts to encourage solidarity as a necessary corrective to the "globalization of indifference" and the "throwaway culture" further underscore the place of solidarity in the formation of personal moral agents.[56] Indeed, he has effectively recontextualized the earlier deference to group actors by describing solidarity as "a basic attitude ... in relationships between persons, peoples and nations," and not just in the last two of these three.[57] Taken together, these developments indicate that the magisterial account of solidarity has begun to acknowledge that solidarity has genuine prescriptive potential at the personal level, even if this is in addition to its more traditional role at the international level. Consequently, although the development of a distinct form of everyday solidarity as a tool for personal agents involves reshaping the earliest understandings of solidarity found in the magisterial tradition, it is not inconsistent with the ongoing evolution of solidarity in papal teaching.

Second, embracing solidarity as a guide for personal moral discernment is consistent with developments in the broader theological tradition as well. For instance, solidarity has been an essential component of Latin American liberation theology, where the term initially emphasized cooperation among local churches, but always in a way that emerged from relationships of personal encounter.[58] Although the end goal of solidarity in liberation theology still remains a form of collective action that can challenge the oppression of the poor, this group response can emerge only from a sense of personal responsibility in the individual members. Thus, Patricia McAuliffe has insisted that ethics in liberation theology is fundamentally "an ethic of social solidarity," which works "to transform oppressive social structures *and personal relations* into liberating ones" (emphasis added).[59]

Other contemporary theologians have advanced similar claims beyond liberation theology as well. Vincent Miller, for instance, has critiqued the emergence of "virtual solidarity," which allows agents to assume that they are doing good for those in need through an established system—like capitalism—without actually embodying the "political solidarity" that would change the structures that create those needs in the first place. Much like the liberation theologians, he has argued that this kind of social action emerges only from "the uncomfortable, challenging, disruptive aspects of face-to-face, shoulder-to-shoulder solidarity," implying that true solidarity has a radically interpersonal basis.[60] Building on Miller's categorization, Christine Firer Hinze has proposed that the theological alternative to virtual solidarity is a richly "incarnational" solidarity that is properly embodied in a personal pursuit of authentic relationships through a practice of "'unclenched' living" that eschews selfishness.[61] Meanwhile, Meghan Clark has defended solidarity as a "social virtue" that aims to correct a society's "structural vices," asserting that in order to achieve this end, "solidarity can exist as both an individual and a communal virtue."[62] Rebecca Todd Peters likewise defines solidarity in the abstract in relation to "distinct communities or groups of people," but she insists that a practical "ethic of solidarity" begins with "a radical transformation of heart, mind, and soul that literally makes one a new person."[63] Finally, M. Shawn Copeland's explanation of solidarity's significance in feminist theology demonstrates an expectation that each individual Christian will embrace a sense of moral obligation to share the suffering of the marginalized and to work with them for liberation from oppression.[64]

Both the magisterial and nonmagisterial accounts of solidarity therefore indicate that there is ample space to identify solidarity's prescriptive potential for personal agents and not just for collective ones. The sense that solidarity exclusively applies to the latter is therefore a superficial obstacle that could only stand in the way of an everyday form of solidarity for personal agents in theory and not in practice. Furthermore, a personal form of solidarity can serve as a helpful complement to the original form for collective agents. All the existing theological reflections on solidarity stress the necessity of small-scale conversion in order to achieve the large-scale aims of concerted group action. Against this background, the notion of everyday solidarity, which is designed to inculcate solidarity in personal agents through their routine practices in ordinary life, has the potential to create precisely the kinds of moral actors that groups and organizations need to pursue the large-scale, intergroup solidarity found in the earliest models. As a result, the development of an everyday form of solidarity is not merely an acceptable complement to the traditional theological notions of solidarity; it is also a necessary addition that will help the existing theology of solidarity achieve its stated goals. The success of this solution to the superficial obstacle, however, still depends on a fuller response to the substantive obstacle that solidarity's function is too ambiguous to consistently inform moral action.

Solidarity's Prescriptive Function

As stated above, the various magisterial descriptions of solidarity as a duty, a principle, an attitude, and a virtue all point to competing explanations of solidarity's normative function. Duty places solidarity in a deontological paradigm, strengthening the moral obligations emanating from its descriptive reality but revealing little about the rationale behind these responsibilities.[65] Framing solidarity as a principle, meanwhile, presents solidarity as an overall guide rather than a single norm because principles are "general frameworks of moral consideration by which particular decisions about action are to be governed."[66] To describe solidarity as a principle, then, suggests that it should not be limited to a finite number of situations where a specific rule might apply, but instead should be used to direct the moral life as a whole. Linking solidarity with an attitude points to similar emphases, but with a less clearly established ethical force, because this term is not a central component of any ethical system the way duties, principles, and virtues are. Finally, the language of virtue introduces another method of ethical analysis, focusing more on the character of the agent and implying a proper moral disposition that is both formed by and embodied in corollary practices.[67] By employing all four of these interpretations simultaneously, the magisterial account of solidarity limits its prescriptive potential, leaving it too ambiguous to inform concrete choices in a uniform fashion.

In order to move from the general idea of solidarity to a specific account of everyday solidarity, then, this substantive obstacle needs to be addressed. The best solution is to treat the diverse magisterial perspectives on solidarity as complementary rather than competing. After all, as Kevin Doran has observed, there may be four different descriptions for the ethical operation of solidarity, but "each reflects an aspect of the reality of solidarity."[68] By seeking overlaps that might put all these aspects together, a simpler, twofold account of the prescriptive functions of solidarity emerges, and the path to a specific form of everyday solidarity becomes clearer.

First, the notion of solidarity as a principle can helpfully incorporate the understanding of solidarity as a duty. Although principles are not always deontological in scope, they nevertheless imply a force of duty in practice. Consider what is perhaps the most famous application of principles as an ethical system, Tom Beauchamp and James Childress's 1979 book *Principles of Biomedical Ethics*.[69] Summarizing the principles approach years after it was first proposed, in a more recent paper, Beauchamp insisted that although principles were not simply reducible to rules or narrow codifications of one's moral duties, they nevertheless entailed moral duties in operation.[70] Hence, he described the principle of beneficence as "express[ing] an obligation to help others further their important and legitimate interests by preventing and removing harm" and associated the principle of nonmaleficence with the "injunction *primum non nocere*: 'Above all [or first] do no harm.'"[71] Unsurprisingly, scholars have noted that the principles approach of Beauchamp and Childress is not antithetical to a deontological system, but at times actually draws upon this—and other—ethical theories.[72] Similarly, the principle of solidarity can encompass the duty of solidarity. If this were not the case, then the principle would have no ethical force, because principles cannot operate as general guides governing specific actions if they never entail specific actions in practice. The duty of solidarity is therefore legitimately conceived as an extension of the principle. Focusing on the principle, then, reduces some of the ambiguity surrounding solidarity's prescriptive functions without losing sight of solidarity's role as a duty.

A similar form of subsuming is possible with regard to the magisterial presentations of solidarity as an attitude and a virtue. There is a natural affinity between these two terms as a result of the classic definition of virtue as a "disposition."[73] As a disposition, virtue affects an agent's character by informing her or his moral evaluations and priming certain moral actions. As a moral concept, attitudes similarly affect an agent's character through habituation, helping "to ensure that evaluative commitments are embedded in behavioural cognition sufficiently to withstand temptation to act against them."[74] One distinction seems to be that attitudes are more explicitly affective than the dispositions of virtues, because observers note that "solidarity as an attitude has a cognitive and emotional component along with a thrust toward praxis."[75]

With the increasing recognition of the role of the emotions in virtue ethics, however, even this separation founders because virtue ethicists stress that virtue, too, must influence both the affective and cognitive aspects of an agent's moral character in order to have a real effect.[76] Hence, attitudes and virtues have much in common, and their true distinctions reside in nuance rather than substance. One can therefore resolve some of the confusion surrounding solidarity as an attitude and solidarity as a virtue by combining these two aspects together. This is readily justified by the fact that John Paul II, who introduced both the idea of solidarity as an attitude and as a virtue, presented the two terms with a kind of functional equivalence, at least with respect to their moral operation.[77]

Given these observations, the fourfold account of solidarity can be distilled into a twofold interpretation that emphasizes solidarity as both a principle and a virtue without denying the insights implied by alternative presentations of solidarity as a duty and as an attitude. Although this might seem to be just as problematic as saying variously that solidarity is a duty, a principle, an attitude, and a virtue, it is not. On the contrary, precisely because principles and virtues are not reducible to each other, there is added value in preserving solidarity as a principle alongside solidarity as a virtue, especially if solidarity is going to turn into a framework for ethical action in everyday life. The value is most apparent in light of a famous aphorism from the philosopher William Frankena, who insisted that "principles without [virtues] are impotent and [virtues] without principles are blind."[78] His claim reveals that virtues and principles need each other in the moral life, for principles provide the guidance, while virtues provide the means. To envision solidarity as a principle on one hand and as a virtue on the other hand is not dangerously inconsistent but emphatically necessary. In fact, solidarity's potential as both a principle and a virtue is the strongest argument in favor of constructing a general ethical framework for ordinary life around this concept. Unlike most other moral resources, solidarity has the potential to resolve Frankena's tension on its own, ensuring comprehensiveness without sacrificing unity. Given that the entire argument for building an ethical framework before moving to specific applications is to create a consistent approach capable of integrating faith and life into a coherent whole, this asset is indispensable. The central implication of this vision is therefore that the general idea of solidarity will most effectively inform the ethics of ordinary life if it is transformed into a form of everyday solidarity that operates as both a principle and a virtue. The last issue, then, is to specify what the principle of everyday solidarity and the virtue of everyday solidarity mean in practice.

The Principle of Everyday Solidarity

As a principle, everyday solidarity can serve as an overarching guide that directs moral discernment in ordinary life to account for the theological reality of humanity's interdependence. In this sense, everyday solidarity is a principle in the same way that the four principles of bioethics are principles, setting the priorities that moral agents ought to pursue and helping them to identify the most appropriate actions in particular situations. Just as the principle of beneficence calls health care professionals to put the well-being of their patients at the forefront of their clinical judgment—and then, more concretely, helps them adjudicate potential conflicts of interest that can arise from certain reimbursement models (for example)—so the principle of everyday solidarity can dictate the commitments that should be central during moral discernment, effectively spelling out the factors one needs to consider to arrive at a suitable solution to a specific dilemma. By functioning this way, the principle of everyday solidarity also has parallels with the traditional principles of discernment in Catholic moral theology, like the principle of cooperation and the principle of double effect, which indicate the specific elements that an agent must evaluate to make a sound moral judgment in a given case. These established principles may have more clearly delineated criteria, but the principle of everyday solidarity nevertheless seeks a similar end in the refinement of moral judgment. Fundamentally, the principle of everyday solidarity adds a more precise orientation to the discernment process, not only directing agents to do good and avoid evil in general but also helping them discover how their relational anthropology creates obligations that define this primary moral objective.

Given its role in moral judgment, everyday solidarity primarily functions as a principle when it shapes the way personal agents evaluate the ethical significance of their actions in conscience. This could occur after the fact, in what James Keenan calls the "judicial conscience," wherein one evaluates prior decisions and actions in order to determine whether he or she has made the correct moral choice.[79] This type of conscience is commonly, though not exclusively, experienced as a guilty conscience, because the discomfort of an ex post facto indictment tends to be more immediately recognizable than the satisfaction that accompanies correct choices. Certainly, the principle of everyday solidarity has a role to play in the judicial conscience, helping agents examine their past actions to find the decisions that failed to properly account for the reality of human interdependence and that therefore embodied the "failure to bother to love" that Keenan describes as the hallmark of sin.[80] When everyday solidarity functions in this capacity, however, it is not merely an idle critique. It is instead an illuminating analysis that reveals how one might act differently in the future. In Keenan's words, "by knowing our sinful history we can in grace respond to it, ask for forgiveness, overcome it and try not to repeat it."[81] Thus, the principle of everyday solidarity can contribute to a faithful examination of conscience that compares past choices against the descriptive dimension of solidarity, bringing the relational convictions of Catholic theological anthropology into contact with the ordinary choices of everyday life in a way that promotes a change of heart.

Despite these helpful operations in the judicial conscience, everyday solidarity's chief function as a principle is to guide moral agents before they act, which means that its most important work is in the reflections of the "actual conscience."[82] The actual conscience refers to the moral deliberations that allow an agent to determine the right thing to do in a particular situation.

Whereas the judicial conscience offers a retrospective analysis, the actual conscience presents a preemptive assessment, ultimately yielding a judgment that is experienced as a binding command telling an individual what he or she must do.[83] Richard Gula describes this aspect of conscience as a "process," and Timothy O'Connell identifies it as "conscience/2," the particularization of the innate desire to do good (which is classically defined as "*synderesis*" and is labeled "conscience/1" in O'Connell's typology) in a fashion that examines a person's immediate context and enables a decision about what it means to do good and avoid evil in the concrete.[84] In order to answer this question, conscience/2 "searches for what is right through accurate perception, and a process of reflection and analysis."[85] As Russell Connors and Patrick McCormick explain, one important aspect of this process is the identification of the ethical issues that are at stake in a given decision, so that agents can accurately weigh their options in light of the appropriate moral values.[86] This evaluation, like all the considerations involved in conscience/2, is particularly prone to error, making the process of conscience/2 "an aspect of humankind that needs all the help it can get."[87] The principle of everyday solidarity ought to be understood as one indispensable form of help for this "fragile reality."[88] Indeed, throughout this book, the process of conscience/2 is a recurring referent as the primary locus of everyday solidarity's operation as a principle, so it is especially important to take note of what the process of conscience/2 designates in ordinary moral discernment and then to understand how everyday solidarity can help to align this process with some of the most fundamental concerns of the Catholic moral tradition.

As an essential contributor to the process of conscience/2, everyday solidarity hedges against error by helping an agent accurately determine which moral values are at stake in a potential course of action. Because it presumes the descriptive fact of the human person's relational anthropology, the principle of everyday solidarity reminds the agent that other persons are invariably affected by every human choice, even the ones that seem the most personal or independent. In practice, then, everyday solidarity is the principle that obliges moral agents to identify the impact of their actions on others as the principal criterion of discernment in conscience/2. The result is an analysis that asks not merely whether the benefits of a proposed course of action outweigh its costs for the individual actor but also for the broader community as well. This latter point is particularly important, for the principle of everyday solidarity is not ordered to a simple utilitarian maximization of benefit to the greatest number, but instead, like all forms of solidarity, is aligned with the common good. Because, again, the common good is defined as "the good of all and of each" in the Catholic tradition, the principle of everyday solidarity asks agents to pursue the course of action that will best contribute to the full flourishing of all, not just the most.[89]

Although the principle of everyday solidarity thus provides a general commitment to help direct moral discernment, it is not restricted to serving as an overarching priority alone. Like other principles, it has corollary expectations that emerge from and support its broad vision. More specifically, there are three logical extensions of the principle of everyday solidarity that the process of conscience/2 should embrace, and significantly, all three reinforce everyday solidarity's work as a portable distillation of broader themes from the Catholic moral tradition, most especially the assertion that the fullness of human flourishing is found in the life lived morally in the service of others. First, a person's very capacity for relationality must become a priority in his or her moral calculus. Although agents in the US context of atomistic individualism are often encouraged to evaluate their choices in light of a rational desire to maximize self-interest, the relational perspective of everyday solidarity asks each person to examine his or her options in order to choose the actions that will provide the maximum benefits for their relationships. Second, this relational evaluation requires a sincere examination of other people's needs in order to assess what would benefit the relationship from their perspective. After all, the theological basis for solidarity is the Incarnation, a form of radical accompaniment manifest most profoundly in God's willingness to share in the experience of suffering through the cross.[90] Following the model of Christ, one can embrace the obligations of everyday solidarity by sincerely trying to imagine how others might assess the options one considers in the conscience/2 process. Finally, following solidarity's close connection with the preferential option for the poor, this task of moral imagination must give special weight to what Sobrino calls the "view from the victims," meaning that agents will need to evaluate the effects of their actions on the most vulnerable and least well off.[91] This analysis must account for not only direct effects but also indirect ones, especially because the latter are often much more significant.[92] Each of these three features thus reveals specific implications of everyday solidarity, and collectively they reaffirm the central demand of the principle by encouraging the moral actor to evaluate options as an inherently relational being. In this way, the principle of everyday solidarity serves as a tool to promote the full human flourishing of each moral agent, allowing all to become the morally good people they are called to be. Although this makes the principle of everyday solidarity a useful resource for the integration of theological ethics and ordinary life, it remains insufficient without the accompanying virtue of everyday solidarity as well.

The Virtue of Everyday Solidarity

Given the existing connections between solidarity and virtue in Catholic theology, the specific form of everyday solidarity can be defined as a virtue in relation to social reform. Significantly, this does not exclude personal conversion. After all, virtues affect agents and thus entail some form of personal transformation. Indeed, the restoration of virtue ethics in theology during the last forty years was premised on the need for more attention to the moral character of personal actors and not just the rightness or wrongness of their acts.[93] To conceive of everyday solidarity as a virtue, then, is to associate this form of solidarity with personal formation, even when it is oriented to the transformation of social life. This association is entirely reasonable, for although the goal may be social change, the means to that end remain personal actors, so there can be no disconnect between personal conversion and social reform in the key of virtue. Moreover, as discussed above, solidarity's response to structural sin has always been connected to the personal conversion of moral agents, so there must be a personal dimension to the virtue of everyday solidarity as well.[94] These points add appropriate nuance to everyday solidarity's operation as a virtue, but they do not negate its ultimate focus. As a virtue, everyday solidarity must include personal formation, but its proper telos remains social transformation.

Notably, everyday solidarity's function as a virtue is directed at a particular kind of social transformation: the correction of structures of sin. The *Compendium of the Social Doctrine of the Church* justifies this description when it identifies solidarity more generally "*as a moral virtue that determines the order of institutions*," and asserts, "on the basis of this principle the '*structures of sin*' that dominate relationships between individuals and peoples must be overcome" (emphasis in the original).[95] These sinful structures are, again, the restrictions and enablements used by social groups to promote problematic actions that undermine the common good. In practice, then, the virtue of everyday solidarity entails a commitment to the transformation of social structures so that they can serve the common good, just as John Paul II suggested in his initial definition of solidarity as a virtue.[96] Following Finn's critical realist account of sinful social structures, this means targeting the causal power of social groups in two distinct yet related directions: first by reforming the enablements and incentives that encourage personal agents to undermine the common good, and second, by challenging the restrictions that limit personal agents' abilities to promote the common good when they want to do so. At times this will require reworking existing structures of sin so that their enablements, incentives, and restrictions are reoriented to the common good. At other times it will entail working proactively to construct new structures that are inherently ordered to this end. Either way the goal remains the emergence of "structures of grace" to counterbalance existing structures of sin.[97]

Given the abovementioned notion of the common good as the good of all and of each, one can say further that the virtue of everyday solidarity must promote not merely structural reforms in general but also structural reforms specifically designed to facilitate the full flourishing of each human being.[98] This flourishing, in turn, must be defined by the presuppositions of theological anthropology, especially the assertion that the human person is properly fulfilled only through the agapic gift of self that mimics Christ's own selfless love on the cross. Everyday solidarity's commitment to flourishing therefore entails transforming structures, so that each person has "relatively thorough and ready access" to opportunities for self-gift, not just through occasional peak experiences but also in all aspects of their ordinary life.[99]

Significantly, this description of the virtue of everyday solidarity and its operative features narrows its function as a virtue. This is an intentional and essential element of the definition of everyday solidarity as a distinct species of solidarity. Thus, though the thoughtful accompaniment of someone in need might represent an act of solidarity in its general sense, the specific virtue of everyday solidarity requires a different kind of action in light of its role in combating structural sin. It must operate with elements of both an intellectual virtue, insofar as it can inform an agent's perception of the world so that they are more attentive to the structural roots of moral problems, and a moral virtue, insofar as it can empower an agent to take action to correct the structural injustices they see more clearly. Of course, these actions are not divorced from the more general form of solidarity, as the removal of structural obstacles makes genuine accompaniment more feasible and the process of accompaniment with the marginalized makes it easier to see structures of sin. Nevertheless, the virtue everyday solidarity operates in a distinctive fashion through its pursuit of structures of grace.

Ultimately, the narrowness of the virtue of everyday solidarity is reasonable because its restricted scope puts it more directly at the service of the principle of everyday solidarity. Cast in terms of flourishing and the common good, the principle represents a form of self-gift because it asks all moral agents to turn their reflections in the conscience/2 process toward others, and thus (at least in part) away from their own self-interest. This is not an easy goal for someone to achieve consistently in their ordinary life. Certainly, there is the challenge of concupiscence as a kind of moral inertia that plagues any effort at moral improvement, but this is not the only obstacle. In addition, there are also systemic forces that variously make it easier or harder for personal agents to cultivate the powers and dispositions necessary for acting rightly. The philosopher Lisa Tessman has appealed to the idea of "moral luck" to explain that systemic forces always influence an agent's ability to do the right thing and thus to construct the kind of personal character that is constitutive of full human flourishing. In some instances, a person's social situation of privilege enables this endeavor; but in other cases, the structural weight of an agent's immediate context results in "moral damage," making the task of personal conversion exponentially more difficult.[100]

Applying these insights to the issue of everyday solidarity, one can say that the incentives, enablements, and restrictions of social structures will apply differently, and unequally, to different people based on their social positions. In some cases, these social positions will make it easier for agents to employ the principle of everyday solidarity in their deliberations of conscience/2, but in many situations the social positions will actively frustrate efforts to evaluate moral choices from a relational perspective. These discrepancies are rightly understood as a form of moral luck because their origin is outside the agent's control. As such, the vagaries of these structural restrictions are inherently unfair, because, according to the criterion of flourishing, all persons should be empowered to analyze their moral choices in the self-giving way that the principle of everyday solidarity facilitates. The virtue of everyday solidarity therefore examines the structures influencing ordinary life in order to determine what would need to change to allow more people to evaluate their everyday decisions through the lens of relationality and to act accordingly. Once the answer is found, the operative aspects of the virtue commence, prompting action to reform the enablements, incentives, and restrictions that create the negative forms of moral luck currently limiting opportunities for self-gift and thus undermining human flourishing.

In sum, the virtue of everyday solidarity works to make the principle of everyday solidarity a more realistic resource for everyone. It pursues this goal with a particular attention to the sinful social structures that incentivize self-interest or otherwise make it more difficult to evaluate one's moral decisions from a relational perspective. Although this process of structural reform will inevitably take a long time to succeed, the fight itself is just as important as the victory, for the desire to transform social structures in order to help others achieve their full human flourishing is a fine illustration of the principle of everyday solidarity at work. The pursuit of structural reforms according to the virtue of everyday solidarity thus encourages more people to live the kind of life that Catholic relational anthropology demands.

CONCLUSION

The twofold operation of everyday solidarity as both a principle and a virtue creates an ideal ethical framework for approaching ordinary life in a more richly theological fashion. As a principle, everyday solidarity brings the relational anthropology of Catholic theology to bear on ordinary life in a meaningful way, reshaping the way moral agents think about themselves and their responsibilities through a process of personal conversion and conscience formation. As a virtue, everyday solidarity highlights the Catholic theological understanding of the common good, promoting a commitment to that common good through a critical examination of the systemic forces of oppression that require structural reform. In this way, everyday solidarity reflects the fullness of solidarity, which is properly oriented to the salvation and liberation of the oppressed, "both as a theory and as a strategy."[101] Just as important, as an overarching ethical framework, everyday solidarity also reflects solidarity's intrinsic connection to subsidiarity by allowing for personal variation as each agent works to discern the applications of the principle and the virtue of everyday solidarity to the concrete circumstances of their own life.[102] To the extent that people embrace this flexibility and embody everyday solidarity in their ordinary lives, they can more fully realize Pope Francis's depiction of solidarity itself as "a new mind-set which thinks in terms of the community and the priority of the life of all over the appropriation of goods by a few."[103] For Catholics, this would mean, simply, living out their faith in their ordinary lives.

Although it is therefore important to think of ways to pursue everyday solidarity throughout ordinary life, the point of discussing such a broad ethical framework in this context is to understand how it might apply to the specific case of free time. The remainder of the book deals with this question in detail, but at this point it is nevertheless helpful to indicate how everyday solidarity can guide the evaluation of leisure and recreation in broad terms. First, the principle of everyday solidarity indicates that relationality must be the primary lens for evaluating the ethical impact of leisure and recreation. This has practical consequences in both areas of free time, but generally it helps to mitigate the tendency to see free time choices as isolated decisions that have effects on the agent alone. Second, the virtue of everyday solidarity demands that one look to improve others' opportunities for relationally rich forms of leisure and recreation, mainly by working to change existing structural forces that limit access to free time or that incentivize problematic recreational pursuits. When both these concerns are held together, leisure and recreation can come closer to their full potential, and free time can be transformed into a genuine opportunity for the greater integration of faith and life.

NOTES

1. Peters, *Solidarity Ethics*, 17–23.
2. Tillman, *Master Calls*.
3. Aquinas, *ST*, II-II.23.8; Gilleman, *Primacy of Charity*.
4. Beyer, "Meaning of Solidarity," 13.
5. Beyer, 9; Doran, *Solidarity: A Synthesis*, 81.
6. Pius XII, *Summi pontificatus*, 15.
7. Pius XII, 35.
8. On the importance of solidarity's descriptive and prescriptive elements in Catholic theology, see Beyer, "Meaning of Solidarity," 15. For an outline of the Magisterium's subsequent usage of solidarity, see Bilgrien, *Solidarity: A Principle*, 4–12.
9. John XXIII, *Mater et magistra*, 155, 157.
10. *Apostolicam actuositatem*, 8; *Gaudium et spes*, 32. On *Gaudium et spes* in particular, Christine Firer Hinze has further highlighted the close relationship between the relational concerns of Catholic theological anthropology and the normative implications of solidarity articulated in the Pastoral Constitution. See Hinze, "Straining toward Solidarity," esp. 168–74.
11. Pontifical Council for Justice and Peace, *Compendium*, 110, 149.
12. Buckley, "Catholic University," 17–18.
13. *Gaudium et spes*, 24.
14. Heyer, "Catholics," 62–63.
15. *Gaudium et spes*, 32.
16. *Gaudium et spes*, 75.
17. Clark, "Anatomy," 34; more generally, see also 31–35.
18. Paul VI, *Populorum progressio*, 64.
19. John Paul II, *Centesimus annus*, 49.
20. Benedict XVI, *Caritas in veritate*, 43.
21. See Hofstede, Hofstede, and Minkov, *Cultures and Organizations*, 93–95; Lipset, *American Exceptionalism*, 18–19. For a critical take on Lipset's historical arguments, see Grabb, Baer, and Curtis, "Origins." Notably, Grabb, Baer, and Curtis merely challenge the pervasiveness of a certain type of individualism at the founding of the United States. They do not dispute its subsequent influence.
22. Machan, "Liberalism," 227; Williams, *Keywords*, 115. On the classical Greek roots of the term "atom," see Van Melsen, *From Atomos to Atom*, 19, 131–32.
23. Taylor, "Atomism," 187–210, at 190–91.
24. Taylor, 188.
25. This description builds on Michael Sandel's notion of the "unencumbered self." Sandel, *Democracy's Discontent*, 11–13.
26. For a summary of the historical development, see Jones and Kelly, "Sloth," 118–22. Atomistic individualism aligns with the category of "liberal individualism" in that article. See also Sandel, *Democracy's Discontent*, which on the whole argues that in the United States this liberal (here atomistic) form of individualism has triumphed over a more "republican" strand, especially since the twentieth century.
27. Taylor, "Atomism," 189.
28. Bellah et al., *Habits of the Heart*, 20.
29. Bellah et al., 23.

30. In further support of the assertion that the cultural power of atomistic individualism has risen in recent years, Bellah and his colleagues argue that this form of individualism was not always the first language of discourse in the United States, and previously competed with other equally influential first languages. Bellah et al., 27–28.
31. Fukuyama, *Great Disruption*, 47; see also Hall and Lindholm, *Is America Breaking Apart?* 104–6.
32. Roberts, *Impulse Society*, 3.
33. Bishop, *Big Sort*, 130–36, 155, 212. Other scholars have documented similar trends, especially when the sorting expands beyond political ideology. See Roberts, *Impulse Society*, 115–18; Dunkelman, *Vanishing Neighbor*, 46–49; cf. Abrams and Fiorina, "Big Sort That Wasn't," 203–9. Notably, Adams and Fiorina do not deny the trend of ideological sorting; they just contest Bishop's overgeneralization of this trend to politically homogenous communities throughout the United States as a whole. Finally, it is worth noting that not everyone has had the freedom to self-sort in the way Bishop identified, because relocation requires a degree of economic security that is unattainable for most lower-income households. Hence, the urban planning and public policy researcher Richard Florida calls this the "means migration." Florida, "Inequality Puzzle"; see also Florida, "Where the Brains Are."
34. Putnam, *Bowling Alone*, 109–12.
35. Peters, *Solidarity Ethics*, 25.
36. Since John XXIII's *Mater et magistra*, the Magisterium had been describing solidarity's prescriptive functions by identifying it explicitly as a moral principle. John XXIII, *Mater et magistra*, 23.
37. Faus, "Sin," esp. 536–39.
38. Scholars note this resistance especially in the Magisterium's reaction to the language of "social sin," of which structural sin is one manifestation. See Pfeil, "Doctrinal Implications," 134. On John Paul II's support, see Curran, *Moral Theology*, 82; and John Paul II, *Reconciliatio et paenitentia*, 16.
39. John Paul II, *Sollicitudo rei socialis*, 36, 37.
40. John Paul II, 38.
41. John Paul II, 38.
42. John Paul II, 38; see also 40.
43. John Paul II, 39.
44. John Paul II, 42, 45.
45. Finn, "What Is a Sinful Social Structure?" 142–54.
46. Elder-Vass, *Causal Power*, 115.
47. Finn, "What Is a Sinful Social Structure?" 154.
48. Finn, 154; see also 152, 153.
49. Haidt, "Emotional Dog and Its Rational Tail," 821; see also Haidt, "Emotional Dog Does Learn New Tricks," 197–98.
50. For more on this process, see Kelly, "Nature and Operation," 313–23.
51. Heyer, "Social Sin and Immigration," 423–24; Himes, "Social Sin and the Role of the Individual," 193.
52. Bilgrien, *Solidarity: A Principle*, 1; Doran, *Solidarity: A Synthesis*, 191–93.
53. See John Paul II, *Sollicitudo rei socialis*, 9, 33, 36, 39.
54. Benedict XVI, *Caritas in veritate*, 38.
55. Francis, *Laudato si'*, 227.

56. Francis, "Message for the Celebration of the 2014 World Day of Peace," 1; Francis, "Address during Visit to the Community at Varginha," 1; Francis, "Address to Participants in the Ecumenical Convention of Bishop-Friends of the Focolare Movement."
57. Francis, "Message for World Food Day 2013."
58. Sobrino, "Communion, Conflict, and Ecclesial Solidarity," 632; Sobrino, "Bearing with One Another," 6, 10, 21.
59. McAuliffe, *Fundamental Ethics*, 109; more generally, see also 92–110.
60. Miller, *Consuming Religion*, 76.
61. Hinze, "Straining toward Solidarity," 174–75, 182–83.
62. Clark, "Anatomy," 37; see also 31–35.
63. Peters, *Solidarity Ethic*, 51, 60.
64. Copeland, "Toward a Critical Christian Feminist Theology," 28–31.
65. Gula, *Reason Informed by Faith*, 21.
66. Hays, *Moral Vision of the New Testament*, 209.
67. Keenan, "Virtue Ethics," 84–94.
68. Doran, *Solidarity: A Synthesis*, 191.
69. Beauchamp and Childress, *Principles*.
70. Beauchamp, "'Four-Principles' Approach," 3.
71. Beauchamp, 4, 5.
72. See Mitchell, "Major Changes," 460–65.
73. Aquinas, *ST*, I-II.55.2 ad 1; see also Aristotle, *Nicomachean Ethics*, 1108b10–15.
74. Webber, "Character, Attitude, and Disposition," 1087; see also 1087–89.
75. Bilgrien, *Solidarity: A Principle*, 53.
76. See Lawler and Salzman, "Virtue Ethics," 450–56; Cochran, "Moral Significance"; Cates, *Aquinas*, 248–54.
77. Bilgrien, *Solidarity: A Principle*, 52.
78. Frankena, *Ethics*, 65.
79. Keenan, "Examining Conscience," 16.
80. Keenan, *Moral Wisdom*, 55–58.
81. Keenan, "Called to Conscience," 16.
82. Connors and McCormick, *Character, Choices, and Community*, 124.
83. Connors and McCormick, 124–30.
84. Gula, *Reason Informed by Faith*, 131–33; O'Connell, *Principles for a Catholic Morality*, 109–11.
85. Gula, *Reason Informed by Faith*, 132.
86. Connors and McCormick, *Character, Choices, and Community*, 126.
87. O'Connell, *Principles for a Catholic Morality*, 111.
88. O'Connell.
89. John Paul II, *Sollicitudo rei socialis*, 38.
90. This aspect of solidarity is highlighted in the work of Jürgen Moltmann. See, e.g., Moltmann, *Jesus Christ for Today's World*, 38–40.
91. Sobrino, *Christ the Liberator*.
92. E.g., environmental degradation is seldom viewed as a direct effect of one's choices, but it has an outsize impact on those who are in poverty throughout the world. Francis, *Laudato si'*, 48.
93. Keenan, "Proposing Cardinal Virtues," 709–10.
94. See, e.g., John Paul II, *Sollicitudo rei socialis*, 38.

95. Pontifical Council for Justice and Peace, *Compendium*, 193.
96. See, again, John Paul II, *Sollicitudo rei socialis*, 38.
97. See Ahern, *Structures of Grace*, 130–36.
98. John Paul II, *Sollicitudo rei socialis*, 38.
99. See *Gaudium et spes*, 26.
100. Tessman, *Burdened Virtues*, 11–31. Significantly, Tessman also critiques the traditional interpretations of "moral damage," cautioning that the uncritical use of this idea might result in a kind of victim shaming that further reinforces the conditions of oppression that limit moral freedom. She ultimately uses this caution, however, to reclaim a more nuanced account of moral damage. Tessman, 33–52.
101. Isasi-Díaz, *Mujerista Theology*, 92.
102. Benedict XVI, *Caritas in veritate*, 58.
103. Francis, *Evangelii gaudium*, 187.

PART II

Applications to Leisure

CHAPTER 3

Leisure and the Principle of Everyday Solidarity

With the overarching ethical framework in place, the next step in an ethical analysis of free time is to consider how both the principle and the virtue of everyday solidarity can generate a more intentional approach to leisure and recreation. In the case of leisure, this is best accomplished by separately applying the principle of everyday solidarity and the virtue of everyday solidarity. The rationale is that leisure, unlike recreation, is a clearly defined concept, so it can therefore be analyzed as a singular category, with both the principle and the virtue of everyday solidarity providing guidance for leisure as a whole. Recreation, in contrast, is a remainder concept that needs to be evaluated in its concrete manifestations, with the principle and the virtue of everyday solidarity working in tandem to assess specific recreational pursuits. These differences justify the structures of the remaining six chapters of this book (two on leisure in general, and four on different recreational pursuits in particular); but they also point to a logical starting point, which is the focus of this chapter: the impact of the principle of everyday solidarity on leisure.

As a principle, everyday solidarity's primary impact is on ethical discernment, where it prompts the conscience to pay particular attention to the relational nature of the human person. By orienting ethical discernment to relationality in this way, the principle of everyday solidarity empowers moral agents to see the effects of their actions on others. In the process, the principle of everyday solidarity also strengthens the relational nature of the moral actor herself or himself, contributing to the fuller flourishing of the agent as a human being. Through these two functions, the principle of everyday solidarity generates a more critical evaluation of leisure that orients both leisure and the one at leisure to their fullest potential. How this occurs is the subject of this chapter—which, first, uses the principle of everyday solidarity's focus on relationality to reinforce the ethical prioritization of leisure over recreation alluded to in chapter 1 and, second, discusses how the pursuit of flow during free time can be helpfully structured around the human person's relational identity. This yields a more complete account of what is at stake in the personal moral evaluation of leisure, setting the stage for the virtue of everyday solidarity's complementary analysis of the ethics of leisure at the structural level.

LEISURE IN THE SERVICE OF RELATIONALITY, AND ITS PRIORITY OVER RECREATION

Because the principle of everyday solidarity promotes the full flourishing of the person at leisure as well as the full potential of leisure itself, the question of how leisure fits properly within the human person's moral life as a whole is one of its central concerns. Naturally, the principle of everyday solidarity's emphasis on relationality indicates that free time ought to be directed at the realization of right relationships, so this serves as the overarching goal for the subcategory of leisure. The achievement of this goal, however, depends in part on preserving the proper relationship between leisure and recreation, because the distinction between these two elements of free time implies an ethical ordering that is perfectly consistent with, and ultimately strengthened by, the principle of everyday solidarity.

Recall from the definitions developed in chapter 1 that leisure and recreation have distinct theological values. Leisure has an intrinsic value, derived from its ability to prefigure heavenly rest; and recreation has an extrinsic value, rooted primarily in its ability to restore the human person for his or her relational obligations. Following the parallels with Augustine's notions of enjoyment and use, these differences justify an ethical prioritization of leisure over recreation—although, again, this is not an absolute prioritization, because one can legitimately use free time for both leisure pursuits and recreational activities. Instead, the effect of this prioritization is to ensure that people do not simply default to recreation, which could easily occur because leisure establishes a higher ideal for free time and is therefore less likely to be sought in the absence of an intentional commitment to seek flow experiences. The principle of everyday solidarity details the practical implications of the proper prioritization, yielding specific practices for putting leisure ahead of recreation in a realistic and sustainable fashion. Before getting to this issue, which is the focus of the second section of this chapter, it is worth discussing how the principle of everyday solidarity supports the prioritization itself, in two ways.

First, the principle of everyday solidarity emphasizes relationality in ethical discernment, ensuring that decisions made in conscience are made in a way that promotes the full flourishing of a relational being. In other words, the principle of everyday solidarity directs the person to the right realization of all his or her relationships, so that a person's relationships with God, with self, and with others can thrive. All these relationships are important, but one's relationship with God holds a certain pride of place in the Christian tradition. Jesus's reflection on the greatest commandment included a twofold call to love God and one's neighbor (and arguably oneself), but there was not complete parity between these objects of love. Love of neighbor and love of self may have been placed on an equal footing, but in the succinct phrasing of Diana Fritz Cates, "Christians are enjoined to love God above all things."[1] Furthermore, this relationship is at the heart of the human person's relational nature. As the *Compendium of the Social Doctrine of the Church* explains, the first chapter of Genesis reveals "that the creation of man and woman is a free and gratuitous gift of God; [and] that man and woman, because they are free and intelligent, represent the 'thou' created by God and that only in relationship with [God] can they discover and fulfill the authentic and complete meaning of their personal and social lives."[2]

As a result, one cannot conceive of the full flourishing of a relational human being without the right realization of the person's relationship with God. The principle of everyday solidarity can therefore justify the prioritization of leisure over recreation because leisure calls attention to one's relationship with God in a particular way, aiding in the fulfillment of this essential aspect of the human person's relational nature.

When conceived theologically, leisure necessarily points to God in an innate way because leisure's intrinsic value stems from the parallels between the experience of flow and the promise of heavenly rest. The value of leisure thus depends on the value of heavenly rest, but heavenly rest has an ultimate value—and serves as the human person's true telos—only because it is rest in union with God. This is the message that theologians typically take from the fact that God rested on the Seventh Day of creation, for the Hebrew verb for this rest, "*shabat*," depicts cessation and implies a sense of completion for all creation.[3] Thus, rest becomes an essential component of the proper teleological vision for every creature, amounting to the "final goal of Creation."[4] For human beings, created in the image and likeness of God and destined for communion with God, this final goal is properly realized in "rest in fellowship with the rest of God, of participation in the freedom, rest and joy of [God's] true deity."[5]

Indeed, if heavenly rest is to be the final fulfillment of the human person, the completion of this creature's true purpose, then it must be rest in union with God. For as Thomas Aquinas famously argued, the human being's "final and perfect happiness [i.e., fulfillment] can consist in nothing else than the vision of the Divine Essence."[6] Hope for heavenly rest, then, is fundamentally hope for rest in the presence of God. To value leisure as a prefiguration of heavenly rest is therefore to value one's relationship with God. Indeed, to seek leisure as a prefiguration of the divine rest one hopes to experience in the next life is a way to honor that relationship. Consistent with the principle of everyday solidarity, then, leisure has a priority over recreation, because leisure inherently accentuates the person's relational connection with God and innately furthers that relationship, whereas recreation can do so only by extension. By prioritizing leisure over recreation, moral agents reaffirm the significance of their relationship with God as a true "ultimate concern," which allows them to acknowledge their relational identity and to pursue its fullness in exactly the manner that the principle of everyday solidarity demands.[7]

Second, the principle of everyday solidarity also supports the prioritization of leisure over recreation as a way of honoring the other dimensions of the human person's relational nature. In particular, leisure can facilitate the realization of right relationships with self and others because one of the essential features of any truly human relationship is the connection that is forged by being fully present to another. This may seem overly intuitive and similarly easy to achieve, but it is not. In fact, as the Anglican priest and theologian Samuel Wells points out, the most common tendency today (at least in the Western world) is to relate to others through doing rather than being. Establishing a contrast between doing something "for" someone and being "with" someone, Wells argues that people are more comfortable with the former than the latter, despite the fact that "'for'... does not dismantle resentment, it does not overcome misunderstanding, it does not deal with alienation, it does not overcome isolation."[8] Even more poignantly, Wells notes, "'for' is not the way God relates to us"; rather, Wells insists, "God's whole life and action and purpose are shaped to be with us," a truth most profoundly evident in the mystery of the Incarnation, which reveals that God is with humanity in everything, even in the darkness of suffering and death.[9] This has significant effects on relationships, and even relationality, because, as Wells acknowledges, "in a lot of ways, 'with' is harder than 'for.' You can do 'for' without a conversation, without a real relationship, without a genuine shaping of your life to accommodate and incorporate the other."[10] In light of the challenge of truly being with others, and in the face of a propensity to do things for others by default, the pursuit of leisure during free time takes on new meaning, for the ideal of leisure (represented in flow) requires an immersion in the moment that serves the demands of being present with someone in a meaningful way.

Leisure, by its very nature, combats the contemporary inclination to relate to others by doing something for them and instead reintroduces the value of being with them. First, because leisure has an intrinsic value, its worth is not dependent on its utility. As a result, leisure questions the utilitarian assumptions underlying the constant desire to do something for others, revealing that there is a value in being and not only in doing.[11] In this way, leisure can strengthen a person's relational nature by preparing him or her to see the significance of simply being with others. Second, leisure can also facilitate the experience of being with others in a genuine way. Although flow is obviously experienced subjectively, it is not necessarily encountered in isolation. A number of shared leisure activities—from games and sports to conversations and time with one's family—are conducive to flow.[12] When people experience flow with others in these ways, they are necessarily encountering the depths of their relationality because flow requires an intensity of focus that allows one to be fully present in the moment. In fact, according to Csikszentmihalyi, "While [flow] lasts, people lose their self-conscious sense of individuality and often report a feeling of union with entities larger than the self," meaning that flow allows not only presence with another but also a meaningful sense of union with the other.[13]

Just as important, flow cannot tolerate distraction, so it also represents a remedy to one of the major obstacles to authentic human connection in the age of ubiquitous technological connectivity: digital distraction.[14] Specifically, flow counteracts what the psychologist Kenneth Gergen has come to define as the problem of "absent presence," whereby people are physically present together in the same space but mentally absent from one another as they turn their attention to screens of one form or another.[15] This phenomenon is easy to imagine, especially in the technologically saturated context of the United States, and it does real damage to people's relational capacities. As the social psychologist and Massachusetts Institute of Technology professor Sherry Turkle observes, "We expect more from technology and less from each other."[16] In this environment, the experience of flow—and thus leisure—presents an invaluable opportunity to build connection with other human beings in a way that counteracts the habituation of multitasking and the prevalence of digital distraction by immersing people in the depth of one activity and in the fullness of their relationships.[17]

Given the possibilities of flow for promoting an awareness of the depth of life, cultivating a person's relational capacities, and nurturing genuine human connections, the principle of everyday solidarity logically supports the prioritization of leisure over recreation. This is not to say that recreation has no relational value. As part III of this book demonstrates, recreation has a similar ability to serve relationships in a manner consistent with the principle of everyday solidarity. Nevertheless, there remains a difference of degree between leisure and recreation on this point. Leisure, because of the characteristics of flow, inherently provides the benefits for relationality outlined above. Recreation, however, cannot promote depth and relationality in the same way because recreation's primary value is extrinsic. Recreation is, by definition, always sought with some other end in mind. The benefits to relationships in recreation are therefore complicated by the fact that these benefits are incidental rather than essential. As a result, recreation has a more limited ability to serve as a corrective to the utilitarian assumptions that make living for others appear so much more attractive than being with them. Consequently, leisure can do more than recreation to help moral agents recognize and esteem their relationality, and it can also do more than recreation to forge relational connections that hinge on being together rather than doing something together. The fact that leisure additionally foregrounds one's relationship with God in this process means that leisure is especially capable of supporting the human person's relational nature in its fullness, nourishing the full range of relationships that constitute an authentically human life. For this reason, the principle of everyday solidarity strengthens the prioritization of leisure over recreation, counseling moral agents to place the former ahead of the latter in the ethical evaluation of free time. At the same time, the principle of everyday solidarity also offers the resources to make sense of this obligation in concrete terms, providing practical guidance for the prioritization of leisure over recreation in ordinary life.

AN ORDERING OF LEISURE IN THE SERVICE OF RELATIONSHIPS

Just as the principle of everyday solidarity supports the prioritization of leisure over recreation as a means to secure the fulfillment of human relationality in general, so too it can justify the relative ordering of specific leisure pursuits in order to promote the full realization of particular relationships. Notably, this strategy also fits leisure's role as a prefiguration of heavenly rest quite well, for Christian interpretations of eternal life are decidedly relational. As Augustine explained, "The supreme reward is that we should enjoy [God] and that all of us who enjoy [God] should also enjoy one another in [God]."[18] Or, as the *Catechism of the Catholic Church* insists, "Heaven is the blessed community of all who are perfectly incorporated into Christ."[19]

Communion is thus central to the Christian understanding of heaven, and consequently, leisure most fully prefigures heavenly rest when flow is encountered in a relational context. For this reason, the principle of everyday solidarity can go beyond the general prioritization of leisure over recreation to commend more specifically the pursuit of those flow-inducing free time activities that foster genuine relationships. Further, through an analogical application of the ordering of love, the principle of everyday solidarity can guide an ordering of leisure that emphasizes the importance of time for God, time for self, and time for others, yielding a practical plan for incarnating the prioritization of leisure over recreation in a meaningful and sustainable way.

From the Ordering of Love to the Ordering of Leisure

Building an ordering of leisure on an analogy with the ordering of love requires an understanding of the more traditional concept. In this endeavor, the work of Thomas Aquinas is especially helpful because his careful consideration of the order of charity "provides the classic account of the ordering of priorities in the Christian moral life."[20] Moreover, his approach is expressly compatible with the principle of everyday solidarity, for he based his ordering of love on a theological anthropology that defined the human person in relation to God as his or her final end.[21] On this basis, he defended an order of charity that placed love of God at the top of the hierarchy, because this was the most fitting form of love according to the human person's created nature.[22] He then proceeded to evaluate love in a variety of relationships, using two criteria: nearness to God and nearness to the moral agent. The latter criterion allowed Aquinas to not only preserve but also emphasize the natural tendencies of human love and the concrete expressions of human relationality.[23] Hence, Aquinas asserted that moral agents should love themselves ahead of their neighbors because the love of self was both more intensely natural and more directly ordered to the realization of spiritual union with God.[24] Likewise, he justified the more detailed ordering of the love of different neighbors by appealing to both criteria, placing the love of one's family members—at least in the intensity of affections and in acts of love—ahead of the love of other individuals, on the presupposition that bonds of blood created closer connections than the bonds of a shared civic heritage or common human nature.[25] In broad strokes, then, Aquinas created a straightforward order of charity: love of God first, love of self second, and love of neighbor third.

Analogically, this ordering of love can turn into an ordering of leisure that encourages people to find flow during their free time in activities that sustain their relationships with God, with self, and with others. Furthermore, the parallel with Aquinas's ordering of love indicates that these pursuits can and should be prioritized with time for God ahead of time for self and ahead of time for others. But the ordering of leisure cannot be applied absolutely, for doing so would undermine the very idea of an ordering. After all, time with an omnipotent, omnipresent God would seem to be a constant possibility, so one would never be able to choose time for self or time for others if the priorities were strictly enforced. Yet the whole point of developing an ordering of leisure as part of the principle of everyday solidarity is to call attention to the multirelational nature of each human person. As a result, the proper application of the ordering of leisure must center on balancing these relationships. In cases of outright conflict, this balancing might require a strict insistence on the basic order, but generally the ordering of leisure should be employed to ensure that none of the three major categories of relationships is neglected during free time. Thus, though the analogy with the ordering of love justifies a prima facie prioritization of time with God ahead of time for self and places both of these ahead of time with others, in practical application, the ordering of leisure must proceed more holistically so that it can function in a manner befitting the principle of everyday solidarity's insistence on the full realization of all of a human person's relationships, not just one type of them.

Even more so than the ordering of love, then, the ordering of leisure should be understood as a tool of moral evaluation that allows the moral agent to assess his or her free time pursuits using the relational perspective that the principle of everyday solidarity incorporates into the discerning work of the conscience/2 process. The ordering of leisure therefore functions best as a spiritual practice, akin to the Ignatian examen, which allows people to evaluate their moral progress over time. Traditionally, the Ignatian examen asks a person to reflect back on the past 24 hours in order to identify moments of "consolation," when God's grace was most evident, and moments of "desolation," when the temptations of sin were most powerful. When incorporated as a daily ritual, the examen allows a person to keep track of the movements of the spirit and to discern the best ways to follow God's will in the concrete particulars of one's life.[26] Everyday solidarity's ordering of leisure can proceed in much the same way, although it will probably be more effective when employed as a weekly diagnostic. Thus, moral agents would examine their free time over the last seven days to see if they had made adequate time for God, time for themselves, and time for others. Then, they would be able to use the insights gleaned from this reflection to plan their free time in the coming week.

Of course, because this ordering of leisure is guided by the principle of everyday solidarity, the basis of evaluation cannot be restricted to quantity of time alone. Quality is in fact more important, because the principle of everyday solidarity is meant to guide relationships to their fullest potential, not merely to acknowledge their existence. In addition, the weekly review is properly an ordering of *leisure*, so quality is an essential focal point in this evaluation because the experience of flow will not emerge without a significant degree of intentional engagement in the activity at hand. Accordingly, everyday solidarity's ordering of leisure invites moral agents to assess their time with God, time with self, and time with others against the standard of flow. Though demanding, this is not an impossible standard, for flow has been associated with activities that would serve each of these relationships in various ways. To illustrate this point, and to provide additional guidance for applying the ordering of leisure in a weekly examen, it is useful to consider specific examples of how a person can use various leisure pursuits to develop his or her relationships with God, with self, and with others.

Time for God

The human person's relationship with God offers fertile ground for the experience of flow, meaning that this relationship can be sustained and strengthened through leisure. In one of his earliest descriptions of the idea of flow, Csikszentmihalyi identified "the grace of God that the mystic seeks to attain" as a paradigmatic example.[27] He has similarly referred to the "ecstasy" of mysticism as simply another word for the experience he calls flow.[28] Sociologists of religion, meanwhile, have argued that flow is a useful hermeneutical concept for those looking to understand and interpret religious experience, noting that "in modern pluralist society there are many avenues to flow, but religions continue to be an important source."[29] To this end, one researcher has asserted that the routines of Catholic religious life, specifically the earliest rules of the Society of Jesus, "provided an optimal set of conditions by which young men could live the entirety of their lives as a single flow experience."[30] As this scholarship indicates, a wide variety of spiritual practices are conducive to flow, for they are able to "combine routine with uncertainty, producing a challenging state 'beyond boredom and anxiety.'"[31] Leisure therefore offers a fine opportunity to foster one's relationship with God, and although there are many leisure pursuits that might serve this end, two—prayer and liturgy—can be examined here in more detail.

First, prayer is an obvious way to use one's free time to relate to God. Prayer is so essential to one's relationship with God that the *Catechism of the Catholic Church* refers to prayer itself as the believer's "vital and personal relationship with the living and true God."[32] Within this relationship, there are a number of ways to pray. Prayers of praise and thanksgiving have deep scriptural roots, and they can generate an experience of flow, if for no other reason than that they require people "to forget self and become open to the primacy of the divine."[33] This mirrors the self-transcendence at the heart of flow while also orienting the person to God in a way that "expresses and celebrates the gift of [their] relationship."[34]

Meditations on Scripture, meanwhile, represent another way to use leisure to strengthen one's relationship with God, for relationships develop when both parties get to know one another as they really are, and Scripture, as a tool of God's self-revelation to the world, represents an incomparable resource for deepening one's understanding of who God really is.[35] Among the various ways of praying with Scripture to encounter God in this way, the traditional practices of *lectio divina* and Ignatian contemplation seem especially well suited to the experience of flow, for both allow an intense immersion in Scripture that orders consciousness to the encounter with God and, in some cases, seems to temporarily transplant the person at prayer into the world of the text itself.[36] Other forms of meditation, like centering prayer, can result in a similar flow state, revealing another way to use leisure to relate well with God.[37] Notably, all these prayer practices are experienced subjectively and therefore admit variation as God meets the individual at prayer as he or she is, such that no one expects the prayer experience of Teresa of Ávila to match that of a young adult trying contemplative prayer for the first time. As a result, prayer can easily facilitate the alignment of skills and challenges from which flow emerges.

Of all the forms of prayer, the one that is probably the most common might seem to facilitate one's relationship with God the least well, for intercessory prayer hinges on asking God *for* something, which seems to contradict the call simply to be with God.[38] Even this form of prayer, however, is fundamentally relational, because "the efficacy of [this] praying is not to be measured in terms of a causal link between petition and response, as if there were an automatic link between request and fulfillment. Rather, it takes place within the relational dynamics between Higher Power and the subject who begs."[39] In other words, intercessory prayer is not so much about the intercession as it is about the relationship it creates and sustains between God and the intercessor. Just as important, intercessory prayer situates this relationship in the broader context of the person's relationality as a whole. As Pope Francis explained in *Gaudete et exsultate*, "Prayer of intercession has particular value, for it is an act of trust in God and, at the same time, an expression of love for our neighbour."[40] In intercessory prayer, then, people strengthen their relationship with God while also honoring their relationships with others (and possibly with the self), making this form of prayer an appropriate way to use leisure in light of the principle of everyday solidarity.

Second, liturgy provides another opportunity to experience flow with God in a way that reflects the priorities of the principle of everyday solidarity. Liturgy is, of course, a form of prayer; but it is so formalized that it deserves distinct treatment. In fact, the ritualization of liturgy is an essential part of its contributions to flow because the routines of rites help to redirect one's concentration to the liturgy itself, combating distraction and facilitating the ordering of consciousness at the heart of flow.[41] Also, though the categories might seem an odd fit in this context, the liturgy nevertheless provides a balancing of skills and activities like other forms of flow as long as one evaluates the skills that are particular to a liturgical context. At least in a Catholic context, liturgical rites are designed to yield the "full and active participation by all the people," specifically enabling the members of the Body of Christ to engage in worship to the fullest extent of the faculties accorded to their state in life.[42] The liturgy therefore presents a legitimate flow experience. However, some might still object to the idea that liturgy is a leisure activity.

The original Greek term, *leitourgia*, means "work of the people," and participation in religious rites has regularly been identified in the Christian tradition as an obligation, either as a derivative of the commandment to "keep holy the Sabbath" or as a matter of the justice creatures owe to their Creator.[43] Both these facts would seem to support identifying liturgy as a form of work, rather than leisure, but there are limits to this assumption. Granted, the word *leitourgia* may literally mean the work of the people, but one cannot simply equate Christian liturgy with *leitourgia*, and even if one could, the "work" of liturgy is not work in the sense that it must be contrasted with leisure.[44] This is most evident in the fact that the Christian obligation to participate in the community's liturgical celebrations quickly became paired with a complementary obligation to refrain from work (understood, with some exceptions, as one's professional occupation) on Sundays.[45] In the Christian tradition, then, the liturgy has been juxtaposed with work, justifying the claim that the liturgy fits within the ordering of leisure as a way of developing one's relationship with God during free time. The definition of leisure further strengthens this assertion, because leisure is meant to serve as prefiguration of heavenly rest, and liturgy is often described theologically as a foretaste of heaven as well.[46] Participation in liturgical rites therefore represents a true form of leisure, one that builds one's relationship with God by recognizing one's proper place before the Creator. Not insignificantly, the liturgy does this in a public context, thereby affirming one's relational links to a community of faith at the same time. To use the liturgy as a means of setting aside time for God is thus to order one's leisure according to the principle of everyday solidarity in its fullest sense.

Naturally, there are other ways to honor one's relationship with God through leisure activities, but prayer and liturgy hold a rightful preeminence, due to both their deep roots in the Christian tradition and their ability to connect one with God in a way that preserves and underscores one's relational connections with others. Together, they both demonstrate the potential that leisure holds for fostering one's relationship with God, indicating prospects for the first part of the ordering of leisure. The second part involves using leisure to strengthen another essential relationship by making time for oneself.

Time for Self

At first glance, the idea that the principle of everyday solidarity should encourage solitary leisure activities might seem a bit counterintuitive, if not completely contradictory. The whole point of the principle is to encourage ethical choices that honor a person's relational nature, so time for self might appear to undermine the aims of the principle. Such an interpretation, however, presumes an overly restricted definition of relationality. The order of charity, on which the ordering of leisure is based, clearly affirms one's moral responsibility for one's own well-being, revealing that the notion of a relationship with oneself is not entirely out of order. Indeed, Aquinas's account of the order of charity places love of self (at least in a spiritual sense) ahead of love of neighbor, on the rationale that even when "a better neighbor is nearer to God, . . . he is not as near to the man who has charity, as this man is to himself."[47] This comparative sense of distance assumes a relational connection between the person and his or her self that is just as real, and just as morally significant, as the relationships they have with others. Hence, when the Catholic ethicist James Keenan sought to redefine the cardinal virtues better to suit a relational conception of the human being, he did so in conversation with Aquinas and proposed that "we are relational in three ways: generally, specifically, and uniquely."[48] On this basis, he identified self-care as the cardinal virtue accounting for "the unique relationship that I as a moral agent have with myself," and he explained that this virtue entails "a unique responsibility to care for ourselves, affectively, mentally, physically, and spiritually."[49] As a tool of ethical discernment, then, the principle of everyday solidarity can, and should, account for this relationship as an essential element of the agent's relational responsibilities.

Furthermore, the principle of everyday solidarity can promote self-care as a way of honoring the totality of one's relationality, for as Aquinas's ordering of charity demonstrates, it is possible to love oneself as a result of one's love for others. Aquinas was most explicit on this point in relation to God, because the entire ordering of charity was premised on the assertion that genuinely loving God—the true object of charity—also requires loving that which God loves.[50] In this sense, the self is loved on account of one's love for God, which puts self-love in a decidedly relational context. Extending this rationale, proper love of self can also serve one's relationships with others, for the truly agapic form of love that Christians are called to show their neighbor requires a self to give in the first place. Moreover, in the context of a reciprocal relationship, self-love reflects the love one has for another. Consider spouses: if a husband loves his wife, he will want what is best for those whom his wife loves, and this must surely include himself. The husband's love of self can thus be motivated, at least in part, by his love for his wife—and vice versa. In these ways, proper love of self is not self-referential but is relationally conditioned. Consequently, the relationship one has with oneself is a fitting concern for the principle of everyday solidarity, and an acceptable point of reference for the ordering of leisure.

In terms of preserving the relationship one has with oneself through leisure, a number of individual free time pursuits are conducive to flow. Physically active pursuits, like exercise, are regularly connected to flow. Running is one of the most common examples, because running is so accessible and its potential for quantifiable goals is almost limitless—one can aim to run a specific distance, strive to achieve a certain pace, or hope to keep moving for a specified period of time, all of which allow a runner to cater the challenges of his or her workout to the skill level they have achieved. As a team of scholars, including Csikszentmihalyi, have argued, "Everyone can find runs and adventures that are personally meaningfully," which is significant because "performing a task that has personal significance makes you more likely to maintain attention for prolonged periods of time," thus creating the ideal conditions for flow.[51] More than any other activity, they contend, "running is unique in that it offers opportunities to experience flow in various settings and with a high degree of frequency."[52]

Although other forms of exercise may not offer the same variety and frequency of flow experiences as running, many are nevertheless conducive to flow as well. One study found close parallels between the experiences of elite figure skaters and Csikszentmihalyi's descriptions of flow, while other research found flow in swimming, track and field, cycling, rowing, and triathlons (as well as two team sports: field hockey and rugby).[53] Golf has been similarly linked to flow, and individual basketball players have reported flow experiences during practice and games.[54] In sum, personal participation in sports represents a significant opportunity to achieve flow and thus to enjoy leisure in a way that benefits one's relationship with oneself.[55]

Though a case can be made for identifying physically active leisure pursuits as a morally obligatory part of time for oneself—given that one's bodily well-being is a legitimate aspect of self-care—physical activity is not the only way to find flow for oneself during free time. Other, more sedentary pursuits can also facilitate the experience of flow, provided a person is doing something more engaging than watching television.[56] Reading, for instance, has been correlated with flow in two significant ways. First, the experience of reading can be so engaging that someone reading a stimulating novel or other text can achieve a flow state.[57] Second, the attention and focus required to read seem to help people cultivate a skill set that allows them to find flow more easily in other areas of life; a "large-scale study in Germany ... found that the more often people report reading books, the more flow experiences they claim to have."[58] Writing, another solitary activity, has been shown to facilitate flow, as have other creative leisure pursuits.[59] In some ways, the possibilities of flow during time spent alone seem to be endless, as long as a person finds a way to set goals and focus on one task at a time.[60] Hence, in order to find flow when taking time for oneself, the real issue is not so much what one does but how one does it.

The preceding examples have all discussed ways of finding flow in solitary leisure pursuits, but there are of course other ways to attend to one's relationship with oneself in a more social context. The studies about flow in sports, for example, show that individual athletes can experience flow for themselves while participating in a game with others or while contributing to a team. These activities are especially valuable from the perspective of everyday solidarity because they serve multiple relationships at once, so one can appropriately incorporate them into the ordering of leisure as part of one's time for self. At the same time, because the principle of everyday solidarity values each relational dimension of the human person *in se*, one's time for self should not be defined solely by leisure pursuits that also serve other relationships. There is something significant about solitude for the development of a healthy self, especially when that self is understood theologically.[61] For this reason, although time for self can consist largely of nonsolitary opportunities for flow, a proper ordering of leisure ought to include at least some form of flow in solitude in order to serve the moral agent's unique relationship with herself or himself as fully as possible.

Time for Others

The category of time for others is probably the most understandable element of an ordering of leisure based on the principle of everyday solidarity. This principle, after all, promotes the full flourishing of a person's relationality, and one's relationships with others are the most obvious and intuitive source of his or her relational identity. Also, people often plan their socializing for their free time, so many are already accustomed to using leisure to foster their relationships with others. The principle of everyday solidarity affirms this instinct and, through the ordering of leisure, introduces additional normative guidance to refine this practice. Specifically, the close parallels between the ordering of leisure and the ordering of love indicate that a person's responsibilities to set aside time for others ought to be conditioned by her or his distinct relational situation. As Keenan acknowledged in his development of new, relationally based cardinal virtues, the human person is not related to all his or her neighbors in the same way. Some relationships are general, and thus governed by justice in Keenan's typology; but other relationships are specific to each agent, and these require fidelity in addition to justice.[62]

Similarly, in his ordering of charity, Aquinas prioritized love of family ahead of love for other neighbors, and he even distinguished between one's responsibilities in love to various family members.[63] Applying these insights to the case of leisure, the principle of everyday solidarity must insist that people who have committed themselves to a romantic relationship have an obligation to prioritize time with their partner or spouse; those with children must include time with them; those in professed religious communities ought to find ways to connect with their confreres; and everyone needs to account for their specific relationships in their ordering of leisure. The exact demands will be different for each person, but the moral responsibility to honor "those special relationships that we enjoy whether by blood, marriage, love, or sacrament" is consistently incumbent on all.[64]

Generally, a person can make time for others during leisure in one of two ways. First, he or she can find flow personally in a group activity or social setting. Second, one can find flow with other people in activities that require intense engagement among all participants. Though both these experiences can serve one's relationships with others, there are qualitative differences between them. According to the psychologist Charles Walker, who has studied these social experiences of flow, the former is an example of "co-active flow" and the latter is an example of "interactive flow." His research found that social flow experiences in general were more enjoyable than solitary ones and that interactive flow and co-active flow were equally enjoyable as long as co-active flow arose in situations that allowed significant social interactions (e.g., conversations) while people performed the same activity.[65] Beyond individual enjoyment, however, Walker revealed a unique feature of interactive flow that makes it particularly significant in an ordering of leisure based on the principle of everyday solidarity. "In highly interdependent situations," he explained, "people may serve as agents of flow for each other. This form of social flow is mutual and reciprocal."[66] Given this reciprocity, interactive flow represents the gold standard for people looking to use their free time to enjoy leisure with others because it allows all the participants in a shared activity to experience the depth of their activity and the intensity of truly being with one another in the moment.

The experience of interactive flow is not limited to any one activity. Walker's study showed a wide range of activities in which participants experienced interactive flow, leading Walker to assert that interactive flow could arise without too much trouble whenever people were engaged in "a task best done by a group of people and impossible to do alone (e.g., playing a pickup game of basketball)."[67] Csikszentmihalyi's work underscores this point, for he argued that joint flow is not a matter of specific activities but can develop "when there is harmony between the goals of the participants, when everyone is investing psychic energy into a joint goal."[68] This might seem to require carefully curated leisure experiences, but in actuality it points to the possibilities of interactive flow in some of the most ordinary free time interactions, provided they are approached with thoughtful intentionality and appreciated for their own sake. One study of women's flow experiences, for example, indicated that mothers found flow in mundane activities with their children whenever they were able to be fully present and invested in what their children were doing.[69] Csikszentmihalyi, meanwhile, highlights the prospects for finding flow in conversations, and although he grants that this "requires both participants to concentrate on the interaction," he simultaneously insists that "the secret of a good conversation is really quite simple: . . . find out what the other person's goals are, . . . [and then] utilize one's own experience or expertise on the topics raised by the other person—without trying to take over the conversation, but developing it jointly."[70] In effect, all it takes to find flow while sharing free time with others is to invest oneself in the interaction and in the other person. This is exactly the kind of "being with" that underlies the principle of everyday solidarity's support for the prioritization of leisure over recreation. By finding flow with others in this way, moral agents can incorporate meaningful time with others into their proper ordering of leisure, strengthening their relationships with others—according to each relationship's needs—and promoting the full flourishing of their relational being as well.

CONCLUSION

In application to leisure, the principle of everyday solidarity provides concrete guidance for Christians committed to embracing free time as a resource for the integration of faith and ordinary life. As this chapter has explained, the relational orientation of the principle supports both the priority of leisure over recreation and an ordering of leisure that empowers the full flourishing of one's relationships with God, self, and others. These two conclusions support one another, for the ordering of leisure offers a realistic way to prioritize leisure over recreation while avoiding the pitfall of assuming that free time can never be used for recreation. In fact, when practiced as an examen, the ordering of leisure asserts that as long as moral agents set aside some time to seek flow in a fashion that deepens their relationships with God, with themselves, and with others in a given week, they need not have qualms about seeking recuperation through recreation during the remainder of their discretionary time. In addition, the ordering of leisure also facilitates flexibility as moral agents pursue this goal. Recognizing that different people will find flow in different contexts—based on their particular skill sets and interests—the ordering of leisure allows each person to find the specific pursuits that will fulfill a person's various relationships without mandating any one activity in particular. This leaves the breadth of leisure activities open while reorienting ethical discernment to the quality of the relationships that form during free time.

Of course, one must not forget that this application of the principle of everyday solidarity is about the ethics of leisure, which adds two dimensions to the analysis. First, the principle of everyday solidarity's promotion of a relational being's full flourishing in leisure must be connected with the theological understanding of leisure's intrinsic value. Consequently, the desire to build and sustain relationships through leisure ultimately needs to be oriented toward the enjoyment of leisure as a prefiguration of heavenly rest. Given the importance of communion in the Christian conception of the afterlife, these two elements of leisure do not have to compete with one another but can instead serve complementary functions. Hence, making time for God, time for self, and time for others can enhance a person's enjoyment of leisure as an intrinsic good, adding to one's appreciation of leisure as a glimpse of heaven, provided one keeps this understanding of leisure in mind. Second, the fact that leisure, by definition, represents the ideal for free time means that the ethical vision developed here demands a lot. The prioritization of leisure in free time sets a high bar, even when nuanced with a realistic ordering of leisure, yet the principle of everyday solidarity indicates that this high bar is essential if free time is going to serve the full flourishing of inherently relational human beings. This creates a paradox of sorts, for it suggests that what is necessary is also impossible—at least in many, if not most, cases. Obviously, this paradox is untenable, especially from the perspective of everyday solidarity, which expects moral agents to concern themselves not only with their own relational flourishing but also with the relational flourishing of all others. For this reason, the ethics of leisure must include not only the insights of the principle of everyday solidarity but also the insights of the virtue of everyday solidarity, so that the principle's high ideal for leisure can become more attainable for all.

NOTES

1. Cates, "Love," 1.
2. Pontifical Council for Justice and Peace, *Compendium*, 36.
3. Bacchiocchi, "Remembering the Sabbath," 75.
4. Hasel, "Sabbath in the Pentateuch," 23.
5. Barth, *Church Dogmatics*, III.1:218.
6. Aquinas, *ST*, I-II, q. 3, a. 8 c. Aquinas has a complex argument to support this claim, based in part on the Aristotelian notion of happiness as *eudaimonia*, or fulfillment. See Aquinas, *ST*, I-II, qq. 1–5, more broadly.
7. On the notion of God as "ultimate concern," see Tillich, *Systematic Theology*, 1:11–13.
8. Wells, "Rethinking Service," 9.
9. Wells, 9, 10.
10. Wells, 10.
11. Pieper, *Leisure*, 45–47, 52, 56–57.
12. Csikszentmihalyi, *Flow*, 50–51; Csikszentmihalyi, *Finding Flow*, 29, 112.
13. Csikszentmihalyi, "Consciousness," 24.
14. For details on the impact of digital distraction, see Turkle, *Alone Together*, 265–67.
15. Gergen, "Challenge," 227.
16. Turkle, *Alone Together*, xii.
17. Not coincidentally, one critical observer of contemporary digital trends points to "depth of thought and feeling, depth in our relationships, our work and everything we do" as the main casualty of the digital age and the essential remedy to digital distraction. Powers, *Hamlet's Blackberry*, 4, see also 11–12, 16.
18. Augustine, *De doctrina Christiana*, I.32.35. There are other defenses of this idea, most notably in the Catholic notion of the "communion of saints," which, as Elizabeth Johnson notes, "is a most relational symbol." Johnson, *Friends of God*, 217, see also 233–36; and *Catechism of the Catholic Church*, 952–59.
19. *Catechism of the Catholic Church*, 1026.
20. Pope, "Order of Love," 262.
21. Pope, *Evolution of Altruism*, 50; see also Aquinas, *ST*, I-II, q. 1, a. 8 c.
22. Aquinas, *ST*, II-II, q. 26, a. 2 c, II-II, q. 26, a. 3 c; see also Pope, *Evolution of Altruism*, 55–56, 58.
23. Pope, *Evolution of Altruism*, 59, 61; Aquinas, *ST*, II-II, q. 26, a. 4 ad 1.
24. Aquinas, *ST*, II-II, q. 26, a. 4 c; see also I-II, q. 27, a. 3 c. Aquinas defended this claim by arguing that love of self should outrank love of neighbor because the actual participation in the divine nature (which is what an agent experiences for himself or herself in heaven) generates a greater union than sharing in that participation (which is how one relates to others in heaven). At the same time, he nuanced this ordering by arguing that one should

love one's spiritual nature ahead of one's neighbor, but one should properly prioritize the neighbor's spiritual welfare over love of one's own bodily nature. Aquinas, *ST*, II-II, q. 26, a. 5 c, ad 1.
25. Aquinas, *ST*, II-II, q. 26, a. 8 c.
26. For a good overview, see Martin, *Jesuit Guide*, 87–100.
27. Csikszentmihalyi, *Beyond Boredom*, 37.
28. Csikszentmihalyi, *Finding Flow*, 29.
29. Neitz and Spickard, "Steps toward a Sociology of Religious Experience," 24, at 23.
30. Csikszentmihalyi, "Flow in a Historical Context," 232.
31. Neitz and Spickard, "Steps toward a Sociology of Religious Experience," 22.
32. *Catechism of the Catholic Church*, 2558.
33. Giordan and Woodhead, "Introduction," 2. For scriptural roots of prayers of praise and thanksgiving, see *Catechism of the Catholic Church*, 2637–43.
34. Giordan and Woodhead, "Introduction," 2.
35. *Dei verbum*, 2, 6, 11–13. For more on the notion of Scripture as God's personal revelation, see Gaillardetz and Clifford, *Keys to the Council*, 32–33.
36. See Martin, *Jesuit Guide*, 145–62.
37. For more on centering prayer, see Keating, "Method of Centering Prayer."
38. Though there are few data on the relative prevalence of different types of prayer, intercessory prayer would seem to have an especially prominent role in the United States today, where according to Christian Smith and Melinda Denton, "moralistic therapeutic deism" is the de facto spirituality, creating an emphasis on intercessory prayer since the therapeutic element reflects the assumption that God only needs to be involved in one's life when one needs God's help. Smith and Denton, *Soul Searching*, 165; and more broadly, 163–70.
39. Giordan and Woodhead, "Introduction," 3.
40. Francis, *Gaudete et exsultate*, 154.
41. Neitz and Spickard, "Steps toward a Sociology of Religious Experience," 22.
42. *Sacrosanctum concilium*, 14.
43. On the etymology of liturgy and *leitourgia*, see Fagerberg, *Theologia Prima*, 11. On the links between an obligation to attend the weekly liturgy and the demands of the Sabbath commandment, see Harline, *Sunday*, 8; and Sullivan, "Sunday Rest," 6–7. On worship as an obligation of justice, see Matthiesen, "'Justice of Christ.'"
44. According to Fagerberg's reflections on the etymology, "liturgy is therefore both our product and not our work." Fagerberg, *Theologia Prima*, 12.
45. Vereecke, "Repos du Dimanche et oeuvres serviles," 54–56.
46. Saliers, *Worship as Theology*, 52–53, 56–60, 210–11; *Sacrosanctum concilium*, 8.
47. Aquinas, *ST*, II-II, q. 26, a. 4 ad 1.
48. Keenan, "Proposing Cardinal Virtues," 723.
49. Keenan, 726, 727. Keenan explicitly argues that his virtue of self-care aligns with Aquinas's order of charity. Keenan, 727n84.
50. Aquinas, *ST*, II-II, q. 25, esp. aa. 1 and 4; see also II-II, q. 26, a. 1.
51. Csikszentmihalyi, Latter, and Duranso, *Running Flow*, 100.
52. Csikszentmihalyi, Latter, and Duranso, 6.
53. Jackson, "Athletes in Flow"; Jackson, "Toward a Conceptual Understanding."
54. Valiante, *Golf Flow*; Oliveira, Gomes, and Miranda, "Flow State."
55. On this point, an entire book has been written about how to find flow in sports in general: Jackson and Csikszentmihalyi, *Flow in Sports*.

56. According to research by Csikszentmihalyi and Robert Kubey, television is inimical to flow because it requires so little engagement from the television viewer. As a result, many people find relaxation while watching television, but only 3 percent of people ever report something close to flow while watching TV. Kubey and Csikszentmihalyi, *Television*, 81–85, 143, 207.
57. Towey, "Flow," esp. 132–34; McQuillan and Conde, "Conditions of Flow"; Kubey and Csikszentmihalyi, *Television*, 99–100, 135.
58. Csikszentmihalyi, *Finding Flow*, 69, citing Noelle-Neumann, "Stationen der Glücksforschung," 15–56. Watching television, meanwhile, has been associated with fewer flow experiences in other areas of life. Kubey and Csikszentmihalyi, *Television*, 129, 137–38.
59. Perry, *Writing in Flow*. On links between creativity and flow more generally, see Csikszentmihalyi, *Creativity*, 113–26.
60. Indeed, one researcher found that prisoners who survived prolonged periods of solitary confinement did so by finding flow alone in their cells. Logan, "Flow in 'Solitary Ordeals,'" 81–83.
61. Kelly, "Depth," 120–21.
62. Keenan, "Proposing Cardinal Virtues," 723.
63. Aquinas, *ST*, II-II, 26, qq. 8–11.
64. Keenan, "Proposing Cardinal Virtues," 724–25.
65. Walker, "Experiencing Flow," 4, 5–6.
66. Walker, 4.
67. Walker, 5.
68. Csikszentmihalyi, *Finding Flow*, 112–13.
69. Allison and Duncan, "Women, Work, and Flow," 129.
70. Csikszentmihalyi, *Finding Flow*, 114–15.

CHAPTER 4

Leisure and the Virtue of Everyday Solidarity

As a complement to the principle, the virtue of everyday solidarity calls attention to the structural constraints limiting a person's ability to make moral decisions in a way that prioritizes relational flourishing. In the context of leisure, this brings one issue to the forefront: free time is a luxury that not everyone has. Unless the ethical analysis of free time can account for this fact, the prioritization of leisure over recreation and the ordering of leisure cannot hope to have any impact. Worse, the entire notion of applying theological ethics to free time will turn into a bourgeois project that is tone deaf to the needs of real people, especially the poor. Given solidarity's close link to the Church's preferential option for the poor, this would be an unacceptable outcome. Hence, the principle of everyday solidarity's promotion of a relational ordering of leisure must be paired with the virtue of everyday solidarity's structural critiques to insist that true leisure cannot be the purview of the few, because its high theological and relational potential are goods that belong to all.

At the same time, because the virtue of solidarity involves "a firm and persevering... [commitment] to the common good,"[1] this structural analysis must be more than just an abstract critique; it must also include an assessment of the actions moral agents can undertake to transform the structural impediments themselves, so that free time will be less of a luxury good and more of an everyday opportunity for moral growth and relational fulfillment for all. Consequently, this chapter analyzes leisure in light of the virtue of everyday solidarity in three sections. The first identifies the structural obstacles that stand in the way of quality free time, detailing an ongoing inversion of resources in the United States that leaves moral agents either time rich and economically poor or economically rich and time poor, limiting people's recourse to leisure during free time. The second and third sections then discuss structural reforms that would address economic poverty and time poverty, respectively, emphasizing the importance of transforming the sphere of work in order to create new opportunities for leisure. In essence, the assumption driving this chapter is that everyone needs enough free time if the ethics of leisure is going to have any real significance, and the corollary message of the virtue of everyday solidarity is that moral agents must therefore take responsibility for effecting the structural changes that would improve access to free time.

STRUCTURAL CONSTRAINTS ON LEISURE

The main structural constraint on people's ability to follow the principle of everyday solidarity's vision for leisure is a lack of high-quality free time. This is the result of two trends, each of which has structural roots. The first trend is an overall decrease in free time. Juliet Schor's influential study, *The Overworked American*, diagnosed this trend, revealing that working hours in the United States had increased steadily since the 1970s, totaling an extra 199 hours (or roughly five additional 40-hour work weeks) each year by the time of a follow-up study in 2000.[2] The corollary effect was, unsurprisingly, a decline in free time, meaning that opportunities for leisure have become scarcer in the United States.[3] Admittedly, not everyone has found Schor's data and interpretations persuasive. Two other sociologists, John Robinson and Geoffrey Godbey, used time diaries to assess free time trends during the 1970s and 1980s, and concluded "that Americans have *more* free time than they did 30 years ago," in direct contradiction to Schor's results (emphasis in the original).[4] Schor has responded by noting that different data sets allow one to study different pieces of a larger picture, and she has shown that although there may have been grounds for disputing the exact number of free time hours people had in the United States in the 1980s or 1990s, there is convincing evidence from multiple data sets to support the claim that at the trend level, working hours have been increasing while free time hours have been decreasing. Indeed, by the late 1990s, even time diary studies corroborated this assertion.[5]

Furthermore, other scholarship has shown that any aggregate gain in free time in the latter half of the twentieth century stalled by the 1980s, resulting in a negative trend since 1985.[6] As Schor points out, this trend has deep structural roots, for workplace power shifts have given employers the ability to set employees' working conditions unilaterally, and they have opted to reward increases in productivity with marginally higher wages rather than additional paid time off.[7] At the same time, the assumptions and pressures of living in a consumerist society give greater rewards to those who choose to work more (and thus earn more), while limiting options for people who genuinely want more free time.[8] For all these reasons, an overall decrease in free time is rightly described as a structural problem limiting the full realization of relational flourishing during leisure.

The second trend that has been having an impact on the availability of high-quality free time is the emergence of what might be called the free time gap, or the inverse relationship between economic resources and temporal opportunities that currently exists in the United States. The clearest example is the growing divergence in free time opportunities according to educational attainment. Between 1985 and 2005, men without a high school diploma gained 14.2 hours of free time per week over their peers with at least a college degree, while women with at least a college degree had 2.9 fewer hours of free time than women who did not complete high school.[9] During roughly the same period, educational attainment was closely tied to wage growth, but in the opposite direction, such that wages grew modestly for college-educated workers between 1979 and 2007 while declining substantially for workers with only a high school diploma or less.[10] As result, the United States now has a free time paradox, where those who have the most free time are least likely to have the financial means to use it for leisure (or recreation), while those who have the most money to use on these activities typically have the least free time to do something with it. As a result, even if there were not an overall decrease in free time in the United States, there would still be significant structural constraints on people's abilities to enjoy leisure during free time. Furthermore, the existence of the free time gap reveals that there are still structural obstacles affecting the quality of free time, even for the outliers whose personal experiences manage to break from the population-level decrease in free time.

Despite the prevalence and impact of these two trends, one must be careful to note that personal freedom remains. Social structures exert a substantial force in people's lives, but an ethical analysis rooted in Catholic theological anthropology cannot abide by the assumption that these structures are deterministic.[11] A perspective that maintains human agency must therefore acknowledge that neither of these trends eliminates the possibility of good free time experiences. For example, the task of constructing and maintaining strong relationships is not contingent on financial expenditures, so those with more time but less money could still pursue a relational sense of flourishing during their free time. At the other end of the spectrum, those with more money but less time could likewise build relationships during the free time that they do have, because the strength of a relationship typically depends less on the sheer amount of time dedicated to it and more on the quality of the time that two people are able to share. Despite these concessions, however, the challenging trade-off between financial and temporal resources remains. Thus, while people could freely choose to prioritize their free time according to the principle of everyday solidarity, they will inevitably have a difficult time doing so because the growing free time gap creates structural pressures that make it easier to default to free time pursuits that fall short of both the lofty ideal of leisure and the relational possibilities of recreation.

Although the free time gap creates different structural constraints at each end, the problems emerge from a type of insufficiency in both cases. For the sake of clarity, then, one can identify the two ends of the free time gap as a resource-poor end and a time-poor end. Of course, one must not conflate these two experiences, because no two types of poverty are fully equivalent.[12] Indeed, as Sandra Schneiders points out, one of the key distinguishing features of true poverty is "the *lack of options*" (emphasis in the original).[13] From this perspective, the economic poverty at the resource-poor end of the free time gap is much more severe because it is almost entirely unchosen. In contrast, the temporal poverty at the other end is not unchosen to the same degree, because possessing more financial resources inherently means one has access to more options. Even without exercising these options, as Schneiders says, "the fact that they can [exercise them] assuages the violent determinism that constitutes real poverty."[14] Still, some unchosen aspects remain in the case of temporal poverty, and thus the time-poor designation is not entirely inappropriate.[15] Furthermore, both these types of poverty represent structural impediments to high-quality free time, and thus to the proper ordering of leisure, meaning that the virtue of everyday solidarity must consider structural reforms for each of these distinct constraints. The remainder of this chapter discusses concrete proposals for these reforms, addressing the resource-poor end of the free time gap before responding to the limitations of time poverty. Notably, all the proposals revolve around work, because this sphere of life represents the common thread behind the structural constraints at both ends of the free time gap. This should not be surprising, because free time is defined in relation to work, and thus the quality and amount of one's work have a direct bearing on the quality and amount of one's free time.

THE STRUCTURAL REFORM OF A LIVING WAGE FLOOR FOR THE RESOURCE POOR

At the resource-poor end of the free time gap, financial constraints represent a serious obstacle to the full realization of free time, undermining the prioritization of leisure over recreation and frustrating the ordering of leisure. Structural reforms for this end of the free time gap should thus aim to increase the resources available for free time activities, a goal best achieved by promoting a living wage floor for all workers in the United States. At first glance, this may seem to require a significant theoretical leap away from the issue at hand; but in truth, wage rates are intimately connected to the question of access to high-quality free time because a lack of financial resources directly affects a person's options for free time pursuits, encouraging a strictly economic evaluation of leisure and recreation rather than the relational one envisioned under the principle of everyday solidarity. Generally, this calculus leads to less fulfilling free time activities because the cheapest free time pursuits are passive forms of recreation that facilitate isolation more than interpersonal engagement. Hence, watching television, which has negligible immediate costs once a television set is present, is the most popular free time activity in the United States, yet this activity yields little satisfaction for viewers and correlates with decreases in social engagement, as the next chapter discusses in detail.[16] More engaging free time pursuits, including the types of flow-inducing activities that constitute genuine leisure, typically require immediate expenditures, especially as leisure becomes privatized through commodification—an increasingly common trend in the United States.[17] Hence, moral agents motivated by the virtue of everyday solidarity must concern themselves not merely with people's access to leisure but also, by necessary extension, with people's access to economic capital. This leads directly to the issue of just wages, because "wages constitute the majority of overall income for families in the middle of the income distribution" and below, meaning that the solution to limited financial resources—especially for the poor who are the virtue of everyday solidarity's prime point of reference—lies in wage rates.[18]

Fortunately, the question of adequate remuneration for labor is not an alien concern for the Catholic theological tradition. Catholic theology has emphatically championed just rewards for workers' labors, most directly through the defense of a living wage for all workers found in the Church's social encyclicals. Rooted in the scholastic conception of the "just price," which sought to establish the proper price that could be charged for a good (or service) in order to ensure that buyers and sellers did not take advantage of each other, the explicit notion of a living wage emerged in the first Catholic social teaching encyclical, *Rerum novarum*.[19] Directly counteracting the arguments in support of free contract that were linked to English philosophers like John Stuart Mill, Leo XIII's famed encyclical described a living wage as a matter of justice for workers, insisting that "there underlies a dictate of natural justice more imperious and ancient than any bargain between [two persons], namely, that wages ought not to be insufficient to support a frugal and well-behaved wage earner."[20] Further reflection led to the refinement of this initial idea, generating an equation between the just wage and a living wage in Catholic social thought, based on the claim that just remuneration must provide a worker with enough resources to secure a basic living from her or his labor.[21]

This traditional priority of Catholic social teaching presents an ideal solution to the structural constraints affecting those at the resource-poor end of the free time gap because a living wage would ensure that all workers have enough money to make real choices about how they will spend their free time, emancipating them from the financial limitations that quickly restrict people to one de facto option. Additionally, a standard living wage would also reduce the need for multiple jobs at the lower end of the wage scale, militating against the possibility that a wage increase would simply move people from the resource-poor end to the time-poor end of the free time gap. For this structural reform to take effect, however, moral agents motivated by the virtue of everyday solidarity will need to champion a living wage for all, and this requires specifying exactly what constitutes a living wage today.

Specifying a Living Wage Floor

There are a number of disputes about how best to define the living wage in practical terms. Early Catholic activists, like the National Council of Catholic Women (NCCW), which was founded in 1922, followed the Church's indication that justice was the basis for the living wage and therefore defined the living wage "qualitatively rather than quantitatively," suggesting that it should allow workers—especially female workers—to achieve the "American standard of living," which included "economic independence, civic participation, working-class character development," and the ability to be a "consumer, not a victim of the marketplace."[22] They based their arguments in part on John A. Ryan's famous 1906 defense of the living wage, which calculated the living wage using government survey data to determine the average amount that a normal family in the United States paid annually for its physical and social necessities.[23] His calculations accounted not only for obvious things like food, clothing, health care, and shelter but also for "a moderate amount of amusement and recreation" and the ability to afford opportunities for further education and personal growth.[24] Unlike the NCCW, however, Ryan used this approach to produce a decidedly quantitative outcome, asserting on the basis of his calculations that $600 per year was the living wage baseline in the United States at the time.[25] Significantly, he also made allowances for geographical variations in the cost of living, explaining that this annual income *"probably"* amounted to a family living wage in areas of the country where food and shelter were cheap (e.g., the South), that it *"possibly"* constituted a family living wage in "moderately sized cities of the West, North, and East," and that it was "certainly *not*" a family living wage in the nation's largest urban areas (emphasis in the original).[26] As these two strategies reveal, one central question about the living wage, then, is whether it should be specified in relation to aspirations, as the NCCW did, or with a particular number, as Ryan did. Although there are benefits to the qualitative approach, the quantitative approach is better suited to the virtue of everyday solidarity because, as a matter of practical expediency, there is a greater likelihood of actual reform when a concrete number is in view because so much of political life revolves around faith in the objectivity of numbers.[27]

Even if one accepts the value of the quantitative approach, however, lingering questions still remain about how to calculate the exact numbers. One of the first decisions is how expansive a living wage should be, given that the costs of meeting one person's basic needs differ rather drastically from the costs of meeting the basic needs of a whole family. In the Catholic tradition, this question has always been decided in favor of the family, under the assumption that parents have an obligation to care for their dependent children, and that a worker's income is the most common means of meeting this demand.[28] More recent developments in the papal tradition of Catholic social teaching have expanded the onus of responsibility, suggesting that if an employer could not or would not pay sufficient wages to a worker to support his or her family, then the state should compensate by offering "family allowances" for those individuals who choose to stay home and raise a family.[29] Over more than a century, then, the Catholic perspective on justice for workers has not wavered from the assertion that the wages for labor should allow workers to provide for their families.[30] Because the framework of everyday solidarity is designed to create a closer connection between one's faith convictions and one's ordinary life, this consistent definition of worker justice ought to inform the application of everyday solidarity to the sphere of work, indicating that the numerical calculations for a living wage floor should account for the costs of raising a family. Furthermore, a family living wage is a better solution to the structural obstacles affecting free time quality, for the principle of everyday solidarity indicates that families should have opportunities to enjoy leisure together, and this will be a more realistic possibility if a worker's job can support his or her family as a whole.

Admittedly, the conclusion that the costs of raising a family should be the guiding concern for the quantitative determination of a living wage elicits at least three significant objections, each of which deserves attention. First, there is a feminist critique, which challenges the idea of a family living wage for its patriarchal heritage, because the earliest arguments in its favor presumed that male workers needed enough money to provide for their family because women were not to work outside the home.[31] This is indeed a problem with some of the Catholic Church's promotions of a family living wage, but it does not need to condemn the notion entirely, given that the basic convictions behind the idea are not incompatible with modern sensibilities.[32] Christine Firer Hinze, for example, has argued for a greater compatibility by reinterpreting the referents of "family," "living," and "wage."[33]

Even without new connotations, however, the traditional argument for a family living wage is still amenable to modern adaptation. After all, the original Catholic argument was substantively about responsibility and only accidentally about gender. Consider *Rerum novarum*, which promoted the family living wage primarily as a means to allow a worker to save prudently for the future. The rationale was that if workers' wages did not allow them to meet all their responsibilities—which included caring not only for themselves but also for any dependents—then they would need to forgo the possibility of future savings in order to meet their immediate basic needs.[34] Similarly, John Ryan's famous defense of the family living wage, which has also been criticized for perpetuating a gendered division of labor, is not intrinsically tied to that split.[35] On the contrary, Ryan's argument for a family living wage was fundamentally about the natural right to marry and have children, a right that gave all workers a concomitant claim to receive sufficient remuneration to support a family so that they might be in a position to realize that right.[36] While Ryan adopted the gendered assumptions of his day and applied this right to adult males only, there is nothing prohibiting the extension of this right to all workers. With a few modifications, then, the traditional case for a family living wage can overcome its feminist critiques, providing a defense of just remuneration for all workers—which is, not coincidentally, how contemporary living wage movements tend to support this policy.[37]

In addition to the feminist critiques, a second major objection to a family living wage is from those who would insist that it imposes an undue burden on employers, who must pay all workers enough to support a family, despite the fact that many of their workers who currently earn less than a family living wage do not have a family to support. Though reasonable on its face, this criticism misunderstands the real purpose of the family living wage. The policy is not just designed to support a worker in his or her individual efforts to provide for a family. More fundamentally, it is intended to create the social conditions that would allow every worker to exercise their right to have a family.[38] As such, those workers who are not currently responsible for a family still deserve sufficient pay to provide for a family so that they will have the resources to support one in the future should they choose to have one. Furthermore, familial responsibilities extend beyond one's nuclear family, despite the tendency—especially in Catholic theological reflection—to theorize family almost exclusively in nuclear terms.[39] A family living wage for all workers is therefore an appropriate application of the virtue of everyday solidarity because it affirms the inherently relational nature of each person. At the same time, when applied to every worker regardless of family situation, a family living wage provides all workers with the resources to sustain their relational identity during free time without preemptively confining the realm of relational responsibilities to the nuclear family alone. Finally, in a true testament to the meaning of solidarity, this policy also conveys that everyone is willing to shoulder the burdens of an increased access to relational flourishing, because a family living wage for every worker would likely entail increases in the costs for goods and services to allow employers to cover the higher labor costs.[40] By embracing the virtue of everyday solidarity, however, advocates of a family living wage acknowledge this possibility and simply describe it as a price worth paying for the good of all and of each.

Finally, there is a third objection to the quantitative specification of a family living wage that challenges the method behind this policy rather than its substance. Noting the goal of securing sufficient remuneration for workers to support themselves and their dependents, some advocates for a family living wage have suggested that it is inadequate to settle on one single quantitative goal, because this leaves workers with larger families in the lurch. In place of a single, quantitative determination of a family living wage, then, these advocates assert that paying workers different wages based on the size of their families is a better solution.[41] This response, however, overlooks two practical stumbling blocks that make such a strategy undesirable. First, a variable wage floor is much harder to realize because the political salience of numbers makes a standardized quantitative goal more feasible. Second, and more important, the strongest resistance to minimum wage laws has come from trade groups representing business owners, which argue that an increased minimum wage will raise the costs of labor too high, forcing them to cut jobs.[42] Given the prevalence of this line of thinking, many business owners would interpret a family living wage floor that differed for each worker as an incentive to hire single, childless workers and to avoid those with dependents, thereby undermining the goals of a family living wage. There is a practical value, then, in advocating for a single, standardized living wage and, from the perspective of everyday solidarity, a legitimate rationale for basing this number on the needs of a family rather than an individual worker, because this strategy reaffirms the central place of relationality in the identity of every worker. Additionally, when the goal is to facilitate greater access to relational flourishing through leisure, a universal family living wage provides the best potential for aiding as many people as possible at the resource-poor end of the free time gap.

Deriving a Number

Even when one grants, against these three objections, that the virtue of everyday solidarity has good reason to champion a family living wage, the question of how to translate this commitment into a specific number remains. The answer hinges on a range of calculations. At one end of the range is the approach adopted by the living wage movement, which has successfully turned the eradication of subpoverty wages into a political goal. The movement's simple yet potent strategy, summarized in slogans like "A job should lift you out of poverty, not keep you in it," is to define the living wage in relation to the federal poverty guidelines, which offer a quantifiable, albeit crude, definition of poverty for households of various sizes in the United States.[43] This approach appeals to commonsense notions of justice and fairness, winning over supporters with what is primarily a moral, rather than an economic, argument.[44] This perspective, which aligns well with the virtue of everyday solidarity's preferential option for the poor, can generate a living wage based on the federal poverty guidelines for a household of four persons. This household size makes sense because the average family size in the United States, according to the most recent census data, is 3.14 persons.[45] By rounding up to four, the living wage calculations allow the labor of one adult to meet the typical family's poverty threshold while also offering extra resources to account for the fact that the federal poverty guidelines are notoriously low, due to both methodological limitations and the fact that these guidelines are designed for a statistical purpose and not meant to capture the actual costs of meeting all of one's needs.[46] These parameters yield a living wage rate of $12.38 per hour, using the current poverty guideline of $25,750 per year for a family of four, and assuming one adult working full time (2,080 hours per year).[47] This provides the bottom end of the living wage range.

At the upper end of the living wage range is a number that derives from an assessment of the actual costs of providing for a family in the United States today, using concrete numbers rather than the statistical interpolation of the federal poverty line. Like Ryan's initial efforts to specify the living wage using a rough estimation of what a typical family would need to spend to achieve a decent standard of living, a team of researchers at the

Massachusetts Institute of Technology has developed a "Living Wage Calculator," which summarizes the costs for basic needs in every county in the United States and then translates these costs into a minimum hourly wage for various household arrangements.[48] At the national level, the calculator's creator and her researchers indicate that the cost of supporting the basic needs of a family of four, with two adults and two children, generates a living wage of $16.14 per hour, provided both adults worked full time.[49] This, obviously, is the high end of the living wage range, because it requires more than doubling the current federal minimum wage of $7.25 per hour; yet it also adds another data point to the virtue of everyday solidarity's pursuit of a more just standard of remuneration that would allow all workers, and not just those at the top end of the wage scale, to embrace their relationality through their free time decisions.

Following this range, moral agents informed by the virtue of everyday solidarity have two helpful reference points for the effort to counteract the structural effects of working conditions at the resource-poor end of the free time gap. Certainly, adequate wages to cover the real (i.e., calculated) costs of caring for a family ought to remain the ultimate goal, even if this generates a somewhat quixotic benchmark given the current federal minimum wage.[50] For this reason, the higher rate of $16.14 must remain in focus, but it cannot be the sole marker of success. After all, the virtue of everyday solidarity is committed to the common good, as specified in light of the preferential option for the poor. When interpreted through this lens, some movement toward a living wage is better than none, and a lower cutoff acknowledges this reality while also ensuring that one's pragmatic instincts do not surrender too much. A poverty-based threshold of $12.38 an hour may be low, due to the methodological limitations of the federal poverty guidelines, but "given the precipitous fall in the national minimum wage over the past thirty years, establishing a living wage minimum *at least* at the poverty line is a substantial step forward" (emphasis in the original).[51] In pursuit of actual structural reform, then, the virtue of everyday solidarity counsels fighting for a family living wage with both $12.38 and $16.14 in mind, encouraging all concerned moral agents to throw their support behind movements like the "Fight for 15," which, at $15.00 an hour, would reach closer to the higher end of the target range while also allowing realistic compromise on any strategy that would raise all workers to at least $12.38, especially if this is the result of local campaigns in areas of the country where the cost of living is lower. Thus, the two numbers provide two poles that, much like Reinhold Niebuhr's love and justice, should be kept in tension with one another so that the ideal does not become the enemy of the real, or vice versa.[52]

Strategies for Structural Reform

In pursuit of this goal, advocates motivated by the virtue of everyday solidarity must remember that there are a variety of ways to achieve living wages. Although a national minimum wage floor might be ideal, because it would ensure sustainable wages for all workers and demonstrate a societal commitment to solidarity—insofar as laws reflect the values of the communities that enact them—a federal law enforcing the higher end of the living wage range is not the most likely outcome.[53] To date, the most effective living wage reforms have occurred at the local level.[54] Consequently, those committed to improving access to free time by transforming work in light of the virtue of everyday solidarity should not ignore national efforts, but they should prioritize local ones. At the same time, they need not confine their hopes to legal efforts alone. After all, the goal is not a specific law but a practical outcome, and more workers could have access to the security of living wages, and thus a better work/life balance, if employers simply paid their employees more.

Of course, there are many reasons why employers do not do this unilaterally, but chief among them is the assumption that higher wages will put them at a disadvantage when compared with their competitors who pay merely the legal minimum wage and therefore have lower labor costs. Although this need not be the case, because increased productivity is a typical by-product of increased wages, there are other changes that employers can make to improve wages while addressing competitive concerns.[55] One such strategy, famously employed by Minnesota's Reell Precision Manufacturing in the 1990s, is to hire employees at market wages while making an intentional, and timely, effort to train them so that their contributions to the company can eventually sustain a higher living wage.[56] As Reell's experience indicates, living wages are possible in the absence of a legal mandate, and personal moral agents can help to make this a more common reality by publicly pressuring businesses and by financially supporting only those companies that commit to paying a living wage. Ultimately, the coercive power of the law will remain the only force capable of guaranteeing a living wage floor for all workers, but even this aim becomes more feasible if more workers are close to a living wage threshold. As a result, anyone interested in securing the type of remuneration from work that can adequately address the resource-poor end of the free time gap needs to consider a variety of complementary approaches instead of focusing on one method of structural change in isolation.

The nuances of a dynamic wage range and a multipronged approach to implementing it thus help to make a living wage floor more viable, allowing the virtue of everyday solidarity to chip away at the structural constraints worsening half the free time gap. By increasing wages for the lowest-paid workers, a living wage floor reduces the pressures of economic insecurity, which frequently hamper a person's ability to evaluate his or her choices with the freedom and intentionality that undergird morally good decisions.[57] Indeed, in the case of free time, this improved economic security can make it easier to evaluate one's free time choices in light of the principle of everyday solidarity, because more disposable income frees up economic resources, affording the opportunity to seek out particular leisure pursuits and recreational activities with the kind of critical awareness that the ordering of leisure entails. Thus, though living wages are obviously a work-related policy change, they nonetheless represent an application of the virtue of everyday solidarity in relation to free time, for they constitute a structural reform that would make it easier for more people to employ the principle of everyday solidarity in their free time decisions. Because low wages represent only one half of the free time gap, however, this structural reform is not the only application of the virtue of everyday solidarity to free time. There are additional reforms, still in the sphere of work, that are also necessary.

THE STRUCTURAL REFORMS OF VACATION TIME AND PARENTAL LEAVE FOR THE TEMPORAL POOR

At the time-poor end of the free time gap, there are a number of root causes behind the limited amount of free time. Some of them are cultural, such as the de facto narrative of busyness that leaves many in the United States feeling as if they need to cultivate a life of constant activity, "as though busyness itself is the point."[58] Just as significantly, however, there are also structural causes, and these serve to reinforce the cultural ones. As with the resource-poor end of the free time gap, the greatest structural challenges at the time-poor end also emerge from the sphere of work, where the United States has a peculiar approach to free time that leaves many without enough of it to embrace the principle of everyday solidarity's vision for leisure and recreation. This is most evident in the lack of guaranteed vacation time and the absence of paid parental leave, two deficiencies that moral agents ought to counteract as an extension of the virtue of everyday solidarity.

Increasing Guaranteed Vacation Time

If one of the biggest factors exacerbating time poverty is the amount of time people spend at work—both in terms of paid employment and the "second shift" at home—then the simplest solution might seem to be to convince people to work less.[59] In some cases, the living wage reforms discussed above might have precisely this effect, allowing more workers to find economic security with a typical forty-hour workweek instead of multiple jobs over long hours. Yet these structural changes only help to ameliorate one part of the problem, for the fact that the free time gap has two sides indicates that limited free time is a persistent obstacle precisely for those who have already achieved a certain degree of financial security through their paid employment. Additional reforms are therefore necessary as a complement to the virtue of everyday solidarity's support for a living wage.

In the Catholic theological tradition, one of the most common proposals for assuring workers' adequate access to free time has been the promotion of a weekly day of rest. In *Rerum novarum*, for instance, Pope Leo XIII connected a weekly day of rest (on Sundays) with his own arguments for a living wage, suggesting that employers could not justly demand, nor workers justly consent to, an employment arrangement that did not guarantee "the cessation from work and labor on Sundays and certain holy days."[60] Pope John XIII's *Mater et magistra* similarly addressed "the question of the Sunday rest" and "call[ed] upon all, public authorities, employers and workers, to observe the precepts of God and His Church and to remember their grave responsibilities before God and society" by taking time off from work on Sundays.[61] Pope John Paul II advanced this priority as well.[62] Such a policy would certainly improve access to free time and increase attainment of the principle of everyday solidarity's vision for leisure and recreation, especially if this day off became a moment "free from mundane cares," when one can "lift up his mind to the things of heaven, and look into the depths of his conscience, to see how he stands with God in respect of those necessary and inviolable relationships which must exist between the creature and [the] Creator."[63] Yet this traditional approach has significant limits in a US context, and, worse, it fails to get to the root of the time poverty preventing the realization of the principle of everyday solidarity's vision for free time.

The limits of championing regular Sunday rest for all workers are twofold. First, this policy would not be amenable to any kind of legal force in the United States, where the laws are supposed to be as neutral as possible with respect to their effects on religious practice.[64] Because different religions propose different days of the week as the appropriate day of rest for their adherents, it would be difficult to justify a legal requirement that all (or most) workers have a specific day off each week without running afoul of the current state of US jurisprudence on religious liberty. Although one might achieve a policy like this without recourse to the force of law, increasing time off for all workers will be most effective if there is a common practice, so there is limited viability for a policy that precludes legal structures from its efforts at structural reform. Second, regulations requiring a specific day off would ultimately reduce flexibility in workers' schedules, potentially complicating families' efforts to spend time together as they scramble to rearrange existing routines. Because the principle of everyday solidarity promotes a relational approach to free time, advocates for the virtue of everyday solidarity must be cautious about championing structural reforms that exacerbate the challenges of spending time together.

Nevertheless, the strongest argument against a simple adoption of the traditional proposal for Sunday as a universal day of rest is that such a policy fails to address the root causes of the time-poverty end of the free time gap. A significant factor behind this problem is not simply an increase in the number of hours a worker must spend at his or her job, but also the expansion of employment responsibilities beyond the confines of the workplace. This form of "job spill" is an acute problem for those at the resource-rich end of the free time gap because smartphones and other internet-enabled devices have made constant connection—even at home during one's supposedly free time—a part of the employment contract for the most financially secure jobs.[65] A mandatory day off from work would not reverse this trend, because data suggest job spill stems chiefly from unwritten rules, which tend to persist even in the face of legal regulation.[66] Such persistence would be especially likely in the case of a weekly day off, because a one-day break from the work routine is not enough time to dismantle established habits.

Truly addressing the structural constraints of contemporary time poverty requires a more analogical application of the traditional Catholic case for time off from work. Although a weekly day of rest on Sunday has been Catholic social teaching's most common policy proposal, it is not the only means to the end of more free time for more workers. After all, the presuppositions behind the Catholic Church's support for regular Sunday rest included the argument that "man has a right to rest a while from work, and indeed a need to do so if he is to renew his bodily strength and to refresh his spirit by suitable recreation. He has also to think of his family, the unity of which depends so much on frequent contact and the peaceful living together of all its members."[67]

This vision for rest can be served by other approaches, including structural reforms that would increase the amount of guaranteed vacation time available to workers, shifting the promotion of free time from a single, weekly day of rest to a more flexible arrangement that would allow workers to seek the full potential of leisure and recreation in accordance with the principle of everyday solidarity. There is already a precedent for this policy in Catholic social teaching, given that Pope John Paul II expanded the "right to rest" to include "also a longer period of rest, namely the holiday or vacation taken once a year or possibly in several shorter periods during the year."[68] Just as important, this policy has the ability to address the larger structural forces behind workers' time poverty because longer breaks from work afford greater freedom from the demands of a job-spill culture, for coworkers and supervisors more readily accept that someone is unavailable during an extended block of time. Consequently, the virtue of everyday solidarity indicates that one of the best structural reforms for the time-poor end of the free time gap would be a universal increase in the number of vacation days accorded to each worker.

An increase in guaranteed vacation time represents a straightforward reform with significant consequences, especially in the United States, which is the only nation among the members of the Organization for Economic Cooperation and Development (OECD) that does not require any paid vacation for employees.[69] Of course, numerous US employers offer paid vacation as a perk to attract employees, despite the lack of a legal mandate, but the overall results vary dramatically. Although US workers average ten paid vacation days and six paid holidays every year, the process of averaging masks the fact that 23 percent of workers have zero paid vacation days and 23 percent similarly report zero paid holidays.[70] Additionally, the average of sixteen paid days off is still less than the legal minimum in all but one of the other OECD countries.[71]

Facing this reality, the virtue of everyday solidarity must critique the US approach to vacation time as a problematic structural constraint. This is true from the perspective of the preferential option for the poor, because the jobs least likely to offer any paid vacation are found at the bottom quarter of the wage scale. Workers in these jobs have an average of four paid vacation days and three paid holidays, and half of these workers have none at all.[72] At the same time, US vacation policies also hinder free time opportunities for higher-wage workers because the absolute number of days is so small compared with other developed nations and because the abovementioned workplace culture can easily pressure people to forgo what little vacation time is available to them. The US approach to vacation thus restricts the free time potential of all US workers, creating an obstacle to the principle of everyday solidarity's vision for relational fulfillment in leisure and recreation. In response, moral agents habituated in the virtue of everyday solidarity should advocate a transformed approach to vacation that guarantees all workers a minimum number of paid days off annually. Here, the legal requirement is especially important, as current US practice clearly indicates what will happen without some enforceable standard.

In terms of particular aims, two general constraints should inform the specific number of vacation days sought by the virtue of everyday solidarity. First, the number of legally protected paid days off ought to exceed the current average, because the existing free time gap demonstrates that today's common practice is inadequate for the full realization of free time. Thus, the number should be higher than sixteen. Second, the statistics from other developed nations should shape US policy, both because prevailing standards show what is possible and because relative parity seems an appropriate way to honor solidarity's affirmation of the interconnections between all humans, not just coworkers. Accounting for both of these factors, the virtue of everyday solidarity can reasonably champion fifteen paid vacation days and ten paid holidays every year for every US worker. This allows workers to observe the nationally recognized holidays listed on the federal calendar (which include major holidays like Thanksgiving, Christmas, and New Year's Day, alongside others like the Fourth of July, Labor Day, and Martin Luther King Jr. Day) without sacrificing their vacation time to do so. Meanwhile, the remaining fifteen vacation days amount to three full weeks of work away from the job every year, adding one week to what the average worker receives under the current system. Obviously, the total of twenty-five paid days off represents a significant increase from the existing averages, but it would not radically transform the relative placement of the United States among its OECD peers. In fact, twenty-five total days would move the nation only four spots, to fifth from the bottom, ahead of the Netherlands and Switzerland (which have twenty total days each) and slightly behind Greece (twenty-six days). Given that fifteen nations are still able to accomplish more, this is hardly an unrealistic standard.

Nevertheless, a legal increase in paid time off will likely be difficult to achieve. In relative terms, twenty-five days off may be unremarkable; but given that the current floor is zero, this new legal requirement would be a big leap. The difficulty of accomplishing this task does not diminish its importance, however. People must have access to free time if they are going to transform it according to the principle of everyday solidarity, and vacation time is a major part of this project. In fact, vacation time might be the type of free time best suited to the vision of everyday solidarity, at least initially, because people tend to view their vacations as a special experience, set apart from their normal routines and thus subject to a different set of standards, when one can intentionally reflect on and strive to become one's "best self." Adding another layer of scrutiny to this natural practice would be simple, so the principle of everyday solidarity could easily become the new standard by which vacation activities are evaluated. If people are then able to see the benefits of this framework while on vacation, the principle might spill over into other types of time off as well, transforming free time more completely.

Increasing Parental Leave

Alongside increases in vacation time, paid parental leave constitutes a second structural reform that could empower more workers to adopt a relational approach to free time. The arrival of a new child represents one of the most malleable moments of a person's life, for "new parents' habits are more flexible than at almost any other time in their adult lives."[73] Because cognitive researchers have discovered "that it is actually people's unthinking routines—or habits—that form the bedrock of everyday life," accounting for nearly half of a person's "everyday behaviors," moments when routines are most likely to be reshaped offer a unique opportunity to inject a sense of conscious discernment into the choices that are often made with limited intentionality.[74] Even more than vacations, then, life with a newborn can serve as an important springboard to a new approach to free time that is more closely aligned with the principle of everyday solidarity, if only people had the chance to develop this new habit of discernment. The problem, of course, is that new parents are hardly awash in free time, but their time poverty does not need to be the case.

Certainly, not all aspects of a new parent's time poverty can be undone. The interruption of sleep routines, for instance, is a constitutive part of welcoming a naturally nocturnal baby into a nonnocturnal world, and the feeding schedules of newborns leave limited flexibility, especially for mothers. Even in the throes of a new child's earliest months, however, there are unstructured moments, many of which become more appreciated because of their sudden rarity. How parents choose to use this time during their initial transition period creates the sorts of lasting habits that can shape their entire family's approach to free time for years to come. Though it may seem like a lot to ask parents to make these choices with a significant amount of intentional discernment, the truth is that they are already making intentional choices about these matters because they can no longer rely on old free time routines. If some of the other, nonessential distractions were reduced, the burden of thinking critically about the formation of these new routines would not be as substantial, and new parents might be able to embrace the principle of everyday solidarity's approach to free time at one of the few moments in a person's life when it would have the best chance to stick.

One significant way to reduce some of these nonessential distractions is to remove the pressures of work from the equation with guaranteed parental leave. Generally speaking, the argument in favor of parental leave is that it allows new parents to focus on bonding with their children at a particularly important—and particularly intensive—time of infant development. Many countries recognize the long-term benefits of family bonding during this period and therefore have legal guarantees to protect a set amount of paid leave from work. The United States, however, does not. Consistent with its approach to vacation, the United States is the only OECD country that does not legally mandate some form of paid parental leave.[75] Of course, this does not mean that paid parental leave is nonexistent for all US workers. On the contrary, a number of companies have made headlines for voluntarily adopting "family friendly" policies like paid parental leave, usually as part of their employee retention efforts.[76] The very fact that these strategies are newsworthy, however, indicates that they are the exception that proves the rule. The reality remains that most workers do not have these protections.

In light of these facts, the virtue of everyday solidarity's application to free time should include a push for legally guaranteed paid parental leave. Although legal reforms are not the only strategy, in the case of parental leave they are arguably the most important for two reasons. First, a legal mandate is the only way to ensure that all workers have access to this benefit. Because the virtue of everyday solidarity is concerned with ensuring the common good of all and of each, complete coverage needs to remain the goal of its structural reforms. After all, the point is to ensure that genuine flourishing during free time is not exclusively the privilege of a select few. Consequently, the virtue of everyday solidarity countenances the creation of standard legal protections for paid parental leave. Second, workplace experience has shown that voluntary leave policies often do not translate into actual parental leave for their workers. Typically, this is due to the unwritten rules of workplace culture, which either make it difficult for employees to ask for the leave available to them or lead workers to conclude that their prospects for career advancement will be harmed by having family leave on their record.[77] Female employees in particular recognize this danger, as it is not unusual to see the effects of what one researcher calls the "maternal wall," where women who take parental leave are given fewer job responsibilities when they return because their coworkers and supervisors interpret their decision to use the company's parental leave policy as a sign of their lack of commitment to the job.[78] As long as parental leave remains the prerogative of the employer, reflecting a corporation's generosity with its employees rather than an authentic right for all workers, these counterpressures will continue to limit workers' access to parental leave. The only way to counteract some of these stigmas in a meaningful way is to make paid parental leave a universally recognized norm, and the most effective way to do this is through legal protection.

In practice, the specifics of legal reforms might vary, both with respect to the amount of time workers should have for their parental leave and how much they will be paid during that time. Discerning the best course of action will require "prudential judgment," but as with vacation time, the experiences of other developed countries can provide a useful benchmark.[79] Though there is a considerable range, "the smallest amount of leave required in any of the other 40 [OECD and similar] nations is about two months."[80] Current US law provides workplace protections for approximately three months of unpaid parental leave, so shifting some or all of that period to paid leave would be a reasonable goal, with two months representing a reasonable minimum threshold. The rate at which employees will be paid is also debatable, but because the goal of these reforms is to free families from external pressures so they can more easily reshape their habits with intentional discernment, full salary replacement is the most desirable outcome. Following the examples of other countries, where successful leave programs typically use government funds to support these payments, this policy would likely require input from a tax fund.[81] From the perspective of everyday solidarity, such an outcome is not a problem, because it can reinforce a sense of common commitment to this policy while also shifting workers' perceptions of paid parental leave so that it becomes their right in part because they have paid into the system.[82] As a result, workers will be more likely to take advantage of their newfound leave protections, thereby counteracting the unwritten norms that currently leave many workers feeling as though they cannot utilize their company's leave policy if they are so lucky to have access to one.

Together, guaranteed vacation time and guaranteed parental leave represent two structural reforms that have the power to challenge the pressures of time poverty that represent one end of the free time gap. There are, undoubtedly, other structural reforms that can also help to chip away at these pressures, and additional efforts will be required to change the culture surrounding free time so that people can recognize the value of leisure and recreation in a way that allows them to resist the valorization of busyness and the almost absolute prioritization of paid employment. This is where the complementary relationship between the virtue and the principle of everyday solidarity becomes especially important, for the aim of these structural reforms is to make it easier for moral agents to take a new view of the value of leisure and recreation, which will in turn reinforce the effects of the structural reforms. Guaranteed vacation time and guaranteed parental leave thus reflect two of the best strategies to help reshape people's perception of their free time, and thus they are the two best policies for transforming the time-poor end of the free time gap.

CONCLUSION

The structural reforms discussed here are all designed to counteract the paradoxical relationship between economic and temporal resources that limit people's ability to assess their free time with the kind of critical analysis that the principle of everyday solidarity encourages. That the proposals are also united by their focus on the workplace is not an accident, for the structures surrounding paid employment have the greatest influence on both a person's financial security and her or his time pressures. It is impossible to defend a new vision for free time without attending to these factors; otherwise, the principle of everyday solidarity's commitment to the ordering of leisure would be an unattainable ideal for virtually everyone except the members of what Thorstein Veblen disparagingly dubbed "the leisure class."[83] Such an outcome would of course be intolerable because the entire message of the principle of everyday solidarity is that moral discernment must be driven by an empathetic concern for the situation of others and not just the agent's own self-interest. Furthermore, insofar as the principle of everyday solidarity proposes an approach to free time that is designed to promote the full human flourishing of each moral agent, this vision cannot remain the luxury of the few who find themselves in the rare position to transcend the free time gap. Instead, this vision must be accompanied by a similarly strong commitment to reforming this gap, so that people will have access to the resources—both financial and temporal—to assess their free time choices with greater intentionality and critical awareness. Shifting the constraints of work through living wages, guaranteed vacation time, and guaranteed parental leave will accomplish exactly this.

Although all these reforms are essential, one must resist the assumption that the principle of everyday solidarity's vision for free time is pointless until these structural changes come to pass. Although the structural constraints of the free time gap do present legitimate obstacles to the full realization of the ordering of leisure, the effects of social structures like these are not fatalistic. Moral agents retain their freedom even in the face of structural obstacles, so people must be encouraged to do what they can with the principle of everyday solidarity's vision for free time even before structural reforms occur. Nevertheless, people should still commit themselves to these structural reforms, because such changes can have a significant impact on everyone's ability to attain the ideal envisioned by the principle of everyday solidarity. In the meantime, a partial realization of the ideal always remains a viable outcome, which means that moral agents must not lose sight of the practical implications of the principle of everyday solidarity for their own free time decisions.

Though the overarching vision for leisure discussed in chapter 3 offers one way to achieve this goal, recreation provides an even more fertile ground for the initial incorporation of the principle of everyday solidarity because most people have greater access to recreation and thus more experience with it. All they need is a little guidance to indicate how the principle of everyday solidarity might inform their use of recreation, and that is what the next half of this book provides.

NOTES

1. See, again, John Paul II, *Sollicitudo rei socialis*, 38.
2. Schor, *Overworked American*, 1–5, 29; Schor, "(Even More) Overworked American," 7.
3. Schor, *Overworked American*, 5, 159–62.
4. Robinson and Godbey, *Time for Life*, 5; see also 4.
5. Schor, "(Even More) Overworked American," 8–9.
6. Aguiar and Hurst, *Increase in Leisure Inequality*, 2.
7. Schor, *Overworked American*, 126. Detailing the imbalance of power in the employer-employee relationship, Schor notes that 85 percent of workers had no input on their working hours. Schor, 128.
8. Schor, 112–24.
9. Aguiar and Hurst, *Increase in Leisure Inequality*, 48; see also 16–19.
10. Mishel et al., *State of Working America*, 214; more generally, see also 211–26.
11. Finn, "What Is a Sinful Social Structure?" 142–44, 153–54.
12. For more on different types of poverty, see Himes, "Poverty and Christian Discipleship," 12–16.
13. Schneiders, "Vow of Poverty," 46.
14. Schneiders.
15. See Harvey and Mukhopadhyay, "When Twenty-Four Hours Is Not Enough."
16. Kubey and Csikszentmihalyi, *Television*, 199–201; Putnam, *Bowling Alone*, 222–36.
17. Kelly, "Commodification of Leisure"; McLean and Hurd, *Kraus' Recreation and Leisure*, 80–81.
18. Mishel et al., *State of Working America*, 129.
19. Noonan, *Scholastic Analysis of Usury*, 82–99.
20. Leo XIII, *Rerum novarum*, 45.
21. Ryan, *Living Wage*, 28–33.
22. Lamoureux, "Justice for Wage Earners," 225.
23. Ryan, *Living Wage*, 125.
24. Ryan, 132–35, at 135. Additionally, as a matter of social necessity, Ryan, on 134, stressed that food needed to be sufficient not just in quantity but also in "quality and variety," and that clothing should be appropriate not only for one's climate but also for one's social environment, so that workers might "appear among their fellows without hurt to that self-respect and natural pride which are indispensable to decent living."
25. Ryan, 139–45.

26. Ryan, 150.
27. Alonso and Starr, "Introduction," 1–6, at 2–3.
28. See Leo XIII, *Rerum novarum*, 46; and Pius XI, *Quadragesimo anno*, 71. Notably, Patricia Lamoureux has suggested that Leo XIII did not support a true family living wage but merely expressed a desire that wages would allow a worker to provide for a family but did not insist upon this in detail. See Lamoureux, "Justice for Wage Earners," 214–15.
29. John Paul II, *Laborem exercens*, 19.
30. For subsequent defenses after *Laborem exercens*, see US Conference of Catholic Bishops, *Economic Justice for All*, 103; and Benedict XVI, *Caritas in veritate*, 63.
31. Hinze, "Bridge Discourse," 511.
32. For a magisterial example of the tendency to presume that women should work in the home, see Pius XI, *Quadragesimo anno*, 71. For a general overview of the phenomenon in Catholic social thought, see Hinze, "Women, Families, and the Legacy of *Laborem exercens*," 74–78, 81–82.
33. Hinze, "Bridge Discourse," 528–30.
34. Leo XIII, *Rerum novarum*, 46.
35. For the critique of Ryan, see Hinze, "Bridge Discourse," 519–23.
36. Ryan, *Living Wage*, 117–19.
37. Bennett, "'Living Wage,'" 50.
38. Ryan, *Living Wage*, 120.
39. Soltis, "*Gaudium et spes* and the Family," 250–51.
40. See Pollin and Luce, *Living Wage*, 10–12.
41. For a classic defense of this position, see Rathbone, *Disinherited Family*, 14–21.
42. This is the basic theoretical conclusion of neoclassic economics, which envisions static supply-and-demand curves in the labor market and concludes that if the costs of the labor supply increase, the demand for workers will decrease. For a basic overview, see Neumark and Wascher, *Minimum Wages*, 39, 50–53.
43. Pollin and Luce, *Living Wage*, 27; Luce, *Fighting for a Living Wage*, 48. The slogan is used by Snarr, *All You That Labor*, 41.
44. Snarr, *All You That Labor*, 37.
45. US Census Bureau, "Households and Families."
46. Federal poverty guidelines are based on a simple multiplier of the cost of basic foods, adjusted for household size. Critics insist that food does not hold the large share of family budgets it once did, yielding an unrealistically low poverty threshold. See Snarr, *All You That Labor*, 26–27; and Lamoureux, "Justice for Wage Earners," 231. In addition, another concern arises from the fact that the guidelines are based on the cost of *basic* foods, because recent studies have shown that healthy foods are more expensive, costing about an additional $1.50 per person per day, or almost $550 more per year for each individual. As a result, the federal guidelines are also out of alignment with the costs of maintaining a sustainable lifestyle. Rao et al., "Do Healthier Foods and Diet Patterns Cost More?" For all these reasons, the use of a four-person household is a common practice in ethical evaluations of the living wage. See Albrecht, *Hitting Home*, 149.
47. Author's calculations from the US Department of Health and Human Services, "Poverty Guidelines."
48. Glasmeier, "Living Wage Calculator."

49. Glasmeier, "New Data Up."
50. In fairness, the goal might not be so idealistic at the local level. Though some states have plans to raise their minimum wage to $15 per hour by 2022, Washington, DC, is on pace for this minimum wage rate by 2020, and New York City has already enacted a $15 minimum wage. National Council of State Legislatures, "State Minimum Wages."
51. Pollin and Luce, *Living Wage*, 163.
52. On the application of love and justice in Niebuhr's theology, see Hinze, "Drama of Social Sin," 453–54; Niebuhr, *Interpretation of Christian Ethics*, 31–32.
53. Kaveny, *Law's Virtues*, 1–2, 28–37.
54. Pollin and Luce, *Living Wage*, 2–3.
55. Pollin and Luce, 124, 150–59; Pollin et al., *Measure of Fairness*, 30–31, 172–73.
56. Naughton, "Distributors of Justice," 165–67, at 165. The company has since had business trouble, but this seems to have been due primarily to larger business issues beyond its commitment to its employees. Burlingham, "Paradise Lost."
57. Ward, "Toward a Christian Virtue Account," esp. 132–33.
58. Powers, *Hamlet's Blackberry*, 9–10, at 10.
59. On the contributions of work to time poverty, see Wolfteich, "Time Poverty," 46–49; and Hochschild, *Second Shift*.
60. Leo XIII, *Rerum novarum*, 40–41, at 41.
61. John XXIII, *Mater et magistra*, 248, 253.
62. John Paul II, *Laborem exercens*, 19.
63. John XXIII, *Mater et magistra*, 249.
64. *Lemon v. Kurtzman*, 403 US 602 (1971); Ravishankar, "Establishment Clause's Hydra," esp. 270–73, 287–89, 291, 297–99.
65. Fraser, *White-Collar Sweatshop*, 24–26, 75–81; Deal, *Always On, Never Done?* 1; Turkle, *Alone Together*, 165.
66. Hewlett, "Addressing the Time Crunch," 167–75; Slaughter, "Why Women Still Can't Have It All."
67. John XXIII, *Mater et magistra*, 250.
68. John Paul II, *Laborem exercens*, 19.
69. Ray, Sanes, and Schmitt, *No-Vacation Nation Revisited*, 2–3.
70. Ray, Sanes, and Schmitt, 4.
71. Ray, Sanes, and Schmitt, 1.
72. Ray, Sanes, and Schmitt, 4.
73. Duhigg, "How Companies Learn Your Secrets."
74. Neal, Wood, and Quinn, "Habits," 198.
75. Livingston, "Among 41 Nations, US Is the Outlier."
76. See, e.g., Wojcicki, "Paid Maternity Leave"; Barney, "15 Companies."
77. Hochschild, *Time Bind*, 132–33, 144.
78. Williams, *Unbending Gender*, 70–72.
79. On the importance of prudential judgment in the moral evaluation of specific proposals for legal reforms, see US Conference of Catholic Bishops, *Forming Consciences*, 31, 33.
80. Livingston, "Among 41 Nations, US Is the Outlier."
81. Gornick and Meyers, "Supporting a Dual-Earner/Dual-Career Society," 395.

82. Thus, people are more protective of and more likely to use programs like Medicare in part because they have put in their "fair share," as the famed "Keep your government hands off my Medicare" critique from Tea Party activists revealed. Skinner, "'Keep Your Government Hands Off My Medicare!'" 609.
83. Veblen, *Theory of the Leisure Class*.

PART III

Applications to Recreation

CHAPTER 5

Television

As people actually use their free time for recreation, one activity dwarfs all other pursuits in the US context: watching television. Statistically, in 2017 everyone over the age of fourteen years in the United States had an average of 4.72 hours of free time each weekday and 6.46 hours each weekend day. More than half this free time (52.97 percent on weekdays and 52.48 percent on weekends) was dedicated to watching TV, and the second-closest activity—socializing—was not even close, accounting for far less than half the amount of time given to television.[1]

Although, admittedly, a variety of demographic differences affect these statistics, nearly every single demographic group spends at least half its free time watching TV, and there is not a single subset of the population whose most popular free time activity is something other than watching television.[2] For reasons discussed in more detail below, this fact points toward the triumph of recreation over leisure for most people in the United States, an inversion of the priority of leisure that emerges from the theological analysis of free time. Moreover, research indicates that watching TV is a particularly isolating activity, so the most popular free time activity also has negative effects on a person's relational well-being. From the perspective of everyday solidarity, then, the prominence of television represents a problematic trend frustrating the full potential of free time.

To provide some guidance on how to evaluate and ultimately to address this trend, this chapter presents a two-section application of everyday solidarity to television. The first explains the principle of everyday solidarity's critique of television as the default free time pursuit while also presenting some ways in which video consumption could be used to serve relational ends. The second considers the broader forces behind the prominence of television during free time, providing a structural challenge to strengthen the principle of everyday solidarity's alternative vision. The end result is a strategy for the proper incorporation of television, film, and video into the moral life in a way that accords with recreation's status as an instrumental good.

TELEVISION IN LIGHT OF THE PRINCIPLE OF EVERYDAY SOLIDARITY

According to the principle of everyday solidarity's emphasis on relational flourishing, the outsize influence of television during free time creates two major problems. First, the act of watching TV is not only unlikely to induce flow; it is often inimical to it. Consequently, watching TV is very much a form of recreation rather than leisure. Though this does not make television inherently problematic as a free time activity, because there is a legitimate place for the use of recreation as an instrumental good, the dedication of more than half the average person's discretionary time to this recreational pursuit is hardly consistent with the priority of leisure as an inherent good. Second, television, along with some but not all other forms of video media, harms relationality, both because this isolating activity drowns out more social pursuits and because it habituates asocial tendencies. This first section of the chapter discusses how the principle of everyday solidarity can shed light on both of these shortcomings in order to develop some practical proposals for a better incorporation of television, film, and video into a more balanced use of recreation during free time. Before proceeding with this analysis, however, a brief note on terminology is appropriate.

The category that captures the average person's largest use of free time in the United States is defined in surveys as "watching TV." Initially, this would have been a very straightforward category, covering the shows regularly available on a person's television set. In recent years, however, the category of television has expanded to include streaming services and other internet content that is sometimes, but not always, accessed through a television set. In the context of this chapter, then, "television" is employed in the colloquial sense to refer to any video content that is consumed via a screen, whether that be the screen on a television set, a computer, a tablet, a smartphone, or some other device. In some cases, however, the means of consumption does matter, so there are moments in this chapter (notably the subsection addressing television's impact on relationality) when television is separated from other categories like film. But unless explicitly noted, television, film, and video can be treated interchangeably, and so the comments about television should be construed to apply broadly to all the various forms of video consumption.

Television as the Triumph of Recreation

The first issue with respect to television stems from its negative relationship with flow, and thus its distance from leisure. On this point, Mihaly Csikszentmihalyi, the psychologist who pioneered the idea of flow, has explicitly evaluated the experience of watching TV, and he and his colleague Robert Kubey have concluded that it is far from optimal. Although a number of viewers have, at times, described getting lost in their TV viewing experience to the point that they do not realize how much time has passed, Kubey and Csikszentmihalyi determined that this experience was not actually one of flow.[3] Instead, they found that watching TV required far less skill than other everyday activities, including both work and leisure ones, and also that it ranked as the least-demanding activity done in the home, requiring less mastery than even eating.[4] Because flow emerges from the perfect alignment of an activity's challenges with a person's skills, these characteristics make it almost impossible for television to lead to flow because the low skill threshold for watching TV is easily crossed, so additional challenges do not arise and personal growth and self-actualization do not proceed.[5]

Ultimately, the contrast between watching TV and the optimal experience of flow is due to the passive nature of television as a medium. Whereas flow represents the complete focus that can emerge from active pursuits, watching television is most commonly reported as a passive (albeit relaxing) experience.[6] Hence, Marie Winn, a journalist who explored the effects of television on children, has likened youth TV viewing to a "trance" that serves as a defense mechanism against overwhelming stimuli, creating "an unmistakable return to the passive mode of functioning" that defines the earliest stages of childhood development.[7] Although passivity during TV viewing is therefore identified in both self-reporting and observation, one could still object that this is an accidental rather than substantial feature of television. Such an objection seems particularly pointed in this internet-connected age, when, for instance, a number of audience-generated websites for popular television shows allow fans to engage each other and to discuss theories related to their favorite programs.[8]

On this point, one study found that greater online activity on message boards for reality TV shows correlated with greater cognitive engagement with the content of those shows, suggesting an active way of watching TV under the right circumstances.[9] Significantly, however, these exceptions to passivity in TV viewing hinge on viewers doing something *in addition to* watching television, which means that these anecdotes do nothing to challenge claims about the nature of the medium itself. On this question, the evidence consistently points toward television's passivity, especially on the cognitive level—a limitation that becomes especially apparent when one compares TV viewing with reading, which has the same sedentary features of television but still constitutes an active pursuit because it requires much higher levels of brain engagement.[10]

Given the contrasts between television's passivity and the active conditions necessary for flow, there is a significant distance between watching TV and the leisure ideal articulated in chapter 1. On some level, people seem to recognize this already. For instance, when Kubey and Csikszentmihalyi asked their study's participants to describe what would actually give them satisfaction, virtually everyone identified experiences that involved much more complexity and demanded much more active engagement than watching TV. The juxtaposition, they argued, was quite revealing, for "compared to such optimal experiences [of flow], much television watching could be deemed a waste of time."[11] These features all indicate that watching TV is properly regarded as a recreational pursuit rather than a leisure activity, for it lacks the flow elements that justify leisure's status as an intrinsic good. Of course, this does not mean that watching TV is all bad, or that it has to be condemned. According to the theological interpretation of free time advanced in this book, leisure remains the ideal, but recreation is also recognized as an appropriate, albeit instrumental, good. Similarly, the principle of everyday solidarity's approach to free time may champion the priority of leisure; but, as discussed in chapter 3, this is not an absolute prioritization. Recreation has a valuable part to play in a well-integrated approach to free time.

As a form of recreation, television has its advantages. The communications professor Jib Fowles has argued that viewers watch TV for a reason, and he suggests that they must be getting what they are looking for because they come back so frequently. In his assessment, television provides "therapeutic benefits," like relaxation, that allow viewers to relieve the stress of their day and ease the "psychic pressure[s]" of cultural expectations.[12] Similarly, Kubey and Csikszentmihalyi suggested that watching TV might constitute an "adaptive regression," like daydreaming, that allows people to take a mental break from the taxing elements of their everyday life so that they can then face them with renewed vigor afterward.[13] In essence, they have described watching TV as a particularly effective form of recreation, because it promotes the kind of renewal that justifies recreation's status as an instrumental good in the moral life. From the perspective of everyday solidarity, then, television is not inimical to a well-ordered approach to free time. The problem, however, is that television is not typically integrated into such a well-ordered approach. Instead, it has come to dominate free time in the United States, to the point that watching TV is often a person's default response to having discretionary time.

In light of the theological potential for free time, it is this trend of defaulting to television that constitutes a problem, for two reasons. First, the tendency to default to one activity during free time habituates an unconscious approach to free time that militates against the intentional and self-critical evaluation of ordinary life that the principle of everyday solidarity is meant to promote. Second, the specific tendency to default to television creates a de facto prioritization of recreation in a way that limits a person's opportunities for genuine leisure. Though this would be a concern for any recreational pursuit that occupied as large a proportion of the population's free time as television does, it is amplified by the fact that television is the particular pursuit in this case, because watching TV (and similar video media) has residual effects on a viewer that make it more difficult to transition to other activities, including leisure pursuits. The negative residual effects of watching TV stem from the way the human brain interacts with television's visual stimuli, which allows a sense of relaxation while one is watching TV but also creates "feelings of passivity and lowered alertness" that continue after the video is turned off.[14] As a result, people have less ability to concentrate after watching TV and less energy for other activities, creating a cycle that makes television, a decidedly low-energy activity, even more appealing.[15] This is not merely a theoretical association. One study of people's behavior before and after the introduction of television in a small town—the closest thing researchers have to a controlled scientific experiment—revealed that more television correlated with a general decline in other leisure pursuits.[16] Not only does the prominence of television during free time lead to an inversion of the priority of leisure over recreation, then; it also habituates this preference, generating additional inertia that agents must overcome before they can reprioritize leisure again. Although television is not per se opposed to the theological vision for integrating free time into the moral life, its outsize prominence during free time in the United States is hard to justify on these terms.

Given these factors, the principle of everyday solidarity has good reason to suggest that people should strive to watch less television. The sheer amount of time people spend watching TV means that they do not yet abide by the priority of leisure over recreation, because viewing video media is too passive to facilitate flow, the hallmark of leisure. At the same time, the "passive spillover" effects of television mean not only that people have less time for leisure when they watch more TV but also that they have less inclination to pursue leisure with whatever free time remains.[17] As a result, television (along with film and video, which also rely on the same visual stimuli behind the passive spillover effect) represents an obstacle to the principle of everyday solidarity's guidance for free time, which includes a prima facie preference for leisure over recreation. This is not the only challenge that television presents to the principle of everyday solidarity's vision for free time, however. In addition to the general preference for leisure over recreation, the principle of everyday solidarity also seeks to promote the full relational flourishing of each human person, and there is evidence to indicate that television also frustrates this aim.

How Television Harms Relationality

The effects of television on a person's relational capacities are overwhelmingly negative. First, the same passive spillover effects that reduce a person's interest in leisure also chip away at a person's relational capacities. Specifically, the low levels of concentration required for television negatively affect a viewer's attention span.[18] This reduced attention span makes it more challenging to have meaningful interactions with others, because the difficulty of concentrating both limits one's abilities for self-reflection, leaving less to talk about with others, and erodes the skills needed to engage in conversation, which requires focusing not only on what one thinks but also on how it relates to what others say.[19] Moreover, the long-term effects of habitual TV viewing include a greater emphasis on material affluence and less interest in seeking happiness through relationships, which unsurprisingly leads to less social involvement with others.[20] In all these ways, a reliance on television during free time leaves one less well equipped for social interactions, which is inherently a problem when one assumes, as Catholic theological anthropology does, that relational connections are essential for human flourishing.

However, the effects of television on relational well-being are not limited to spillover effects. As with television's impact on leisure, there are also crowding-out effects that result from television's ability to replace more social pursuits. Significantly, though the spillover effects are associated with any video media, there are indications that the crowding-out effects leaving less time for socializing are distinct for television, revealing that this free time pursuit is of particular concern from the perspective of everyday solidarity.

Television's effects on social behavior have been most well documented by the sociologist Robert Putnam, whose research has chronicled a persistent decline in social capital—the invisible bonds that knit a community together—in the United States that has been aligned directly with the increasing availability of television during the twentieth century.[21] His initial foray into the topic suggested that watching television was "strongly and negatively related to social trust and group membership."[22] Further study, which resulted in the influential book *Bowling Alone*, led to the even stronger claim that "dependence on television for entertainment is not merely *a* significant predictor of civic disengagement. It is *the single most consistent* predictor that I have discovered" (emphasis in the original).[23] Specifically, those who affirmed that watching TV was their "primary form of entertainment" were consistently less involved in community organizations, less invested in political issues, and less frequently in contact with their friends than those who denied this statement.[24] These negative effects on social engagement increased as average daily viewing hours increased, and they were most strongly associated with those who watched TV habitually instead of turning on the television to watch a specific show. Unfortunately, heavy TV viewers (those watching TV for more than three hours per day) outnumbered light TV viewers (less than one and a half hours per day) at least two to one in every demographic, and habitual viewing has been on the rise with each successive generation.[25] By Putnam's estimation, these TV trends offer a reasonable explanation for the generationally driven decline in social capital, accounting for about one-quarter of the overall loss.[26]

Putnam's research thus reveals that watching television has a dramatic effect on a community's interconnections, eroding relationships by isolating individuals during their free time. What is particularly striking about this revelation is that free time activities normally perpetuate one another, such that more time in one free time activity usually correlates with more time spent in other free time pursuits, even those of a qualitatively different type.[27] In contrast, TV viewing has isolating effects, as indicated by the fact that the number of people in the US asserting that they would prefer a "quiet evening at home" to time spent in communal interactions has increased in tandem with the spread of television.[28] In fairness, there are indications that some of these effects cannot be entirely, uniformly ascribed to all types of TV programming. Watching the news, for instance, has been linked to more involvement in one's community, and another study suggested that the content, and even television station, likely affected the relationship between TV viewing and communal engagement.[29]

These caveats, however, do not radically change the diagnosis, because news viewership is both small and declining, and the overall effects of watching TV on one's attitude toward community involvement are negative.[30] This latter point is underscored by the fact that watching films (at least in theaters) is not associated with the same kind of social disengagement; in fact, increased movie attendance aligns with increased participation in a host of communal activities during one's free time.[31] The best conclusion, then, is that watching TV is *in se* negatively associated with civic engagement, and *in addition*, certain types of programming exacerbate this problem.[32] Hence, TV viewing is an isolating free time activity that leads individuals to become less involved in their communities.[33]

Unfortunately, from the perspective of everyday solidarity, television's problematic effects on relational flourishing are not limited to its negative effects on social capital. In addition to facilitating civic disengagement, watching TV also crowds out more informal social interactions with friends, neighbors, and family members. Though this might be an intuitive extension of the fact that the amount of time people in the United States spend watching television greatly exceeds the amount of time they spend socializing, it is also evident from more detailed data as well. First, according to time diary studies, the amount of time married individuals spend watching TV is three to four times higher than the amount of time they spend in conversation with their spouses.[34] Second, as the number of households with more than one TV set has increased, the tendency to watch TV alone has also risen.[35] Even studies that estimate higher rates of shared TV viewing—about 60 percent of total TV viewing hours—suggest that much of this is "parallel viewing," where social interaction is limited.[36] Third, TV viewing has been linked to declines in socializing, and not simply as part of its larger spillover effects.[37] For instance, the above-mentioned study of one Canadian town during the initial introduction of television found that people spent less time in group leisure activities and also specifically noted that they attended fewer social events, like dinners and parties, after TV arrived.[38]

From the other side of the equation, research has shown that families that have given up television spend more time together in conversation and in active leisure pursuits than they did when they watched TV—two changes that dissipate if a family returns to watching TV.[39] Finally, these trends are consistent with research showing that people often use TV as a buffer against negative feelings, a process that is not problematic per se but that in practice can lead to less social interaction with others.[40] In all these ways, television has a displacement effect on socialization, which constitutes an obstacle to one's relational flourishing.[41]

The ethical assessment of television, then, is negative, at least insofar as watching TV is the primary free time activity for most people in the United States. Not only does watching television leave people with less time—and less motivation—for the flow-inducing free time activities that constitute leisure's ideal; it also crowds out time with other people, isolating individuals from their community and undermining their interpersonal relationships. Consequently, the heavy reliance on television is doubly problematic, at least according to the principle of everyday solidarity's vision for free time, for it both limits the likelihood that people will abide by the priority of leisure over recreation and also frustrates a person's full flourishing as a relational human being. Fortunately, however, the principle of everyday solidarity can offer more than a simple indictment of the tendency to default to television during free time. When one adopts the principle's standard of relational flourishing for one's ethical discernment, alternative options for a more relationally fulfilling use of recreation appear.

Television and the Principle of Everyday Solidarity

Between television's inversion of the priority of leisure over recreation and its negative effects on relationality, the simplest advice to emerge from the principle of everyday solidarity is that people should spend less time watching television. This strategy obviously would address the tendency to default to recreation instead of intentionally seeking out leisure, restoring some balance to free time overall, so that the enjoyment of leisure as an intrinsic good might more regularly accompany the use of recreation for more instrumental ends. These observations do not mean that moral agents should strive to completely eliminate television from their free time, however, for this is both unrealistic and unnecessary. It is unrealistic because television is such an outsize part of free time at the moment. A no-TV goal would require not merely challenging current free time trends but completely reversing them, which is unlikely to occur.

At the same time, this no-TV goal is unnecessary, because there is a place for recreation in the theological vision for free time, and a complete assault on the principal form of recreation for most people in the United States would unfortunately imply otherwise. Moreover, watching TV is a particularly relaxing experience, so it has the potential to help one realize the instrumental good of recuperation, to which recreation is partially ordered. Admittedly, television's contributions to relaxation diminish during prolonged viewing, and there are concerns about the impact of TV's passive spillover effect on other forms of recreation and also leisure, but both these factors reflect problems that emerge most acutely from watching too much television. They are not fatal flaws, provided one is attentive to these risks and uses television with an intentional focus on the instrumental goods one wants to attain.

The goal for an ethical approach to free time is therefore not zero television but a more moderate use of television that better incorporates it into a well-ordered use of recreation that coexists with adequate time to enjoy leisure. The best way to quantify this goal is not in absolute numbers but in relative terms. Specifically, one should aim to reorder free time so that watching TV is not one's principal free time activity. This is a more moderate, and thus more realistic, goal than zero television. It also creates flexibility for personal variations in free time and allows for times when a person might decide that he or she needs more opportunities for recuperation, and thus more recreation than leisure, to balance out extra stressors. More important, the tipping point for television's impact on communal disengagement and social disintegration occurs when someone declares that watching TV is their "primary form of entertainment."[42] Reducing one's reliance on television so that it is no longer one's principal free time activity is therefore a quantifiable goal that will have a substantial positive effect, reversing the declines in social capital and connectivity that arise from watching too much TV while also freeing up more time for the enjoyment of leisure.

In addition to reducing the time one spends watching TV, moral agents have other ways to adjust their use of recreation so that it better aligns with the impulses of the principle of everyday solidarity. First, they might consider seeking the relaxation that television can provide through other forms of video media in different settings. As Putnam's study revealed, spending more time watching TV at home was associated with declines in social capital and civic engagement, but spending time watching movies (at a movie theater) was not. The distinction seems to be where the activity occurs, because the viewing experience is virtually identical apart from that. For those who would like to experience the relaxation of television while also abiding by the principle of everyday solidarity, then, an appropriate alternative would be to search for opportunities to watch television shows, films, and other video content in a social setting. This could mean watching more movies in public settings, which might seem prohibitively expensive, especially when one thinks of the high ticket prices for blockbuster films. But this is not the only way to get out of the house to watch movies. There are often smaller, independent cinemas that charge less for tickets or, in some cases, that have their own memberships available to decrease costs.

Similarly, many communities have film appreciation societies that either screen free films for their members or offer discounts at independent theaters. Though the costs of these two types of memberships are not negligible, they are often less than the amount of money people in the United States typically spend on cable television annually.[43] For even less money, one can seek out free public film screenings at the local public library, in parks during the summer, or at other community institutions. Finally, depending on the type of television programming one wants to see, there could be ample opportunities to watch TV in more social settings—for example, by going to a bar or restaurant to watch a sporting event with other fans. All these avenues, not to mention other creative opportunities, represent ways to use television, film, and video for their recuperative effects without isolating oneself from the community in the process.

Second, there are ways to use television more intentionally so that it can contribute to relational flourishing while providing its restorative benefit. Specifically, one can turn TV viewing into a communal experience. This requires moving beyond parallel viewing, where two or more people watch the same thing side-by-side with little to no interaction, to engaged viewing. In some cases, this could involve watching a show together and discussing its content, its plotlines, or new issues that it stimulates. The current "golden age" of television is particularly well suited to this end, for an impressive number of shows are now introducing complex characters and exploring consequential themes, leaving much for fans to discuss together.[44] In other cases, television could simply become an excuse to gather friends together, with a shared show generating a regular routine when people can see each other and talk about other things, especially if there is built-in time for socializing before or after viewing—perhaps even with a shared meal. Although all these strategies work with traditional cable television shows, they also work with new content on streaming services and online videos. The point, of course, is to use television, film, and video in a way that contributes to rather than detracts from relational connections, which means that these options hardly constitute an exhaustive list for implementing this strategy.

With a greater degree of intentionality, and a greater reliance on the principle of everyday solidarity, people can incorporate television, film, and video into a well-ordered approach to free time. Though the goal is not a complete elimination of television, the vision just articulated still requires substantial changes in personal free time choices, particularly in the United States. This will not be an easy shift, both because the reliance on television during free time has been habituated for individuals and because watching TV at home is now so popular that the public events and social settings where one might seek to watch TV with others are harder to find. There needs to be a critical mass of people who are similarly interested in a more social context for recreation, but this will occur only if more people have the time to evaluate their free time choices critically and intentionally. As a result, the structural reforms to improve access to leisure discussed in the last chapter are essential not only for the proper ordering of leisure but also for the proper ordering of free time as a whole. At the same time, the principle of everyday solidarity's specific vision for television requires more than just additional time for people to examine their recreational decisions but also alternatives to watching TV at home alone. Beyond the general structural reforms that would increase access to free time, then, moral agents can also support a more fulfilling use of recreation by addressing some of the distinct structures that currently encourage the excessive emphasis on television in the United States. As a tool for social analysis and structural reform, the virtue of everyday solidarity can help to add specificity to this project.

TELEVISION IN LIGHT OF THE VIRTUE OF EVERYDAY SOLIDARITY

There are two factors contributing to the popularity of television during free time in the United States. One is the ease of access. The other is its low cost. Although there are structural forces behind both these factors, the latter is much more important to address than the former, for two reasons. First, there are few things anyone can do about the ease with which people can now access television in the United States. Once TV succeeded in penetrating a critical mass of households in the United States—which it did by 1955—there was no turning back.[45] From a pragmatic point of view, there is little point wasting energy on reducing ease of access to television. Second, there is also limited justification for trying to do so, even if it were more feasible. After all, ease of access to television is not inherently a problem, given that TV has the potential to serve recreation's instrumental goods appropriately if it is used with greater intentionality, as just discussed. Moral agents thus have little need to counteract television's ease of access. They do, however, have good reasons to address the structural causes underlying television's low costs, because this is a significant factor in its outsize influence during free time.

To be more precise about the effects of television's low costs, it is really the *relatively* cheap cost of television that makes watching TV more appealing and more common than other forms of recreation and leisure. Once a person has a television set, basic broadcast channels are free with a digital antenna. Meanwhile, anyone who pays for cable TV service does so upfront, which means that the immediate costs of watching TV is next to nothing (likely a few cents to cover the amount of electricity used). In contrast, more active forms of recreation and new opportunities for leisure tend to require an immediate financial outlay, especially in an atomistic context, where the tendency toward personalization and privatization has led to the increasing commodification of leisure.[46]

Hence, the tendency to default to television during free time becomes easy to justify because the energy and economic resources required to pursue other activities seem too extreme by comparison. As a result, there is something of an inverse between a recreational activity's costs and its abilities to contribute to the relational flourishing of the people who participate in it. From the perspective of everyday solidarity, this structural reality is particularly problematic because the mismatch in costs suggests that the proper integration of free time into a life of relational flourishing will become an exclusive luxury of those with means. There is hardly any point in countenancing a different approach to free time if it is inaccessible to so many. In order for the principle of everyday solidarity's vision for free time to have legitimacy as a guide for this sphere of ordinary life, then, structural reforms to alleviate the mismatched costs of watching TV must be part of the ethical response to the prominence of television during free time.

The Need to Reform Mismatched Costs

Given that the structural incentives supporting the prominence of television arise from its relative, rather than absolute, costs, one could employ two potential strategies to counteract this problem. One could either attempt to increase the costs associated with television, or one could work to lower the costs associated with other, more relationally fulfilling, free time activities. Although each of these approaches would counteract the cost gap, the second is more practical, and ultimately much more desirable, than the first. To begin with, there is little reason to assume that an increase in the cost of television will prompt people to watch less television, let alone encourage them to seek out new leisure activities or alternative recreational pursuits. As cable TV companies seem to have discovered already, the demand for television content is relatively inelastic. The costs of a cable TV subscription have increased annually, and quite dramatically, since the early 2000s, but these rising costs did not have immediate effects on viewership rates.[47] Indeed, the number of households subscribing to traditional cable TV services increased just as steadily through 2012, at which point things did eventually begin to shift.[48]

More recently, there has been a decline in people paying for traditional cable TV service, but virtually all analysts connect this to the new availability of Netflix, Amazon Prime, and other streaming services that provide similar content at dramatically reduced prices.[49] Together, both these trends reveal the larger point that increases in the costs of television are unlikely to have any practical effect on people's penchant for watching TV. They will either suffer through the cost increases, as most subscribers did before the advent of online video, or they will find new ways to access the same type of content at a lower cost with some combination of streaming services and perhaps broadcast TV, with its proliferating digital subchannels. Thus, although an increase in the costs associated with watching TV might provide a theoretical response to TV's low relative costs, it does not do enough to counteract the effects of this structural imbalance in practice.

The better solution, then, is to address television's low relative costs from the other side of the equation by working to reduce the costs associated with other free time activities so that additional forms of recreation—as well as genuine leisure activities—might be more readily available to more people. This approach is preferable, for two reasons. First, it can challenge the typical, troubling assumptions about the value of free time, paving the way for a more sympathetic response to the theological vision for leisure and recreation. Second, it can ultimately promote not only new forms of recreation in place of television but also new opportunities for leisure, making the prioritization of leisure over recreation at the heart of the theological vision for free time more attainable. A brief explanation can defend both these advantages.

First, by making the enjoyment of leisure and the appropriate use of recreation cheaper, this strategy chips away at the commodification of free time, which is one of the larger forces limiting people's appreciation of leisure and recreation as theological goods whose value extends beyond their utility. In contrast, the attempt to make television more expensive simply increases the cost pressures, underscoring a strictly economic assessment of value. At the same time, such cost increases serve as a blunt instrument, making television more expensive without discriminating between mindless default viewing, which one would want to decrease, and an intentional effort to use TV to serve relational ends, which one ought to encourage. In other words, an increase in the costs of television might actually create new obstacles to an agent's efforts to prioritize their use of recreation according to the principle of everyday solidarity. Because the aim of the virtue of everyday solidarity is to remove such obstacles, there is more to be gained by reducing the costs associated with other free time activities than there is by increasing the costs of watching TV.

Second, decreasing the costs associated with a variety of free time activities has the potential to encourage not only alternative forms of recreation but also new opportunities for leisure. Although there are a wide variety of ways to achieve the flow state that characterizes leisure, not all of them are equally accessible. In fact, many of them are hard to come by, either because they are expensive in their own right or because they are available primarily in more affluent communities. Consider sports, which are an important form of leisure because the rules and clearly defined objectives of games provide parameters that are especially conducive to flow.[50] Although a person could conceivably play a sport like baseball for minimal costs, especially if she or he is willing to improvise, they will still need to find other people with whom to play. In the current cultural context of the United States, this is where new costs factor into the equation. At one time, finding teammates for an informal game of baseball might have been as easy as walking down the street, but as the ethos of atomistic individualism described in chapter 2 has gained influence, collective pursuits like this now increasingly require organization through some external authority like a recreation department or travel league. Though this trend is not isolated to any one sport, it is especially pronounced in the case of baseball, where informal "sandlot" games, which were once a very visible staple of community life in the United States, have all but disappeared in the face of carefully structured little leagues and travel teams.[51]

Certainly, there is nothing inherently problematic about structured games and organized leagues, which can actually promote both leisure and recreation in a relational context. The problem, however, is that they create structural impediments to equal access, further tilting the cost mismatch of recreational activities in television's favor. As Joseph Ellis and Hemant Sharma explain in relation to similar shifts in soccer, "the trappings of [organized] league play have created an exclusionary process whereby those with money can afford the leagues, and moreover, those leagues have monopolized public spaces for private function."[52] The result is that a major avenue for access to leisure has been foreclosed for those with limited resources, making the recourse to passive forms of recreation—like watching TV—easier, and thus more likely.

Sports, however, are only one example. A similar shift toward privatization and commodification can also be seen in numerous other free time pursuits.[53] With each shift toward fee-based leisure pursuits, the obstacles to leisure increase, and the low costs of watching television look more appealing on a relative scale. By working to defray the costs associated not simply with active forms of recreation but also with flow-inducing leisure pursuits, moral agents can counteract the structural pressures that make the primacy of television during free time so appealing and common. In the process, they can counteract not only television's crowding-out effects on more relationally fulfilling opportunities for recreation but also its de facto inversion of the priority of leisure over recreation. By applying their energies to reduce the costs of more fulfilling free time activities, moral agents can make it easier for both themselves and others to embrace the vision for free time that emerges from the principle of everyday solidarity, just as the virtue of everyday solidarity is designed to do.

Concrete Strategies for Reform

Naturally, one can imagine various strategies to reduce the costs associated with both active leisure pursuits and more relationally fulfilling forms of recreation. Among the many options, three in particular are discussed here because they have the ability to achieve this immediate goal in a fashion that can also create new bonds of communal responsibility, paving the way for more agents to internalize the relational sense of their own moral obligations that solidarity promotes.

First, there is the personal strategy of offsetting costs on a small scale. For instance, someone who can afford to pay the registration fees and other upfront costs associated with more relationally fulfilling free time pursuits could use those resources to decrease economic obstacles for others. Thus, to return to the baseball example, in addition to paying his or her own entry fee, a person could also sponsor another spot on the team, thereby reducing the league's barriers to entry—at least for one other player. In this way, the person would embrace a small-scale commitment to the common good, recognizing that even in the case of free time, others deserve the same "thorough and ready access to their own fulfillment" that one wishes to enjoy for oneself.[54]

Second, direct ancillary support for public goods offers another way to decrease costs and cultivate a similar sense of solidarity vis-à-vis the benefits of free time. In this strategy, the goal would not be to reduce barriers to access—given that many public goods are already free—but rather to raise the quality of these low-cost resources for leisure so that they will be able to provide a level of fulfillment similar to that of their costlier counterparts. Of the many institutions that might benefit from this strategy, public libraries are an exceptional illustration because they are usually open to all of an area's residents and offer both opportunities for flow, through their reading materials and other media, and options for relationally fulfilling forms of recreation, through their community programming. A direct donation to the local library could strengthen either of these, providing more (or better) books and new (or bigger) programs, which might make this common resource appealing enough to at least chip away at the hegemony of private, passive free time pursuits like watching TV at home.

At the same time, donations to these kinds of free public goods can help to ensure that they remain free, creating an additional bulwark against the ongoing privatization of leisure and recreation. Ideally, given the virtue of solidarity's affinity with the preferential option for the poor, one would make it a priority to direct these donations to the libraries and other public goods that serve the most resource-poor populations and not merely the institutions with which one is most familiar. Regardless of the specific institutions one chooses to support, however, the simple choice to contribute more intentionally to the maintenance of a public good has the ability to promote a sense of solidarity and an awareness of one's responsibility to the common good.

Although both these strategies have the potential to raise people's awareness of their relational obligations, they are still somewhat one-sided insofar as they require private resources and are therefore feasible only for those who have sufficient income to make personal donations. Because the virtue of everyday solidarity presumes that a sense of shared responsibility for the well-being of others is a constitutive element of each person's full flourishing as a human being, these two strategies cannot be the only avenues for structural reform. Concern for access to genuine forms of leisure and relationally fulfilling forms of recreation must move beyond a patronizing form of charity offered *for* those with limited resources in order to generate a new sense of solidarity *with* those in need.[55] Fortunately, there is a third strategy, which is open to all, that can reduce barriers and promote shared responsibility. In addition to personal donations, moral agents can embody the virtue of everyday solidarity's efforts to offset the high relative costs of more fulfilling free time pursuits by supporting public policies that improve access to high-quality free time activities at little to no cost.

These public policies will obviously look different at the various levels of government in the United States. Locally, supporting these types of policies might mean encouraging the community's recreation department to leave soccer fields or baseball diamonds unscheduled at specific times throughout the week to facilitate pickup games apart from the fees of the structured leagues. It could also entail persuading one's neighbors to vote for the use of community funds to update parks and other leisure spaces. At the state and national levels, this aspect of the virtue of everyday solidarity will more typically apply to funding questions, because state and federal support for the programs that facilitate widespread access to high-quality forms of leisure and recreation are often on the chopping block. Although these often seem like inconsequential trade-offs, if one is concerned about reducing the economic barriers to leisure and recreation, threats to programs like the National Endowment for the Arts and the National Endowment for the Humanities, which each help fund numerous museums, will be acutely felt and fervently resisted.

Notably, all three of these strategies combine the goal of reducing the costs of higher-quality free time pursuits with the added benefit of instilling a greater personal sense of solidarity. Collectively, they strengthen the claim that the better solution to the structural influence of television's low relative costs is not to raise the costs of TV but to decrease the costs of other free time activities. Even if these new incentives—or at least reduced restrictions—do not prompt people to take more time for leisure or to adopt alternative recreational activities, they will at least create the social conditions to view free time as an opportunity for relational connection rather than private isolation. By highlighting a community's shared commitment to creating opportunities for leisure and recreation in public spaces and through public institutions, this approach can combat the privatization and commodification of free time in a way that encourages moral agents to recognize their interconnectedness and to take a more active role in promoting the common good. To the extent that they can internalize this orientation as part of their ethical discernment in the process of conscience/2, they will have a much better foundation for judging their moral responsibilities in ordinary life, whether they apply this directly to their use of television or not. Ideally, this change in social conditions will have an impact on the prominence of television during free time in the United States; but even if it did not, the cultivation of a greater awareness of the common good is enough to justify these emphases from the virtue of everyday solidarity.

CONCLUSION

The overall message from this analysis of television, film, and video is that there is a problem not with these recreational pursuits per se but with their outsize influence during free time. Watching television or other video media actually has the potential to provide the kind of relaxation that contributes to recreation's status as an instrumental good, and, under the right circumstances, this activity even has the potential to serve relational ends. These abstract benefits, however, need to be weighed against the actual liabilities that accompany television, film, and video. Such liabilities include the passive spillover effect, which is perhaps most acute in the case of television but still also applies to film and other forms of video. By depressing interest in more active free time pursuits, passive spillover creates a cycle in which selected forms of recreation become more appealing than leisure, directly contradicting the theological vision for the proper ordering of free time. Television in particular also has the added liability of decreasing communal engagement and decreasing relational connections, further undermining the theological vision for free time as an opportunity for relational flourishing.

The solution, according to the application of the principle of everyday solidarity, is to spend less time with these passive media. Time spent with television, which is the most problematic of the three, serves as an important benchmark, so people ought to strive concretely to arrive at the point where watching TV is no longer their primary form of entertainment. Though this goal is theoretically attainable for anyone who is willing to strive for it, it will be easier for some than for others. In fact, this aim will be especially difficult for people who find that they have access to few alternative free time pursuits. In order to countenance this goal as an ethical good, then, one must also recognize that part of television's current appeal in the United States is its low relative costs when compared with other free time activities. Counteracting this factor becomes the work of the virtue of everyday solidarity, which recognizes the cost mismatch as a structural incentive facilitating television's outsize influence on free time. The best path for structural reform therefore lies in efforts to reduce the costs of other, more relationally fulfilling, free time activities—a process that not only helps to remove some of the structural incentives supporting the primacy of television but also adds to the development of an agent's awareness of his or her responsibilities for the well-being of others and the common good. Thus, simply by recognizing that free time can provide much more than just the diminishing returns of television, one has the ability to challenge the hegemony of passive recreational pursuits while cultivating solidarity in the process. Significantly, however, television is not the only popular form of recreation that has greater influence than the benefits it generates. Other forms of recreation therefore require reevaluation in light of a commitment to everyday solidarity, as the next three chapters show.

NOTES

1. Bureau of Labor Statistics, "Time Spent in Leisure and Sports." All percentage calculations are the author's own, from the American Time Use Survey's 2017 data.
2. Bureau of Labor Statistics. Out of the thirty-seven different demographic groupings in the survey, only those age 15–19 years and 20–24 years spent less than 40 percent of their free time watching TV on weekdays or weekends. They are unlikely to represent a consequential exception, however, because longitudinal research shows that people watch more TV as they age, so this cohort will likely spend more than 50 percent of their free time watching TV as they transition into older demographic groupings. See Mares and Woodard, "In Search of the Older Audience," 610–11.
3. Kubey and Csikszentmihalyi, *Television*, 38, 144; see also Kubey and Csikszentmihalyi, "Television Addiction," 77, 80.
4. Kubey and Csikszentmihalyi, *Television*, 81, 85.
5. Kubey and Csikszentmihalyi, 141–44.
6. Kubey and Csikszentmihalyi, 174–75; Kubey and Csikszentmihalyi, "Television Addiction," 76; Csikszentmihalyi, *Flow*, 64.
7. Winn, *Plug-In Drug*, 17–21, at 21.

8. In one pioneering example, fans of the show *Lost* created their own website, "Lostpedia," to discuss details of the show. See Shirky, *Cognitive Surplus*, 11.
9. Godlewski and Perse, "Audience Activity," 162, 165.
10. Kubey and Csikszentmihalyi, *Television*, 85, 99–100, 135–40; Kubey and Csikszentmihalyi, "Television Addiction," 76; see also Carr, *Shallows*, 51–66; and Jackson, *Distracted*, 78–79, 166–74.
11. Kubey and Csikszentmihalyi, *Television*, 199–201, at 201.
12. Fowles, *Why Viewers Watch*, 6–8, 33–59, esp. 47–49.
13. Kubey and Csikszentmihalyi, *Television*, 103.
14. Kubey and Csikszentmihalyi, "Television Addiction," 76.
15. Kubey and Csikszentmihalyi; Kubey and Csikszentmihalyi, *Television*, 123–29.
16. Williams and Handford, "Television," 175.
17. Kubey and Csikszentmihalyi, *Television*, 137.
18. Winn, *Plug-In Drug*, 61–62.
19. Postman, *Amusing Ourselves to Death*, 16, 28, 75–80, 87–97, 109–13.
20. Frey, Benesch, and Stutzer, "Does Watching TV Make Us Happy?" 284–85, 287–88, 300–302, 305; Bruni and Stanca, "Income Aspirations," 209–10, 212–13, 216–17.
21. Putnam, *Bowling Alone*, 19–22, 247–76, 283; Putnam, "Tuning In, Tuning Out," 666, 674–77.
22. Putnam, "Tuning In, Tuning Out," 678.
23. Putnam, *Bowling Alone*, 231.
24. Putnam, 231. These trends were also evident when individuals were compared with earlier periods in their own lives when they watched less TV. Campbell, Yonish, and Putnam, "Tuning In, Tuning Out Revisited."
25. Putnam, *Bowling Alone*, 229, 224–25.
26. Putnam, 283.
27. Putnam, 237. See also Meyersohn, "Television," esp. 103–4.
28. Putnam, *Bowling Alone*, 223.
29. Putnam, 220; Campbell, Yonish, and Putnam, "Tuning In, Tuning Out Revisited"; Hooghe, "Watching Television," 95–97. The distinction between TV stations compared for-profit commercial stations with not-for-profit public broadcasting.
30. Putnam, *Bowling Alone*, 221; Hooghe, "Watching Television," 100.
31. Putnam, *Bowling Alone*, 237.
32. Campbell, Yonish, and Putnam, "Tuning In, Tuning Out Revisited." Other studies have shown this general link as well: Bruni and Stanca, "Watching Alone," 523.
33. It is worth noting that the direction of causality is hard to pin down in the absence of controlled experimentation. Nevertheless, the close correlation between TV viewing and civic engagement found, in the midst of multivariate analyses, increases the likelihood that watching TV exacerbates the decline of social capital, rather than vice versa. Additionally, studies that have managed to examine communities before and after the introduction of television have documented a noticeable decline in civic engagement, indicating TV was a prime factor in causality. Campbell, Yonish, and Putnam, "Tuning In, Tuning Out Revisited"; Putnam, *Bowling Alone*, 235–36; Williams and Handford, "Television," 166.
34. Putnam, *Bowling Alone*, 224.
35. Putnam, 224; Robinson and Martin, "Of Time and Television," 83. This trend is not conducive to family engagement, because one study calculated that 50 percent of US

children between the age of six and seventeen had their own TV in their bedrooms. Taylor, "Recapturing Childhood," 50.
36. Kubey and Csikszentmihalyi, *Television*, 74, 117. Kubey and Csikszentmihalyi indicate that talking was reported during only 21 percent of the co-viewing time. Kubey and Csikszentmihalyi, 110.
37. Putnam, *Bowling Alone*, 238; Robinson and Martin, "Of Time and Television," 75; Bruni and Stanca, "Watching Alone," 523–24.
38. Williams and Handford, "Television," 158–59, 162, 165.
39. Winn, *Plug-In Drug*, 244–52, 266–80.
40. Derrick, Gabriel, and Hugenberg, "Social Surrogacy," esp. 353–54, 357–59; McIlwraith, "'I'm Addicted to Television,'" 384; Bruni and Stanca, "Watching Alone," 511.
41. On the issue of spurious conclusions—such as the possibility that TV viewing is more common among lonely, isolated individuals—one study looking at precisely this question found that the chronically lonely were drawn to certain types of TV programming, but they were not drawn to watching more TV overall. Perse and Rubin, "Chronic Loneliness."
42. See again, Putnam, *Bowling Alone*, 231.
43. The average monthly cost for cable TV was $107 in 2018. For about half as much money, one can afford an independent theater membership that includes unlimited access to movies at the theater (for both the individual and a spouse or friend). For less than a quarter, one can become a member of a film appreciation society that offers discounts at a local theater plus monthly free screenings with the society (again, for both the individual and a spouse or friend). Pressman, "Why the Price of Cable TV Stopped Going Up So Fast"; Coolidge Corner Theatre, "Membership Information"; Milwaukee Film, "Milwaukee Film Membership."
44. Leslie, "Watch It While It Lasts."
45. Putnam, *Bowling Alone*, 217.
46. Kelly, "Commodification of Leisure"; McLean and Hurd, *Kraus' Recreation and Leisure*, 80–81.
47. Farrell, "Kagan."
48. McAlone, "Get Ready."
49. McAlone and Morris, "Viewers Are Ditching Cable."
50. Csikszentmihalyi, *Flow*, 50–51.
51. Kimiecik, "Play Ball?" See also Ellis and Sharma, "Can't Play Here," 364–69.
52. Ellis and Sharma, "Can't Play Here," 377.
53. McLean and Hurd, Kraus' *Recreation and Leisure*, 80–81.
54. *Gaudium et spes*, 26.
55. Again, the theological and ethical significance of the distinction between doing something "for" someone and doing something "with" someone comes from Wells, "Rethinking Service."

CHAPTER 6

Digital Media Use

Although the primacy of television during free time is easy to establish, there is greater dispute about what constitutes the second-most-common use of free time in the United States. As mentioned briefly at the start of chapter 5, the American Time Use Survey suggests that socializing is the second-most-popular free time activity for the average person in the United States.[1] There are, however, reasons to believe that this is not the most accurate picture of the ways people in the United States actually spend their free time.

Specifically, the American Time Use Survey asks participants exclusively about their primary activities, a method that tends to overrepresent certain free time activities and underrepresent others, especially in an environment as rife with multitasking as contemporary life in the United States.[2] Granted, it is difficult to know exactly how much the focus on primary activities skews the statistics, but there is anecdotal evidence to suspect that this methodology would overemphasize social conversations and visiting and underrepresent time spent with digital media.[3] Just as important, there are other empirical reasons to conclude that technology use is underrepresented, because recent data incorporating multitasking shows that time spent with digital media is beginning to exceed time spent watching TV.[4] Given that socializing was a distant second to television in the traditional data, the fact that digital media use is not only close to but actually exceeds television viewing according to more comprehensive measurements suggests that this activity has a better claim to the second spot than socializing.[5] Bolstering this claim is the fact that even in the American Time Use Survey, demographic breakdowns reveal that socializing is not the second-most-common activity for every group, because "playing games and computer use for leisure" fills this slot for a not insignificant number of the survey's demographic segments.[6] The next question for the ethical analysis of free time, then, is how to evaluate digital media use—defined here as "screen time" (i.e., time spent in front of a computer, tablet, or smartphone screen) that is not exclusively used to watch video content (because the ethical analysis of this form of digital media use aligns with the evaluation of television discussed in the last chapter).

Much like watching TV, digital media use has its benefits in theory, but they have to be balanced with significant downsides in practice. In fact, just as television is concerning primarily because of its outsize influence during free time, so digital media use is not problematic *in se*, but it becomes worrisome when it is relied on uncritically too often. The challenge for this chapter is therefore to explore how this popular free time activity might promote the relational flourishing that free time, at its fullest potential, can serve so well. This requires navigating both the power of social networking and the flow-inducing possibilities of video games to arrive at a sense of how digital technologies and the internet might better align with an agent's efforts to abide by the vision of everyday solidarity in ordinary life. In concrete terms, this will mean increasing one's awareness of both the tendency to rely on digital technologies and the larger consequences of digital media use on in-person interactions. It will also require attending to the structural implications of participating in a society that is primarily driven by technologically mediated connections. This chapter addresses all these questions in two sections, the first outlining how the principle of everyday solidarity can facilitate a more nuanced ethical discernment of the prospects and perils of digital media use, and the second exploring how the virtue of everyday solidarity can pinpoint structural reforms that would empower more people to follow through on these recommendations.

DIGITAL MEDIA USE IN LIGHT OF THE PRINCIPLE OF EVERYDAY SOLIDARITY

From the perspective of everyday solidarity, the ethical analysis of digital media use during free time varies significantly, depending on what people do with their digital technologies. After all, when the goal is relational flourishing, there is a substantive distinction between using FaceTime to connect with a friend who happens to live far away and mindlessly surfing clickbait. Because most digital activity falls between these extremes, the principle of everyday solidarity needs to generate a more nuanced analysis that can attend to people's actual digital media use. When it does, two major concerns emerge. First, there are specific problems associated with each of the three most popular digital activities people pursue during their free time, all of which frustrate relational fulfillment or threaten the priority of leisure to some degree. Second, there are general worries about the heavy reliance on digital media during free time, because mounting evidence reveals that increased digital media use has negative consequences for face-to-face interactions that are essential for genuine human connection.

In order to justify these two claims, one needs first to have a sense of how people actually spend their time with digital technologies and the internet. Unfortunately, the data regarding specific uses of digital media are neither as thorough nor as granular as the data found in the American Time Use Survey, but there are still some resources with which to develop a fuller picture of digital media use. Marketing firms, for instance, dedicate a considerable amount of energy to the question of how people spend their time online because they want to find the best virtual locales to reach consumers' eyeballs. Data from these companies show that social media, video, and video games are the most common ways people use digital media during their free time. Different methodologies and different ways of categorizing online activities mean that there is some disagreement about precisely which of these three takes the top spot, but the prevalence of each is uniformly recognized.[7] This indicates that most people are not using digital technologies to build their relationships directly but that they are instead dedicating their free time online to alternative pursuits that each raise issues from the perspective of everyday solidarity.

To begin, the prominence of video does not need much attention here, because it raises relatively straightforward concerns. Essentially, watching video content on the internet is indistinguishable from watching video content on a television. (In fact, with the advent of internet-enabled "Smart TVs," many people now watch video content from the internet on their television.) Hence, the same worries about television's inversion of the priority of leisure over recreation and its facilitation of isolation apply to watching video content on digital devices. The last chapter's suggestion that people reorder their free time to ensure that watching TV is not their primary form of entertainment offers sufficient guidance for an ethical approach to this form of digital media use—provided, that is, that watching video content online is included in the definition of "watching TV." The implications of social media and video games, however, are more complicated, so each of these needs a more detailed analysis.

Social Media versus Relational Fulfillment

Social media use, which typically rivals watching video as the most popular online activity, presents a challenge for the ethical analysis of digital media use during people's free time. At first glance, its place at the top of the list of digital media activities would seem to suggest that digital technology use during free time is already ordered to the sort of relational fulfillment that the principle of everyday solidarity encourages. Such an interpretation presumes that social networking sites actually generate social experiences, which is far from a guarantee. In fact, the opposite is more likely to be the case, because three features of social media's everyday usage create an opposition with relational fulfillment. As a result, the prominence of social media use during free time is a concern from the perspective of everyday solidarity and not a promising sign of efforts to embrace Catholicism's relational anthropology.

First, the large amount of time people dedicate to social media is not an indication that they are using their free time to pursue relational connections, because there are many ways to interact with social media, and many of them have negative social effects. In relation to this point, research into Facebook, the world's largest social networking site, has found that most people use the site for a passive review of its content rather than for active contributions that would initiate new connections with one's online "friends." The majority of Facebook posts, comments, messages, and friend requests come from a minority of "power users," who account for at most 30 percent of the people on the platform.[8] Thus, most of the time, most people are not using their social media accounts to forge direct social connections. Instead, they treat social media like any other website, collecting information without doing much to engage the people behind the content they see. As a result, there is not much that is truly social about the primary way people engage with social media.

Second, the tendency to collect information from others' posts without reaching out or contributing to the conversation—what is sometimes described as "lurking" on Facebook—not only reflects a penchant for a non-social interaction with social media; it also has implications that can negatively affect a person's relationships offline. One study, for instance, found that passive browsing on Facebook produced significantly less pleasant experiences for users than more targeted interactions on a specific friend's profile page, and another study linked greater satisfaction with posting to Facebook and lower satisfaction with scanning others' posts.[9] These effects have the potential to frustrate relational flourishing because sadness can prompt people to withdraw from their real-life social networks and leave them less motivated to seek out friendships.[10]

Beyond the generic possibility for social withdrawal that can accompany lower affective well-being, however, passive social media use also has a specific propensity to harm relationships more directly. In the case of Facebook, at least, the principal source of this negative impact on affective well-being is the feeling of envy that passive viewing elicits when a user sees others having a desirable, and seemingly happier, experience online.[11] The effect stems from the social comparison that is practically built into the passive review of social media content, because people carefully curate the content they post to social media sites and thus create an unrealistic standard that is seldom recognized as such.[12] Envy, of course, is not conducive to a healthy relationship. As a vice, it triggers not simply the longing to have something others have but also (and arguably more so) creates the desire to see that the other person no longer has it as well.[13] By fostering a spirit of rivalry, and a zero-sum approach to happiness, envy puts two people at odds with each other, evaporating the benevolence on which true friendship depends. When social media use is the cause of this envy, the problem is further exacerbated because the envied individual has almost no way of knowing that his or her friend has begun to harbor this ill will, because the negative feelings emerge from an asynchronous virtual interaction that lacks the nonverbal cues that reveal someone's veiled displeasure in face-to-face contexts. Given that people spend much more time on passive social media use than they do on active social media engagement, the high rate of social media use during free time indicates an unfortunate erosion of the foundations of healthy social interactions.

Third, even when social media users do find ways to connect with others online, this free time activity still has a harmful effect on the broader context for social interaction. By pushing some of the ordinary tasks of relationship maintenance online, social media may facilitate certain kinds of connections, but only at the cost of reinforcing an atomistic sense of personal identity. More specifically, social media contributes to the broader personalization of communication that is enabled by other technological devices, allowing individuals to connect directly with one another in a one-to-one fashion, reducing people's reliance on intermediary organizations and decreasing their estimation of the importance of community structures.[14] The result has been the development of what the sociologist Barry Wellman calls "networked individualism," whereby people devote less attention to the web of social connections that create and sustain their local community and instead focus more on maintaining one-to-one ties with other people in their own social network.[15] This type of interaction, which is the de facto norm of interpersonal connection on the internet, has a disruptive effect on personal identity and communal ties, encouraging people to view their community as a series of voluntary links that can be called upon when convenient and ignored when not, rather than as a group of human beings to whom one has at least some irreducible responsibilities.[16] If social media were but one way people chose to connect during their free time, this might not be a significant concern. But because social media use is one of the most popular ways people spend time online, the replacement of communally mediated ties with a new networked individualism poses a problem for the theological vision that sees recreation as a resource for relational flourishing.

In light of these three features, the social nature of social media is more a myth than a reality. Certainly, social media still has the potential to serve relationships, but there are strong indications that this potential is seldom realized under normal conditions. As a form of recreation, then, this particular form of digital media use is problematic in much the same way that watching TV is a concern, which is to say more for its prominence than its existence. If people were using social media as a tool to connect with others, it would obviously still have its limitations, but it could serve an important function as a complement to more organic community interactions. The data just discussed, however, reveal that this is not how most people use social media. Because the large amount of free time dedicated to this and other forms of digital media leaves little time for in-person interactions to complement online forms of relationship maintenance, social media's prominence during free time reveals that recreation is not the source of relational flourishing that it could be.

Video Games versus the Full Potential of Free Time

Video games, it turns out, are a more complicated form of digital media use, generating both assets and liabilities from the perspective of everyday solidarity. In public narratives, video games are often criticized for promoting antisocial behaviors, but at the same time they provide the means to connect players in immersive experiences, sometimes generating genuine offline relationships. Additionally, because the games themselves tend to be task oriented and offer immediate feedback to players, they present the kinds of challenges that can be conducive to flow under the right circumstances. Video games therefore have the features to turn digital media use into a form of leisure, which could prompt one to identify the prominence of video games as a positive step toward the priority of leisure over recreation that the principle of everyday solidarity encourages. Even when they do serve as a form of leisure, however, video games have peculiar features that muddle their contributions to the full potential of free time. Consequently, the overall ethical assessment of video games is one of critical optimism.

In terms of video games' effects on relationality, their real impact depends on the type of video game that a person is playing. Violent video games, for instance, have been the subject of much research, based on the theory that the content of these games can lead people to exhibit violent behavior in real life. A number of studies have found that playing violent video games correlates with increased aggression, not only in the immediate aftermath of gameplay but also over longer periods of time.[17] The exact nature of this relationship is contested, and some studies reveal no significant link between violent video games and aggression, but the most recent meta-analysis of the literature on the social effects of different kinds of video games supports a connection between violent video games and aggressive tendencies.[18] Video games with violent content therefore present a problematic use of free time because they promote the kinds of behaviors and thinking that close people off from relationships.

Not all video games are violent, however, and many of the others instead promote an openness to relationships. Thus, video games that require players to cooperate with one another to succeed, or that revolve around helping characters in the game, have been shown to reduce aggressive thoughts and to contribute to an increase in prosocial behaviors.[19] One study found that simply playing the same game with another player (or players) led to more social cooperation, not only with one's partners from the game but also with new partners.[20] Within family relationships, meanwhile, playing video games together has been linked to stronger parent–child relationships and more empathetic reactions between siblings.[21] Given these ways in which video games can contribute to relational fulfillment, they can have a place within the vision for recreation as an instrumental good. Of course, this optimistic assessment needs to be tempered by the realization that some video games also have decidedly antisocial effects. As moral agents assess their interest in playing video games during free time, then, they must think about both the content of the game and the context in which it is played, because these are the factors that define whether video games will undermine or promote relational flourishing.[22]

Beyond the possibility of helping players strengthen relational skills, video games also have the theoretical capacity to bring free time closer to its full potential in another way: by providing access to the flow state that defines leisure. This is a significant capacity because it suggests a different approach might be required for a complete assessment of the ethical significance of video games during free time. Evidence for flow in video games has grown over time as scholars have sought to account for the high levels of enjoyment that people often report from playing them. Analyses have focused on how video games offer different challenges based on a user's experience, which creates the optimal balance between difficulty and competence at the heart of flow, and on the fact that these games provide so much sensory input that they leave little room for outside stimuli to distract players from the task at hand, which facilitates (and preserves) the ordering of consciousness that is another hallmark of flow.[23] As one study noted, "Video games are unique in their opportunity for the balance between challenge and skill that can stimulate the neural processes responsible for flow."[24]

In terms of the ethical assessment of free time, these studies suggest that playing video games does not fit neatly, or exclusively, into the category of recreation. Instead, video games can serve as a form of leisure; in fact, they are likely to provide opportunities for flow for many, if not most, users. To the extent that this is the case, video games could facilitate the priority of leisure over recreation, and their use would be better evaluated against the ordering of leisure. This evaluation does not, however, suggest that there is an absolute license to play video games during free time whenever one wants. Leisure may be an intrinsic good, but this does not mean that moral agents can abdicate their responsibility to assess the ethical implications of their leisure pursuits. Indeed, the ordering of leisure is meant to ensure that leisure, and free time more generally, is oriented to its proper telos. From this perspective, the positive value of video games as an avenue for flow and thus a form of leisure needs to be balanced by two additional concerns that reflect the same focus on content and context that informs the ethical evaluation of video games as a form of recreation.

First, the effects of video game content do not disappear when someone experiences flow while playing them. The antisocial implications of violent games persist, as do the interpersonal benefits of prosocial games. This means that one must not simply seek flow from any game without discrimination; instead, one must be aware of the various side effects of game content and then prioritize those with prosocial content ahead of those with violent features. This approach introduces an important caveat to the evaluation of gaming as a form of leisure, because one study suggests that so-called first-person shooter games are especially effective at maximizing immersion and generating flow for players.[25] If one were to seek flow at all costs, these games might become one's method of choice because of their effectiveness. When the value of flow is set within the context of a commitment to everyday solidarity, however, the evidence suggesting that violent game content exacerbates antisocial thoughts and behaviors tempers one's enthusiasm and implies that it might be better to seek flow in other, prosocial games, which would allow players to experience flow while also promoting their relational capacities. This analysis does not need to translate into an absolute prohibition on games with any violent content, because there is the possibility of some positive social benefits when these games are played cooperatively.[26] Unless one assumes that everyone in his or her peer group will adopt a critical impression of all violent video games, there may come a time when a person is invited to choose between playing one of these games with his or her friends and sacrificing time with others, and it is not clear that he or she would always have to choose the latter. Instead, the takeaway from this analysis is that people ought to spend less time with violent video games (ideally, with a goal of zero) and instead seek flow from games with nonviolent content when they are interested in enjoying gaming as a form of leisure.

Second, as this last point about violent video games reveals, the context in which one plays a game also has an important impact on a game's flow experience. These games can provide access to flow in both single-player and multiplayer environments, which means they could theoretically fit into either the time-for-self or time-with-others categories in the ordering of leisure. In practice, however, playing video games alone has dangers that are not attached to playing games with others. Specifically, the immersive power of these games has the potential to suck players in so much that they exhibit something like addictive behavior, possibly to the point that gaming negatively affects players' daily lives.[27] Naturally, a number of elements exacerbate this problem and mediate the likelihood that a particular player will develop an addiction, but loneliness and social isolation are significant factors.[28] Playing games solo, then, carries more risk factors for video game addiction than playing games in social settings, which suggests that one must be wary of relying too much on gaming as a form of time for self in the ordering of leisure. They are, instead, best embraced as a form of time with others, which better reflects the values at the heart of the priority of leisure over recreation, because although social and solo game play generate similar levels of flow, social game play provides a more rewarding experience in the process.[29]

Given all these factors, the best way to capture the ethical approach to video games during free time is to think about minimizing risks. As a form of recreation, gaming can help people recuperate in a way that not only sustains but also strengthens their relationality, but this is not a foreordained outcome. As a form of leisure, gaming can similarly, under the right circumstances, provide access to flow in a manner that serves relationality. The content and context in which these games are played, however, determine whether these potential benefits are ever realized. Consequently, those who are motivated by the principle of everyday solidarity and who would also like to preserve gaming as one of their preferred free time activities ought to opt for prosocial games in social settings. In the process, however, they must also be mindful of the addictive potential of video games, chiefly by paying attention to how much time they are spending on this activity. Though there are benefits to this free time pursuit, no single activity can serve all of a person's relational needs; therefore, balance is also a necessary element in the more intentional approach to free time that theological ethics advocates. This recognition leads to the final point of consideration for the principle of everyday solidarity's evaluation of digital media use, namely, the relational consequences of spending large amounts of time with digital technologies, regardless of how one uses them.

The Relational Consequences of Spending Too Much Time with Digital Technologies

Apart from the effects of any specific technologies, digital media use has two negative effects on relationships: it can displace time spent building personal relationships, and it can erode the skills needed to foster meaningful human connections. Initially, claims about displacement may seem counterintuitive, because the internet is a communication technology at its core, and data even indicate that social interactions online are often used to maintain preexisting offline relationships.[30] The implications for these offline relationships are not all equal, however, creating a displacement effect as some relationships are served at the expense of others. For example, one study of preexisting social groups found that shifts to internet interactions did sometimes create connections between group members who had previously been one degree of separation apart (e.g., an unknown friend of a friend), but a number of "weak ties" (i.e., acquaintances) were lost along the way.[31] Though the data from this study suggested that "strong ties" between close friends could remain unaffected by internet use,[32] other studies indicate that internet communications favor friends over family[33] and that the frequency of online interactions negatively affects time spent with family and neighbors in person.[34] Most significantly, a recent analysis of time use data determined that there was a negative correlation between time spent online for recreation and time spent socializing "in more traditional ways."[35] Taken together, these data points reveal that, much like television, digital media use has a displacement effect on the informal social interactions upon which community is built. Although the addition of new online relationships might seem to mitigate these losses, displacement is a genuine ethical concern because trading offline relationships for online interactions is hardly a pathway to relational flourishing.

To assert a qualitative distinction between online and offline relationships is not to capitulate to Luddism but simply to acknowledge that online interactions remove the social cues of intonation and body language that are so essential to empathetic connections between human beings.[36] This difference results in changed behavior online, leading people to "so lessen [their] expectations of other people that [they] can feel utterly alone."[37] Unsurprisingly, people tend to rate face-to-face communication as more intimate than either telephone or internet communications precisely because co-present interactions allow more access to a broader range of social cues.[38] Of course, this relative assessment does not entail that connections established through digital media are "emotionally or socially impoverished," but it does mean that they are qualitatively different.[39] Given that the increased reliance on technologically mediated communication has created a cultural context in which "people readily admit that they would rather leave a voicemail or send an e-mail than talk face-to-face," there is a real way in which the prominence of digital technologies threatens relational flourishing through displacement, even when this displacement tries to replace face-to-face connections with digitally mediated ones.[40] The issue of erosion further highlights this concern.

The problem of erosion, in which time spent online weakens social skills, emerges from the omnipresence of screens, especially mobile devices, which makes immediate access to the internet possible in almost any situation.[41] As a result, in-person social interactions are increasingly interrupted by phone calls, text messages, and other internet intrusions, and this weakens people's ability to focus on their face-to-face interaction. Much like cell phone conversations, which have always occurred at the expense of "co-present" individuals, the frequency of smartphone interruptions means that screens shift "our attention away from those who are co-located, ... hampering the ability to generate a common sense of the mood in these co-located settings."[42] The psychologist Kenneth Gergen has coined the phrase "absent presence" to describe this phenomenon, noting that technology allows people to be physically present but mentally absent whenever their attention is directed to a screen.[43] The effect is palpable on families, where parents are increasingly aware of what one author describes as "the Vanishing Family Trick," whereby everyone slowly disappears from a common space in order to check an email, make a phone call, or surf the Web.[44] Indeed, sociologists have argued that the presence of and reliance on digital technologies has created "postfamilial families," in which homes become "hubs of communication" where relatives gather to share an internet connection that allows each individual to remain in contact with others outside the home at the expense of those within it.[45]

All these trends point to an erosion of relational capabilities, as the Massachusetts Institute of Technology psychologist Sherry Turkle has documented through careful ethnography. Today, people are so accustomed to interruptions from smartphones and tablets that, on those rare occasions when they do meet in person, they have shifted their conversations to allow for distraction. "The mere presence of a phone on the table (even a turned off phone)," Turkle explains, "changes what people talk about.... If two people are speaking and there is a phone on a nearby desk, each feels less connected to the other than when there is no phone present."[46] Unfortunately, the pull of technology's novelty is hard to overcome, so recourse to a phone or the internet remains a ubiquitous option. As a result, people stop investing in conversations when they become boring or start to falter; and in the process, they miss out on the insights that can emerge from being with someone and acknowledging a worth that transcends their entertainment value.[47] This development reflects not only a loss in the ability to focus on a sustained conversation but also a diminishment of the broader skill set for genuine human connection. For instance, Turkle notes that "research shows that those who use social media the most have difficulty reading human emotions, including their own."[48] Because empathy is the entrée to intimacy, one does not need a crystal ball to see where these technological developments are leading: to a place where conversation and connection are too hard to sustain because few have enough practice with either. This is the problem of erosion that a heavy reliance on digital technologies during free time exacerbates.

Although these losses are thus risks of technology, they are not a predetermined outcome. Even Turkle, after all her critical research on technology's disruptive effects on human relationships, remains an optimist, provided people recognize the damage being done. "Once aware," she asserts, "we can begin to rethink our practices. When we do, conversation is there to reclaim."[49] The question, then, is how to rethink these practices, and the principle of everyday solidarity proves a useful tool to this end, providing the emphasis on relationality that can transform one's ethical discernment about online decisions.

Using Digital Technologies and the Internet to Serve Relational Ends

In practical terms, the best way to preserve the principle of everyday solidarity's theological presuppositions in the realm of digital media use is to incorporate Pope Francis's reflections on communication technologies as a tool for an "authentic culture of encounter."[50] Because he is a realist about the dangers of technology—including displacement—Pope Francis has eschewed complete rejection and instead championed a theological approach to internet technologies that amounts to a practical guide for those who wish to make digital technologies serve relational ends. Appealing to the parable of the Good Samaritan, Pope Francis has summoned Christians "to see communication in terms of 'neighbourliness,'" by which he means that people should model the Good Samaritan's empathy in their online interactions so that they might see themselves in others' struggles and honor the innate human dignity of all their interlocutors.[51] Obviously, this would mean a rejection of the "trolling" and abuse that the anonymity of internet interactions has a habit of enabling, for empathy highlights the fact that there is an actual human person, with all the concomitant feelings and vulnerabilities that come with the human condition, at the other end of every comment and critique.

However, Pope Francis's vision involves more than just a sense of which behaviors to refuse. It also reveals a starting point for a more holistic online engagement. Connecting neighborliness to dialogue, for instance, he explains, "To dialogue means to believe that the 'other' has something worthwhile to say, and to entertain his or her point of view and perspective."[52] Genuine empathy, in other words, is the main objective when communication online is ordered to an "authentic culture of encounter."[53] To a certain extent, this emphasis on empathy may seem trite, but given the damage that an excessive reliance on digital technologies can inflict on real-life relationships, a more intentional emphasis on empathy in internet interactions is essential. In addition, underscoring empathy aligns with the principle of everyday solidarity, which encourages moral agents to recognize the effects of their actions on others and to account for this impact in their ethical evaluation. Pope Francis has even made this link explicit, effectively championing a more careful discernment process online when he asserts that "we need, for example, to recover a certain sense of deliberateness and calm. This calls for time and the ability to be silent."[54] His response to the pitfalls of digital technologies thus entails more than an exclusive appeal to empathy. In fact, when interpreted alongside the principle of everyday solidarity, it can yield two concrete suggestions for the reorientation of time spent with digital technologies to relational flourishing.

First, Pope Francis's vision for an authentic culture of encounter indicates that people should approach their time online with greater intentionality, seriously considering the ends they want this time to serve and using digital technologies only to the extent that they serve not simply desired but also genuinely worthwhile ends. In all likelihood, this application of the principle of everyday solidarity will lead to less time spent online for most people, which would counteract the displacement (and erosion) effects associated with an excessive reliance on digital technologies. Though not unwelcome, such a development is properly regarded as an ancillary benefit rather than the main goal, for unintentionality itself is a much bigger stumbling block to the full realization of free time's potential than the sheer quantity of time one spends in a given recreational pursuit. Hence, those who closely study technology's perils recommend intentionality, rather than rejection, as the most appropriate solution.[55] This view is theologically defensible as well, for greater intentionality—especially the kind shaped by an awareness of one's inherently relational nature—equips moral agents with the opportunity to reorient their free time choices to their full flourishing, generating a more integrated moral life.

Second, intentionality about how much time one spends online should be coupled with a greater intentionality about how one uses online resources. Consistent with the principle of everyday solidarity, this second form of intentionality can be realized by recalling that digital technologies are a tool of communication and by choosing to use them as such. In other words, people can better move toward the flourishing that the principle of everyday solidarity promotes when they remember that their online lives are opportunities for human connection and that this opportunity persists for both better and worse. Some of the worst digital behavior emerges when one forgets this fact, as people lob insults, pass judgments, and (in the most extreme examples) actively attack other users without thinking about the human consequences for the recipients of this harassment because there is not a human there to see directly. When people imagine their fellow humans at the other end of their online interactions, however, they can reclaim this significant portion of their free time for more moral, and more fulfilling, ends. For instance, they can fight against the temptation to present only their carefully curated "best selves" to their social media followers, instead admitting to something of their vulnerability. Or they can counteract some of the emotional damage that competitive video games can inflict by recognizing the humanity of their online opponents alongside their teammates'. Finally, they can work to make their online communication mimic their face-to-face discussions and not vice versa, so that they might build human relationships and combat erosion at the same time. In these ways, moral agents can orient their digital media use to authentic communication, which as Pope Francis reminds us, "is really about realizing that we are all human beings, children of God."[56]

Together, these two strategies reveal how moral agents can reorient time spent online to more relationally fulfilling ends. In the process, they can combat some of the pitfalls of digital technology, replacing the envy-inducing facades of social media with a more honest invitation to connection and communication, or flipping the script on the sometimes-divisive impact of video games. To the extent that agents succeed in these endeavors, they will begin to turn digital media use—the second-most-popular recreational pursuit in the United States—into a tool of relational connection rather than a source of social disintegration. Although the dangers will not disappear, these strategies reveal that with the guidance of the principle of everyday solidarity, digital media use can become a beneficial form of recreation. The perspective of everyday solidarity cannot stop here, however, for insofar as digital technologies can serve as both a means of connection and a positive free time pursuit, then one must also be concerned with the structures affecting who has access to this potential good, which is a question for the virtue of everyday solidarity.

THE VIRTUE OF EVERYDAY SOLIDARITY AND ACCESS TO DIGITAL TECHNOLOGY

The question of access to the digital technologies is ethically significant, for two reasons. First, as a free time activity, digital technologies obviously have their limitations, but they also have a way of serving relational ends—at least under the right circumstances. If digital technologies provide a good way of using recreation, then it would be selfish to try and take advantage of this opportunity without at least considering whether others have ways of doing so as well. Second, as more communication moves online, there is a very real possibility that those without access to the internet will become estranged from civic discourse, and from their communities more generally, as virtual meeting places replace traditional public forums. Though this trend is a cause of concern overall, it is especially worrisome from the perspective of the preferential option for the poor that the Catholic understanding of the common good champions. Because variations in internet access reflect not simply personal preferences but also structural factors, they are an essential target of the virtue of everyday solidarity's vision for structural reform.

At the outset, it is important to note that access to digital technology can mean many things, and not all of them are equally a cause of concern. For instance, as discussed above, video games provide a way to encounter flow, creating a meaningful leisure experience that one can enjoy in the theological sense. Not everyone has equal access to this technology, but that is not sufficient evidence of a moral crisis. Precisely because video games are not good *in se*, but valuable insofar as they serve as a means to the fulfilling ends of leisure, a lack of access to video games is not inherently a problem, as long as people do have genuine access to the enjoyment of leisure via other means. The structural reforms discussed in chapter 4 are meant to address this problem, mitigating some of the concerns about the mere existence of discrepancies in access to specific digital technologies. For the internet itself, however, the calculus is not the same.

Given how much free time people spend online, and the sheer amount of essential information that has moved to the internet, access to the internet poses an acute moral problem in a way that access to video games does not. The reason is that, as Pope Francis has said, "those who for whatever reason lack access to social media run the risk of being left behind."[57] For all its pitfalls, the internet has become a primary form of communication for all kinds of communities. Consequently, a lack of internet access reflects more than simply a missed opportunity for a particular type of recreation. In a real way, a lack of access to this digital technology presents an obstacle to one's personal fulfillment as it is theologically understood, because complete absence from the internet in today's context means exclusion from the conversations (however imperfect) that are shaping the communities one inhabits offline. Additionally, given the sheer number of people online and both the displacement and erosion effects that this free time activity has on in-person conversations, a lack of access to the internet means fewer opportunities for social connection in general, not just a smaller number of online "friends." In these ways, a lack of access to the digital technologies that connect people online crosses the threshold to become a threat to the common good, although, notably, this concern must also be held in tension with the recognition that there are other losses and limitations to a society's increasing reliance on digitally mediated forms of communication, a point reassessed in more detail at the end of this section.

Structural Forces Shaping Internet Access

Evaluating the internet access problem requires attending to the structural influences that affect internet availability in the United States. Generally speaking, most US adults (89 percent) do have access to the internet in the United States today, so it is not the sheer numbers that create a moral problem but their distribution.[58] More specifically, age, educational attainment, geographic location, and income all affect access, given that those over the age of sixty-five, those with less than a high school diploma, those who live in rural areas, and those who make less than $30,000 per year are all more likely than their demographic counterparts to lack access to the internet.[59] None of this is coincidental. In some cases, the divergences reflect different structural incentives. For example, those under the age of eighteen are online at a much higher rate than those over the age of sixty-five, but the former depend on the internet not simply for keeping in touch with friends but also for access to the schoolwork and job prospects on which their future success will depend. Seniors, meanwhile, do not have the same immediate gains. In other cases, however, the patterns of divergent internet access reflect more corrosive structural influences, such as the uneven investment in internet services in the United States, which leaves rural populations behind and also makes cost a barrier in many cases.

The best way to see the structural forces shaping internet access is to compare internet service in the United States to the rest of the world. In terms of speed, the Federal Communications Commission, which oversees internet service providers, determined that the United States had the tenth-fastest internet speeds among developed economies in 2016 and the fifth-slowest speeds for mobile internet services.[60] In terms of pricing, however, the United States ranked near the bottom of the list, depending on how costs are compared internationally.[61] The factors behind this value discrepancy are most evident in a now-classic comparison between the United States and South Korea, the nation with some of the best, and cheapest, internet access. In South Korea, the average cost for "the fastest internet in the world" is "$17 less than what the average American pays for a much slower internet hookup."[62] The difference traces back to a strategic commitment on the part of South Korea to make "equal access for all citizens" a public policy goal, which resulted in "generous subsidies designed to incentivize [internet service providers] to serve communities across the country."[63] In addition, the South Korean government set strict speed standards, and enforced them for urban and rural areas alike, while also supporting the construction of infrastructure so that multiple companies could compete with one another to drive down costs on a level playing field.[64] In the United States, meanwhile, local monopolies are the most common source of internet service, yet the government has resisted regulation of these companies.[65] The result is that most people in the United States overpay for access to the internet—at least when compared with their peers in other parts of the world—and this hampers access for the poor and those on the geographic peripheries.

Structural Reforms to Address Digital Divides

The solution to this digital-divide problem is hardly straightforward, but one thing that the South Korean experience reveals is that viewing internet access as a public good is essential. One way to enshrine this perspective structurally would be to reclassify the internet as a public utility, allowing stricter regulation and thus greater public force in shaping who should have access, to what, and at what cost. This view, which gained significant attention during the "net neutrality" fight, has a number of strong proponents, including some of the largest internet platforms (like Google, Netflix, and others), which champion the greater protections that utility classification could provide, albeit for self-interested reasons.[66] There is, indeed, much to be said for this approach; from the perspective of everyday solidarity's commitment to greater access, the power to regulate is an important asset that should not be ignored. Thus, although there are risks to too much interference when regulation is permissible, it is better to have the ability to regulate and to deal with mistakes along the way than to abdicate the power entirely out of a fear of overregulation.

Utility classification is not the only way to embrace internet access as a public good, however. Although this strategy would help to address the financial obstacles to access, and also potentially the geographic discrepancies, it still fails to address two of the problems underlying insufficient access. First, it does not provide a clear response to the ways that age and educational attainment affect access. Though cost is undoubtedly a concern for both these demographic groups, it is not the only aggravating factor. Indeed, nearly a third of those people who did not use the internet in 2013 reported in a survey that they found the internet "too difficult to use," and another 8 percent believed they were simply "too old to learn."[67] Addressing this problem requires more than just cutting costs; it necessitates helping people more directly so that they can confidently approach changing technologies and use them to connect with others in new ways. This problem can be solved with more formal training programs, especially at public libraries and senior centers; but in the spirit of both subsidiarity and solidarity, this work should not remain the purview of institutions alone. Behind the significant generational gap in internet adoption lies the reality that younger users are digital natives, whose immersion in technology from a young age allows them to approach the internet with familiarity and ease. If some of these digital natives took it upon themselves to help the older adults or those with different educational attainments navigate the internet, they could decrease the accessibility gap and build interpersonal solidarity in the process.

Second, the pursuit of utility classification might help to reduce cost as a structural barrier, but an exclusive reliance on this strategy has the potential to reinforce, rather than to challenge, the displacement effects currently associated with digital technologies. After all, this approach still treats the internet as a private good and looks for ways to make this private good more affordable. Although this is a laudable goal, it does not necessarily help people to use the internet to forge new social connections with more intentionality during their free time. Obviously, the principle of everyday solidarity can help with this side of the equation, for it can guide agents as they discern how to use their newly attainable access in a responsible and relationally fulfilling way. Nevertheless, for the virtue of everyday solidarity to complement the principle more fully, it should promote structural reforms that make it easier for people to see themselves as inherently relational agents. Utility classification does not achieve this goal on its own. One additional way to help people see the internet as a public good, then, is to provide public access in more places. Currently, public libraries typically have free wireless internet (and free computer access), but this is not the only shared space that can offer this good. Virtually any public place, from a park to the street corner, is just as viable a candidate for free Wi-Fi as any library, and municipal access could even extend to some of the "third places," like coffee shops and informal meeting places, that help knit a community together.[68] By turning internet access into a shared good in these spaces, people can begin to challenge their assumptions about the social functions digital technologies can serve. Additionally, they will have new incentives to come outside their homes when they are connecting online, which will create new opportunities for the kinds of incidental contact on which social capital depends. As a result, a new set of structures can emerge around internet access, making it more widely accessible while also counteracting some of the traditional displacement effects that accompany a strictly private approach to digital technologies during free time.[69]

Naturally, as with the earlier applications of the virtue of everyday solidarity, there are other structural reforms that could strengthen people's ability to embrace the principle of everyday solidarity in their evaluation of this recreational activity, but the three changes articulated here provide a helpful start. Collectively, they represent a holistic approach to the problems limiting access to the internet for certain groups and not others. If implemented carefully, these solutions offer the hope of bringing what is at best a helpful social tool to more people, so that no one is left behind during their free time. Notably, however, greater access will not eliminate the pitfalls of digital technologies, so one must always remember that the benefits of digital media use during free time remain a conditional good. The structural reforms improving access must therefore be accompanied by the personal conversions identified by the principle of everyday solidarity, so that more people on the internet will not simply yield more people experiencing the internet's worst problems. To the extent that improved access can reshape people's perceptions of the internet as a public good, however, it can also help with personal conversion, prompting people to cultivate a shared sense of responsibility online, thereby reinforcing the complementarity of the virtue and the principle of everyday solidarity in ordinary life.

At the same time, moral agents must also guard against the danger of taking these efforts to equalize access to the internet too far. Although the virtue of everyday solidarity indicates that people should rightly question who is excluded from the ongoing shifts to online communication, the principle of everyday solidarity's orientation to full human flourishing also reveals the need to question the value of these shifts themselves. Given the ways in which digital media use can erode relational capacities, there is a loss when so much communication moves online, which means that responsible moral agents must complement their attention to inequalities of internet access with a similar attention to inequalities in access to genuine human connection beyond the internet. After all, there is a temptation to utilize technology to solve all kinds of human problems, including problems like loneliness and isolation that cry out for more basic, human solutions. For instance, there are now robots that have been designed as companions for the elderly, relieving other humans of the responsibility of caring for—or at least being present with—those who are deemed particularly dependent and therefore burdensome. This, as Turkle, the MIT psychologist, points out, means that "we ask technology to perform what used to be 'love's labor': taking care of each other."[70] In the process, society reveals something of how it values the elderly and the dependent more generally because the intentional creation of robots as companions highlights "that our allocation of resources is a social choice," suggesting that some people are not worth the time, money, and energy required for human companionship but should instead be left to settle for the next best thing.[71]

This implicit indication of (lesser) value is not merely a problem for people confined to a nursing home, however, but is instead becoming the reality for a significant majority in the modern world, now that digital technologies are an ever more cost-effective way of delivering the goods and services that once required a human mediator. "All of this," the technology reporter Nellie Bowles observes, "has led to a curious new reality: Human contact is becoming a luxury good."[72] This, too, creates a problem from the perspective of everyday solidarity, just as much if not more so than the lack of access to online resources among those with fewer economic means. Consequently, at a structural level, the pursuit of expanded access to digital technologies must be tempered by a readiness to resist the assumption that everything should be done online. Naturally, as suggested above, the larger theological vision for free time, with its priority of leisure over recreation, challenges this assumption and champions an alternative through the promotion of reforms designed to increase leisure opportunities for all. Nevertheless, there is still a need to translate this commitment into the context of recreation, particularly to the concrete circumstances of digital media use, which the moral agent can do by remembering that the pursuit of improved internet access is only a means to the more important end of facilitating flourishing for inherently relational creatures and not an end in itself.

CONCLUSION

As this chapter has shown, time spent with digital technologies and the internet, the second-most-popular free time activity, is a recreational pursuit that has some significant limitations from the perspective of everyday solidarity, but also some genuine potential. Streaming video content, a common online activity, shares the same burdens as watching television, which means it ought to be approached in much the same way, with both a more critical attitude and an interest in limiting the amount of time one spends streaming videos. Social media sites and video games, however, are more complex. Although the ways people typically use social media fail to contribute to their relational flourishing, a more intentional approach, modeled on Pope Francis's vision for communication as a component of an authentic culture of encounter, has the potential to reclaim these and other online platforms as a means of human connection and relational fulfillment. Similarly, video games can be isolating and can exacerbate antisocial behavior, but when one chooses the content and context for these games more judiciously, there is an opportunity to serve relational ends. In both cases, the key feature is to remember and to recognize the humanity of the people behind the usernames and the avatars. When the humanity of the other is honored, genuine empathy is possible, allowing moral discernment in this sphere of ordinary life to reinforce the inherently relational notion of the human person that is at the heart of Catholic theological anthropology. To the extent that the structural reforms of the virtue of everyday solidarity can provide this kind of moral training ground to more people, they strengthen the prospects for a more theologically rooted form of moral discernment in ordinary life.

Naturally, none of these changes will make digital media use the perfect free time activity. The theological vision for free time still champions the priority of leisure over recreation, after all, and with the exception of some video games in some circumstances, most digital media use remains a form of recreation. Nevertheless, digital technologies are communication technologies at their core, and, as a result, they have greater capacities to serve as a relationally fulfilling form of recreation, provided the right conditions are met. The work of the principle and the virtue of everyday solidarity is to ensure that these conditions are met by more people more often.

NOTES

1. See, again, Bureau of Labor Statistics, "Time Spent in Leisure and Sports."
2. Wallsten, *What Are We Not Doing?* 6; Robinson and Godbey, *Time for Life*, 38–39; Jackson, *Distracted*, 74; *Wall Street Journal*, "Data Point."
3. After all, one thing technology enables is multitasking in the presence of others, and if this were the case, it is unlikely that someone would report checking their email on their phone as their primary activity over socializing. See Baym, *Personal Connections*, 36; and Turkle, *Alone Together*, 155.

4. eMarketer, "Growth in Time Spent."
5. Bureau of Labor Statistics, "Time Spent in Leisure and Sports." In fairness, this may not be as consistent across demographics as the primacy of television, for reasons discussed in the last section of this chapter.
6. Bureau of Labor Statistics.
7. Nielsen, "Time Flies"; Hwong, "How Consumers Spend." For data that include international sources, see Limelight Networks, "State of User Experience."
8. Hampton et al., "Why Most Facebook Users Get More than They Give."
9. Wise, Alhaash, and Park, "Emotional Responses," esp. 560–61; Burke, Marlow, and Lento, "Social Network Activity"; Verduyn et al., "Passive Facebook Use."
10. The social psychologists Heather M. Gray, Keiko Ishii, and Nalini Ambady describe this as the traditional interpretation of the effects of sadness. Their recent work argues that this effect varies, depending on the cause of one's sadness. According to data from their experiments, social loss (e.g., the death of a loved one) more typically generates the sort of sadness that elicits responses from one's friends and has the potential to strengthen relationships. Sadness that results from a sense of failure or status loss, however, often prompts social withdrawal. The distinction comes into play in relation to social media use because it is primarily the comparative sense of failure, or what Gray, Ishii, and Ambady describe as "status loss" that triggers the negative affective response in social media users. Gray, Ishii, and Ambady, "Misery Loves Company," 1438–39, 1445.
11. Verduyn et al., "Passive Facebook Use," 483–86.
12. Verduyn et al., 487–88; Steers, Wickham, and Acitelli, "Seeing Everyone Else's Highlight Reels."
13. DeYoung, Glittering Vices, 43.
14. Wellman and Hogan, "Connected Lives," 161–216, at 163–64; Ling, New Tech, 3.
15. Wellman and Hogan, "Connected Lives," 165–66; Wellman et al., "Does the Internet Increase?" 450–51.
16. Song, Virtual Communities, 26, 115–16, 125, 130.
17. You, Kim, and No, "Impact," 104; Willoughby, Adachi, and Good, "Longitudinal Study," 1044–57.
18. Greitemeyer and Mügge, "Video Games," 581, 583–86; cf. Ferguson, "Good, the Bad, and the Ugly."
19. Greitemeyer and Osswald, "Effects of Prosocial Video Games"; Greitemeyer and Osswald, "Prosocial Video Games"; Greitemeyer and Mügge, "Video Games," 586.
20. Greitemeyer and Cox, "There's No 'I' in Team," esp. 226–27.
21. Buswell et al., "Relationship," 184; Coyne et al., "Game On"; Coyne et al., "Super Mario Brothers and Sisters."
22. Coyne et al., "Super Mario Brothers and Sisters," 49.
23. Sherry, "Flow," 339–40. See also Cowley et al., "Toward an Understanding," esp. 20:13–20:17; and Abuhamdeh, Csikszentmihalyi, and Jalal, "Enjoying the Possibility of Defeat."
24. Weber et al., "Theorizing Flow," 398.
25. Cowley et al., "Toward an Understanding," 20:24; Konnikova, "Why Gamers Can't Stop." This effect appears to be moderated by gender—males tend to find flow in first-person shooters more easily than females. See Sherry, "Flow," 340–44.
26. Greitemeyer, Traut-Mattausch, and Osswald, "How to Ameliorate Negative Effects."
27. Gorman, Gentile, and Green, "Problem Gaming," 311–13.
28. Jeong, Kim, and Lee, "Why Do Some People Become Addicted?" 199, 201, 207.

29. Kaye and Bryce, "Go with the Flow."
30. Baym, *Personal Connections*, 132.
31. Haythornthwaite, "Social Networks," 136–38, 140–41; see also Haythornthwaite, "Strong, Weak, and Latent Ties."
32. Haythornthwaite, "Strong, Weak, and Latent Ties," 138.
33. Baym, *Personal Connections*, 138. Additionally, heavy Facebook use has been correlated with greater levels of "family loneliness," while nonusers report higher levels of "social loneliness." Ryan and Xenos, "Who Uses Facebook?" 1661–62.
34. Baym, *Personal Connections*, 140; Katz and Rice, "Project Syntopia," 173.
35. Wallsten, *What Are We Not Doing?* 23.
36. See Brignall and Van Valey, "Impact," 338–39; Baym, *Personal Connection*, 53.
37. Turkle, *Alone Together*, 226.
38. Baym, *Personal Connections*, 50.
39. Baym, 57.
40. Turkle, *Alone Together*, 15.
41. Data trends indicate that having an internet-enabled mobile device increases the frequency of internet use relative to other technologies. Perrin and Jiang, "About a Quarter of US Adults Say They Are 'Almost Constantly' Online."
42. Ling, *New Tech*, 100, 102, 115.
43. Gergen, "Challenge," 227.
44. Powers, *Hamlet's Blackberry*, 52.
45. Wellman and Hogan, "Connected Lives," 172.
46. Turkle, *Reclaiming Conversation*, 21, citing Przybyliski and Weinstein, "Can You Connect with Me Now?"; Misra et al., "iPhone Effect"; Ling, *New Tech*, 115.
47. Turkle, *Reclaiming Conversation*, 23, 26.
48. Turkle, 25.
49. Turkle, 4–5.
50. Francis, "Message of Pope Francis for the 48th World Communications Day."
51. Francis.
52. Francis.
53. Francis.
54. Francis.
55. Turkle, *Reclaiming Conversation*, 25.
56. Francis, "Message of Pope Francis for the 48th World Communications Day."
57. Francis.
58. Pew Research Center, "Internet/Broadband."
59. Anderson, Perrin, and Jiang, "11% of Americans Don't Use the Internet."
60. Federal Communications Commission, *2018 International Broadband Data Report*, §§9, 10.
61. Federal Communications Commission, §§14–15.
62. Lee, "Why Does South Korea Have Faster Internet?"
63. Laravea, "South Korea's Internet Infrastructure."
64. Laravea.
65. To illustrate the power of regional monopolies, in 2015 Time Warner Cable and Comcast announced plans to merge. Although they represented the two largest internet service providers in the country, they attempted to downplay antitrust concerns by underscoring the fact that they competed in virtually zero zip codes in the United States.

Cohen, "Comcast and Time Warner Cable Announce Merger." The deal ultimately fell through as a result of regulatory roadblocks. The interest in internet regulation has since waned significantly, as indicated by the recent reversal of the FCC's "net neutrality" provisions, which would have identified internet service providers as utilities. Collins, "Net Neutrality."

66. Ruiz and Lohr, "FCC Approves Net Neutrality Rules."
67. Anderson, Perrin, and Jiang, "11% of Americans Don't Use the Internet."
68. Oldenburg, *Great Good Place*.
69. In 2016, New York City rolled out free Wi-Fi in a number of public spaces using internet kiosks, and although there have been bumps along the way, one reporter found evidence that "these kiosks are indeed mostly used by the city's least privileged," providing them "a space of comfort and connection." Huber, "Is New York City's Public Wi-Fi Actually Connecting the Poor?"
70. Turkle, *Alone Together*, 107.
71. Turkle, 108, 119.
72. Bowles, "Human Contact."

CHAPTER 7

Spectator Sports

Alongside television and digital technologies, sports constitute one of the most popular free time diversions in the United States, where they carry great cultural influence. According to an estimate by Pricewaterhouse-Coopers, the sports industry in the United States was expected to be worth more than $73 billion in 2019.[1] Every major newspaper in the country has a sports section. The Super Bowl is the most watched event on television every year. Participation in highly organized, and highly competitive, youth sports is increasing, and one investigation found that "the United States routinely spends more tax dollars per high school athlete than per high school math student."[2] Conceiving of free time without sports is therefore a difficult, if not impossible, prospect. Hence, this chapter addresses sports as a third example of how theological ethics can inform recreation in concrete ways. More precisely, this chapter assesses spectator sports from the perspective of everyday solidarity, assuming that participation in sports as a player is more likely to be a form of leisure and thus can be assessed using the ordering of leisure and the commitment to structural reforms for free time developed in chapters 3 and 4 of this book.

Set against the theological vision for free time, spectator sports represent an opportunity for novel kinds of solidarity, and thus relational flourishing; but their potential is often frustrated by human sinfulness in both its personal and structural embodiments. The first section of this chapter captures one piece of this puzzle, applying the principle of everyday solidarity to insist that the most ethical use of spectator sports is to connect with others in a way that expands one's sense of concern for others, a goal that requires approaching sports in a particular fashion. The chapter's second section then discusses the social structures shaping spectator sports, employing the virtue of everyday solidarity to challenge the damaging effects of spectator sports' outsize influence on culture and economics and recommending appropriate reforms. Much like the last two chapters, this chapter shows how to approach spectator sports with more critical scrutiny, creating another sphere in which to forge stronger connections between faith and ordinary life.

SPORTS AND THE PRINCIPLE OF EVERYDAY SOLIDARITY

In the context of spectator sports, the principle of everyday solidarity's emphasis on a concern for others in moral discernment highlights the effects of one's recreational decisions on two sets of people: other spectators who are also watching the game, and the people playing the game for one's entertainment. In a number of striking ways, sports can unite a spectator with both these groups of people, but this outcome is not foreordained, because sports can just as easily drive a wedge between the agent and each of these types of companions. At its core, the ethical approach to spectator sports comes down to how one navigates this tension. Fortunately, the principle of everyday solidarity provides the right resources to identify both the potential for meaningful human connections latent in spectator sports and the temptation toward a narrower sense of self-concern that often undermines this potential. A fuller analysis of both these prospects and these perils can therefore empower moral agents to embrace the former and resist the latter so that this form of recreation can remain a genuine, yet still instrumental, good.

Solidarity between Spectators

Anyone who follows a sports team with any regularity is aware of the first type of solidarity that spectator sports can reinforce. Simply at the experiential level, a sports fan can intuit the development of a new bond with the other people who cheer for the same team. There is more than just intuition and anecdote behind this connection, however, and scholars regularly point to the bonding power of spectator sports using the sociological notion of civil religion. Although there are various interpretations of this term, the one most pertinent to spectator sports appeals to Émile Durkheim's functional definition of religion to emphasize the ways that public events and traditions can bind people together in much the same way that religions connect their adherents through common practices.[3] Scholars adopting this Durkheimian view point to a host of communal activities that constitute displays of civil religion, not because of their embrace of religious content but because of their parallels with the unifying role that religions serve in social groups.[4] This interpretation of civil religion creates a novel way to evaluate the role of sports in society, laying the foundation for a more detailed account of how spectator sports can strengthen solidarity under the right circumstances.

Consider baseball, the "national pastime" in the United States. Christopher Evans has argued that baseball amounts to a civil religion in the United States because its mythology (especially its origin story, which misconstrues baseball as a US creation) unites people around a set of shared values.[5] According to Evans, the mythological version of baseball's birth, which helped to cement its status as the national pastime, gave people a way to embrace the virtues they already associated with the US way of life: discipline, diligence, the purity of rural life, and a belief in the exceptionalism of the country itself.[6] By thus aligning its history with the values of the nation, baseball became the lowest common denominator, creating a new civil religion to bind citizens together with a (manufactured) sense of common cause. But this mythology is not the only way scholars have identified baseball as a civil religion. Craig Forney, for instance, has asserted that a spirit of transcendence imbues baseball, because things that break the boundaries of the game (e.g., home runs, foul balls) still affect the game itself, and he notes that the game has a timeless character because it is played according to the theoretically unending rhythms of innings instead of the strictures of a clock.[7] The result, according to Forney, is a quasi-eschatological experience that allows fans to hold out hope for both the perfect game and a better future outside the game as well.[8] This tightens the bonds between fans who have the sense that their commitment to the sport holds much more significance than the simple love of a game. He is hardly the first to locate baseball's binding force in its religious parallels.[9] By offering an encounter with the transcendent and a sense of shared emotional experience, baseball has a way of uniting its fans, creating a spirit of solidarity among those cheering for their team.

Although baseball has evident dimensions of civil religion for its spectators, the fullest example of how sports can bind fans together comes from Eric Bain-Selbo, who has extensively researched football's status as a civil religion in the United States. Focusing on the distinctive experience of college football in the South, Bain-Selbo notes that the ritualization of events surrounding the football game, especially elaborate tailgating practices, creates implicit parallels with overt religious practices, turning college football into "a sacrament" that "became an important communal event."[10] Elaborating on this point, Bain-Selbo incorporates Mircea Eliade's notion of the sacred as that which is set apart from the profane (i.e., the ordinary aspects of life) to assert that college football constitutes a sacred event because it pulls both athletes and fans out of their ordinary lives and unites them in "the transcendent pursuit . . . of something greater than the [individual] athlete or spectator."[11]

The fan experience is a key feature of this transcendence of self because it provides spectators with a communal identity. Moreover, Bain-Selbo explains that the team itself serves as a "totem," or "most sacred" object, for college football fans, uniting disparate spectators through their common belief in the deeper significance of their fandom.[12] The result is the same "collective effervescence" that Durkheim identified in religion, which creates a sense of bondedness and common identity to hold a group together in spite of its other divisions.[13] The effect is not merely theoretical, however. In surveys, college football fans self-report a strong sense of communal attachment as a result of their game day experience, rating the bonds with other fans stronger than the bonds they have at their work and at their churches.[14] As a result, Bain-Selbo has concluded that Durkheim's account of "the social-psychological function of religion in communal life provides an excellent blueprint for understanding how sports, and college football in the South as one example, function religiously."[15] In other words, spectator sports share in the bonding function that sociologists identify with religious experience, thus creating a civil religion that is quite effective at uniting fans together.

Similar claims can be made for other sports, indicating that the experience of being a fan of a particular team, with all its rituals and its emotion, can create real and meaningful bonds between people. Consequently, spectator sports provide an effective context for the cultivation of solidarity, as fans begin to see themselves as part of a larger whole. Watching sports thus constitutes a particularly promising recreational activity, insofar as it can strengthen one's relational identity and thus contribute to the moral agent's awareness of and attentiveness to others, just as the principle of everyday solidarity envisions. There is not, however, a guarantee that sports will serve this role completely or consistently. In fact, there is a real danger that the bonds fans share will emerge too easily, creating the sorts of connections that can paper over some divisions and exacerbate others, leaving larger problems unaddressed and ultimately resulting in only a semblance of solidarity rather than its genuine manifestation. In theological terms, the solidarity of spectator sports can devolve into sinful forms of "collective egotism" that prioritize the insularity and self-interest of a group above the well-being of others.[16] Moral agents must therefore guard against two temptations as they pursue the benefits of everyday solidarity through spectator sports.

The first temptation is to derive a warped sense of solidarity with fans of one's own team at the expense of solidarity with others, typically through a cultivated disdain for fans of rival teams. Though a little bit of pseudo-animosity employed in a jocular fashion might not be a major concern, the us-versus-them mentality that sports rivalries tend to instill can quickly escalate into something more damaging. The worst illustrations of this tendency end in violence, like the assault on a Boston Red Sox fan allegedly perpetrated by a small group of Los Angeles Dodgers fans after the 2018 World Series, or like the plight soccer's hooligans inflict on opposing fans (and often their own communities) after games.[17] Even when physical violence is not involved, however, the stoking of division is still problematic, for there is a stark contrast between the sense of relational responsibility that the principle of everyday solidarity is designed to promote and the assumptions that rivalry-based sports bonding habituates. Specifically, the principle of everyday solidarity affirms relational anthropology by empowering moral agents to identify their shared responsibility for the common good, and thus the well-being "of all and of each."[18] When the Durkheimian collective effervescence of sports is used to separate insiders from outsiders in an exclusive way, however, the moral agent is encouraged to assume that those who support a rival team are not worthy of one's consideration. Even though the thought is not always internalized as such, and despite the fact that many fans are able to overcome this artificial division and reaffirm the humanity of their rivals after a game, the fact that they need to fight to make this their default position is indicative of the ways that the solidarity of sports can subvert the deeper solidarity to which all human beings are called if one is not careful.

The second temptation hidden in the bonding power of spectator sports is subtler and, for that reason, more dangerous. Precisely because sports are so effective at building a certain kind of bond between fans, they are also distinctly capable of distracting people from the deeper fractures that continue to divide them, even when they share the same stadium and have feelings of mutual affection in the stands. This phenomenon is hardly a new feature of sports. The ancient Romans, after all, supposedly provided *panem et circenses*—which is to say, not just food but also opportunities to be spectators at entertainment events—as a means of distracting the masses so that the government could keep to its own devices.[19] Today, sports serve a similar function when they generate superficial bonds that allow a group of fans to ignore the social problems and divisions that exist below the surface. Two divisions in particular, those of race and those of socioeconomic status, are especially prone to this type of deceit. In the context of college football, for instance, Bain-Selbo notes that everyone acts as equals during the tailgating that happens before the game, but inside the stadium the effects of economic inequalities persist, with luxury boxes for the rich and nosebleed seats for the poor.[20] Similarly, fans of different races mingle in the stands and share a common cause that may seem helpful but goes only so far. If the temporary solidarity of game day soothes a fan's conscience into thinking that everything outside the stadium is equally blissful, the civil religion of sports will undermine solidarity by effectively sweeping injustices under the rug.[21] Much like Dietrich Bonhoeffer's "cheap grace," which wants the benefits of forgiveness without the responsibilities of conversion and reconciliation, the bonds forged in the civil religion of sports can become a form of "cheap solidarity" that undermines the real thing, which is far more honest about conflict and division.[22]

The solution to these two temptations is to preserve a critical perspective on the bonding power of spectator sports. Sports may serve as a form of civil religion, but they are not religious goods. As a result, neither sports nor the bonds that they create can stand on their own; they need to be ordered to the human person's higher ends. Recognizing spectator sports as a form of recreation can help in this process, because recreation fits into the theological approach to free time as an instrumental good. This means that the moral value of recreation is contingent upon its ability to serve other, more ultimate ends appropriately. When one places spectator sports within this framework, a critical consciousness can emerge because the burden of proof shifts. No longer can one assume that an experience of watching sports will be neutral, or that it will be inherently good. Instead, one must approach each opportunity to watch sports with the presupposition that its acceptability rises or falls on the basis of the more fundamental goods it is able to facilitate. By employing this approach, sports fans can begin to see themselves first as human beings, with deeply human purposes to fulfill, and then only secondarily as fans of a particular sport or team. This shift will then guard against the temptation to let one's interest in a team become the ultimate marker of her or his identity, which is precisely how spectator sports' two deficient forms of bonding emerge. By working more intentionally to combat these dangerous tendencies, one can embrace spectator sports as a healthy form of recreation that will serve not only the goal of rejuvenation but also the end of relational fulfillment. Yet the ethical approach to spectator sports cannot stop at the effort to ensure that one bonds well with other fans. If spectator sports are to be embraced as a means of relational flourishing, then fans will also need to attend to the relationships they develop (or fail to develop) with the players they are watching.

Solidarity with Players

Spectator sports are inherently relational because they connect people watching with the people who are playing the game. From the perspective of everyday solidarity, then, spectators must be aware of both sides of this relationship and factor the well-being of participants into their ethical discernment. How this should happen is a delicate question, because there is a risk of paternalism if a spectator assumes that she or he knows what is best for a player without accounting for the player's own wishes and agency. This is a particularly poignant concern for those seeking to integrate faith and ordinary life, because the Christian understanding of solidarity always regards a relationship with others as a two-way street in which both parties can and should enrich each other. Instead of a static, or colonialist model, wherein one party decides how to help the other, the Christian vision for true solidarity requires honoring the agency of those one seeks to help, working to empower them to contribute to their own solutions and not just trying to solve problems for them by assuming that an outsider knows best.[23]

Generally, spectators who wish to attend to the well-being of those who are playing for their entertainment in a nonpaternalistic fashion ought to attend to two factors. First, spectators who genuinely care about the people performing for their entertainment should think about how the love of the game compares with the costs professional athletes must pay to pursue this love in front of others. Spectators need to be mindful of these trade-offs, but in order to avoid paternalism, the proper evaluation of this equation should remain in the hands of the participants themselves. In general, then, a spectator's moral responsibility is not to evaluate these trade-offs for a participant but rather to look for signs that the participants have in fact taken this question seriously. If the answer is yes, the spectators might be able to watch in good conscience, even when there is a lot of sacrifice, or risk, involved for the participants.

To give a quick illustration of this point, consider the 2018 documentary *Free Solo*, which follows a young man's attempts to become the first person to climb the California mountain El Capitan without the assistance (and protection) of ropes. This was an especially risky proposition, but as the movie unfolds, two things become clear: Alex Honnold, the climber, is acutely aware of these risks, and he is going to free solo anyway. The enjoyment of the climb, with all its challenges and its preparations, is so great for him that the sacrifice of avoiding its risks altogether would be too unbearable in his case. As one reviewer explains, "It's his mother who . . . best understands why her son constantly puts his life at risk—and why she doesn't quarrel with the choice. 'When he's free soloing is when he feels most alive, the most everything,' she says. 'How can you even think about taking that away from somebody.'"[24] When one appreciates this reality, which is quite particular to Honnold, one quickly comes to challenge a paternalistic temptation to deny him this sporting activity because it is dangerous. Instead, one can accept the relationship that comes with being a spectator of this remarkable attempt, concluding, as the reviewer did, that Honnold's climb "wasn't a useless stunt but a reminder that utility alone is a poor way to measure the grandeur of one man's spirit."[25] This is exactly the reason that spectators cannot be too quick to make the evaluation of a sport's worthiness for its participants without an awareness of the participants' own evaluations.

Of course, just because a participant has deemed a sport worthy of the sacrifices it demands, it does not follow that a spectator's responsibilities of solidarity have been fulfilled, which leads to the second factor spectators must consider: structural constraints. Specifically, as spectators examine the costs borne and benefits gained by the participants, they must ask if two larger structures—the structures of professional leagues and the structures of the sport itself—shift the calculus in unjust ways.

In the case of league structures, the question is whether the costs and burdens of participation in a particular sport are distributed fairly. For example, consider the recent disputes over working conditions for the US Women's National Team in soccer. In March 2019, the team made headlines for suing the US Soccer Federation, the sport's national governing body, for "institutionalized gender discrimination," noting that women players make far less money than players on the men's team, despite greater tournament success. Though one might be tempted to argue, as US Soccer once did, that different "market realities" between men's and women's soccer make it impossible to pay the women's team the same as the men's, that argument falls apart because the women's team generated more revenue than the men's in the three years immediately preceding the lawsuit. Furthermore, the lawsuit alleges that the women's team faced more risks than the men's team because US soccer often scheduled their games on artificial fields, which observers generally agree lead to more injuries. The men's team, in contrast, has had to play only one home game on artificial turf since 1994 (a game that seems to have been scheduled on artificial turf only after the women's team raised concerns about this disparity).[26] These conditions drastically reshape the costs of playing professional soccer for women compared with men, meaning that the women have to pay greater costs to realize their love of the game, even when their commitment to the sport and the enjoyment they receive from it are equal to their male counterparts. Some of the women have obviously decided that they will still accept this arrangement, likely because they have such a strong passion for the sport, but a solidarity-based analysis recognizes that they should not have to make such a steep trade-off. The differences between the men's and women's teams are not innate; US soccer could easily improve the women's conditions to create greater parity if the organization so chose. When fans take solidarity with the participants seriously, they will attend to these kinds of complaints, and look for ways to support the players in their efforts to improve their working conditions, so that they do not have to pay such significant costs to enjoy the sports they love. Other sports have similar structural limitations that could also be changed, so it is important that spectators consider this question even as they embrace a propensity to defer to players' judgments about the benefits and sacrifices of the game in order to avoid a paternalistic attitude.

Beyond the structures of a sport's league, spectators must also evaluate whether the structure of the game itself can create undue, or even intolerable, sacrifices. The clearest example of this problem would be the case of professional football, which, in its current iteration, requires its players to accept an unjustifiable risk of serious brain injury. The problem is not merely the rates of concussions, which are high, but also the ways in which the structures of the game of football make it virtually impossible to avoid long-term brain damage. Recent research into chronic traumatic encephalopathy (CTE), a neurodegenerative disease, illustrate this point. Not only has CTE been diagnosed in an alarming number of former professional football players (110 out of 111, in one study), but "available data ... indicate that exposure to [repetitive brain trauma] represents the greatest risk factor for CTE pathological characteristics."[27] Tackle football, it turns out, regularly exposes its players to repetitive brain trauma, especially the "repetitive *subclinical* brain trauma, often referred to as 'subconcussive blows'" that researchers suspect are at the root of CTE (emphasis added).[28] Unlike concussions, these subclinical injuries do not present with consistent signs and symptoms, so they are hard to diagnose in the moment and therefore more likely to recur, further increasing the risks of CTE. Thus, the National Football League's concussion protocols, which have been touted as a way to reduce players' risks of brain injuries, do little to combat the problem because it is the repeated subconcussive blows that football still requires that will lead to CTE and not simply repeated concussions.[29] As long as there are hits to the head, real risks of CTE and similar conditions persist, and this is a problem that football is not yet ready to solve.

Ultimately, it is the combination of the danger of repetitive brain injuries—even more minor ones—and the nature of football that make the sport particularly problematic for spectators who are informed by the principle of everyday solidarity. There are, of course, any number of sporting activities that could expose a participant to head trauma. According to the professional association of neurosurgeons, for instance, cycling results in more head injuries every year than football.[30] Heading the ball in soccer, meanwhile, carries concussion risks, as do the collisions that sometimes happen during the game.[31] The difference, however, is that the factors aggravating head injuries in these and other sports are incidental to the activity. Nobody sets off cycling with the intent to fall off a bike, although this is a risk; one could play soccer without heading the ball; and colliding with other players is not an intended consequence of the game. In football, however, direct physical contact, including head-on contact, is an essential rather than accidental feature. It is not possible to play football—at least not in its tackle variety—without being exposed directly to head injuries.[32]

This is the reality that fans of the game need to assess out of a spirit of solidarity with those who play. They must recognize that the structure of the game makes football an ethically questionable spectator sport because it effectively requires those who watch it to accept the fact that those who are playing for their entertainment take on an extraordinary risk as an inherent part of the game. Though one might be tempted to argue that the love of the game or the high compensation for professional players could offset these risks, that would not be a sufficient argument for someone motivated by the principle of everyday solidarity, because it is too abstract and aloof. The point of everyday solidarity is to put oneself in someone else's shoes during moral discernment. The more appropriate way to assess the situation, then, is to ask how one would respond if the responsibility for these risks fell more squarely on one's shoulders. When this is the perspective, there is evidence that the calculus changes quite quickly. Parents, for instance, have a much more negative view of football when their children are the focus of the evaluation. A 2018 poll found that almost half the population would encourage their own children to play another sport if they expressed an interest in football because of concerns about head injuries.[33] Even those with a clear love of the game, like Hall of Fame quarterback Brett Favre, have expressed this sentiment.[34] If a person shares this conviction, then it will be difficult to justify watching football as recreational activity, for there is a jarring incongruity in effectively saying, "I would not want to watch my own child play football, but I have no problem watching other people's children take on that risk." Insofar as the structural features of the game itself lead people to this conclusion for their own children, they should, in the spirit of solidarity, be also led to a corollary conclusion for those they do not know so well.

Football is, in many ways, an easy illustration of this approach, but it is not necessarily the only sport where spectators would want to avoid unnecessary complicity. The key factor in all cases, however, must be that certain risks are both so damaging and so fundamental to the sport itself that removing them would end the sport as it is known (at least in its spectator version). This is what it means to consider risks that are inherent in the structures of the game itself. A good way to think about this problem is through an analogy with the concept of intrinsic evil found in Catholic moral theology. This notion claims that there are some human actions whose "object" is so diametrically opposed to the moral good that no changes to exigent factors (like an agent's intention or external circumstances) could ever redeem the act. The only way such an act could be something other than intrinsically evil is if it were a completely different act.[35] Although there is a whole series of debates about whether these sorts of actions exist and how people can identify them,[36] the theoretical concept remains, and it helps to direct an agent's moral response, because no one should willingly participate in an intrinsically evil act.[37] Intolerable risks that are part of the very structure of a spectator sport operate in a similar way, and therefore a similar response is justified. Hence, when spectators identify these sorts of untenable burdens at the essential level of a sport they like, they should end their association with that sport out of compassionate concern for its participants, because the problem goes so deep that even the passive support of a bystander sends the wrong message—just as a person's cooperation with another's intrinsically evil act raises a serious danger of scandal.[38] As long as this judgment is indeed based on the structures of the sport, then a spectator's response will not represent a paternalistic imposition but rather a clear-eyed assessment that some risks are too great to be offset even by extraordinary rewards. If someone is willing to make this claim for her or his own children, they should also be willing to follow through on its implications for other players. The principle of everyday solidarity demands nothing less.

Spectator's Responsibilities in Light of the Principle of Everyday Solidarity

Taken together, these suggestions for how spectators can approach their relationships with other spectators and with players in a spirit of solidarity provide a viable outline for integrating spectator sports into the moral life. By attending to these two relationships with a critical eye, agents have the opportunity more fully to embody the relational understanding of the human person that sits at the heart of the Catholic theological tradition. The interpersonal connections are not the only factors affecting relational flourishing, however. Spectator sports are inherently social activities, which means that they are always shaped by larger social influences. As a result, broader social structures also affect the prospects for relational flourishing when one chooses to watch sports. If one is committed to evaluating this element of free time from the perspective of everyday solidarity, then the virtue of everyday solidarity must enter into the conversation as well.

168 CHAPTER 7

SPORTS AND THE VIRTUE OF EVERYDAY SOLIDARITY

Applying the virtue of everyday solidarity to spectator sports requires dealing with the outsize influence of professional sports in US culture, particularly the sizable economic rewards that sports command vis-à-vis the negative effects of concentrating all that money in one free time pursuit. If spectators are truly motivated by the concern for others that defines the principle of everyday solidarity, then they will not ignore these effects; instead, they will work to grapple with the repercussions that an overemphasis on sports can have for the common good. In the United States, these repercussions are most evident in the economic structures that currently support spectator sports, because they create a series of perverse incentives that can put self-interest ahead of the collective good. As I have explained elsewhere, this is a defining feature of what makes a particular social structure a structure of sin.[39] When moral agents approach spectator sports from the perspective of everyday solidarity, then, they must attend to these economic structures in particular, promoting reforms to change the structures while also taking steps to disentangle themselves from the systems of perverse incentives that give spectator sports a social and cultural influence that outpaces their contribution to the common good.

In truth, a host of economic incentives surround spectator sports, and many of them compromise the common good through what economists call opportunity costs. When significant resources go to spectator sports, they do not go to other things, many of which would be a worthy investment, and this creates a lost opportunity, or opportunity cost. Consider the astronomical salaries of professional athletes. A report in late 2016 determined that the average salaries for professional athletes in the NFL, NHL, MLB, and NBA ranged from $2.1 to $6.2 million, depending on the league.[40] For comparison, the median *household* income in 2016 was $60,309.[41] There is obviously a significant gap between the compensation of professional athletes and that of more typical workers, yet "few people believe that the social contribution of a lavishly paid NBA star is really a thousand times more valuable than that of a nurse or kindergarten teacher."[42] At first glance, the discrepancy may seem inconsequential; but as a structural incentive, this dramatic gap encourages people to view the possibility of a career path in professional sports differently than the possibility of a career path in health care, education, or almost any other field. With the possibility of much greater rewards in the former, more people end up dedicating their time and talent to sports than would otherwise be the case, and this ultimately means that fewer people are left to do the jobs that contribute more directly to the health and well-being of the community and its members.[43] The economic power of spectator sports is thus more than a mere annoyance; it is a structural concern that fans must address when they take their responsibility to solidarity seriously. The question of how to change these opportunity costs comes down to two structures—broadcasting revenues and stadium financing deals—because these two economic structures generate the most benefit for sports at the greatest opportunity cost to the common good.

Broadcasting Revenues and Outsize Rewards

If someone had to pinpoint one source for the dramatic increase in the amount of money surrounding professional sports at the end of the twentieth century and the start of the twenty-first century, television contracts would be the most identifiable culprit. Certainly, other features of sports economics have shaped the system as well. Free agency, for instance, has had a role to play. By allowing players to negotiate new contracts with other teams, this arrangement has dramatically increased the players' share of their sport's revenues, eventually leading to the high salaries seen today. Yet this is not the root of the virtue of everyday solidarity's concerns about opportunity costs, for two reasons. First, from the perspective of everyday solidarity, it is better that players have a more equitable sharing in the rewards of their labor, meaning that free agency is an improvement over the old system, where players received a meager share of the profits that went to the teams and their owners. Second, a shift in the share of a league's revenues going to players could not result in the outsize influence of sports on its own. The total revenues also had to increase alongside the share, and that is only tangentially related to free agency. It is, however, directly related to television.

Initially, broadcasting rights were a minor feature of spectator sports. In the early years of television, for example, individual baseball teams negotiated broadcasting deals with their local stations, which led to wide variations in team revenues, depending on their local market's size. As television evolved, however, and nationwide live broadcasts became feasible, the possibilities for higher revenues across the whole league exploded.[44] Other leagues found the same result, as they began to coordinate their own nationwide—and eventually worldwide—broadcast contracts. Over time, the values of these deals increased exponentially, to the point that "revenues from broadcasting rights became the single most important source of income for professional team sports in the USA," and for professional sports teams worldwide, broadcasting revenues are more important than ticket sales today.[45] In the United States, the absolute numbers are staggering. In 2018 the existing nationwide television deals translated to annual payouts of $450 million for the NHL, $1.5 billion for the MLB, $2.6 billion for the NBA, and $4.5 billion for the NFL.[46]

Significantly, these numbers are possible only as a result of structural factors. First, the most direct structural support is the 1961 Sports Broadcasting Act, which provided professional leagues exemptions from antitrust laws so that all their teams could coordinate and negotiate a single television contract together.[47] In theory, as the NFL argued in the initial hearings that led to the law, this exemption helps to protect small market teams, who can share in the revenue from a league's more powerful players.[48] In practice, however, the structural arrangement has had serious economic effects. By essentially creating a "cartel" that regulates access to the television rights, the Sports Broadcasting Act has legalized what "'amount[s] to a price fixing mechanism,' ... which leads to inflated prices."[49] On its own, however, this legal structure could take television rights only so far. In order to maximize the impact of this price-fixing mechanism, leagues need to find broadcasters that are both willing and able to pay the inflated prices. These have been provided by a second set of structural factors, which affect the broadcasters' resources.

The most profound of these economic structures is the system of cable TV contracts, which bundles channels and sells them to households with little consumer input. The result is that cable TV channels—the ones that come in packages and are not the traditional "free TV" broadcasters like NBC, ABC, CBS, and FOX—are funded by licensing fees that get bundled together. Because cable TV service providers resist an à la carte model that would allow subscribers to pick the channels they want, every subscriber ends up paying for all the content on all the channels, even the ones they would rather not watch. This creates a powerful financial base for sports rights' bidding wars, because a cable TV channel can spread out the costs of its increased licensing fees across a broader population than if it had to rely on sports fans alone. Indeed, one economist's estimates concluded that the fees for sports channels would triple if viewers had to pay for them in isolation, because cable TV providers would need to offset the loss of both people who never wanted to pay for sports in the first place and the occasional sports fans who would not be willing to pay anything more than they already do.[50] In 2017 this model would have pushed the distribution cost for ESPN and its suite of networks to over $27 per month, with customers likely paying a premium on top of that, perhaps as much as $81 per month.[51] At that point, viewers' cost consciousness would become a much greater concern, meaning that cable TV channels would no longer be able to count on their customer's money to bankroll increased sports licensing fees. Because cable networks can currently mask these fees in cable bundles and diffuse them across larger populations, however, they feel less pressure to rein in their spending. Instead, the structural incentives encourage a win-at-all-costs mentality that fuels bidding wars for sports broadcasting rights, further driving up the costs and thus the money pouring into professional sports.[52]

Again, all this may seem like an inconsequential issue, because the costs of TV contracts appear to affect only the people who choose to buy cable TV packages, which is unquestionably a luxury good at a global level. One might be hard pressed to accept that price gouging in this market is really an appropriate area of concern for solidarity, especially when it is closely linked to the preferential option for the poor. If one were concerned exclusively with costs to cable TV subscribers, this critique would make sense; but the issue is not about the effects of these contracts on the people who pay for cable. Instead, the question is how the structures behind these costs affect the common good, and at this level, two problems emerge that do present serious concerns. First, this whole system bankrolls professional sports in an unsustainable fashion, which skews social and economic incentives in the ways discussed above, pushing some people away from work that would have more immediate and lasting social benefits. Second, the bidding wars facilitated by this system affect the costs of sports broadcasting rights throughout the world, which can have a serious and direct impact on the availability of other public goods in certain countries. After all, not all countries operate with the same market assumptions that drive television in the United States. Many, in fact, view television as an important public resource for both social connection and civic education, and they structure their broadcast systems accordingly, with robust public service broadcasters, some of which are funded directly by the government. The British Broadcasting Corporation, for example, is government funded, and it has to compete in the same bidding wars for the sports content that it identifies "as an important part of [its] public service remit."[53] If the BBC were to keep up with the escalating fees for sports broadcasting rights, it would leave less money for other government services. Because this is not an acceptable outcome, the BBC has instead accepted the loss of some of its sports broadcasting rights because it cannot compete in the open bidding wars, particularly at times when government funding is reduced across the board.[54] At a structural level, then, sports fans in the United States have to deal with the fact that their participation in the broadcast TV system not only supports perverse incentives but also forces public service broadcasters elsewhere to choose between offering their citizens access to sports or resources for other public goods. If one accepts the bonding potential of spectator sports, this becomes a lamentable trade-off, especially given that public service broadcasters have a broader reach than subscription channels and thus "are uniquely placed to maximise the social and cultural value to be gained from sport."[55] Hence, the trade-off itself is a serious concern for those committed to solidarity.

The obvious question is how one should address this. Given the ways broadcasting rights underwrite the perverse incentives of professional sports, the virtue of everyday solidarity points toward structural reforms in the cable TV model for sports. In practice, sports fans have three ways of challenging the current system while still finding ways to enjoy the recreational benefits of spectator sports. First, they can redirect their allegiances to smaller market sports and teams. Although large professional leagues command large broadcasting deals, less popular sports are not as susceptible to the same type of commercialization and thus avoid some of the perverse incentives associated with spectator sports. Consequently, a basketball fan can avoid some of the problematic complicity involved in watching the NBA, with its multibillion-dollar annual TV contract, by tuning in to women's basketball, which makes far less money in TV rights.[56] Of course, this still raises the issue of how one will access this content, because the same cable TV channels that use subscriber fees to engage in bidding wars are the ones that show these less popular sports alongside their marquee matchups. (For instance, the WNBA is televised by ESPN.) The second strategy helps address this problem, as sports fans can select the platforms they use to watch sports carefully. Given that the cable TV bundle masks the true costs of sports, fans should look for streaming services or cable packages that allow them to pay à la carte, so that the funding model can begin to change. In all likelihood, this would mean spending more money for sports, but a fan can offset this by selecting the sports he or she wants to watch judiciously. When deployed in tandem with the first solution, this strategy might actually open more sporting events for less money. Third, sports fans can avoid the problems associated with TV broadcasting structures altogether by watching sports in person. This, too, will likely be more expensive than watching sports on TV, although once again the costs will depend on which sports and at what level. Though this last strategy offers the most distance from the broadcast deals that create structures of perverse incentives, it also highlights the challenges of avoiding complicity in the problematic economics of spectator sports because attendance at live sporting events puts fans in contact with the second major structure creating opportunity costs for the common good: public subsidies for professional stadiums.

Stadium Subsidies and the Common Good

Sports stadiums and arenas are essential to spectator sports, and they are also extremely expensive to build. These two factors regularly combine to put pressure on local and state governments to subsidize stadium construction, because teams point out that they need a place to play if a city is going to continue to be their hometown, and they do not want to foot the bill for construction alone if they can avoid it. The teams, it turns out, are normally quite successful in convincing civic leaders to support their construction projects. Between 1970 and 2017, local and state subsidies—in the form of bond borrowing and tax incentives for teams—covered approximately two-thirds of the costs to build 129 stadiums for professional sports teams in the United States and Canada, at a combined cost of more than $52 billion.[57] Although the percentage of construction costs covered by subsidies appears to have decreased to closer to one-third in the aftermath of the Great Recession, the age of stadiums replaced has also decreased, leaving state and local governments on the hook more regularly.[58] The central question, from the perspective of everyday solidarity, is whether these subsidies are a benefit or a burden to the common good. The data, unfortunately, indicate that they are a burden, which means that these subsidies are another structural factor that sports fans need to consider if everyday solidarity is going to transform their free time.

Generally, the argument in favor of stadium subsidies relies on the claim that sports stadiums can generate economic activity and greater name recognition for the cities that are their hosts. As a result, proponents argue, local and state governments ought to support professional sports teams with stadium subsidies so that they can lure or keep a local team and reap the benefits of heightened economic activity, which should ultimately be good for the city both directly (through an expanded tax base) and indirectly (through the civic pride and sense of place that a professional team and a stadium district can provide).[59] The actual numbers to support these claims are missing, however, and any tangible benefits that do occur often come at greater costs to the common good. Thus, in terms of a strict cost-benefit analysis, the economic argument for stadium subsidies is nonexistent. Professional sports teams and local governments typically justify large taxpayer subsidies on the basis of faulty (or intentionally misrepresented) predictions of highly inflated returns, only a fraction of which materialize.[60] The consensus of economists is that stadium subsidies do not generate enough benefits to offset their costs.[61]

This observation is not to suggest that there are no economic benefits. The teams obviously reap exceptional economic rewards, gaining state-of-the-art facilities at a fraction of the cost. There are also, arguably, some benefits to the cities that host professional teams, albeit not at a level that matches the cost. A closer look at these benefits, however, indicates that they are also problematic on their own terms, especially when solidarity is the standard by which the pursuit of these goods is evaluated. For example, there is an argument that teams generate economic activity, and thus tax revenues, for the area immediately around their new stadiums, usually through increased real estate prices and additional commercial opportunities.[62] But most of the activity is not new economic input; it is simply a relocation that occurs when people who used to spend their discretionary income in one part of a county or metropolitan region choose to spend it near the stadium instead.[63] Depending on the context, different municipalities might find a way to use subsidies to boost economic activity in their jurisdiction, but only at the expense of neighboring communities.[64] This would essentially turn stadium subsidies into a direct structure of sin, insofar as it would exploit economic incentives to serve the self-interest of one municipality in isolation while harming the collective good of its larger region.[65] The sinful impact of these structures is further exacerbated by the fact that the real estate benefits are concentrated in the hands of homeowners and landlords. Consequently, although there might be a value to building a stadium in an impoverished area in order to bring increased economic activity to the neighborhood, the people who live there are unlikely to benefit, because renters get pushed out in these gentrification situations and only investors reap the rewards.[66] Because solidarity is rooted in the preferential option for the poor, this unequal distribution of a stadium subsidy's meager benefits is problematic, to say the least.

Beyond the unequal distribution of benefits, there is also a larger inequality problem behind stadium subsidies. As one economist points out, "public subsidization of professional sports teams represents a transfer of income from tax payers to the owners of professional sports teams, most of whom are billionaires."[67] As with the TV broadcasting deals, this structure creates significant opportunity costs. Although the structure of subsidy deals often involves restricted resources, so there is not a one-to-one comparison, every subsidy still requires governments to spend resources on a private endeavor, even if they are mainly time and energy. Additionally, stadium subsidies can have two trickle-down effects. First, because they involve large sums of money in bond issues, they can push a municipality's rate of borrowing higher, forcing the city to pay more for future projects supported by borrowing. Second, because voters tend to oppose stadium subsidies, ones that go into effect over voter opposition (as they often do) can erode support for spending increases in other areas, like schools.[68] As a result, stadium subsidies represent a trade-off between money for sports franchises and money for public services either directly or indirectly, depending on the nature of the subsidy agreement.

How might a sports fan deal with this structure of sin? Given that the virtue of everyday solidarity countenances structural reform, concerned moral agents ought to look to the structural roots of these subsidies. The reasons cities continue to offer subsidies over all the objections come down to one simple fact: cities and sports teams compete on an uneven playing field. There are a limited number of professional sports teams as a result of the antitrust exemptions that allow professional leagues to dictate the terms of their teams' business, so cities must compete with one another to lure new teams or keep existing ones.[69] Teams are therefore in a position to extort subsidies from cities with the threat of relocation, because the economic benefits may be minimal, but they are better to have than to forfeit. The solution, then, lies in rearranging the balance of power. To this end, two potential structural reforms could assist in transforming the incentives that lead cities to believe they have no choice but to subsidize stadium construction.

First, the antitrust protections currently enjoyed by professional sports leagues could change. If leagues were less empowered to restrict the number of potential teams, the bidding wars between cities would be less intense, because supply would more closely match demand. A shift in antitrust protections would also transform the economic pressures that lead to bidding wars for broadcasting rights, further addressing the outsize social influence of sports. Second, teams could become genuine public goods. At the moment, one problem with stadium subsidies is that they are ostensibly designed to achieve at least some public good—like urban revitalization, or the sense of camaraderie that comes from having a hometown team to support—but the money still goes directly and primarily to "privately controlled facilities."[70] This stands in stark contrast to the earlier model of stadium construction, which involved significant public expenditures but yielded publicly owned and operated venues that were used for civic purposes in addition to any private sporting events.[71] Building stadiums as genuine public venues would counteract this tendency, but few major league teams are likely to accept a city-owned-and-operated stadium, which would leave them with only a share of ticket sales, when they could find a subsidy for their own independently owned-and-operated stadium elsewhere. The better solution, then, is to treat the team and not just the stadium as the public good. Structurally, this could be achieved with community ownership, which the philosopher Michael Sandel has advanced as a "promising solution" to the problem of enormous stadium subsidies and teams' extortionary threats of relocation.[72] His logic makes sense, because if the public owns the team, there is no risk of moving for a better deal, and thus less leverage to extract outrageous subsidies. The problem, again structurally, is that leagues either outright prohibit community ownership or have policies militating against it. At one time, there was a legislative proposal to make leagues' antitrust exemptions contingent on their openness to community ownership.[73] Such a policy would advance the second solution proposed here at the expense of the first, but given that there is little appetite for challenging antitrust policies outright, this seems like an effective compromise.

These solutions, like those discussed in relation to the challenges created by broadcasting rights, are obviously large scale and are potentially hard to envision coming to fruition. Such is the nature of structural reforms, however, so the difficulties do not remove responsibility. But the difficulties do affect the pace of change, because wholesale structural transformation is unlikely to occur quickly. Fortunately, there are steps moral agents can take in the interim to chip away at some of the imbalances of power that sports leagues wield and to live out their commitment to solidarity in ordinary life. By way of conclusion, then, this chapter closes with an account of how all these insights into the work of everyday solidarity in spectator sports can translate into new practices for ordinary moral agents.

CONCLUSION

In effect, the principle of everyday solidarity and the virtue of everyday solidarity each provides two key insights for spectators. As a tool for moral discernment, the principle indicates that spectators should look to strengthen their relationships with other fans and to cultivate an active spirit of compassion for the athletes performing for their entertainment. Practically, these two concerns raise the questions of how one watches sports and which sports one watches. The virtue of everyday solidarity's emphasis on reforming structural sins, meanwhile, highlights the problematic influence of subsidies for broadcasting rights and stadium construction. This adds another dimension to the question of how one watches sports, and it also suggests where there is an issue.

Stating these questions is important, for these morally significant questions are precisely the ones that go unasked in the uncritical approach to free time. Answering them is a little more complicated, so one must leave space for each moral agent's personal discernment in conscience. Nevertheless, the commitment to relational flourishing at the heart of everyday solidarity reveals three helpful parameters for this discernment.

First, spectators should seriously evaluate the effects of their preferred sports on the athletes who perform for their entertainment. When risks are inherent and severe, to the point that success in the sport amplifies rather than diminishes one's exposure to the risks, spectators need to be willing to walk away from the sport. Spectators who cannot at least entertain this possibility, and who cannot clearly articulate the point at which they would abandon the sport, fail to show an adequate concern for the athletes they observe. Second, spectators should have a preference for communal viewing opportunities. This amplifies the possibilities for solidarity among spectators, because they will be in direct contact with other fans. It also challenges the current structures that facilitate bidding wars for broadcasting rights by taking people away from their private television sets (and thus reducing the reliance on private TV subscription bundles) or from TV altogether (if they watch in person). Third, spectators should seek out opportunities to watch sports in-person, especially in nonsubsidized or minimally subsidized stadiums. This would mean more attendance at minor league games or even at local sports events, where the other spectators are more likely to be members of one's regular community and thus are more likely to benefit from the bonding power of sports in a way that will persist beyond the games. Although attendance at major league events involves greater complicity in the system of stadium subsidies, everyday solidarity does not necessitate abandoning these stadiums completely. After all, once a stadium has been built, the public dollars have already been spent, so going to games onsite has no impact on the larger problem. In fact, if one were hoping to create the possibility for public ownership at some point, there is greater value in having a vibrant fan base in the stands. Under the current structures, purchasing season tickets at a major league stadium (at least one that receives subsidies) would be more problematic, however.

There are, of course, a number of factors for fans to consider as they evaluate the central questions raised by the perspective of everyday solidarity. The three matters outlined here offer a good start and a useful framework, however. The rationale behind both the questions and the guidelines is that sports provide a means for human connection, and this needs to be honored and developed when people spend their time watching sports. By preserving and amplifying this connection, spectator sports can serve as a tool that helps fans become more fully the relational human beings God created them to be.

NOTES

1. Heitner, "Sports Industry."
2. Ripley, "Case against High-School Sports."
3. The original definition was first proposed by Robert Bellah, who appealed to the work of Jean Jacques Rousseau to argue that the United States had its own "elaborate and

well-institutionalized civil religion" that borrowed generic religious concepts (e.g., the generic existence of God) to connect citizens with one another through the lowest common denominator. See Bellah, "Civil Religion," esp. 1–7, 12–13; quotation at 1.
4. See Cristi, *From Civil to Political Religion*, 30–40.
5. Evans, "Baseball as Civil Religion."
6. Evans, 27–30.
7. Forney, *Holy Trinity of American Sports*, 70–71.
8. Forney, 67, 76.
9. A similar defense appeared in the early twentieth century, when Morris Cohen proclaimed baseball a "national religion." See Price, *Rounding the Bases*, 111–12.
10. Bain-Selbo, "From Lost Cause to Third-and-Long."
11. Bain-Selbo, *Game Day and God*, 2–3, at 3.
12. Bain-Selbo, 29–31, 47.
13. Bain-Selbo, 34–35.
14. Bain-Selbo, 41–42, 51.
15. Bain-Selbo, 51.
16. For the notion of "collective egotism," see Niebuhr, *Nature and Destiny of Man*, 208–13.
17. Kovacik and Levin, "Red Sox Fan Recovering"; Frosdick and Marsh, *Football Hooliganism*.
18. John Paul II, *Sollicitudo rei socialis*, 38.
19. Borchard and Ferri, "When in Las Vegas," 721.
20. Bain-Selbo, *Game Day and God*, 188.
21. Bain-Selbo, 192–94.
22. Bonhoeffer, *Cost of Discipleship*, 43–56. On the often-necessary role of conflict in solidarity, see Massingale, "Vox victimarum vox Dei," 82–83.
23. Sobrino, "Bearing with One Another," 17–21.
24. Stephens, "Alex Honnold."
25. Stephens.
26. Murray, "Here Are the Strongest Arguments."
27. Mez, Daneshvar, and Kiernan, "Clinicopathological Evaluation"; Asken et al., "Research Gaps," 1260.
28. Asken et al., "Research Gaps," 1257.
29. Additionally, there are issues with the protocols even as a response to concussions, both because the NFL's history suggests a greater interest in preserving its image than in player safety and because there is evidence that teams have kept players on the field in spite of the protocols. *Frontline*, "League of Denial"; Stites, "How Does the NFL's Concussion Protocol Work?"
30. American Association of Neurological Surgeons, "Sports-Related Head Injury."
31. Stewart et al., "Symptoms."
32. A study of college football players, for instance, estimated that players on average experience a head impact on roughly every third play during a game. Kuo et al., "Comparison."
33. Murray, "Poll."
34. Brett Favre is on the record supporting legislative efforts to outlaw tackle football for children under the age of twelve. Carroll, "Brett Favre."
35. See John Paul II, *Veritatis splendor*, 79–83, esp. 80–81.
36. See Fuchs, *Personal Responsibility*, 115–52; Knauer, "Hermeneutic Function," 7–8. For a succinct explanation of the overarching debates, see Cahill, "Teleology," 610–11, 617.

37. The degree to which one could cooperate with someone else's intrinsically evil act, however, is governed by the principle of cooperation, which assesses proportionate reason in relation more to the gravity of the evil act than to its intrinsic or extrinsic evil. For a succinct overview of the principle, see Häring, *Law of Christ*, 292–94. On the importance of gravity, see Slater, *Manual*, 1:204. For an example of how the Congregation for the Doctrine of the Faith accepts the possibility that material cooperation with an intrinsically evil act could be permissible, see *Origins*, "Sterilization."
38. Scandal is such a concern in the case of cooperating with evil that, as the US Conference of Catholic Bishops proclaims in its directives for Catholic health care, "Cooperation, which in all other respects is morally licit, may need to be refused because of the scandal that might be caused." US Conference of Catholic Bishops, *Ethical and Religious Directives*, no. 71; see also no. 45.
39. Kelly, "Nature and Operation," 309–12.
40. The report also included data from Major League Soccer, where the average salary was $308,969. Although this is still a considerable amount of money, it represents such an outlier from the other leagues that it fails to represent the statistical trends effectively. Kurt Badenhausen, "Average Player Salary."
41. Fontenot, Semega, and Kollar, "Income and Poverty."
42. Sandel, "Moral Economy," 337.
43. This structural effect of income inequality is more commonly identified in the financial services industry, where large salaries draw talented workers away from more "socially desirable" jobs, harming the economy as a whole. Shakhnov, "How Wealth Inequality Entices Talent into Finance."
44. Walker and Bellamy, *Center Field Shot*, xii–xv, 43. Even early on, national broadcast rights nearly doubled the league's revenues. Walker and Bellamy, 107.
45. Gratton and Solberg, *Economics*, 1.
46. Pledge Sports, "Biggest TV Rights."
47. Taylor and Thomass, "Sports Rights," 113; see also Surdam, *Big Leagues*, 178–85.
48. Surdam, *Big Leagues*, 182.
49. Evans, Iosifidis, and Smith, *Political Economy*, 90, quoting Mario Monti, as head of the European Union Competition Commission.
50. Byzalov, "Unbundling," 41.
51. This is based on the 2017 monthly subscriber fee of $9.06 for ESPN, ESPN2, ESPNU, and the SEC Network. Gaines, "Cable TV." Most industry observers expect that customers would pay more than the subscriber fee alone because those fees are charged to cable providers, who in turn need to cover their costs. For Byzalov, this meant retail prices for customers were between two to three times the costs cable companies paid in subscriber fees. In the case of ESPN, this would be somewhere between $54 and $81 per month for each à la carte subscriber. Byzalov, "Unbundling," 41.
52. On the impact of bidding wars and the mentality and incentives they create, see Evans, Iosifidis, and Smith, *Political Economy*, 34–35, 37–38, 46–47.
53. Smith, "Playing," 204.
54. Smith, 208.
55. Evans, Iosifidis, and Smith, *Political Economy*, 75.
56. The WNBA's contract was $25 million a year. Though not insignificant, this is a mere fraction of the NBA's $2.6 billion a year, although the WNBA's contract appears to

benefit from some of the NBA's clout. Ourand, "ESPN's New Deal"; Waldron, "NBA's New TV Deal."
57. Humphreys, "Should the Construction of New Professional Sports Facilities Be Subsidized?" 264.
58. Matheson, "Is There a Case?" 271; Humphreys, "Should the Construction of New Professional Sports Facilities Be Subsidized?" 264–65.
59. Matheson, "Is There a Case?" 271–74.
60. Eisinger, "Politics"; Delaney and Eckstein, *Public Dollars*, 34–38; Humphreys, "Should the Construction of New Professional Sports Facilities Be Subsidized?" 265.
61. Coates and Humphreys, "Do Economists Reach a Conclusion?" 310.
62. Matheson, "Is There a Case?" 273; cf. Harger, Humphreys, and Ross, "Do New Sports Facilities Attract New Businesses?" esp. 497–98.
63. Matheson, "Is There a Case?"; Humphreys, "Should the Construction of New Professional Sports Facilities Be Subsidized?" 266.
64. Matheson, "Is There a Case?" 274.
65. See again Kelly, "Nature and Operation," 309–12.
66. Humphreys, "Should the Construction of New Professional Sports Facilities Be Subsidized?" 266.
67. Humphreys, "Facility Subsidies Redux," 278.
68. Eisinger, "Politics," 325–26.
69. Humphreys, "Facility Subsidies Redux," 278.
70. Coates and Humphreys, "Do Economists Reach a Conclusion?" 294. On the potential public goods stadiums provide, see Matheson, "Response to Professor Humphreys," 279–80; Matheson, "Is There a Case?" 271–72.
71. Coates and Humphreys, "Do Economists Reach a Conclusion?" 294.
72. Sandel, "Sports," 83.
73. Sandel, 84.

CHAPTER 8

Travel

Like sports, travel has the ability to contribute greatly to one's relational flourishing and therefore is quite amenable to the framework of everyday solidarity. At the same time, travel is often defined "by the effort to escape one's milieu, calling, everyday life, with all their obligations and stresses."[1] Travel can therefore distract a person from his or her moral commitments, to the extent that time away from normal routines invites a trivialization, or even a suspension, of one's usual values. Moreover, though travel brings a person into contact with others from a variety of backgrounds, these interactions do not always unfold in a spirit that recognizes the equal dignity of all. Consequently, everyday solidarity is not only amenable to the topic of travel; it is also necessary to ensure that travel respects the relational nature of both travelers and those whom they encounter on the way.

Hence, this chapter evaluates travel in light of both the principle and the virtue of everyday solidarity. In the first section, travel is considered as a valuable opportunity to cultivate existing relationships—especially family ties—insofar as it can provide the time and space for moral agents to focus on these relationships in a more direct and intentional fashion. There is also a caution, however, that this attention to preexisting relationships can go too far if the focus on one's traveling companions comes at the expense of one's awareness of and respect for those one encounters on a trip. The chapter's second section then discusses the ways that structural factors ought to influence the moral assessment of travel, giving special attention to its environmental and economic impact. Here the virtue of everyday solidarity indicates that moral concern for these structures can work at cross purposes, because travel's heavy toll on the environment could be interpreted as a demand for local travel (or none at all), while the importance of tourism for the economic health of many international destinations could be understood to promote travel to more distant locales. Acknowledging these tensions, and recognizing the fact that one moral agent can do only so much, the chapter refrains from universal norms and instead appeals to the importance of prayerful discernment, providing a sense of the factors one ought to consider when planning vacation trips. The result, as with the other chapters, is a better sense of how this recreational activity can promote a traveler's full flourishing as a relational human being and thus how travel can contribute to closer connections between theology, ethics, and ordinary life.

TRAVEL ACCORDING TO THE PRINCIPLE OF EVERYDAY SOLIDARITY

There is a strong theological case to be made for the value of travel. In Scripture alone, there is ample basis for evaluating travel in light of one's relationship with a personal God. After all, "the Hebrew Bible ... cannot be imagined without travel stories, as travel is deeply interwoven with its messages."[2] Of course, there is a substantive difference between the type of travel at the heart of the biblical narratives—which included permanent migrations and travel to flee natural disasters and wars—and the recreational travel of today. A contemporary theological evaluation of travel therefore requires more than just biblical reflection, but unfortunately there has not been much analysis of recreational travel to date.[3]

Although there are some exceptions in both Vatican documents and academic theology, a true theological case for recreational travel that is capable of integrating its various ethical challenges still needs to be made. Fortunately, the ethical framework of everyday solidarity and the theological vision for free time provide the resources to identify the value of travel as an instrumental good that promotes recuperation and relational flourishing. The ethical implications of travel can therefore be evaluated according to its ability to serve these purposes. The principle of everyday then adds specificity to this assessment, indicating that moral agents should consider how travel affects two relationships in particular: the relationships they can build with family members and other traveling companions, and the relationships they can build with the people they encounter while traveling. By attending to each of these relationships, the principle of everyday solidarity reveals how travelers can proceed with their travels in a way that honors their identity as human beings created in the image of a relational God.

Using Travel to Build Relationships

Regarding the first set of relationships, travel provides distinct opportunities for bonding with one's traveling companions. The intensity of sharing all of one's time with one's companions, often in a small space, can create new insights into the people with whom one has a preexisting relationship, including the family members with whom one already shares a life and a home outside travel. Perhaps unsurprisingly, many people turn to travel with the intention of strengthening their preexisting relationships. In fact, one early study of people's motivations for travel identified the "enhancement of kinship relationships" as one of the "seven socio-psychological motives which served to direct pleasure vacation behavior."[4] And these are more than just idle hopes and anecdotal aspirations. Empirical research supports these instincts and reveals in more detail how and why travel can contribute to the bonds between traveling companions. This research helps to define the relational potential that the principle of everyday solidarity insists travel ought to fulfill.

In many ways, the relational potential of recreational travel arises from the relational contributions of shared free time activities more broadly. On this more general point, "researchers have reported, with little variation, significant positive relationships between participation in joint leisure activities and satisfaction with family life."[5] The typical point of reference for this research has been married couples, but one study investigating the effects of joint leisure experiences on parents and children concluded that family leisure activities positively affect these relationships as well, although the effect is typically stronger on parents' family satisfaction than it is on children's. This divergence seems to arise from the fact that children and parents have two different scales for assessing family satisfaction, with children defining family satisfaction in reference to "their own personal satisfaction of the activity at the moment," while parents interpret family satisfaction as a measure of the functioning of their family as a whole.[6] The higher impact of shared free time activities on parents' perceptions of family satisfaction thus suggests that increased family cohesion is a genuine result of these experiences. Although this study did not evaluate travel in particular, it nevertheless has relevance to this recreational pursuit because the study also sought to assess whether different types of free time activities would affect family satisfaction differently. Drawing on a model that distinguishes "core" free time pursuits (which are part of a person's or a family's regular routine) from "balance" free time pursuits (which are more atypical), the study's authors ultimately determined "that relatively equal amounts of both patterns are essential to promote healthy functioning families."[7] Given that vacations are a paradigmatic example of balance free time pursuits, this discovery indicates that travel can contribute positively to a family's sense of cohesion and thus life satisfaction.

Other research has amplified these assertions about the importance of shared balance free time activities with specific reference to travel. A study of Canadian children, for instance, determined that the activities in which children engaged during vacations had the largest impact on their perceptions of whether a vacation was satisfying, reinforcing the value of shared leisure experiences.[8] More important, although the study's authors quickly discovered that, unlike adults, "children did not typically talk directly about social relationships" in their evaluations of vacation time, "their discussion of other family members and how they enjoyed their time and activities with them highlighted the importance of this aspect of family vacations."[9] In other words, these researchers found that vacations had the same positive effect on family cohesion as other joint free time pursuits, to the point that parents seek out this bonding intentionally and appreciate it explicitly, while children value it significantly but implicitly. A 2009 survey of leisure travelers similarly found that vacationing as a family increased a family's sense of bondedness and overall satisfaction.[10]

Given common intuitions—and idealizations—about travel's relational benefits, these findings are hardly surprising, but there is also a certain logic to the data indicating that family travel strengthens family relationships because vacations provide four mechanisms to facilitate this outcome. First, they offer more time for family members to be together without the usual distractions. Vacations thus have a particularly powerful effect on the strength of relationships with family members whose work or other responsibilities limit their regular time at home, but it is not limited to these situations alone.[11] "It is inevitable," one recreation scholar observed, "that a much greater exchange and understanding of each other is likely to occur [on vacation] than in the normal routine situation in which family members go in different directions interacting only spasmodically."[12]

Second, and relatedly, vacations can prompt improvements in a family's communication style and skills because the distance from regular routines removes many of the more common flashpoints in a relationship.[13] Third, although it is a free time activity itself, travel with others also affords a host of opportunities to engage in shared forms of leisure and recreation, from sports to games to conversations and more. Because shared free time activities are a valuable resource for relationship maintenance and have a direct impact on social bondedness, the increased number and frequency of joint leisure and recreation during vacations are especially poignant tools for increasing a family's sense of togetherness.[14] Fourth, family travel involves new experiences, which in turn create the conditions for building lasting memories that can "provide meaning into the future" and even "become a basis for future life decisions."[15] In fact, these memories can become the basis for restoring family bonds when subsequent trips bring people back to a familiar place imbued with nostalgia and happy memories. One interviewee in a dissertation project on family vacations and family cohesion, for instance, commented on the significance of returning to Cape Cod with his teenage children after years had passed since their regular vacations there, claiming, "I felt it was important to reconnect by visiting the Cape, where we had strong memories. The old, familiar closeness helped heal some disagreements that had come up [in the intervening time]."[16]

With these four mechanisms—several of which overlap—family vacations offer clear and effective tools for bringing family members closer together. Perhaps even more so than other recreational activities, family travel is therefore expressly compatible with everyday solidarity's understanding of the nature of free time and its purpose in the moral life. Indeed, from the perspective of Catholic theological anthropology, family travel is particularly well suited to the task of contributing to the moral agent's full flourishing as an inherently relational human being. After all, the Catholic moral tradition recognizes that the human person is constituted relationally not just in general terms but also in her or his particularity. As described in chapter 3, the traditional ordering of charity was designed to acknowledge this fact and to help Christians navigate the tensions that it inevitably produces. One key insight from that ordering, at least as it was fleshed out by Thomas Aquinas, is that one's familial relationships deserve an additional degree of attention. "We ought out of charity," he wrote, "to love those who are more closely united to us more, both because our love for them is more intense, and because there are more reasons for loving them."[17]

Applying this logic, Aquinas underscored the importance of kinship bonds, which he described as "prior to, and more stable than, all others, because it is something affecting the very substance, whereas other unions supervene and may cease altogether."[18] He therefore concluded that although other relationships may legitimately place more demands on the moral agent in certain circumstances, everyone remains "more beholden to [kinship bonds] in the providing of necessaries."[19] Attention, of course, is one of these basic needs, especially for children. As a result, the ordering of charity creates a moral obligation to set aside time to sustain one's familial relationships. Because family travel creates the conditions for more meaningful interactions between family members, there is a case to be made for it as an important part of the integration of faith and ordinary life.

Significantly, this recasting of the value of family travel can generate practical guidance for those wishing to approach this form of recreation as an opportunity to cultivate everyday solidarity. To begin, the desire to strengthen family bonds can help to shape trip planning. Destinations can be selected not simply on the basis of what one hopes to see but also on the basis of how much intimate family time a place or resort can facilitate. This could, potentially, justify using one's time and money to experience things, like fancier accommodations or more expensive activities, that would be less appropriate in other circumstances. David Cloutier's critique of luxury as a morally inappropriate indulgence for Christians actually provides a certain kind of rationale for this claim, given that he entertained "the idea that luxury might also be appropriate on special occasions," when it serves a more legitimate end.[20] Defending this position, he noted that, morally, "one can distinguish habitual use from intentional occasional use," and he explicitly allowed that "a luxurious vacation may be morally different from a luxurious apartment or home."[21] Second, he asserted that "refusing luxury is more than a call to stop buying; it is a call to buy differently, to take pleasure not in mocha lattes but in the human connections of a just economy."[22] With the principle of everyday solidarity applied to travel, it is possible to imagine that a family could choose a luxurious vacation destination in a morally justifiable way as an intentional occasional use of luxury designed to pursue the pleasures of human connection. They would obviously still have to make this selection precisely for the greater bonding opportunities they might gain from setting aside their usual mundane tasks more completely, and their temporary indulgence would also need to be set against a larger habit of using money in morally responsible ways. Even in cases like this, however, one would need to remain on guard, lest the luxury—or the recreation—become the end rather than the means.

Beyond having an impact on where one decides to travel, the framework of everyday solidarity can also affect what one decides to do when on vacation. Researchers note that children in particular experience and assess their vacations through the activities they get to do while traveling.[23] Consequently, parents planning family vacations need to consider the activities that will help their children experience the family bonding that makes travel morally justifiable. The activities do not need to be expensive or complicated; in fact, given the importance of regular joint leisure activities for children's satisfaction in the family, the activities would probably be most effective if they were to incorporate one or more of a family's typical free time pursuits in a new locale. The guiding question should be what the children will enjoy, and what parents can enjoy with them, so that everyone can be together and bond in the process.

Naturally, when families are traveling with grown children, or without children (e.g., as empty nesters), moral agents may not need to focus as much on selecting carefully curated activities, because adults tend to have a preference for more unstructured time to relax.[24] Even in these instances, however, one can still cultivate the principle of everyday solidarity by planning trips with the enjoyment of one's traveling companions in mind. This is not to say that a traveler should never think of her or his own desires, for vacations are especially conducive to the type of recuperation that can prepare one to return to one's vocational responsibilities with the energy that prevents burnout.[25] It is appropriate to consider how one can realize this goal while traveling, but the message of the principle of everyday solidarity is to remember that this is not the only relationship that matters for one's flourishing. By focusing on one's relationships, and making relationship quality the goal of one's travel, the moral agent creates the conditions to use travel appropriately as a form of recreation that is ordered to one's overall well-being as a relational creature of God.

Although using recreational travel to strengthen one's preexisting relationships is thus an appropriate aim, the principle of everyday solidarity must also caution against prioritizing these relationships too exclusively. The human person is certainly constituted by his or her particular relationships, but these are not the only facet of relationality. Each person is also defined by the capacity for relationships in general, a propensity that demands honoring justice alongside fidelity.[26] Moral agents motivated by the principle of everyday solidarity must therefore attend to other relational responsibilities, and not just familial obligations, as they discern how to shape their recreational pursuits in light of their faith commitments. This inclusive discernment is especially incumbent on Christians, for Jesus's message to his followers included an emphatic challenge to the exclusive focus on one's kinship responsibilities. "Whoever loves father or mother more than me is not worthy of me; and whoever loves son or daughter more than me is not worthy of me" (Matthew 10:37), Jesus insisted in one of his more memorable and challenging teachings. Read in context, these striking words reveal a critique of the absolutization of family ties, creating the expectation that Christians will not use their legitimate obligations to their kin as an excuse to avoid attending to the needs of those who do not happen to be their immediate relatives.[27]

When traveling, then, Christians must ensure that their appropriate desire for family connectivity does not transform into an inappropriate "égoïsme à deux" (in the relationship between spouses) or an "égoïsme à la famille" more broadly.[28] Such an outcome would contradict the order of love, which must "attend to the multitude of interacting relations within which we are immersed."[29] Hence, travelers should consider not only their responsibilities to their traveling companions but also their obligations to the people they meet in their new locale. The question of how to relate to one's hosts is thus the second essential element of the principle of everyday solidarity's assessment of travel.

The Relationship between Traveler and Host

In addition to strengthening family bonds, travel also creates the conditions for meaningful encounters with others and thus a deeper sense of the depth and breadth of the human person's inherently relational nature. "Contact with others," John Paul II insisted, "leads to discovering their 'secret,' to being open to them in order to welcome their valid aspects and thus contribute to knowing each one better."[30] Recognizing this potential as a central purpose of travel, moral agents motivated by the principle of everyday solidarity must give special attention to the hosts they encounter on their journey. The best way to honor this relationship between traveler and host is to reimagine the virtue of hospitality, as Patrick McCormick has emphatically insisted, so that it can serve as a moral guide for the person who visits and not just the one who is visited.[31]

In the biblical tradition, hospitality is an essential virtue that invites the faithful to imitate the work of God, whose care and concern for the Israelites in particular revealed how hospitality is designed to protect those in need.[32] The traditional understanding of hospitality, of course, lays the onus on the host, who has the benefits of stability, familiarity with the local environment, and a network of social relationships that travelers lack. Sharing these resources with travelers, who were vulnerable precisely because they had left these assets behind, became an important way for hosts to honor the humanity of the nomads who came into their home.[33] Hence, "offering care to strangers became one of the distinguishing marks of the authenticity of the Christian gospel and of the church"—a commitment that has been preserved in the tradition of the corporal works of mercy, which includes a summons to "shelter the homeless" as an outgrowth of the biblical understanding of hospitality.[34] This traditional virtue therefore offers an exceptional opportunity for Christian travelers to incorporate their faith convictions into their ordinary life while on the move.

At first glance, the biblical notion of hospitality would seem to apply most fittingly to hosts. But the most obvious parallel is not always the most apt application of a moral summons. As William Spohn outlines in his book on the intersection of Scripture and ethics, the movement from scriptural command to contemporary application is best navigated by an appeal to the analogical imagination that can preserve the spirit and not just the letter of the theological and ethical convictions found in revelation.[35] Using the example of contemporary efforts to imitate Jesus's washing of the disciples' feet during the Holy Thursday liturgy, Spohn juxtaposes the pope's washing the feet of twelve priests at the Vatican with a white inner-city pastor's decision to shine the shoes of some black laborers in his parish. The former is a far more literal reenactment than the latter, but the latter much more faithfully embodies the message of selfless service on display in Jesus's humble gesture.[36]

So it is with the biblical message of hospitality. Granted, insisting on the duty of hosts to welcome guests may be the most direct application of the biblical vision of hospitality, but the spirit of this precept is often much more faithfully captured in a reversal of this standard expectation today. This is especially true when one recognizes the contours of contemporary international travel, which increasingly brings wealthier tourists from the Global North to struggling economic areas in the Global South.[37] In this context, biblical hospitality—which "commands believers to provide needy aliens with adequate food, shelter, and protection; demands that the stranger be welcomed as a companion and friend and offered a place at the table; and requires that hosts breach and dismantle the walls of privilege or exclusion by becoming servants of those in need"—looks a bit different.[38] In fact, while not discounting the expectations that this tradition places on hosts, "biblical hospitality generates parallel obligations on modern travelers," who bear the greater burden of "the duty to be hospitable," which in the biblical tradition "was generated by the need and vulnerability of the other, not by their status as a sojourner."[39]

The practical question, of course, is how travelers can live out this call to embody hospitality toward their hosts. Part of the answer lies in the mindset travelers bring with them on vacation. The biblical vision of hospitality originally asked hosts to respond to the vulnerability of travelers by "extending the welcome and protection of one's home to the outsider, [by] treating the stranger *as if* he or she were a member of one's household, tribe, or community" (emphasis in the original).[40] This is certainly a vision travelers can embrace in their interactions with their hosts. Although the typical model of international travel is to sequester tourists from locals and limit interactions to service work that "reinforce[s] hierarchies of class, race, and gender," the traveler who embodies the principle of everyday solidarity will look for ways to challenge this model.[41] Specifically, he or she can "take steps to protect and provide for the basic needs of host communities serving them in emerging economies, welcome these hosts as friends and companions, and take steps to dismantle colonial and exploitative structures imposed on these communities."[42] Each of these is important, but the first two speak to the heart of the principle of everyday solidarity's impact on ethical discernment because they represent a conscious attempt to consider the well-being of the other as one contemplates moral action.

In concrete terms, travelers might manifest this commitment in tips for housekeepers and other staff who often depend on additional support to augment their regular wages but who tend to be excluded from travelers' tips a majority of the time.⁴³ This small gesture would be a way of recognizing one's own responsibility as a traveler to help hosts secure their basic needs. It also sends a message to these workers that their labor is valued, which is an appropriate outgrowth of both the principle of everyday solidarity and the notion of the dignity of work inherent in Catholic social teaching.⁴⁴ Additionally, travelers can honor the dignity of these workers by taking the time to have conversations with them, to ask them their names, and to give a bit more human detail to the people they encounter.

Of course, one must be cognizant of the ways these interactions can prevent workers from fulfilling the jobs their managers are often carefully scrutinizing, so this is a strategy that can be taken too far if the emphasis is not on the needs of the hosts. There is much to be said for the value of a simple "Hello," however—especially for staff members whose presence is often ignored. The image that comes to mind is a housekeeper, albeit in a movie, who jokes with one of her colleagues about possessing "magical powers—to become invisible," presumably as hotel guests walk down the hallway and ignore the cleaning staff.⁴⁵ To leave workers feeling this way is hardly an incarnation of hospitality or solidarity. Treating each person one encounters while traveling as a human being who is worthy of one's attention, conversely, is an essential way to welcome one's hosts as friends and companions; and, as the experience of service workers can attest, it is a gift that can go a long way.

Showing respect to hotel workers is not the only way that travelers can, or should, embody hospitality toward their hosts, however. One of the implications of the hospitality McCormick envisions is a challenge to colonial and exploitative structures. Although the virtue of everyday solidarity has much to offer this effort, as discussed below, this concern also falls under the purview of the principle, insofar as one's mind-set and disposition can inculcate or challenge a colonialist approach. As Pope John Paul II noted in his comments for the Twenty-Second World Tourism Day, "There is no doubt that, when properly oriented, tourism becomes an opportunity for dialogue between cultures and a valuable service to peace."⁴⁶

The problem, however, is that this potential is seldom realized. Travelers often ensconce themselves in resorts and venture out into the local culture only on carefully curated trips, which have a tendency to "reduce a way of life to a 'Kodak moment,' interesting only for its oddity or cuteness."⁴⁷ This approach applies a decidedly consumerist mind-set to intercultural encounters, perpetuating the colonial assumption that virtually every element of the Global South is for sale to the Global North. When travelers are truly motivated by the principle of everyday solidarity, then, they must combat this tendency, seeking out opportunities for cultural tourism that pave the way for a deeper understanding of the other and not just a simple commodification of the exotic. As Pope John Paul II explained, "This solidarity is expressed above all in respect for the personal dignity of the local people, their culture and customs, in a willingness to get to know them through dialogue, aimed at promoting the integral development of each one."[48] This will typically mean resisting the convenience of packaged tours in favor of more personalized experiences, which could be more difficult to arrange. The inconvenience is worth it, however, because direct arrangements with locals present more opportunities for genuine encounters and also provide a greater share of the financial rewards to the hosts themselves.[49] Both these results are fitting manifestations of everyday solidarity.

The steps travelers can take to respect the relational connections they inevitably have with their hosts are essential to ensure that travel can be rightly ordered to moral agents' full human flourishing. Although much of the discussion here has focused on the case of international tourism, the same principles of respect for the dignity of one's hosts, and the same practices of hospitality, can and do apply when people travel domestically or to other countries in the Global North. The central question remains how to approach the interactions one has with those who are working to serve travelers and who make a home in the place a tourist visits only temporarily. This question is essential because the principle of everyday solidarity operates in the sphere of conscience, where one's dispositions affect the pertinent factors one identifies in the conscience/2 process. Cultivating the virtue of hospitality as a traveler is an appropriate way to prioritize relationality in this process. In fact, when this disposition of attentiveness to and concern for the needs of one's hosts complements one's commitment to the bonds one has with one's traveling companions, travelers have the opportunity to honor their relationality in the broadest sense, resisting the fallacy of an égoïsme à la famille to which one can easily succumb without a critical perspective on travel.

Although this line of thinking promotes the relational flourishing of the moral agent, it does not exhaust a traveler's ability to show concern for the well-being of others while away from home. Travelers who are genuinely concerned for the flourishing of all must also wrestle with the fact that tourism today makes one complicit in larger structural injustices that will simultaneously undermine much of the good one can seek to accomplish on a personal level. Alongside their desire to strengthen relationships with their traveling companions and to respect the relationships they have with their hosts, travelers should also consider ways they can contribute to structural transformations for the common good, which leads to the implications of the virtue of everyday solidarity for recreational travel.

TRAVEL IN LIGHT OF THE VIRTUE OF EVERYDAY SOLIDARITY

Among the various structural effects of travel, the two that stand out the most are its environmental impact and its economic impact. These two are repeatedly identified in theological evaluations of travel. Pope John Paul II, for instance, readily connected tourism with environmental concerns. "A certain kind of savage tourism," he wrote, "has contributed to and still contributes to this unwanted destruction [of the environment] by way of tourist installations built without any planning that respects their impact on the environment."[50] In response, he called for "forms of tourism that show greater respect for the environment, greater moderation in the use of natural resources and greater solidarity with local cultures."[51] In his later writings, he also acknowledged travel's contributions to economic life, affirming that "tourist activity can play an important role in the fight against poverty, from the financial as well as the social and cultural viewpoints."[52]

Under the pontificate of Francis, both these themes have been linked to travel in explicit ways. In 2017, for instance, the Dicastery for Promoting Integral Development addressed the theme of "sustainable tourism" and promoted the Church's vision for "integrality" in development in order to ensure that in travel, "three dimensions of sustainability are promoted: the ecological, aiming for the maintenance of ecosystems; the social, which develops in harmony with the host community; and the economic, which stimulates inclusive growth."[53] Outside these official channels, meanwhile, McCormick's vision for travelers' hospitality stresses the need for travelers to attend to both the environmental effects of their activities as well as the economic implications of their choices so they can honor their moral responsibilities to their hosts.[54] There is, clearly, a special concern from theologians for these two structural dimensions of travel.

The attention Catholic theological ethics gives to the environmental and economic effects of travel should hardly be surprising, for globally, travel has an impact on these two areas of life more than any other. Transportation, which is an essential feature of travel, is tied with electricity production as the largest producer of greenhouse gases in the United States, according to data from the US Environmental Protection Agency.[55] When flying is involved, as it is in nearly half of international trips, the impact on the environment is especially pronounced, because "commercial airliners are dirtier polluters than any other form of passenger transport."[56] Even more dramatically, researchers recently concluded that when assessed holistically, the travel industry contributes to global emissions at a much higher rate than initially estimated, accounting for roughly 8 percent of total greenhouse gas emissions, an astounding share for one industry.[57]

Travel's economic effects are just as profound. In 2013, tourism represented the "world's largest industry and employer," accounting for nearly 10 percent of global gross domestic product and one in every eleven jobs.[58] Since then, the industry's influence has only grown, and it now encompasses more than 10 percent of global gross domestic product and employs one in ten workers.[59] Given the enormous impact of travel on both the environment and the global economy, moral agents have a responsibility to consider how they influence each of these spheres with their own travel decisions. The virtue of everyday solidarity is the best tool for this task, because travel's ecological and economic effects occur primarily at the structural level.

Travel's Impact on the Environment and the Economy

The structural nature of travel's impact on the environment and the economy is evident in two ways. First, there is a systemic nature to both the environment and the economy, which ensures that a negative effect in either one is not isolated to that sphere alone. Like a web, where pulling on one strand moves the whole lattice, the environment and the economy are intertwined with other areas of life, to the point that a person's impact in one of these dimensions has ripple effects that extend to other aspects of the common good.

Second, in part because the environment and the economy are both such large-scale spheres, the effects of human actions on each are most pronounced at the collective level. One person's choices in isolation are not going to shift the environment or the economy dramatically, but when combined into a structural force, everyone's collective actions can have a profound effect. Moral agents need to assess their contributions to these collective effects, and they therefore need to embrace a structural approach like the one advocated by the virtue of everyday solidarity. Fortunately, theologians have already laid the groundwork for this approach to the environment and to the economy by highlighting the systemic nature of these spheres and by identifying the collective nature of humanity's effects on them. A fuller account of one's moral responsibilities while traveling can therefore emerge from a closer analysis of this work.

To date, the best account of the systemic nature of environmental concerns in the field of theology has come from Pope Francis. His 2015 encyclical

Laudato si' provided a nuanced account of humanity's shared responsibility for "our common home."[60] Because the pope is especially attentive to the systemic nature of environmental problems, he proposed the idea of "integral ecology" as the necessary framework for "taking into account every aspect of the global crisis."[61] For him, the necessity of this framework emerged from the fact that "everything is interconnected," to the point that "it is no longer possible to find a specific, discrete answer for each part of the problem. It is essential to seek comprehensive solutions which consider the interactions within natural systems themselves and with social systems."[62] In justifying this approach, he explained that the environment both affects and is affected by economic development, civic life, public institutions, and social practices.[63] The solutions to environmental degradation, he argued, must be systemic because the problem itself is systemic. For this reason, one moral theologian has directly linked Pope Francis's appeals to integral ecology with the notion of structural sin, arguing that both highlight the complex relationships between the agency of moral actors and the structural ways this agency plays out in social life.[64] The systemic nature of environmental concerns is thus emphasized in contemporary theological discourse in a way that underscores the structural features of this sphere of life.

The structural nature of environmental effects is also evident in theological attempts to parse out agents' moral responsibilities for ongoing environmental degradation, which note the collective rather than individual nature of this problem. The clearest account of this dynamic comes from Mark Graham, who has noted that a strictly act-based analysis of moral responsibility misdiagnoses the severity of an agent's impact on the environment and undermines effective solutions.[65] At the level of personal moral action, Graham points out, one person's decision to drive his or her children to the park to play seems to have no environmental significance, because "the negative effects of the pollution caused by this one act of driving a car are so trivial and inconsequential that they are virtually morally meaningless."[66] Hence, moral agents cannot be faulted for reaching the conclusion that "virtually any good realized by [this] act of driving... to the park will justify the pollutants created in the process."[67]

However, as Graham highlights, the real impact of the environmental "side effects" of one's actions is much more significant than this act-based assessment would imply, because these actions do not occur in isolation. "Harm suffered as a result of environmental degradation," he explains, "usually results from patterns of behavior, not individual actions. One act of driving a car to the park does not hurt anyone; on the other hand, driving a car as much as the economic elite of first world countries do, day after day, and year after year, really is injurious."⁶⁸ In other words, the moral import of human actions on the environment stems from the cumulative effect of collective actions. The proper place to analyze moral responsibility for the environment is thus the structural level. This means that travelers who wish to take their moral responsibilities seriously must employ the virtue of everyday solidarity to assess the environmental effects of their trips.

Theological reflection on the economy similarly emphasizes the systemic nature of economic operations and stresses the significant influence of collective agency in this sphere of life. The systemic aspects of economic forces are especially evident in the notion of integral development found in Catholic social teaching. First proposed as "man's complete development" in Pope Paul VI's *Populorum progressio*, the concept has since become a mainstay in the Catholic Church's approach to economic life, under the moniker "integral human development."⁶⁹ Essentially, this concept highlights the impact of economic changes, especially large-scale changes at the national level, on human well-being, characterizing economic growth as a necessary but not sufficient condition for genuine human flourishing. In this case, the necessary is due to the fact that economics is inherently interconnected with other spheres of life, to the point that economic factors create the conditions for people not only "to improve their lot" but also "to further their moral growth and to develop their spiritual endowments."⁷⁰

In other words, economic policies affect moral and spiritual dimensions, meaning that economic concerns cannot be isolated from other aspects of life because they operate with a larger systemic influence. Pope Benedict XVI indicated the flipside of this point in *Caritas in veritate*, noting that "*human costs always include economic costs*, and economic dysfunction always involves human costs" (emphasis in the original).⁷¹ These claims about the unavoidable effects of economics on the rest of life have only been reinforced by research in other disciplines. Political scientists, for instance, note that economic resources correlate with greater political participation, revealing a way in which economics is systemically entangled with other social dimensions.⁷² In the field of public health, meanwhile, the discussion of social determinants of health has shown that socioeconomic status affects health outcomes, yielding worse health for those with fewer economic and social resources and better health for those with more.⁷³ Thus, in the context of economics, everything truly is interconnected.

At the same time, the structural nature of economic forces is also apparent in the fundamentally collective nature of economic activity. Much like the environment, where individual choices have minimal immediate effects in isolation but significant implications in connection, the economy also operates as a structure amplifying individual inputs. This is especially true in the case of economic harm, which is mediated by the market, creating "a synergistic dynamic in which the total harm is, in fact, much larger than the sum of individuals' respective contributions."[74] Often, however, the market mechanism obscures these types of harm from the individual agents involved.[75] Thus, a parent buys a soccer ball at a big box store in the United States and unwittingly facilitates sweatshop labor in a Central American factory, because enough parents are looking for a deal on sports equipment and manufacturers have found cheap labor in foreign nations to meet their collective demand. Situations like this, which are all too common, are the result of a confluence of factors, so assessing both an agent's responsibility for the types of harm that are caused through the marketplace and an agent's capacities to rectify these injustices requires attending not only to individual but also to collective forms of agency.[76] Consequently, economics functions much like the environment, insofar as both require a structural perspective for a complete moral analysis. The most appropriate way to assess travel's significant economic effects is therefore at the structural level, which means that travelers must incorporate economics alongside the environment in their dutiful application of the virtue of everyday solidarity.

Accounting for Travel's Impact

In light of the structural nature of environmental and economic choices, moral agents need to focus not only on the immediate effects of their travel plans but also on the collective impact of these personal decisions. This requires assessing their travel choices as part of larger patterns of behavior and not just as isolated decisions. When proceeding in this way, agents will consider not simply the effects of their own personal behaviors at a vacation destination but also the environment and economic effects that result from a swarm of tourists descending on a particular locale year after year. From this vantage point, the environmental and economic harm associated with travel becomes much clearer, and the means of addressing it at a structural level become even more important. The succinct version of how this responsibility can play out is in an effort to reduce environmental harm and to improve economic benefits when traveling.

At the outset, one might want to argue that an agent's moral responsibility to the environment should include not merely minimizing harm while traveling but also bringing new benefits. Although this may be appealing in theory, in practice any positive effects of travel are indirect and therefore are unsuitable as a basis for specifying moral responsibility. For example, many travelers are drawn to locations with remarkable natural beauty out of a desire to appreciate the local environment. Such interactions can stimulate a renewed appreciation for the environment and thereby encourage "people to approach it with respect and to enjoy it without altering its balance."[77] People might be prompted to donate money to environmental preservation programs, either at their destination or back home, and thus travel and the unique encounters with the natural world it provides can help form the moral "consciousness" that acknowledges humanity's responsibility to cooperate with God in caring for creation.[78] Any transformation that occurs as a result of these experiences, however, will be mediated through economic structures.

Meanwhile, the interactions with nature will still have a negative effect on the natural environment, especially when evaluated as part of larger patterns of behavior. After all, at this collective level, there is the agglomerated effect of countless hours of air travel and car emissions, plus infrastructure developments, which often interrupt natural growth in tourist destinations.[79] Furthermore, "busloads and caravans of tourists often overwhelm the fragile ecosystems and habitats they have come to visit. Automobile and foot traffic wear down the lush green of rainforests and national parks and reserves, and wear out the paths and steps to ancient sites."[80] There is always going to be an environmental cost to travel, so the question is not so much how to eliminate it but how to minimize it, so that these costs do not exceed the sustainable threshold at which they can still be offset.

The economic case, however, is more nuanced. Tourism can have substantive benefits for a local (or even national) economy, and some destinations are reliant on tourism for their survival. When properly ordered, travel can therefore contribute to the integral vision of development that the Catholic Church advocates in its social teaching. It can, at the structural level of economic life, provide the resources to open opportunities for fuller flourishing to more people in more places around the globe.[81] Unfortunately, the structures of economic life are seldom organized to allow destinations to realize these benefits. Despite the large share of the global economy attributed to travel activity, "much of the wealth generated by this industry stays in or leaks back to industrial nations," typically through multinational corporations that can keep upward of 80 percent of tourist income out of the local economy.[82] In other cases, the money is reinvested in the tourist economy rather than meeting the needs of the local community, exacerbating both economic inequality and environmental degradation.[83]

The question, then, is how to counteract these tendencies so that travel can become the tool for authentic development and economic solidarity that the Catholic Church envisions it can be under the right conditions. Certainly, travelers must seek to avoid contributing to types of economic harm, like subhuman wages and other unjust working conditions for those in the hospitality industry, but minimizing harm alone sets the bar too low.[84] Travelers truly committed to solidarity will seek ways to do good with their economic activity, not simply avoid evil.

A desire to limit environmental harm and maximize economic benefits can lead to practical strategies for travelers who are motivated by everyday solidarity. Admittedly, however, these two impulses might seem to contradict one another. Given the sizable role that transportation plays in contributing to greenhouse gas emissions, one could be tempted to conclude that travel should be limited to the shortest distances possible. Meanwhile, a penchant for maximizing economic benefits might be interpreted as license for longer trips, because the economies that have the most to gain from tourist dollars are typically smaller nations in the Global South. Though it would be overly reductionistic to conclude that the desires to minimize environmental harm and maximize economic benefit must cancel each other out, there is nevertheless value in recognizing that these two commitments often coexist in an uneasy tension. The proper response is therefore for travelers to weigh both of these concerns in prudence. This is where some of the traditional categories of Catholic act-centered moral thinking can be quite useful, as long as they are used in reference to patterns of behavior and not simply personal decisions in isolation. Specifically, the notion of "proportionate reason" that is integral to the principle of double effect and the principle of cooperation can be a valuable category for moral agents looking to preserve the tension between environmental and economic concerns when traveling—provided, that is, that the agent assumes a structural perspective on these questions.

In the context of traditional moral principles like the principle of double effect and the principle of cooperation, the basic function of proportionate reason is to ensure that the types of harm done by (in the case of double effect) or facilitated by (in the case of cooperation) a moral agent are tolerated only when necessary to the pursuit of some justifiable good. Importantly, the other elements of these principles function to narrow the situations in which this weighing of proportionate reason is appropriate, so that moral discernment does not devolve into strictly consequentialist ethics. Indeed, the entire premise of the principle of double effect's second restriction, that "the evil effect [of an action] must not be the means of producing the good effect," is to ensure that one does not engage in an ends-justify-the-means evaluation but instead only weighs both good and bad outcomes against one another when they are genuinely described as inseparable effects of the same action.[85] The categories of the principle of cooperation, which seek to limit the degree of an agent's participation in the wrongdoing of another, function similarly to narrow the circumstances under which an assessment of proportionate reason would be appropriate.[86]

When it is applicable, however, the idea of proportionate reason highlights a moral tension, indicating that foreseen but unintended negative consequences can sometimes be legitimately offset by foreseen and intended good effects.[87] This is the impulse that ought to guide moral discernment about travel in light of the virtue of everyday solidarity. In essence, moral agents can respect and preserve the tension between concerns about the environmental and economic effects of travel by focusing on proportionate reason. That is, they can seek to strike a balance whereby the goods generated by their economic activity can outweigh the harm caused by their environmental effects.

In practice, this pursuit of proportionate reason could justify travel closer to home, where one can limit environmental effects with fewer miles, even though the economic effects are unlikely to be quite as strong as they might be for an international destination. At the same time, one could still choose among local destinations, with a preference for places that depend on tourist revenues, and one could seek out specific hotels that are known to treat their employees fairly or that are actively working to embrace green operations, so that economic rewards can flow to the people who live in the local economies and strengthen efforts to develop a more sustainable tourist industry. Consistent with the virtue of everyday solidarity, these decisions can serve as a sort of structural reform, insofar as they realign incentives for companies to pursue policies that benefit the common good.[88]

At the other end of the spectrum, the interest in achieving structural goods with one's tourism dollars can legitimate international trips, provided one takes steps to reduce or offset the overall environmental impact of the patterns of behavior that bring travelers from the Global North to destinations in the Global South in unsustainable ways. Here, the practice of purchasing carbon offsets is a helpful way to bring economic benefits into closer alignment with environmental harm. Although this is not to suggest that one can buy one's way out of responsibility for environmental degradation, some of the offset programs do create substantive environmental benefits, and those programs need money to run. Of course, in terms of structural thinking, the best outcome would be if an airline (or the entire airline industry) embraced carbon offsets as a way of working toward carbon neutrality, so travelers should look to support airlines currently pursuing this goal and work to prod others in this direction.[89]

However, travelers will need to look beyond transportation if they wish to minimize environmental harm and maximize economic benefits. They should also consider how their money flows into structures in their host country, looking for smaller hotels and local businesses to support, so that they can combat the drain of tourism dollars from a local economy that often accompanies multinational operations. They might also want to consider the amount of time they spend in a distant location, figuring that a longer trip (to a smaller resort) could generate greater economic benefits that would outweigh the fixed environmental impact of the travel itself.

As this discussion suggests, the tension between travel's structural effects on the environment and the economy yields no easy answers. Instead, travel creates a certain kind of moral ambiguity at the structural level, and travelers who embrace the virtue of everyday solidarity as part of their approach to ordinary life must find ways to respect this reality. The pursuit of proportionate reason provides the means for preserving the tension, suggesting that the best response is not to craft a one-size-fits-all solution in advance but to instead pursue a reasoned application of prudence. Ultimately, this is quite appropriate, for it not only leads to a better, and more honest, analysis of the interactions between environmental and economic concerns at the structural level but also provides agents with the chance to practice the kind of conscientious critical discernment that is the ultimate purpose of connecting theological ethics to ordinary life.

CONCLUSION

In light of the theological vision for free time, and consistent with the ethical framework for ordinary life as a whole, travel presents a striking opportunity for encouraging the fullness of both recreation and relationality. As a form of recreation, travel can provide the rest and recuperation that rejuvenates agents to return to their vocational responsibilities with renewed energy. This capacity aligns well with the theological notion of recreation as an instrumental good that is designed to provide the means to the ends of other, more intrinsic goods. Also, travel can provide focused time for building relationships, both with one's traveling companions and with local hosts. This potential reveals that travel is able to promote relational flourishing, which makes it an especially valuable activity for connecting theological ethics and ordinary life. The positive possibilities of travel are far from guarantees, however. Human sinfulness, in both its personal and structural forms, can frustrate the healthy forms of recreation and relational connection that travel can provide. And the goods of travel can sometimes carry unjustifiable ancillary costs.

Attentive moral agents must therefore evaluate travel with careful ethical discernment. At the personal level, travelers must ensure that their desire for recuperation is an appropriate pursuit of self-care, which restores them for their relational responsibilities, and not a needless indulgence of selfishness, which will close them off from others. They must resist the temptation to absolutize the good of connections with their fellow travelers and instead work to honor the relational connections they can forge with the new people they encounter on their journey. Accepting that the responsibility of hospitality applies to all parties, travelers must be conscious of how their mobility creates new obligations to account for the well-being of their hosts if they are to embrace the principle of everyday solidarity.

At the structural level, meanwhile, travelers must also attend to the fact that their personal choices are part of larger patterns of behavior that have significant effects on the environment and the economy, both locally and globally. They need to embrace a desire to mitigate environmental harm and to maximize economic benefits, and they should pursue a strategy of proportionate reason to incarnate this desire in concrete practices. Where possible, they can use this disposition to transform some of the structural elements that exacerbate travel's harm to the environment and divert its economic benefits. Even when they cannot shift these structures directly, however, they can still find ways to work within alternative structures that are more amenable to the sustainable type of travel that protects the environment and promotes integral human development for all involved.

This is, of course, a lofty vision, and few travelers will find the perfect combination of decisions to make this vision a reality in toto on any given trip, let alone all of them. Nevertheless, if they willingly embrace the principle of everyday solidarity in their ethical discernment and pursue the virtue of everyday solidarity in their structural assessments, this will enable travel to contribute to both their well-being and that of the people they encounter. By genuinely bringing faith and ordinary life closer together during this recreational pursuit, a commitment to everyday solidarity can ensure that "holidays and journeys can be beneficial times for filling gaps in one's humanity and spirituality," just as Pope John Paul II once proposed.[90]

NOTES

1. Bleinstein, "Leisure II," 302.
2. Rieger, *Faith on the Road*, 24.

3. On this point, a 2011 book on the intersection of religion and tourism pitched itself as "the first book from religious studies to deal systematically with a topic which is right in front of everybody's eyes: the vibrant interface between modern tourism and religion." Stausberg, *Religion and Tourism*, x. There have been other studies of general links between religion and travel, especially through the lens of pilgrimage, but little engagement with recreational travel from an explicitly theological perspective. See Norman and Cusack, *Religion*, 4 vols.; and Timothy and Olsen, *Tourism*.
4. Crompton, "Motivations," 418, 416.
5. Zabriskie and McCormick, "Parent and Child Perspectives," 164.
6. Zabriskie and McCormick, 180.
7. Zabriskie and McCormick, 183. On the distinctions between core and balance free time pursuits, see Zabriskie and McCormick, 167–69.
8. Hilbrecht et al., "Experiences," 551.
9. Hilbrecht et al., 564–65.
10. Lehto et al., "Family Vacation Activities."
11. Hilbrecht et al., "Experiences," 563.
12. Crompton, "Motivations," 418.
13. Poff, Zabriskie, and Townsend, "Modeling Family Leisure," 368–69.
14. In addition to Zabriskie and McCormick, "Parent and Child Perspectives," see also Hornberger, Zabriskie, and Freeman, "Contributions of Family Leisure"; and Poff, Zabriskie, and Townsend, "Modeling Family Leisure," 367–70.
15. Shaw, Havitz, and Delemere, "'I Decided to Invest in My Kids' Memories,'" 20.
16. Kruenegel-Farr, "Perceptions of Family Vacation," 16.
17. Aquinas, *ST*, I-II.26.8 c. Aquinas here is actually summarizing the argument he developed in I-II.26.7.
18. Aquinas, *ST*, I-II.26.8 c.
19. Aquinas, *ST*, I-II.26.8 ad 1.
20. Cloutier, "Problem of Luxury," 16.
21. Cloutier, 16–17.
22. Cloutier, 16.
23. Hilbrecht et al., "Experiences," 551.
24. Hilbrecht et al., 546.
25. Strauss-Blasche, Ekmekcioglu, and Marktl, "Does Vacation Enable Recuperation?"
26. These are James Keenan's two cardinal virtues for perfecting these different types of relationships. Keenan, "Proposing Cardinal Virtues," 723.
27. Barton, *Discipleship*, 169–70; Rubio, *Christian Theology*, 49–54.
28. Pope, "Order of Love," 261.
29. Pope, 261.
30. John Paul II, "Message for the World Day of Migrants and Refugees 2005."
31. McCormick, "Good Sojourner."
32. McCormick, 91.
33. Pohl, *Making Room*, 17–20, 39.
34. Pohl, 33; see also Keenan, *Works of Mercy*, 21–26.
35. Spohn, *Go and Do Likewise*, 4, 50–51.
36. Spohn, 51–54.
37. McCormick, "Good Sojourner," 97.
38. McCormick, "Fair Trade Tourism," 167.

39. McCormick, 167.
40. McCormick, "Good Sojourner," 101.
41. McCormick, 101–2, at 102.
42. McCormick, "Fair Trade Tourism," 167.
43. Surveys and other research suggest that only about one-third of hotel guests in the United States tip their housekeepers. La Gorce, "Tipping."
44. Pontifical Council for Justice and Peace, *Compendium*, 270–75.
45. From *Bread and Roses*, directed by Ken Loach (2000), quoted by Snarr, *All You That Labor*, 10.
46. John Paul II, "Message for the 22nd World Tourism Day 2001," 3.
47. McCormick, "Good Sojourner," 99; see also John Paul II, "Message for the 22nd World Tourism Day 2001," 2.
48. John Paul II, "Message for the 24th World Day of Tourism 2003," 3.
49. Arrangements through multinational corporations are largely responsible for the fact that "overall, about half the income from international tourism leaks out of developing countries." McCormick, "Fair Trade Tourism," 163–64.
50. John Paul II, "Message for the 23rd World Day of Tourism 2002," 2.
51. John Paul II, 3.
52. John Paul II, "Message for the 24th World Day of Tourism 2003," 2.
53. Dicastery for the Promotion of Integral Human Development, "Sustainable Tourism," 3.
54. McCormick, "Good Sojourner," 98–100; McCormick, "Fair Trade Tourism," 163–66.
55. US Environmental Protection Agency, "Sources."
56. McCormick, "Good Sojourner," 99.
57. Lenzen et al., "Carbon Footprint," 522–28.
58. McCormick, "Fair Trade Tourism," 162.
59. World Travel and Tourism Council, "Economic Impact."
60. Francis, *Laudato si'*, 3.
61. Francis, 137.
62. Francis, 138, 139.
63. Francis, 141–42, 145.
64. Shadle, "Where Is Structural Sin in *Laudato si'*?"
65. Graham, "Environmental Burden," 102.
66. Graham, 104.
67. Graham, 105.
68. Graham, 107.
69. Paul VI, *Populorum progressio*, 5; Benedict XVI, *Caritas in veritate*, 8.
70. Paul VI, *Populorum progressio*, 34.
71. Benedict XVI, *Caritas in veritate*, 32.
72. Schlozman, Verba, and Brady, *Unheavenly Chorus*, esp. 147–76.
73. For an overview of the research into social determinants of health, see Daniels, *Just Health*, 79–81, 83–88.
74. Barrera, "Individuating Collective Responsibility," 222.
75. Finn, "Social Causality," 243–44.
76. Finn, 247–48. See also Hirschfeld, "How a Thomistic Moral Framework," 160–63; and Barrera, "Individuating Collective Responsibility."
77. John Paul II, "Message for the 23rd World Day of Tourism 2002," 2.
78. John Paul II, 5.

79. McCormick, "Good Sojourner," 99–100.
80. McCormick, 100.
81. Dicastery for the Promotion of Integral Human Development, "Sustainable Tourism," 2–3; John Paul II, "Message for the 22nd World Tourism Day 2001," 4.
82. McCormick, "Good Sojourner," 98.
83. McCormick, 98.
84. These are significant concerns, given that the travel industry pays on average 20 percent less than other industries and often employs child workers. McCormick, "Fair Trade Tourism," 164.
85. Kelly, *Medico-Moral Problems*, 13.
86. Thus, David DeCosse has described the traditional categories of mediate/immediate and proximate/remote used in the principle of cooperation as factors weighing an agent's proximity in time and space to the sinful act of another. DeCosse, "Conscience," 181.
87. Much more can be said about the nuanced application of these principles and of proportionate reason within them, not to mention controversies surrounding the principles and the contested areas to which they ought to apply. For a fuller account of these issues, begin with Bretzke, *Handbook*, 39–40, 72–73, 153, 190.
88. On the role of incentives as morally significant social structures, see Kelly, "Nature and Operation," 306–9; and Finn, "What Is a Sinful Social Structure?" 151–54, 161.
89. See Stewart, "Stop Worrying."
90. John Paul II, "Message of Pope John Paul II for World Day of Tourism 2000."

CONCLUSION

Training in Moral Discernment

The best way to capture what has been done in this book is to return again to the assertion from the introduction that the significance of this project is twofold. First, there is the immediate benefit of bringing free time closer to its full potential. Often approached without much critical scrutiny, free time tends to be a sphere of life where people default to patterns of behavior—like watching television or surfing the internet—that have emerged for the sake of convenience. When the theological perspective advocated in this book is brought to bear, however, the deeper potential and significance of free time can come into view. Attentive to the divisions between leisure and recreation, moral agents can approach their free time with the kind of intentionality that will allow this area of life to support their full flourishing instead of becoming a passive way of killing time. The practical resource for effecting this shift is the ethical framework of everyday solidarity, which helps to put the relational anthropology of the Catholic theological tradition at the center of moral reflection, building a practice of ethical discernment that has implications not simply for free time but also for ordinary life more broadly. This framework and its application reveal the second aspect of the significance of this project, which is the possibility of forging closer connections between theological ethics and ordinary life.

Like the task of assessing the ethical importance of free time, the task of linking ethics and the everyday is one that demands more attention than it has typically received. Fortunately, the notion of everyday solidarity has much to add to this endeavor, particularly in the context of the United States, where the challenges that make everyday solidarity so valuable for the analysis of free time are just as pertinent to and influential in other areas of ordinary life. In light of these connections, the point of this conclusion is not simply to recapitulate the central arguments of this book about the theological and ethical potential of free time but also to discuss the ways this analysis can extend analogically into other areas of life. The latter is especially important, because the real value of assessing free time from the perspective of theological ethics is to help ordinary people link their faith and their ordinary life more completely. Though free time has an essential role to play in this process, the pursuit of greater theological and ethical integration cannot stop at leisure and recreation alone.

A REVIEW OF THE CASE FOR THEOLOGICAL ETHICS AND FREE TIME

The assessment of free time began with the distinction between leisure and recreation. The tradition of the leisure ideal found in philosophical works from Aristotle to Pieper generated the idea that leisure ought to be identified for its intrinsic value, while recreation would be better categorized as an instrumental good. Mihaly Csikszentmihalyi's concept of flow then helped to specify the initial distinction, creating the definition of leisure as flow-inducing free time activities and supporting the notion of recreation as a remainder concept. In theological terms, the intrinsic and instrumental divide between leisure and recreation found justification in the split between enjoyment and use famously advocated by Augustine in *De doctrina Christiana*. Augustine's assertion that God alone is to be enjoyed led to the claim that leisure could be enjoyed for the ways that flow creates a temporal glimpse of heavenly rest, which is an intrinsic good in the life of the Christian. The use of recreation, meanwhile, was linked to the fact that time away from one's normal routines and responsibilities can lead to renewed energies for those duties upon one's return.

Although the theological assessments provided the means to discuss the larger purpose of leisure and recreation, the theological vision alone did not produce sufficient resources for the ethical evaluation of specific free time pursuits. As a result, chapter 2 outlined a framework for ordinary life in general that could yield the necessary nuance for applications to different circumstances and activities. Dubbed everyday solidarity, this framework brings the relational vision of Catholic theological anthropology to the forefront of moral discernment. It can thus act as a bridge to one of the most fundamental convictions of the Catholic faith, namely, that human beings are created in the image and likeness of a relational God and are therefore unable to find fulfillment except in a communion of self-gift. It also serves a critical function in the US context, where cultural and structural pressures valorize an individualistic ethos that can easily overshadow the relational anthropology at the heart of Catholic theology. Everyday solidarity counteracts this tendency with its twofold emphasis on personal and social responsibility. As a principle, it promotes recognition of one's relationality during the process of moral discernment in conscience/2, insisting that moral agents evaluate decisions in light of others' well-being as well as their own. As a virtue, it also highlights the need to defend this well-being through structural reform, indicating the practical significance of embracing a genuine commitment to the common good. In this way, everyday solidarity preserves the multifaceted theological understanding of solidarity as a principle that affirms the fact of humanity's interconnectedness as children of God and as a virtue that orients moral agents toward the common good. Though not constitutive of the fullness of the moral life on its own, when understood in light of, and in service to, the presuppositions that shape the Catholic moral tradition, everyday solidarity nevertheless provides a portable distillation of the main features that people of faith are called to prioritize in the moral life, yielding a reasonably comprehensive framework for practical applications.

In relation to free time, the framework of everyday solidarity translated to an intentional pursuit of relational flourishing during leisure and recreation. Chapters 3 and 4 outlined the significance of this goal for leisure, indicating first that the general priority of leisure over recreation was an appropriate extension of the distinction between leisure as an intrinsic good and recreation as an instrumental one. It also reflected a commitment to relational flourishing, because shared flow experiences are especially conducive to social bonding. Further amplifying leisure's role in the pursuit of relational flourishing, chapter 3 explained how the principle of everyday solidarity could yield an ordering of leisure that promotes the enjoyment of flow-like free time activities to sustain one's relationship with God, with self, and with others. The notion of a leisure examen then offered the means to respond to this vision in a realistic way, ensuring that people could prioritize the enjoyment of leisure without rejecting the use of recreation. Augmenting this plan for leisure, chapter 4 discussed the importance of championing structural changes in the sphere of work that would make free time for leisure, and the resources to do something with it, more readily available to all. These structural changes, like a living wage floor and guaranteed vacation and parental leave, are an essential component of everyday solidarity's applications to free time because one can hardly justify a vision for moral discernment in a sphere of life to which few people have ready access. Consequently, chapter 4 showed that the virtue of everyday solidarity must accompany the principle, lest the incorporation of a concern for others into one's ordinary moral discernment would be incomplete and insincere.

Taking the complementarity of the principle of everyday solidarity and the virtue seriously, part III of this book explored four discreet recreational pursuits in light of everyday solidarity. Beginning with television, the most common free time activity in the United States, chapter 5 explained television's negative effects on both the priority of leisure over recreation and one's relational capacities. This led to a general recommendation that agents should reduce time spent watching TV so that this would no longer be their primary free time activity. Finding ways to turn television viewing into social occasions also emerged as a concrete strategy for living out the principle of everyday solidarity in this recreational pursuit. The virtue of everyday solidarity's structural perspective then led to support for more public recreational opportunities, in order to counteract the privatization of leisure that has played a major role in the rise of television as the principal free time activity in the United States.

Chapter 6 discussed how some of the same pitfalls of television emerge in the second-most-common free time activity: digital media use. Noting that an excessive reliance on technological mediation for human connections undermines authentic relationships, this chapter critiqued the tendency to spend large amounts of time in mindless activity online, recommending instead that people approach their online interactions with a greater intentionality so that they might realize the "authentic culture of encounter" advocated by Pope Francis in his 2014 World Communications Day message. This hopeful vision for a new way of engaging online led to an argument in favor of expanding structural access to the internet, chiefly through more public support for expanded resources in rural areas and new connections in common spaces. Though this structural goal still needs to strike a balance so that increased access does not encourage more people to rely exclusively on the more superficial connections of online life, it reflects an honest appraisal of the reality that many of the avenues for participation in communal life are currently channeled through digital technologies. Insofar as the internet is increasingly the gateway to in-person interaction, access to the internet is a structural concern to which anyone committed to relational flourishing—both their own and that of the people in the community around them—must attend.

Moving beyond the strictly technological realm, chapter 7 assessed recreational sports in light of the principle and the virtue of everyday solidarity, identifying two relationships for spectators to incorporate into their moral discernment. The first, relationships with other spectators, could be honored by embracing the civil religion elements of sporting events, provided spectators resisted the temptation to narrow their bonding too exclusively. The second relationship, with the players, required attending to the larger structural features of professional leagues and the sports themselves to ensure that players were not required to take unnecessary or unjustifiable risks simply for the entertainment of others. The virtue of everyday solidarity's commitment to the common good, meanwhile, indicated that the outsize cultural and economic influence of spectator sports in the United States constitutes a structural concern because of the perverse incentives it creates. Transforming these constraints would mean challenging the traditional cable television model and the practice of diverting public money to private teams through stadium subsidies. Combining these structural critiques with the principle of everyday solidarity's promotion of stronger connections between spectators and greater compassion for athletes, chapter 7 closed with the assertion that moral agents ought to develop a preference for watching sports in social settings—in person, where possible—and that they ought to pick the sports they watch with an eye toward the well-being of the athletes and the effects on the local community.

Finally, chapter 8 examined travel and noted that this recreational activity holds great potential for relational flourishing. Specifically, time spent away from home can facilitate social bonding between family members and other traveling companions, and it can also yield meaningful interactions between tourists and hosts. The principle of everyday solidarity therefore encouraged the intentional pursuit of family bonding while traveling alongside the cultivation of a spirit of hospitality toward one's hosts. The latter was especially important in order to ensure that a legitimate concern for one's family did not devolve into an exclusive type of egoism that ignores the responsibilities moral agents have to people beyond their kinship networks. Extending this commitment to hospitality, the virtue of everyday solidarity indicated that travelers also have a responsibility to consider the environmental and economic effects of their trips. Importantly, they must apply a structural perspective to this assessment, evaluating not simply the effects of their individual journey but rather their role in larger patterns of behavior that regularly bring masses to tourist destinations. The chapter noted that this evaluation might seem to create contradictory impulses, because a commitment to reducing environmental harm could prompt people to travel less, while the desire to maximize economic benefits could prompt people to travel more frequently to more distant places. The solution, chapter 8 suggested, was to preserve this tension, chiefly by appealing to the category of proportionate reason, which can help moral agents weigh the various positive and negative effects of their travel choices so that they can best contribute to the well-being of others.

The book as a whole thus offers a practical road map for the transformation of free time. The theological vision for leisure and recreation reorients free time to a higher end, providing the resources for believers to see this area of ordinary life as an opportunity for growth in faith and not simply as a break from the rest of life. The ideal of leisure as a foretaste of heavenly rest offers a reminder of the human person's ultimate calling and encourages moral agents to prioritize their system of values properly. The notion of recreation as an instrumental good helpfully reinforces this message, preserving the value of recreation while underscoring the greater relative benefits of an experience that offers a glimpse of the future God has planned for creation. The framework of everyday solidarity adds to this reorientation of values, calling the faithful to embrace a decidedly theological anthropology that understands the human person as an inherently relational creature. Its implications for leisure, embodied in both the priority of leisure over recreation and the ordering of leisure, and its effects on recreation suggest a way to take this view of the human person seriously so that it can guide one's everyday life.

This book's vision for free time is therefore detailed and practically relevant, but it is not exhaustive. Many other forms of recreation could benefit from everyday solidarity's twofold analysis, and there are additional nuances in the ways agents might apply the ordering of leisure to their own lives. The point, however, was never to provide answers to every possible conundrum during free time, but instead to provide direction for moral discernment. The theoretical aims identified here and the practical examples offered throughout are sufficient for this task, yielding a process that moral agents can adapt to their own lives so that their free time can reach its fullest potential, offering them opportunities to appreciate the generosity of God's goodness and the flourishing of their relational nature. At the same time, to the extent that moral agents experience these benefits through the application of the theological and ethical resources developed here, they will necessarily begin cultivating new skills for moral discernment. The critical evaluation of free time outlined in this book can thus benefit not simply this one sphere of life but rather a person's approach to ordinary life as a whole by creating more substantive links to one's faith commitments. This is ultimately the real value of examining something as quotidian as free time, so the final point to explore is how the skills and practices of moral discernment described here, especially the framework of everyday solidarity, can contribute to a greater integration of faith and life more broadly.

FROM FREE TIME TO THE REST OF LIFE

Beyond the immediate impact on leisure and recreation, the process of subjecting one's free time decisions to more critical scrutiny, as described in this book, can generate transferable skills for the revitalization of moral discernment more generally. First, the notion of intrinsic and instrumental goods can habituate a mind-set that identifies value in relation to humanity's ultimate end. By prioritizing leisure over recreation based on the former's spiritual significance, moral agents both reaffirm the inherent value of a connection with God and begin to embody a way of life that says that God, rather than another of the many tempting idols, really is one's "ultimate concern."[1] Such a perspective is a prerequisite for a closer connection between faith and ordinary life. Second, evaluating leisure and recreation in light of the framework of everyday solidarity gives moral agents the practical experience of making ethical decisions with an emphasis on relational responsibilities. Much like the recognition of intrinsic and instrumental goods, the adoption of this framework helps to solidify God as one's ultimate concern because caring for others is precisely what Jesus, God incarnate, commanded his followers to do. At the same time, this approach also paves the way for a stronger connection between faith and everyday life in a different fashion, because the recognition of relational responsibilities is premised on the intrinsically relational nature of the human person created in the image and likeness of God. To embrace this relationality in one's ethical discernment is to situate one's fundamental identity in one's status as a creature of God rather than any other contingent status.

The work of analyzing free time can thus reinforce basic links between faith and ordinary life. Just as important, it provides a way to practice moral discernment with greater regularity. This also contributes to the integration of faith and life because one of the most important ways in which a person's faith convictions become incarnated is through the values they prioritize and the ethical choices they make. Unfortunately, there is a temptation, especially in Catholic moral theology, to emphasize the role that some of the weightiest moral choices play in this process. Thus, for instance, the well-publicized case of Terri Schiavo in the early 2000s brought numerous Catholic voices into the public sphere to assert that how one interpreted the removal of a feeding tube for a patient in a persistent vegetative state could define one's status as a faithful Catholic.[2]

Although there are many reasons to challenge the assumption that isolated decisions have the greatest impact on one's faith life, even if one were to accept this argument on its own terms, a larger concern would emerge. In order to be prepared to make these consequential choices in a manner that attends to one's faith convictions, a moral agent would need some experience of navigating moral decisions in a theological fashion upon which they could draw. Thus, if the moral decision a person makes about end-of-life care at a family member's bedside is supposed to embody their theological commitments, then they need training for this process before they arrive at the hospital door. The account developed in this book of how theological ethics can inform an agent's free time choices creates one place for this type of training to occur, but one space will hardly be sufficient alone. There is a need to extend this process of moral discernment more broadly, and fortunately the two transferable skills identified above can quite effectively contribute to this goal, if moral agents also work to cultivate these skills in other areas of their ordinary life.

First, agents ought to preserve the vision of God as the ultimate end who motivates the priority of leisure over recreation. This orientation obviously reinforces a more transcendent worldview and thus opens agents to the practical significance of faith for their own lives, but it also instructs agents in a new system of values that transcends mere utility. This is a consequential contribution to the integration of faith and life because there is an increasing temptation to define the value of experiences, things, and even people in relation to their—chiefly economic—utility. This temptation is particularly prominent in the United States, where utility has a certain pride of place in civic discourse, often serving as the default mode of public reasoning. This perspective, though potentially useful for generating an "overlapping consensus" in a pluralistic setting and thereby propelling necessary conversations, is nevertheless reductionistic, especially when contrasted with the theological vision that identifies at least some intrinsic value in all created things that have been given their existence by God.[3] Truly embodying this alternate vision requires embracing an alternate scale of values, specifically one that recognizes transcendence as an inherent good. To the extent that agents identify the value of the things, people, and experiences around them in relation to God, and seek to order their life according to the sort of use/enjoyment distinction that Augustine proposed, they have the means to overcome the reductionism of a strictly utilitarian outlook, and thus the ability to make moral choices with a clearer sense of what is at stake.

Second, openness to transcendence must be complemented by attentiveness to the common good that the principle and the virtue of everyday solidarity represent. Much like the emphasis on God as the ultimate end, this commitment to the common good is an especially important contribution in the United States, where an ethos of self-sufficiency and a spirit of rugged individualism tend to militate against a consistent awareness of and concern for the common good. Habituating an alternate disposition—which recognizes one's relational nature and prompts one to think in terms of relational responsibilities and not just individual rights—has the power to retrain the moral agent in a much more overtly Catholic way of thinking. As a result, the framework of everyday solidarity can yield a distinctly Catholic approach to moral discernment, helping moral agents strengthen their consciences through practical judgments in areas beyond leisure and recreation. To illustrate this point, consider how this process of discernment might play out in two additional spheres of ordinary life.

Perhaps the most appropriate sphere of ordinary life to explore beyond free time is the world of work, which has been the counterpart to many of the discussions in this book and which occupies an even greater share of a person's time, on average, than leisure and recreation. This area has received more explicit theological attention, but it is not always a place where people of faith internalize the connections to their religious convictions. As a result, work can benefit from the framework of everyday solidarity, if for no other reason than to raise awareness of the theological understanding of work already advanced by various Christian communities. The Roman Catholic view of work, for instance, champions the dignity of work on the basis of both the inherent value of the worker as a human being made in the image of God and the human fulfillment that comes from contributing to a project (like a job) that is necessarily larger than oneself.[4] Both these elements come to the forefront when a moral agent assesses work in light of the principle and the virtue of everyday solidarity.

For example, if a person were to decide what job to take based strictly on economic utility alone, then the decision would come down to the job providing the best remuneration, even though, as the discussion of sports' warped incentives revealed, the highest-paying jobs might not produce the best social outcomes. If a person were to use the framework of everyday solidarity to approach this question, however, the pertinent issues would need to change. The question of how a person might be able to use her or his talents (and passions) to make the world a better place becomes the guiding principle instead, prompting an agent to assess a potential job as a vocation rather than simply as a means of making money.[5] In this way, the worker's decision would be informed by the principle of everyday solidarity, since they would incorporate the needs of others into this vocational discernment process. At the same time, the concrete evaluation of this impulse would also require attentiveness to the impact of larger structural forces, just as the virtue of everyday solidarity would demand. Specifically, a person would need to consider the possibility that unjust structures might be behind the problems in the world that they feel called to address.[6] Also, a concern for others' ability to choose jobs based on vocational concerns rather than economic necessities would prompt a structural evaluation, at the very least to determine if larger forces were constraining people's choices. To the extent that workers recognized these forces and committed themselves to doing something about them, they would embody the virtue of everyday solidarity's emphasis on structural transformation for the benefit of the common good.

The impact of this application of everyday solidarity would be twofold. First, by reshaping the choice of a job into a more intentional form of vocational discernment, everyday solidarity would bring the Catholic theology of work to bear on workers' practical decisions. The question of how one's talents and interests can translate into action for the betterment of society obviously embraces the Catholic emphasis on the social significance of work as a means of contributing to the common good. It thereby calls attention to the dignity of work, but it also underscores the dignity of workers by helping moral agents to see them as human beings. This understanding of the human value of the worker is especially apparent when the vocational vision prompts an assessment of the social structures affecting work, because the desire to reform working conditions so that more people can embrace a vocational view of their jobs reflects an effort to ensure dignified experiences for all workers. The principle and the virtue of everyday solidarity can therefore combine to promote renewed attention to the theology of work and thus can help forge a stronger connection between faith and life. In the process, an even more fundamental change occurs, for behind this shift from a transactional view of work to a more vocational one lies a recognition of the human person's inherently relational nature. The question of how one's talents and passions might effect positive social change is meaningless without the deeper assumption that human flourishing depends on self-gift in relationship and on an ability to participate in the realization of the common good. In the sphere of work, then, the framework of everyday solidarity can reinforce a decidedly theological anthropology, creating a distinctively theological way of being a worker that amounts to a closer connection between faith and ordinary life.

To give a second example, the sphere of health can be transformed by everyday solidarity just as much as the sphere of work. Though this might seem to be a non sequitur, health care is an especially pertinent sphere for testing the potential of everyday solidarity, for two reasons. First, in the United States at least, health care costs are an everyday concern for most people, meaning that questions of health already occupy significant space in ordinary life. Second, decisions surrounding health and health care are the ones where people feel the moral weight of their decisions most acutely, as the prevalence and prominence of ethics committees at health care institutions attests. If the aim is to get people to practice a robustly theological form of moral discernment in their ordinary lives, then health is an appropriate sphere to consider.

The first way that everyday solidarity can transform moral discernment in the sphere of health is by expanding the notion of which health care choices constitute morally significant matters and therefore demand moral discernment in the first place. The typical assumption is that ethical concerns emerge in the sphere of health when people confront major decisions about treatment options, particularly decisions about whether and when to start or stop medical interventions. Of course, the framework of everyday solidarity can, and should, help to enrich moral discernment surrounding these questions, but its chief impact is to challenge this default assumption. Though not denigrating the importance of discerning well in these cases, everyday solidarity indicates that other choices in the sphere of health often have an even greater effect on the common good.

For example, diet and exercise are increasingly understood to be two of the most important factors shaping overall health, yet one rarely views the question of how one eats or how often one exercises as an ethical concern. To the extent that someone did recognize a moral dimension to either of these choices, he or she would seldom identify it as a social ethics concern. Nevertheless, there is a social aspect to these decisions that should not be ignored. In a finite health system, not everyone's demands can be met at the same time. Seeking care therefore has an effect on others. Admittedly, this effect is minor in most instances and hard to pinpoint in isolation; but when one thinks in terms of patterns of behavior, there is more at stake. The little decisions one makes now about diet and exercise will develop the patterns of behavior that affect whether one has the sort of serious medical condition that will tax the system, affecting not only one's own personal experience of health but others' as well. To the extent that some of these situations can be avoided by making better choices now, there is a moral weight to decisions about diet and exercise not only as a matter of self-care but also as a matter of social responsibility. The framework of everyday solidarity helps to highlight this latter dimension, so people can approach this everyday decision with a more holistic view of both its implications and themselves.

A similar way of thinking can shift the analysis of other common health care choices. The emphasis on concern for others at the heart of the principle of everyday solidarity can, for instance, help parents to remember that pediatric vaccines are not just for their children but for other children as well, thereby combating the growing influence of the antivaccination movement's unsupported fears and generating a better outcome for the common good, especially from the perspective of the preferential option for the poor.[7] Likewise, the attention to the structural implications of one's actions that undergirds the virtue of everyday solidarity can prompt people to be a little more judicious in their use of antibiotics, and a little less pushy about them in a health care setting, so that they might minimize their contributions to the growing problem of antibiotic resistance. This kind of prioritization of solidarity in everyday choices has the effect of creating a genuinely Catholic way of thinking in health care, wherein the theological anthropology at the heart of Catholicism informs the entire approach to health-related decisions. Importantly, this everyday approach can then lead to a more critical application of Catholic principles in precisely the areas of health care—like end-of-life care—where the Catholic Church so ardently encourages the faithful to be attentive to the teachings of the Church.[8] The practice of habituating discernment in small matters can thus prepare agents for stronger discernment in bigger ones as well.[9]

Obviously, there are other areas of ordinary life that could be the subject to discernment in light of everyday solidarity. And there are more ways in which everyday solidarity could make an impact on moral discernment in work and health as well. The point here is simply to give a general sense of how everyday solidarity can have a consequential effect on moral thinking throughout ordinary life, beyond just free time. The brief discussions here of work and health support this point, showing that the larger value of inculcating everyday solidarity for moral discernment in free time is in the development of transferable skills that can bring fundamental convictions of Catholic faith, like its relational conception of the human person, to bear on ordinary life as a whole. Of course, none of this is meant to suggest that everyday solidarity can fulfill the demands of the moral life on its own. It has the benefit of translating some of the most important Catholic theological claims for practical application to ordinary life, but it remains a finite tool. Even as a virtue, everyday solidarity is but one virtue among many, and the traditional notion of the unity of the virtues serves, at the very least, as a reminder of the fact that many virtues are supposed to be interconnected in a good life.[10] For everyday solidarity to function well—as both a principle for moral discernment in the process of conscience/2, and as a virtue empowering the necessary pursuit of social transformation—this overarching framework must complement, and be complemented by, larger commitments to charity and the demands of discipleship as a dynamic call from God. When it operates in this context, however, everyday solidarity can helpfully highlight the essential concerns that Christians ought to prioritize in their moral decisions as a result of these larger commitments. In this way, everyday solidarity can helpfully contribute to the grace-filled process of conscience formation as it habituates attention to the concerns of others in moral decisions.

Ultimately, everyday solidarity's contributions to the formation of conscience represent its real significance as an overarching framework for theological ethics in ordinary life, for insofar as everyday solidarity can guide decisions in free time, work, health, and other areas, it can facilitate the development of mature moral agents who are capable of responsible, nuanced discernment in conscience. This is an emphatically necessary task, if conscience is truly the place where one is "alone with God, Whose voice echoes in [one's] depths."[11] Moreover, if the Catholic Church is going to preserve Pope Francis's expansive vision of the role of conscience in the moral life, which acknowledges conscience's ability to conditionally countenance a person's temporary distance from the objective ideal, this kind of maturity and training throughout everyday life is the only way for ordinary Catholics to be able to fulfill their high calling.[12] By laying the groundwork for the cultivation of both the principle and the virtue of everyday solidarity during free time, this book is designed to contribute to this end. The best-case scenario is that it will be only one of an ever-expanding set of tools to make this vision of a more morally mature community a reality, and not the last or only word.

NOTES

1. Tillich, *Systematic Theology*, 1:13.
2. See Kaveny, *Prophecy without Contempt*, 72; and, more generally, 65–72.
3. On the idea of an "overlapping consensus" and its significance in pluralistic society, see Rawls, "Idea of an Overlapping Consensus."
4. John Paul II, *Laborem exercens*, 6, 9–10.
5. For the importance of these questions for the analysis of vocation, see Himes, *Doing the Truth in Love*, 57–58.
6. Himes, 59.
7. For more nuance on this point, see Kelly, "On Pediatric Vaccines."
8. This point is illustrated by Kelly, "Grace at the End of Life."
9. These implications of everyday solidarity for health care are outlined in more detail by Kelly, "From Quandary Cases to Ordinary Life."
10. Aquinas, *ST*, I-II.65.
11. *Gaudium et spes*, 16.
12. Francis, *Amoris laetitia*, 303.

BIBLIOGRAPHY

Abrams, Samuel J., and Morris P. Fiorina. "The Big Sort That Wasn't: A Skeptical Reexamination." *PS: Political Science and Politics* 45, no. 2 (April 2012): 203–9.

Abuhamdeh, Sami, Mihaly Csikszentmihalyi, and Baland Jalal. "Enjoying the Possibility of Defeat: Outcome Uncertainty, Suspense, and Intrinsic Motivation." *Motivation and Emotion* 39, no. 1 (February 2015): 1–10.

Aguiar, Mark, and Erik Hurst. *The Increase in Leisure Inequality*. Cambridge, MA: National Bureau of Economic Research, 2008.

Ahern, Kevin. *Structures of Grace: Catholic Organizations Serving the Global Common Good*. Maryknoll, NY: Orbis Books, 2015.

Albrecht, Gloria. *Hitting Home: Feminist Ethics, Women's Work, and the Betrayal of "Family Values."* New York: Continuum, 2002.

Allison, Maria T., and Margaret Carlisle Duncan. "Women, Work, and Flow." In Csikszentmihalyi and Csikszentmihalyi, *Optimal Experience*, 118–37.

Alonso, William, and Paul Starr. "Introduction." In *Politics and Number*, edited by William Alonso and Paul Starr, 1–6. Ithaca, NY: Russell Sage Foundation, 1987.

American Association of Neurological Surgeons. "Sports-Related Head Injury." March 20, 2019. www.aans.org/Patients/Neurosurgical-Conditions-and-Treatments/Sports-related-Head-Injury.

Anderson, Monica, Andrew Perrin, and Jingjing Jiang. "11% of Americans Don't Use the Internet; Who Are They?" Pew Research Center, March 5, 2018. www.pewresearch.org/fact-tank/2018/03/05/some-americans-dont-use-the-internet-who-are-they/.

Apostolicam actuositatem (Decree on the Apostolate of the Laity). November 18, 1965. www.vatican.va/archive/hist_councils/ii_vatican_council/documents/vat-ii_decree_19651118_apostolicam-actuositatem_en.html.

Aquinas, Thomas. *Summa Theologiae*. 2nd ed. Translated by Fathers of the English Dominican Province. Denver: New Advent, 2000. www.newadvent.org/summa/.

Aristotle. *Nicomachean Ethics*. Translated by Robert C. Bartlett and Susan D. Collins. Chicago: University of Chicago Press, 2011.

———. *Politics*. Translated by H. Rackham. Loeb Classical Library. London: William Heinemann, 1932.

Asken, Breton M., Molly J. Sullan, Steven T. DeKosky, Michael S. Jaffee, and Russell M. Bauer. "Research Gaps and Controversies in Chronic Traumatic Encephalopathy: A Review." *JAMA Neurology* 74, no. 10 (October 2017): 1255–62.

Augustine. *Confessions*. Translated by Henry Chadwick. Oxford: Oxford University Press, 1998.

———. *De doctrina Christiana*. Translated by Edmund Hill. Edited by John E. Rotelle. Hyde Park, NY: New City Press, 1996.

———. *The Literal Meaning of Genesis*. In *On Genesis*. Translated by Edmund Hill. Hyde Park, NY: New City Press, 2002.
Austin, Michael W., and R. Douglas Geivett, eds. *Being Good: Christian Virtues for Everyday Life*. Grand Rapids: Wm. B. Eerdmans, 2011.
Bacchiocchi, Samuele. "Remembering the Sabbath: The Creation-Sabbath in Jewish and Christian History." In *The Sabbath in Jewish and Christian Traditions*, edited by Tamara C. Eskenazi, Daniel J. Harrington, and William H. Shea, 69–97. New York: Crossroad, 1991.
Badenhausen, Kurt. "The Average Player Salary and Highest-Paid in NBA, MLB, NHL, NFL, and MLS." *Forbes*, December 15, 2016. www.forbes.com/sites/kurtbadenhausen/2016/12/15/average-player-salaries-in-major-american-sports-leagues/#31da3fed1050.
Baer, Helmut David. "The Fruit of Charity: Using the Neighbor in *De doctrina Christiana*." *Journal of Religious Ethics* 24, no. 1 (Spring 1996): 47–64.
Bain-Selbo, Eric. "From Lost Cause to Third-and-Long: College Football and the Civil Religion of the South." *Journal of Southern Religion* 11 (2009). http://jsr.fsu.edu/Volume11/Selbo.htm.
———. *Game Day and God: Football, Faith, and Politics in the American South*. Macon, GA: Mercer University Press, 2009.
Banner, Michael. *The Ethics of Everyday Life: Moral Theology, Social Anthropology, and the Imagination of the Human*. Oxford: Oxford University Press, 2013.
Barney, Alicia. "15 Companies with Innovative Parent-Friendly Policies." Parents, 2015. www.parents.com/parenting/work/parent-friendly-companies/.
Barrera, Albino. "Individuating Collective Responsibility." In Finn, *Distant Markets*, 220–40.
Barth, Karl. *Church Dogmatics*. Edited by Geoffrey William Bromiley and Thomas Forsyth Torrance. Translated by J. W. Edwards, O. Bussey, and Harold Knight. Edinburgh: T. & T. Clark, 1958.
Barton, Stephen C. *Discipleship and Family Ties in Mark and Matthew*. Cambridge: Cambridge University Press, 1994.
Baum, Gregory. "Structures of Sin." In *The Logic of Solidarity: Commentaries on Pope John Paul II's Encyclical On Social Concern*, edited by Gregory Baum and Robert Ellsberg, 110–26. Maryknoll, NY: Orbis Books, 1989.
Baym, Nancy K. *Personal Connections in the Digital Age*. Cambridge: Polity Press, 2010.
Beauchamp, Tom L. "The 'Four-Principles' Approach." In *Principles of Health Care Ethics*, edited by Raanan Gillon with Ann Lloyd, 3–12. New York: John Wiley & Sons, 1994.
Beauchamp, Tom L., and James F. Childress. *Principles of Biomedical Ethics*. Oxford: Oxford University Press, 1979.
Bellah, Robert. "Civil Religion in America." *Daedalus: Journal of the American Academy of Arts and Sciences* 96, no. 1 (Winter 1967): 1–21.
Bellah, Robert, Richard Madsen, William M. Sullivan, Ann Swidler, and Steven M. Tipton. *Habits of the Heart: Individualism and Commitment in American Life*. Berkeley: University of California Press, 1985.
Benedict XVI. *Caritas in veritate* (On Integral Human Development in Charity and Truth). June 29, 2009. http://w2.vatican.va/content/benedict-xvi/en/encyclicals/documents/hf_ben-xvi_enc_20090629_caritas-in-veritate.html.
Bennett, Fran. "The 'Living Wage,' Low Pay, and in Work Poverty: Rethinking the Relationships." *Critical Social Policy* 34, no. 1 (February 2014): 46–65.
Best, Shawn. *Leisure Studies: Themes and Perspectives*. Los Angeles: Sage, 2010.

Beyer, Gerald J. "The Meaning of Solidarity in Catholic Social Teaching." *Political Theology* 15, no. 1 (2014): 7–25.
Bilgrien, Marie Vianney. *Solidarity: A Principle, an Attitude, a Duty? Or the Virtue for an Interdependent World?* New York: Peter Lang, 1999.
Bishop, Bill. *The Big Sort: Why the Clustering of Like-Minded America Is Tearing Us Apart*. With Robert G. Cushing. Boston: Houghton Mifflin, 2008.
Black, C. Clifton. *Mark*. Nashville: Abingdon Press, 2011.
Bleinstein, Roman. "Leisure II: Tourism." In *Sacramentum Mundi: An Encyclopedia of Theology*, edited by Karl Rahner, 301–3. New York: Herder & Herder, 1970.
Bonhoeffer, Dietrich. *The Cost of Discipleship*. New York: Touchstone, 1995.
Borchard, Gregory A., and Anthony J. Ferri. "When in Las Vegas, Do as the Ancient Romans Did: Bread and Circuses Then and Now." *Journal of Popular Culture* 44, no. 4 (August 2011): 717–31.
Bowles, Nellie. "Human Contact Is Now a Luxury Good." *New York Times*, March 23, 2019. www.nytimes.com/2019/03/23/sunday-review/human-contact-luxury-screens.html.
Bretzke, James. *A Handbook of Roman Catholic Moral Terms*. Washington, DC: Georgetown University Press, 2013.
Brignall, Thomas Wells, III, and Thomas Van Valey. "The Impact of Internet Communications on Social Interaction." *Sociological Spectrum: Mid-South Sociological Association* 25, no. 3 (2005): 335–48.
Bruni, Luigino, and Luca Stanca. "Income Aspirations, Television, and Happiness: Evidence from the World Values Survey." *Kyklos* 59, no. 2 (2009): 209–25.
———. "Watching Alone: Relational Goods, Television and Happiness." *Journal of Economic Behavior and Organization* 65, nos. 3–4 (2008): 506–28.
Buckley, Michael J. "The Catholic University and the Promise Inherent in Its Identity." In *The Catholic University as Promise and Project: Reflections in a Jesuit Idiom*, 3–25. Washington, DC: Georgetown University Press, 1998.
Bureau of Labor Statistics. "Time Spent in Leisure and Sports Activities for the Civilian Population by Selected Characteristics, Averages Per Day on Weekdays and Weekends, 2017 Annual Averages." American Time Use Survey, June 28, 2018. https://web.archive.org/web/20190111181820/https://www.bls.gov/news.release/atus.t11b.htm.
Burke, Moira, Cameron Marlow, and Thomas Lento. "Social Network Activity and Social Well-Being." Paper presented at Conference on Human Factors in Computing Systems, Atlanta, April 10–15, 2010. www.cameronmarlow.com/media/burke-2010-social-well-being.pdf.
Burlingham, Bo. "Paradise Lost." *Inc.*, February 1, 2008. www.inc.com/magazine/20080201/paradise-lost.html.
Buswell, Lydia, Ramon B. Zabriskie, Neil Lundberg, and Alan J. Hawkins. "The Relationship between Father Involvement in Family Leisure and Family Functioning: The Importance of Daily Family Leisure." *Leisure Sciences* 34, no. 2 (March 2012): 172–90.
Byzalov, Dimitry. "Unbundling Cable Television: An Empirical Investigation." Working paper, Temple University, July 2010. https://astro.temple.edu/~dbyzalov/cable.pdf.
Cahill, Lisa Sowle. "Teleology, Utilitarianism, and Christian Ethics." *Theological Studies* 42, no. 4 (December 1981): 601–29.
Campbell, David E., Steven Yonish, and Robert D. Putnam. "Tuning In, Tuning Out Revisited: A Closer Look at the Causal Links between Television and Social Capital." Paper presented at annual meeting of American Political Science Association, Atlanta, September 2–5, 1999. www.hks.harvard.edu/fs/pnorris/Acrobat/TVAPSA99.PDF.

Carr, Nicholas. *The Shallows: What the Internet Is Doing to Our Brains*. New York: W. W. Norton, 2010.
Carroll, Charlotte. "Brett Favre on Youth Tackle Football: 'They Look like They're Going to Break in Half.'" *Sports Illustrated*, June 20, 2018. www.si.com/nfl/2018/06/20/brett-favre-wants-end-youth-tackle-football.
Catechism of the Catholic Church. 2nd ed. Vatican City: Libreria Editrice Vaticana, 2000.
Cates, Diana Fritz. *Aquinas on the Emotions: A Religious-Ethical Inquiry*. Washington, DC: Georgetown University Press, 2009.
———. "Love: A Thomistic Analysis." *Journal of Moral Theology* 1, no. 2 (June 2012): 1–30.
Clark, Meghan J. "Anatomy of a Social Virtue: Solidarity and Corresponding Vices." *Political Theology* 15, no. 1 (2014): 26–39.
Cloutier, David. "The Problem of Luxury in the Christian Life." *Journal of the Society of Christian Ethics* 32, no. 1 (Spring–Summer 2012): 3–20.
Coates, Dennis, and Brad R. Humphreys. "Do Economists Reach a Conclusion on Subsidies for Sports Franchises, Stadiums, and Mega-Events?" *Economic Journal Watch* 5, no. 3 (September 2008): 294–315.
Cochran, Elizabeth A. "The Moral Significance of Religious Affections: A Reformed Perspective on Emotion and Moral Formation." *Studies in Christian Ethics* 28, no. 2 (May 2015): 150–62.
Cohen, David L. "Comcast and Time Warner Cable Announce Merger, Detail Public Interest Benefits and Undertakings." Comcast, February 13, 2014. https://corporate.comcast.com/comcast-voices/comcast-and-time-warner-announce-merger-detail-public-interest-benefits-and-undertakings.
Collins, Keith. "Net Neutrality Has Officially Been Repealed: Here's How That Could Affect You." *New York Times*, June 11, 2018. www.nytimes.com/2018/06/11/technology/net-neutrality-repeal.html.
Commercial Café. "Work-Life Balance Survey: Gen Z, Millennials Are the Unhappiest Generations." March 26, 2019. www.commercialcafe.com/blog/work-life-balance-survey-2019/.
Connors, Russell, and Patrick McCormick. *Character, Choices, and Community: The Three Faces of Christian Ethics*. New York: Paulist Press, 1998.
Coolidge Corner Theatre. "Membership Information and Benefits." No date. www.coolidge.org/membership/benefits.
Copeland, M. Shawn. "Toward a Critical Christian Feminist Theology of Solidarity." In *Women and Theology*, edited by Mary Ann Hinsdale and Phyllis H. Kaminski, 3–38. Maryknoll, NY: Orbis Books, 1995.
Cowley, Ben, Darryl Charles, Michaela Black, and Ray Hickey. "Toward an Understanding of Flow in Video Games." *ACM Computers in Entertainment* 6, no. 2 (July 2008): 20:1–27.
Coyne, Sarah M., Alexander C. Jensen, Nathan J. Smith, and Daniel H. Erikson. "Super Mario Brothers and Sisters: Associations between Coplaying Video Games and Sibling Conflict and Affection." *Journal of Adolescence* 47 (February 2016): 48–56.
Coyne, Sarah M., Laura M. Padilla Walker, Laura Stockdale, and Randal D. Day. "Game On... Girls: Associations between Co-Playing Video Games and Adolescent Behavior and Family Outcomes." *Journal of Adolescent Health* 49, no. 2 (August 2011): 160–65.
Cristi, Marcela. *From Civil to Political Religion: The Intersection of Culture, Religion and Politics*. Waterloo, ON: Wilfrid Laurier University Press, 2001.
Crompton, John L. "Motivations for Pleasure Vacation." *Annals of Tourism Research* 6, no. 4 (October–December 1979): 408–24.

Crowe, Frederick E. "Complacency and Concern in the Thought of St. Thomas [1]." *Theological Studies* 20, no. 1 (March 1959): 1-39.
———. "Complacency and Concern in the Thought of St. Thomas [3]." *Theological Studies* 20, no. 3 (September 1959): 343-95.
Csikszentmihalyi, Isabella. "Flow in a Historical Context: The Case of the Jesuits." In Csikszentmihalyi and Csikszentmihalyi, *Optimal Experience*, 232-48.
Csikszentmihalyi, Mihaly. *Beyond Boredom and Anxiety: Experience Flow in Work and Play*. 25th anniversary ed. San Francisco: Jossey-Bass, 2000.
———. "Consciousness for the Twenty-First Century." *Zygon* 26, no. 1 (March 1991): 7-25.
———. *Creativity: Flow and the Psychology of Discovery and Invention*. New York: HarperCollins, 2013.
———. *Finding Flow: The Psychology of Engagement with Everyday Life*. New York: Basic Books, 1997.
———. *Flow: The Psychology of Optimal Experience*. New York: Harper & Row, 1990.
Csikszentmihalyi, Mihaly, and Isabella Csikszentmihalyi, eds. *Optimal Experience: Psychological Studies of Flow in Consciousness*. Cambridge: Cambridge University Press, 1988.
Csikszentmihalyi, Mihaly, and Douglas A. Kleiber. "Leisure and Self-Actualization." In Driver, Brown, and Peterson, *Benefits of Leisure*, 91-102.
Csikszentmihalyi, Mihaly, and Reed Larson. "Validity and Reliability of the Experience-Sampling Method." *Journal of Nervous and Mental Disease* 175, no. 9 (September 1987): 526-36.
Csikszentmihalyi, Mihaly, Philip Latter, and Christine Weinkauff Duranso. *Running Flow: Mental Immersion Techniques for Better Running*. Champaign, IL: Human Kinetics, 2017.
Curran, Charles E. *The Moral Theology of Pope John Paul II*. Washington, DC: Georgetown University Press, 2005.
Daniels, Norman. *Just Health: Meeting Health Needs Fairly*. Cambridge: Cambridge University Press, 2008.
Deal, Jennifer J. *Always On, Never Done? Don't Blame the Smartphone*. Greensboro, NC: Center for Creative Leadership, 2015.
DeCosse, David. "Conscience, Catholicism, and Politics." *Theological Studies* 78, no. 1 (March 2017): 171-92.
de Graaf, John, ed. *Take Back Your Time: Fighting Overwork and Time Poverty in America*. San Francisco: Berrett-Koehler, 2003.
de Grazia, Sebastian. *Of Time, Work, and Leisure*. New York: Twentieth Century Fund, 1962.
Dei verbum (Dogmatic Constitution on Divine Revelation). November 18, 1965. www.vatican.va/archive/hist_councils/ii_vatican_council/documents/vat-ii_const_19651118_dei-verbum_en.html.
Delaney, Kevin J., and Rick Eckstein. *Public Dollars, Private Stadiums: The Battle over Building Sports Stadiums*. New Brunswick, NJ: Rutgers University Press, 2003.
Derrick, Jaye L., Shira Gabriel, and Kurt Hugenberg. "Social Surrogacy: How Favored Television Programs Provide the Experience of Belonging." *Journal of Experimental Psychology* 45, no. 2 (February 2009): 352-62.
DeYoung, Rebecca Konyndyk. *Glittering Vices: A New Look at the Seven Deadly Sins and Their Remedies*. Grand Rapids: Brazos Press, 2009.
Dicastery for the Promotion of Integral Human Development. "Sustainable Tourism: A Tool for Development." August 1, 2017. https://press.vatican.va/content/salastampa/en/bollettino/pubblico/2017/08/01/170801c.html.

Donahue, John R., and Daniel J. Harrington. *The Gospel of Mark*. Collegeville, MN: Liturgical Press, 2002.
Doohan, Leonard. *Leisure: A Spiritual Need*. Eugene, OR: Wipf and Stock, 2016.
Doran, Kevin P. *Solidarity: A Synthesis of Personalism and Communalism in the Thought of Karol Wojtyla / Pope John Paul II*. New York: Peter Lang, 1996.
Driver, B. L., Perry J. Brown, and George L. Peterson, eds. *Benefits of Leisure*. State College, PA: Venture Publishing, 1991.
Duhigg, Charles. "How Companies Learn Your Secrets." *New York Times Magazine*, February 16, 2012. www.nytimes.com/2012/02/19/magazine/shopping-habits.html?page wanted=1&_r=1&hp.
Dunkelman, Marc J. *The Vanishing Neighbor: The Transformation of an American Community*. New York: W. W. Norton, 2014.
Dupont, Anthony. "To Use or Enjoy Humans? *Uti* and *Frui* in Augustine." In *Studia Patristica*. Vol. 43. Edited by Frances M. Young, M. J. Edwards, and P. M. Parvis. Leuven: Peeters, 2006.
Eisinger, Peter. "The Politics of Bread and Circuses: Building the City for the Visitor Class." *Urban Affairs Review* 35, no. 3 (January 2000): 316–33.
Elder-Vass, Dave. *The Causal Power of Social Structures: Emergence, Structure, and Agency*. Cambridge: Cambridge University Press, 2010.
Eliade, Mircea. *The Sacred and the Profane: The Nature of Religion*. Translated by Willard R. Trask. Orlando: Harcourt, 1987.
Ellacuría, Ignacio, and Jon Sobrino, eds. *Mysterium liberationis: Fundamental Concepts of Liberation Theology*. Maryknoll, NY: Orbis Books, 1993.
Ellis, Joseph M., and Hemant Sharma. "Can't Play Here: The Decline of Pick-up Soccer and Social Capital in the USA." *Soccer & Society* 14, no. 3 (2013): 364–85.
eMarketer. "Growth in Time Spent with Media Is Slowing." June 6, 2016. www.emarketer.com/Article/Growth-Time-Spent-with-Media-Slowing/1014042.
Evans, Christopher H. "Baseball as Civil Religion: The Genesis of an American Story." In *The Faith of Fifty Million: Baseball, Religion, and American Culture*, edited by Christopher H. Evans and William R. Herzog II, 13–33. Louisville: Westminster John Knox Press, 2002.
Evans, Tom, Petros Iosifidis, and Paul Smith. *The Political Economy of Television Sports Rights*. New York: Palgrave Macmillan, 2013.
Fagerberg, David. *Theologia Prima: What Is Liturgical Theology*. 2nd ed. Chicago: Liturgy Training Publications, 2004.
Farrell, Mike. "Kagan: Multichannel Affordability Plummets." *Multichannel News*, April 25, 2018. www.multichannel.com/news/kagan-multichannel-affordability-plummets.
Faus, José Ignacio González. "Sin." In Ellacuría and Sobrino, *Mysterium liberationis*, 532–42.
Federal Communications Commission. *2018 International Broadband Data Report*. www.fcc.gov/reports-research/reports/international-broadband-data-reports/international-broadband-data-report-4.
Ferguson, Christopher. "The Good, the Bad, and the Ugly: A Meta-Analytic Review of Positive and Negative Effects of Violent Video Games." *Psychiatric Quarterly* 78, no. 4 (December 2007): 309–16.
Finn, Daniel K. "Social Causality and Market Complicity: Specifying the Causal Roles of Persons and Structures." In Finn, *Distant Markets*, 243–58.
———. "What Is a Sinful Social Structure?" *Theological Studies* 77, no. 1 (March 2016): 136–64.

BIBLIOGRAPHY 225

Finn, Daniel K., ed. *Distant Markets, Distant Harms: Economic Complicity and Christian Ethics*. Oxford: Oxford University Press, 2014.
Florida, Richard. "The Inequality Puzzle in US Cities." *City Lab*, March 7, 2012. www.citylab.com/work/2012/03/inequality-puzzle-us-cities/858/.
———. "Where the Brains Are." *The Atlantic*, October 2006. www.theatlantic.com/magazine/archive/2006/10/where-the-brains-are/305202/.
Fontenot, Kayla, Jessica Semega, and Melissa Kollar. "Income and Poverty in the United States: 2017." US Census Bureau, September 12, 2018. www.census.gov/library/publications/2018/demo/p60-263.html.
Forney, Craig A. *The Holy Trinity of American Sports: Civil Religion in Football, Baseball, and Basketball*. Macon, GA: Mercer University Press, 2007.
Fowles, Jib. *Why Viewers Watch: A Reappraisal of Television's Effects*. Rev. ed. Newbury Park, CA: Sage, 1992.
France, R. T. *The Gospel of Mark: A Commentary on the Greek Text*. Grand Rapids: Wm. B. Eerdmans, 2002.
Francis. "Address during Visit to the Community at Varginha." July 25, 2013. http://w2.vatican.va/content/francesco/en/speeches/2013/july/documents/papa-francesco_20130725_gmg-comunita-varginha.html.
———. "Address to Participants in the Ecumenical Convention of Bishop-Friends of the Focolare Movement." November 7, 2014. http://w2.vatican.va/content/francesco/en/speeches/2014/november/documents/papa-francesco_20141107_vescovi-amici-movimento-focolari.html.
———. *Amoris laetitia* (On Love in the Family). March 19, 2016. https://w2.vatican.va/content/dam/francesco/pdf/apost_exhortations/documents/papa-francesco_esortazione-ap_20160319_amoris-laetitia_en.pdf.
———. *Evangelii gaudium* (The Joy of the Gospel). November 24, 2013. https://w2.vatican.va/content/francesco/en/apost_exhortations/documents/papa-francesco_esortazione-ap_20131124_evangelii-gaudium.html.
———. *Gaudete et exsultate* (On the Call to Holiness in Today's World). March 19, 2019. http://w2.vatican.va/content/francesco/en/apost_exhortations/documents/papa-francesco_esortazione-ap_20180319_gaudete-et-exsultate.html.
———. *Laudato si'* (On Care for Our Common Home). May 24, 2015. http://w2.vatican.va/content/francesco/en/encyclicals/documents/papa-francesco_20150524_enciclica-laudato-si.html.
———. "Message for the Celebration of the 2014 World Day of Peace." December 8, 2013. http://w2.vatican.va/content/francesco/en/messages/peace/documents/papa-francesco_20131208_messaggio-xlvii-giornata-mondiale-pace-2014.html.
———. "Message for World Food Day 2013." October 16, 2013. http://w2.vatican.va/content/francesco/en/messages/food/documents/papa-francesco_20131016_messaggio-giornata-alimentazione.html.
———. "Message of Pope Francis for the 48th World Communications Day: Communication at the Service of an Authentic Culture of Encounter." June 1, 2014. http://w2.vatican.va/content/francesco/en/messages/communications/documents/papa-francesco_20140124_messaggio-comunicazioni-sociali.html.
Frankena, William K. *Ethics*. 2nd ed. Englewood Cliffs, NJ: Prentice Hall, 1973.
Fraser, Jill Andresky. *White-Collar Sweatshop: The Deterioration of Work and Its Rewards in Corporate America*. New York: W. W. Norton, 2001.

Frey, Bruon S., Christine Benesch, and Alois Stutzer. "Does Watching TV Make Us Happy?" *Journal of Economic Psychology* 28, no. 3 (2007): 283–313.

Frontline. "League of Denial: The NFL's Concussion Crisis." PBS-TV, produced by Michael Kirk, Jim Gilmore, and Mike Wiser. October 3, 2013.

Frosdick, Steve, and Peter Marsh. *Football Hooliganism.* Portland, OR: Willan Publishing, 2005.

Fuchs, Josef. *Personal Responsibility and Christian Morality.* Translated by William Cleves et al. Washington, DC: Georgetown University Press, 1983.

Fukuyama, Francis. *The Great Disruption: Human Nature and the Reconstitution of the Social Order.* New York: Touchstone, 2000.

Gaillardetz, Richard, and Catherine E. Clifford. *Keys to the Council: Unlocking the Teaching of Vatican II.* Collegeville, MN: Liturgical Press, 2012.

Gaines, Cork. "Cable TV Customers Pay More than $9 Per Month for ESPN Whether They Watch or Not." *Business Insider,* April 27, 2017. www.businessinsider.com/cable-satellite-tv-sub-fees-espn-networks-2017-4.

Gaudium et spes (Pastoral Constitution on the Church in the Modern World). December 7, 1965. www.vatican.va/archive/hist_councils/ii_vatican_council/documents/vat-ii_cons_19651207_gaudium-et-spes_en.html.

Gergen, Kenneth J. "The Challenge of Absent Presence." In *Perpetual Contact: Mobile Communication, Private Talk, Public Performance,* edited by James E. Katz and Mark Aakhus, 226–41. Cambridge: Cambridge University Press, 2002.

Gilleman, Gérard. *The Primacy of Charity in Moral Theology.* Translated by William F. Ryan and André Vachon. Westminster, MD: Newman Press, 1959.

Giordan, Giuseppe, and Linda Woodhead. "Introduction: Prayer in Religion and Spirituality." In *Annual Review of the Sociology of Religion, Volume 4: Prayer in Religion and Spirituality.* Edited by Giuseppe Giordan and Linda Woodhead. Leiden: Brill, 2013.

Glasmeier, Amy K. "Living Wage Calculator." No date. http://livingwage.mit.edu.

Goergen, Donald. *A Theology of Jesus, Volume 1: The Mission and Ministry of Jesus.* Wilmington: Michael Glazier, 1986.

Goldstein, Valerie Saiving. "The Human Situation: A Feminist View." *Journal of Religion* 40, no. 2 (April 1960): 100–112.

Goodale, Thomas L., and Wes Cooper. "Philosophical Perspectives on Leisure in English-Speaking Countries." In Driver, Brown, and Peterson, *Benefits of Leisure,* 21–35.

———. "New Data Up: Calculation of the Living Wage." Living Wage Calculator, January 24, 2019. http://livingwage.mit.edu/articles/37-new-data-up-calculation-of-the-living-wage.

Godlewski, Lisa R., and Elizabeth M. Perse. "Audience Activity and Reality Television: Identification, Online Activity, and Satisfaction." *Communication Quarterly* 58, no. 2 (2010): 148–69.

Gorman, Thomas E., Douglas A. Gentile, and C. Shawn Green. "Problem Gaming: A Short Primer." *American Journal of Play* 10, no. 3 (Spring 2018): 309–27.

Gornick, Janet C., and Marica K. Meyers. "Supporting a Dual-Earner/Dual-Career Society." In Heymann and Beem, *Unfinished Work,* 371–408.

Grabb, Edward, Douglas Baer, and James Curtis. "The Origins of American Individualism: Reconsidering the Historical Evidence." *Canadian Journal of Sociology* 24, no. 4 (1999): 511–33.

Graham, Mark. "The Environmental Burden (Disaster?) of Catholic Act Analysis." *Political Theology* 10, no. 1 (2009): 101–14.

Gratton, Chris, and Harry Arne Solberg. *The Economics of Sports Broadcasting*. London: Routledge, 2007.
Gray, Christopher Berry. *Philosophy of Man at Recreation and Leisure*. New York: Peter Lang, 2007.
Gray, Heather M., Keiko Ishii, and Nalini Ambady. "Misery Loves Company: When Sadness Increases the Desire for Social Connectedness." *Personality and Social Psychology Bulletin* 37, no. 11 (November 2011): 1438–48.
Greitemeyer, Tobias, and Christopher Cox. "There's No 'I' in Team: Effects of Cooperative Video Games on Cooperative Behavior." *European Journal of Social Psychology* 43, no. 3 (April 2013): 224–28.
Greitemeyer, Tobias, and Dirk O. Mügge. "Video Games Do Affect Social Outcomes: A Meta-Analytic Review of the Effects of Violent and Prosocial Video Game Play." *Personality and Social Psychology Bulletin* 40, no. 5 (May 2014): 578–89.
Greitemeyer, Tobias, and Silvia Osswald. "Effects of Prosocial Video Games on Prosocial Behavior." *Journal of Personality and Social Psychology* 98, no. (2010): 211–21.
———. "Prosocial Video Games Reduce Aggressive Cognitions." *Journal of Experimental Social Psychology* 45, no. 4 (July 2009): 896–900.
Greitemeyer, Tobias, Eva Traut-Mattausch, and Silvia Osswald. "How to Ameliorate Negative Effects of Violent Video Games on Cooperation: Play It Cooperatively in a Team." *Computers in Human Behavior* 28, no. 4 (July 2012): 1465–70.
Gula, Richard. *Reason Informed by Faith: Foundations of Catholic Morality*. New York: Paulist Press, 1989.
Haidt, Jonathan. "The Emotional Dog and Its Rational Tail: A Social Intuitionist Approach to Moral Judgment." *Psychological Review* 108, no. 4 (2001): 814–34.
———. "The Emotional Dog Does Learn New Tricks: A Reply to Pizarro and Bloom (2003)." *Psychological Review* 110, no. 1 (2003): 197–98.
Hall, John A., and Charles Lindholm. *Is America Breaking Apart?* Princeton, NJ: Princeton University Press, 1999.
Hammerstein, Oscar, II. "Happy Talk." In *This I Believe: The Personal Philosophies of Remarkable Men and Women*, edited by Jay Allison and Dan Gediman, 106–8. New York: Henry Holt, 2006.
Hampton, Keith, Lauren Sessions Goulet, Cameron Marlow, and Lee Rainie. "Why Most Facebook Users Get More than They Give." Pew Research Center, February 3, 2012. www.pewinternet.org/2012/02/03/why-most-facebook-users-get-more-than-they-give/.
Hannam, Walter A. "*Ad illud ubi permanendum est*: The Metaphysics of St. Augustine's *Usus/Fruitio* Distinction in Relation to Love of Neighbour, *De doctrina Christiana*, I." In *Studia Patristica*. Vol. 38. Edited by Maurice F. Wiles, Edward Yarnold, and P. M. Parvis. Leuven: Peeters, 2001.
Harger, Kaitlyn, Brad R. Humphreys, and Amanda Ros. "Do New Sports Facilities Attract New Businesses?" *Journal of Sports Economics* 17, no. 5 (June 2016): 483–500.
Häring, Bernard. *The Law of Christ*. Westminster, MD: Newman Press, 1960.
Harline, Craig. *Sunday: A History of the First Day from Babylonia to the Super Bowl*. New York: Doubleday, 2007.
Harvey, Andrew S., and Arun K. Mukhopadhyay. "When Twenty-Four Hours Is Not Enough: Time Poverty of Working Parents." *Social Indicators Research* 82, no. 1 (May 2007): 57–77.
Hasel, Gerhard F. "The Sabbath in the Pentateuch." In *The Sabbath in Scripture and History*, edited by Kenneth A. Strand, 21–43. Washington, DC: Review and Herald Publishing, 1982.

Hays, Richard B. *The Moral Vision of the New Testament: Community, Cross, New Creation—A Contemporary Introduction to New Testament Ethics*. New York: HarperCollins, 1996.
Haythornthwaite, Caroline. "Social Networks and Internet Connectivity Effects." *Information, Communication & Society* 8, no. 2 (2005): 125–47.
———. "Strong, Weak, and Latent Ties and the Impact of New Media." *Information Society* 18 (2002): 385–401.
Heintzman, Paul. *Leisure and Spirituality: Biblical, Historical, and Contemporary Perspectives*. Grand Rapids: Baker Academic, 2015.
Heintzman, Paul, and Glen E. Van Andel. *Christianity and Leisure, Volume 2: Issues for the Twenty-First Century*. Sioux Center, IA: Dordt College Press, 2017.
Heintzman, Paul, Glen E. Van Andel, and Thomas L. Visker, eds. *Christianity and Leisure, Volume 1: Issues in a Pluralistic Society*. Sioux Center, IA: Dordt College Press, 2006.
Heitner, Darren. "Sports Industry to Reach $73.5 Billion by 2019." *Forbes*, October 19, 2015. www.forbes.com/sites/darrenheitner/2015/10/19/sports-industry-to-reach-73-5-billion-by-2019/#3d6ec7eb1b4b.
Hewlett, Sylvia Ann. "Addressing the Time Crunch of High Earners." In Heymann and Beem, *Unfinished Work*, 156–79.
Heyer, Kristin E. "Catholics in the Public Arena: How Faith Should Inform Catholic Voters and Politicians." In *Catholics and Politics: The Dynamic Tension between Faith and Power*. Edited by Kristin E. Heyer, Mark J. Rozell, and Michael A. Genovese. Washington, DC: Georgetown University Press, 2008.
———. "Social Sin and Immigration: Good Fences Make Bad Neighbors." *Theological Studies* 71, no. 2 (May 2010): 410–36.
Heymann, Jody, and Christopher Beem, eds. *Unfinished Work: Building Equality and Democracy in an Era of Working Families*. New York: New Press, 2005.
Hilbrecht, Margo, Susan M. Shaw, Fern M. Delamere, and Mark E. Havitz. "Experiences, Perspectives, and Meanings of Family Vacations for Children." *Leisure/Loisir* 32, no. 2 (2008): 541–71.
Himes, Kenneth. "Introduction." In Himes, *Modern Catholic Social Teaching*, 1–6.
———. "Poverty and Christian Discipleship." In Himes and Kelly, *Poverty*, 11–20.
———. "Social Sin and the Role of the Individual." *Annual of the Society of Christian Ethics* 6 (1996): 183–218.
Himes, Kenneth, ed. *Modern Catholic Social Teaching: Commentaries and Interpretations*. Washington, DC: Georgetown University Press, 2005.
Himes, Kenneth, and Conor M. Kelly, eds. *Poverty: Responding like Jesus*. Brewster, MA: Paraclete Press, 2018.
Himes, Michael. *Doing the Truth in Love: Conversations about God, Relationships, and Service*, with Don McNeill, Andrea Smith Shappell, Jan Pilarksi, Stacy Hennessy, Katie Bergin, and Sarah Keyes. New York: Paulist Press, 1995.
Hinze, Christine Firer. "Bridge Discourse on Wage Justice: Roman Catholic and Feminist Perspectives on the Family Living Wage." In *Feminist Ethics and the Catholic Moral Tradition*. Edited by Charles E. Curran, Margaret A. Farley, and Richard A. McCormick. New York: Paulist Press, 1996.
———. "The Drama of Social Sin and the (Im)possibility of Solidarity: Reinhold Niebuhr and Modern Catholic Social Teaching." *Studies in Christian Ethics* 22, no. 4 (2009): 442–60.

———. "Straining toward Solidarity in a Suffering World: *Gaudium et spes* 'After Forty Years.'" In *Vatican II: Forty Years Later*, edited by William Madges, 165–95. Maryknoll, NY: Orbis Books, 2006.
———. "Women, Families, and the Legacy of *Laborem exercens*: An Unfinished Agenda." *Journal of Catholic Social Thought* 6, no. 1 (2006): 63–92.
Hirschfeld, Mary. "How a Thomistic Moral Framework Can Take Social Causality Seriously." In Finn, *Distant Markets*, 146–70.
Hochschild, Arlie Russell. *The Second Shift*. With Anne Machung. Rev. ed. New York: Penguin Books, 2003.
———. *The Time Bind: When Work Becomes Home and Home Becomes Work*. New York: Metropolitan Books, 1997.
Hofstede, Geert, Gert Jan Hofstede, and Michael Minkov. *Cultures and Organizations: Software of the Mind; Intercultural Cooperation and Its Importance for Survival*. 3rd ed. New York: McGraw-Hill, 2010.
Hooghe, Marc. "Watching Television and Civic Engagement: Disentangling the Effects of Time, Programs, and Stations." *Harvard International Journal of Press/Politics* 7, no. 2 (Spring 2002): 84–104.
Hornberger, Laurel B., Ramon B. Zabriskie, and Patti Freeman. "Contributions of Family Leisure to Family Functioning among Single-Parent Families." *Leisure Sciences* 32, no. 2 (2010): 143–61.
Huber, Linda. "Is New York City's Public Wi-Fi Actually Connecting the Poor?" Motherboard, September 14, 2016. https://motherboard.vice.com/en_us/article/vv7pw3/linknyc-is-bringing-internet-to-new-yorks-most-disconnected-people.
Humphreys, Brad R. "Facility Subsidies Redux." *Journal of Policy Analysis and Management* 38, no. 1 (Winter 2019): 277–79.
———. "Should the Construction of New Professional Sports Facilities Be Subsidized?" *Journal of Policy Analysis and Management* 38, no. 1 (Winter 2019): 264–70.
Hwong, Connie. "How Consumers Spend Their Time Online." Verto Analytics, February 2, 2018. www.vertoanalytics.com/how-consumers-spend-time-online/.
Isasi-Díaz, Ada María. *Mujerista Theology: A Theology for the Twenty-First Century*. Maryknoll, NY: Orbis Books, 1996.
Iso-Ahola, Seppo E. "On the Theoretical Link between Personality and Leisure." *Psychology Reports* 39, no. 1 (August 1976): 3–10.
———. *The Social Psychology of Leisure and Recreation*. Dubuque, IA: W. C. Brown, 1980.
Jackson, Maggie. *Distracted: The Erosion of Attention and the Coming Dark Age*. Amherst, NY: Prometheus Books, 2008.
Jackson, Susan A. "Athletes in Flow: A Qualitative Investigation of Flow States in Elite Figure Skaters." *Journal of Applied Sport Psychology* 4, no. 2 (1992): 161–80.
Jackson, Susan, and Mihaly Csikszentmihalyi. *Flow in Sports: The Keys to Optimal Experiences and Performances*. Champaign, IL: Human Kinetics, 1999.
———. *The Social Psychology of Leisure and Recreation*. Dubuque, IA: W. C. Brown, 1980.
———. "Toward a Conceptual Understanding of the Flow Experience in Elite Athletes." *Research Quarterly for Exercise and Sport* 67, no. 1 (March 1996): 76–90.
Jeong, Eui Jun, Dan J. Kim, and Dong Min Lee. "Why Do Some People Become Addicted to Digital Games More Easily? A Study of Digital Game Addiction from a Psychosocial Health Perspective." *International Journal of Human-Computer Interaction* 33, no. 3 (2017): 199–214.

John Paul II. *Centesimus annus* (On the Hundredth Anniversary of *Rerum novarum*). May 1, 1991. www.vatican.va/holy_father/john_paul_ii/encyclicals/documents/hf_jp-ii_enc_01051991_centesimus-annus_en.html.

———. *Laborem exercens* (On Human Work). September 14, 1981. www.vatican.va/holy_father/john_paul_ii/encyclicals/documents/hf_jp-ii_enc_14091981_laborem-exercens_en.html.

———. "Message for the 22nd World Tourism Day 2001." June 9, 2001. https://w2.vatican.va/content/john-paul-ii/en/messages/tourism/documents/hf_jp-ii_mes_20010619_giornata-mondiale-turismo.html.

———. "Message for the 23rd World Day of Tourism 2002." June 24, 2002. https://w2.vatican.va/content/john-paul-ii/en/messages/tourism/documents/hf_jp-ii_mes_20020625_xxiii-giornata-mondiale-turismo.html.

———. "Message for the 24th World Day of Tourism 2003. June 11, 2003. https://w2.vatican.va/content/john-paul-ii/en/messages/tourism/documents/hf_jp-ii_mes_20030626_xxiv-giornata-mondiale-turismo.html.

———. "Message for the World Day of Migrants and Refugees 2005." November 24, 2004. https://w2.vatican.va/content/john-paul-ii/en/messages/migration/documents/hf_jp-ii_mes_20041124_world-migration-day-2005.html.

———. "Message of Pope John Paul II for World Day of Tourism 2000." July 29, 2000. https://w2.vatican.va/content/john-paul-ii/en/messages/tourism/documents/hf_jp-ii_mes_20000801_giornata-mondiale-turismo.html.

———. *Reconciliatio et paenitentia* (On Reconciliation and Penance in the Mission of the Church Today). December 2, 1984. http://w2.vatican.va/content/john-paul-ii/en/apost_exhortations/documents/hf_jp-ii_exh_02121984_reconciliatio-et-paenitentia.html.

———. *Sollicitudo rei socialis* (On Social Concern). December 30, 1987. www.vatican.va/holy_father/john_paul_ii/encyclicals/documents/hf_jp-ii_enc_30121987_sollicitudo-rei-socialis_en.html.

———. *Veritatis splendor* (On the Splendor of Truth). August 6, 1993. http://w2.vatican.va/content/john-paul-ii/en/encyclicals/documents/hf_jp-ii_enc_06081993_veritatis-splendor.html.

John XXIII. *Mater et magistra* (On Christianity and Social Progress). May 15, 1961. www.vatican.va/holy_father/john_xxiii/encyclicals/documents/hf_j-xxiii_enc_15051961_mater_en.html.

———. *Pacem in terris* (On Establishing Universal Peace in Truth, Justice, Charity, and Liberty). April 11, 1963. http://w2.vatican.va/content/john-xxiii/en/encyclicals/documents/hf_j-xxiii_enc_11041963_pacem.html.

Johnson, Elizabeth. *Friends of God and Prophets: A Feminist Theological Reading of the Communion of the Saints*. New York: Continuum, 1998.

Jones, Christopher D., and Conor M. Kelly. "Sloth: America's Ironic Structural Vice." *Journal of the Society of Christian Ethics* 37, no. 2 (Fall 2017): 117–34.

Katz, James E., and Ronald E. Rice. "Project Syntopia: Social Consequences of Internet Use." *IT & Society* 1, no. 1 (Summer 2002): 166–79. http://rrice.faculty.comm.ucsb.edu/A74KatzRice2002.pdf.

Kaveny, Cathleen. *Law's Virtues: Fostering Autonomy and Solidarity in American Society*. Washington, DC: Georgetown University Press, 2012.

———. *Prophecy without Contempt: Religious Discourse in the Public Square*. Cambridge, MA: Harvard University Press, 2016.

Kaye, Lynda K., and Jo Bryce. "Go with the Flow: The Experience and Affective Outcomes of Solo versus Social Gameplay." *Journal of Gaming and Virtual Worlds* 6, no. 1 (March 2014): 49–60.
Keating, Thomas. "The Method of Centering Prayer: The Prayer of Consent." *Contemplative Outreach.* No date. www.contemplativeoutreach.org/sites/default/files/private/method_cp_eng-2016-06_0.pdf.
Keenan, James F. "Called to Conscience." *America* 216, no. 1 (January 2, 2017): 14–18.
———. "Examining Conscience." *America* 214, no. 12 (April 4–11, 2016): 15–17.
———. *Moral Wisdom: Lessons and Texts from the Catholic Tradition.* 2nd ed. Lanham, MD: Rowman & Littlefield, 2010.
———. "Proposing Cardinal Virtues." *Theological Studies* 56, no. 4 (December 1995): 709–29.
———. "Virtue Ethics." In *Christian Ethics: An Introduction*, edited by Bernard Hoose, 84–94. London: Cassell, 1998.
———. *Virtues for Ordinary Christians.* Franklin, WI: Sheed and Ward, 1996.
———. *The Works of Mercy: The Heart of Catholicism.* 2nd ed. Lanham, MD: Sheed & Ward, 2008.
Kelly, Conor M. "Depth in an Age of Digital Distraction: The Value of a Catholic College in Today's World." *Journal of Catholic Higher Education* 34, no. 2 (Summer 2015): 113–33.
———. "From Quandary Cases to Ordinary Life: New Opportunities to Connect Social Ethics and Health Care Ethics in a Lasting Way." Paper presented at Annual Meeting of Society of Christian Ethics, Washington, DC, January 2020.
———. "Grace at the End of Life: Rethinking Ordinary and Extraordinary Means in a Global Context." *Journal of Moral Theology* 8, no. 1 (January 2019): 89–113.
———. "The Nature and Operation of Structural Sin: Additional Insights from Theology and Moral Psychology." *Theological Studies* 80, no. 2 (June 2019): 293–327.
———. "On Pediatric Vaccines and Catholic Social Teaching." *Horizons* 45, no. 2 (December 2018): 287–316.
———. "The Role of the Moral Theologian in the Church." *Theological Studies* 77, no. 4 (December 2016): 922–48.
Kelly, David. *Medico-Moral Problems.* Saint Louis: Catholic Hospital Association of the United States and Canada, 1958.
Kelly, John R. "Commodification of Leisure: Trend or Tract." *Loisir et Société* 9, no. 2 (1986): 455–76.
Kimiecik, Jay C. "Play Ball? Reflections on My Father's Youth Baseball Experiences and Why They Matter." *American Journal of Play* 8, no. 3 (April 2016): 379–95.
Knauer, Peter. "The Hermeneutic Function of the Principle of Double Effect." In *Readings in Moral Theology No. 1: Moral Norms and the Catholic Tradition*, edited by Charles Curran and Richard McCormick, 1–39. New York: Paulist Press, 1979.
Konnikova, Maria. "Why Gamers Can't Stop Playing First-Person Shooters." *New Yorker*, November 26, 2013. www.newyorker.com/online/blogs/elements/2013/11/the-psychology-of-first-person-shooter-games.html.
Kotva, Joseph, Jr. *The Christian Case for Virtue Ethics.* Washington, DC: Georgetown University Press, 1996.
Kovacik, Robert, and Jake Levin. "Red Sox Fan Recovering after Assault by Dodgers Fans." NECN, November 1, 2018. www.necn.com/news/sports/Red-Sox-Fan-Recovering-After-Assault-by-Dodgers-Fans-499131191.html.

Kraus, Richard. *Recreation and Leisure in Modern Society.* New York: Appleton-Century-Crofts, 1971.

Kruenegel-Farr, Dabbie S. "Perceptions of Family Vacation and Family Cohesion and the Moderating Effects of Parenting Style." PhD diss., University of North Texas, 2014.

Kubey, Robert, and Mihaly Csikszentmihalyi. "Television Addiction Is No Mere Metaphor." *Scientific American* 286, no. 2 (February 2002): 74–80.

———. *Television and Quality of Life: How Viewing Shapes Everyday Experience.* Hillsdale, NJ: Lawrence Erlbaum Associates, 1990.

Kuo, Calvin, Lyndia Wu, Jesus Loza, Daniel Senif, Scott C. Anderson, and David B. Camarillo. "Comparison of Video-Based and Sensor-Based Head Impact Exposure." *PLoS One* 13, no. 6 (June 2018): e0199238.

La Gorce, Tammy. "Tipping May Be the Norm, but Not for Hotel Housekeepers." *New York Times*, October 30, 2017. www.nytimes.com/2017/10/30/business/hotel-housekeeper-tipping.html.

Lamoureux, Patricia A. "Commentary on *Laborem exercens* (On Human Work)." In Himes, *Modern Catholic Social Teaching*, 389–414.

———. "Justice for Wage Earners: Retrieving Insights from the Catholic Community." *Horizons* 28, no. 2 (2001): 211–36.

Laravea, Merrick. "South Korea's Internet Infrastructure Shows How Net Neutrality Should Be Done." *Forbes*, January 26, 2018. www.forbes.com/sites/outofasia/2018/01/26/south-koreas-internet-infrastructure-shows-the-fcc-how-neutrality-should-be-done/#ae0646f581bc.

Lawler, Michael, and Todd Salzman. "Virtue Ethics: Natural and Christian." *Theological Studies* 74, no. 2 (June 2013): 442–73.

Lee, Jane. "Why Does South Korea Have Faster Internet for a Cheaper Price Tag?" Public Knowledge, July 19, 2017. www.publicknowledge.org/news-blog/blogs/why-does-south-korea-have-faster-internet-for-a-cheaper-price-tag.

Lehto, Xinran Y., Y-Chin Lin, Yi Chen, and Soojin Choi. "Family Vacation Activities and Family Cohesion." *Journal of Travel and Tourism Marketing* 29, no. 8 (2012): 835–50.

Lemon v. Kurtzman. 403 US 602 (1971).

Lenzen, Manfred, Ya-Yen Sun, Futu Faturay, Yuan-Peng Ting, Arne Geschke, and Arunima Malik. "The Carbon Footprint of Global Tourism." *Nature Climate Change* 8 (2018): 522–28.

Leo XIII. *Rerum novarum* (On Capital and Labor). May 15, 1981. http://w2.vatican.va/content/leo-xiii/en/encyclicals/documents/hf_l-xiii_enc_15051891_rerum-novarum.html.

Leslie, Ian. "Watch It While It Lasts: Our Golden Age of Television," *Financial Times*, April 13, 2017. www.ft.com/content/68309b3a-1f02-11e7-a454-ab04428977f9.

Limelight Networks. "The State of User Experience 2017." February 14, 2019. www.limelight.com/resources/white-paper/state-of-user-experience-2017/#socialmedia.

Ling, Richard. *New Tech, New Ties: How Mobile Communication Is Reshaping Social Cohesion.* Cambridge, MA: MIT Press, 2008.

Lipset, Seymour Martin. *American Exceptionalism: A Double-Edged Sword.* New York: W. W. Norton, 1996.

Livingston, Gretchen. "Among 41 Nations, US Is the Outlier When It Comes to Paid Parental Leave." Pew Research Center, September 26, 2016. www.pewresearch.org/fact-tank/2016/09/26/u-s-lacks-mandated-paid-parental-leave/.

Logan, Richard D. "Flow in 'Solitary Ordeals.'" *Journal of Humanistic Psychology* 25, no. 4 (Fall 1997): 79–89.
Luce, Stephanie. *Fighting for a Living Wage*. Ithaca, NY: ILR Press, 2004.
Lumen gentium (Dogmatic Constitution on the Church). November 21, 1964. www.vatican.va /archive/hist_councils/ii_vatican_council/documents/vat-ii_const_19641121_lumen -gentium_en.html.
Machan, Tibor. "Liberalism and Atomistic Individualism." *Journal of Value Inquiry* 34, nos. 2–3 (September 2000): 227–47.
MacIntyre, Alasdair. *After Virtue: A Study in Moral Theory*. 3rd ed. Notre Dame, IN: University of Notre Dame Press, 2007.
Malesic, Jonathan. "Taming the Demon." *Commonweal* 146, no. 3 (February 8, 2019): 10–15.
———. "When Work and Meaning Part Ways." *Hedgehog Review* 20, no. 3 (Fall 2018): 120–29.
Mares, Marie-Louise, and Emory H. Woodard IV. "In Search of the Older Audience: Adult Age Differences in Television Viewing." *Journal of Broadcasting and Electronic Media* 50, no. 4 (December 2006): 595–614.
Martin, James. *The Jesuit Guide to (Almost) Everything: A Spirituality for Real Life*. New York: HarperCollins, 2010.
Massingale, Bryan. "*Vox victimarum vox Dei*: Malcolm X as Neglected 'Classic' for Catholic Theological Reflection." *Proceedings of the Catholic Theological Society of America* 65 (2010): 63–88.
Matheson, Victor. "Is There a Case for Subsidizing Sports Stadiums?" *Journal of Policy Analysis and Management* 38, no. 1 (Winter 2019): 271–77.
———. "Response to Professor Humphreys." *Journal of Policy Analysis and Management* 38, no. 1 (Winter 2019): 279–81.
Matthiesen, Michon M. "'The Justice of Christ Become Fruitful': Thomas Aquinas and Romano Guardini on the *Iustitia* of Worship." *Antiphon* 20, no. 2 (2016): 96–122.
May, William E. "Work, Theology of." In *The New Dictionary of Catholic Social Thought*, edited by Judith A. Dwyer, 991–1002. Collegeville, MN: Liturgical Press, 1994.
McAlone, Nathan. "Get Ready for Traditional TV to Have Historically Brutal Subscriber Losses This Quarter." *Business Insider*, June 6, 2017. www.businessinsider.com/cable-tv -subscriber-losses-q2-chart-2017-6.
McAlone, Nathan, and David Z. Morris. "Viewers Are Ditching Cable for Streaming Faster than Anyone Expected." *Fortune*, April 29, 2018. http://fortune.com/2018/04/29 /viewers-cable-streaming/.
McAuliffe, Patricia. *Fundamental Ethics: A Liberationist Approach*. Washington, DC: Georgetown University Press, 1993.
McCormick, Patrick. "Fair Trade Tourism: Practicing Hospitality and Keeping the Sabbath in a Foreign Land." In *Living with(out) Borders: Catholic Theological Ethics on the Migrations of Peoples*, edited by Agnes M. Brazal and María Teresa Dávila, 162–72. Maryknoll, NY: Orbis Books, 2016.
———. "The Good Sojourner: Third World Tourism and the Call of Hospitality." *Journal of the Society of Christian Ethics* 24, no. 1 (2004): 89–104.
McGowan, Andrew B. "To Use and to Enjoy: Augustine and Ecology." *St. Mark's Review* 212, no. 2 (May 2010): 89–99.
McIlwraith, Robert D. "'I'm Addicted to Television': The Personality, Imagination, and TV Watching Patterns of Self-Identified TV Addicts." *Journal of Broadcasting & Electronic Media* 42, no. 3 (1998): 371–86.

McLean, Daniel D., and Amy R. Hurd. *Kraus' Recreation and Leisure in Modern Society*. 10th ed. Burlington, MA: Jones and Bartlet Learning, 2015.
McQuillan, Jeff, and Gisela Conde. "The Conditions of Flow in Reading; Two Studies of Optimal Experience." *Reading Psychology* 17, no. 2 (1996): 109–35.
Meier, John P. *A Marginal Jew: Rethinking the Historical Jesus, Volume 3: Companions and Competitors*. New York: Doubleday, 2001.
Meyersohn, Rolf. "Television and the Rest of Leisure." *Public Opinion Quarterly* 32, no. 1 (1968): 102–12.
Mez, Jesse, Daniel H. Daneshvar, and Patrick T. Kiernan. "Clinicopathological Evaluation of Chronic Traumatic Encephalopathy in Players of American Football." *Journal of the American Medical Association* 318, no. 4 (July 25, 2017): 360–70.
Miller, Vincent J. *Consuming Religion: Christian Faith and Practice in a Consumer Culture* New York: Continuum, 2004.
Milwaukee Film. "Milwaukee Film Membership Levels." No date. https://mkefilm.org/memberships.
Mishel, Lawrence, Josh Bivens, Elise Gould, and Heidi Shierholz. *The State of Working America*. 12th ed. Ithaca, NY: Cornell University Press, 2012.
Misra, Shalini, Lulu Cheng, Jamie Genevie, and Miao Yuan. "The iPhone Effect: The Quality of In-Person Social Interactions in the Presence of Mobile Devices." *Environment and Behavior* 48, no. 2 (2014): 275–98.
Mitchell, Louise A. "Major Changes in *Principles of Biomedical Ethics*: A Review of Seven Editions of Beauchamp and Childress." *National Catholic Bioethics Quarterly* 14, no. 3 (Autumn 2014): 459–75.
Moltmann, Jürgen. *Jesus Christ for Today's World*. Translated by Margaret Kohl. Minneapolis: Fortress Press, 1994.
Murray, Caitlin. "Here Are the Strongest Arguments the USWNT Makes in Its Discrimination Lawsuit." *Yahoo Sports*, March 11, 2019. https://sports.yahoo.com/here-are-the-strongest-arguments-the-uswnt-makes-in-its-discrimination-lawsuit-230443224.html.
Murray, Mark. "Poll: Nearly Half of Parents Would Discourage Football Due to Concussions." NBC News, February 2, 2018. www.nbcnews.com/politics/first-read/poll-nearly-half-parents-would-discourage-football-due-concussions-n843836.
National Council of State Legislatures. "State Minimum Wages." January 7, 2019. www.ncsl.org/research/labor-and-employment/state-minimum-wage-chart.aspx.
Naughton, Michael. "Distributors of Justice: A Case for a Just Wage." In *A Worker Justice Reader: Essential Writings on Religion and Labor*, edited by Joy Heine and Cynthia Brooke, 165–67. Maryknoll, NY: Orbis Books, 2010.
Neal, David T., Wendy Wood, and Jeffrey M. Quinn. "Habits: A Repeat Performance." *Current Directions in Psychological Science* 15, no. 4 (August 2006): 198–202.
Neel, Douglas E., and Joel A. Pugh. *The Food and Feasts of Jesus: Inside the World of First-Century Fare*. Lanham, MD: Rowman & Littlefield, 2012.
Neitz, Mary Jo, and James V. Spickard. "Steps toward a Sociology of Religious Experience: The Theories of Mihaly Csiksentmihalyi and Alfred Schutz." *Sociological Analysis* 51, no. 1 (Spring 1990): 15–33.
Neulinger, John. *The Psychology of Leisure*. 2nd ed. Springfield, IL: C. C. Thomas, 1981.
Neumark, David, and William L. Wascher. *Minimum Wages*. Cambridge, MA: MIT Press, 2008.
Neumeyer, Martin H., and Esther S. Neumeyer. *Leisure and Recreation*. 3rd ed. New York: Ronald Press, 1958.

Neville, Graham. *Free Time: Toward a Theology of Leisure*. Birmingham: Birmingham University Press, 2004.
Niebuhr, Reinhold. *An Interpretation of Christian Ethics*. New York: Harper & Brothers, 1935.
———. *The Nature and Destiny of Man, Volume 1: Human Nature*. Louisville: Westminster John Knox Press, 1974.
Nielsen. "Time Flies: US Adults Now Spend Nearly Half a Day Interacting with Media." July 31, 2018. www.nielsen.com/us/en/insights/news/2018/time-flies-us-adults-now-spend-nearly-half-a-day-interacting-with-media.print.html.
Noelle-Neumann, E. "Stationen der Glücksforschung." In *Lesegluck: Eine vergessene Erfahrung?* Edited by A. Bellebaum and L. Muth. Opladen: Westdeutscher Verlag, 1996.
Noonan, John T. *The Scholastic Analysis of Usury*. Cambridge, MA: Harvard University Press, 1957.
Norman, Alex, and Carole M. Cusack, eds. *Religion, Pilgrimage, and Tourism*. 4 vols. New York: Routledge, 2015.
O'Connell, Timothy E. *Principles for a Catholic Morality*. Rev. ed. San Francisco: Harper and Row, 1990.
O'Connor, Brian. *Idleness: A Philosophical Essay*. Princeton, NJ: Princeton University Press, 2018.
O'Connor, William Riordan. "The Uti/Frui Distinction in Augustine's Ethics." *Augustinian Studies* 14 (1983): 45–62.
O'Donovan, Oliver. "*Usus* and *Fruitio* in Augustine, *De doctrina Christiana* I." *Journal of Theological Studies* 33, no. 2 (October 1982): 361–97.
Oldenburg, Ray. *The Great Good Place: Cafés, Coffee Shops, Community Centers, Beauty Parlors, General Stores, Bars, Hangouts, and How They Get You through the Day*. 2nd ed. New York: Marlowe, 1997.
Oliveira, Helder Zimmermann, Victor Fernandes Pinto Gomes, and Renato Miranda. "The Flow State in Young Basketball Players." *Psicologia em Estudo* 20, no. 1 (2015): 95–106.
Origins. "Sterilization in Catholic Hospitals, Statement of the Vatican Doctrinal Congregation." 6, no. 3 (1976): 33–35.
Ourand, John. "ESPN's New Deal Doubles Rights Fee." *Sports Business Daily*, May 9, 2016. www.sportsbusinessdaily.com/Journal/Issues/2016/05/09/Media/ESPN-WNBA.aspx.
Paul VI. *Populorum progressio* (On the Development of Peoples). March 26, 1967. http://w2.vatican.va/content/paul-vi/en/encyclicals/documents/hf_p-vi_enc_26031967_populorum.html.
Perrin, Andrew, and Jingjing Jiang. "About a Quarter of US Adults Say They Are 'Almost Constantly' Online." Pew Research Center, March 14, 2018. https://web.archive.org/web/20180306012502/http://www.pewresearch.org/fact-tank/2018/03/05/some-americans-dont-use-the-internet-who-are-they/.
Perry, Susan K. *Writing in Flow: Keys to Enhanced Creativity*. Cincinnati: Writer's Digest Books, 1999.
Perse, Elizabeth M., and Alan M. Rubin. "Chronic Loneliness and Television Use." *Journal of Broadcasting and Electronic Media* 34, no. 1 (Winter 1990): 37–53.
Peters, Rebecca Todd. *Solidarity Ethics: Transformation in a Globalized World*. Minneapolis: Fortress Press, 2014.
Pew Research Center. "Internet/Broadband Fact Sheet." February 5, 2018. www.pewinternet.org/fact-sheet/internet-broadband/.
Pfeil, Margaret. "Doctrinal Implications of Magisterial Use of the Language of Social Sin." *Louvain Studies* 27, no. 2 (Summer 2002): 132–52.

Pieper, Josef. *Leisure: The Basis of Culture*. Translated by Alexander Dru. New York: Pantheon Books, 1952.

Pius XI. *Quadragesimo anno* (On Reconstruction of the Social Order). May 15, 1931. http://w2.vatican.va/content/pius-xi/en/encyclicals/documents/hf_p-xi_enc_19310515_quadragesimo-anno.html.

Pius XII. *Summi pontificatus* (On the Unity of Human Society). October 20, 1939. http://w2.vatican.va/content/pius-xii/en/encyclicals/documents/hf_p-xii_enc_20101939_summi-pontificatus.html.

Pledge Sports. "Biggest TV Rights Deals in Sports." January 2018. www.pledgesports.org/2018/01/biggest-tv-rights-deals-in-sport/.

Poff, Raymond A., Ramon B. Zabriskie, and Jasmine A. Townsend. "Modeling Family Leisure and Related Family Constructs: A National Survey of US Parent and Youth Perspectives." *Journal of Leisure Research* 42, no. 3 (2010): 365–91.

Pohl, Christine. *Making Room: Recovering Hospitality as a Christian Tradition*. Grand Rapids: Wm. B. Eerdmans, 1999.

Pollin, Robert, Mark Brenner, Jeannette Wicks-Linn, and Stephanie Luce. *A Measure of Fairness: The Economics of Living Wages and Minimum Wages in the United States*. Ithaca, NY: ILR Press, 2008.

Pollin, Robert, and Stephanie Luce. *The Living Wage: Building a Fair Economy*. New York: New Press, 1998.

Pontifical Council for Justice and Peace. *Compendium of the Social Doctrine of the Church*. Washington, DC: US Conference of Catholic Bishops, 2004.

Pope, Stephen J. *The Evolution of Altruism and the Ordering of Love*. Washington, DC: Georgetown University Press, 1994.

———. "The Order of Love and Recent Catholic Ethics: A Constructive Proposal." *Theological Studies* 52, no. 2 (June 1991): 255–88.

Postman, Neil. *Amusing Ourselves to Death: Public Discourse in the Age of Show Business*. 20th annual ed. New York: Penguin Books, 2005.

Powers, William. *Hamlet's Blackberry: A Practical Philosophy for Building a Good Life in the Digital Age*. New York: HarperCollins, 2010.

Pressman, Aaron. "Why the Price of Cable TV Stopped Going Up So Fast This Year." *Fortune*, November 15, 2018. http://fortune.com/2018/11/15/average-cable-tv-bill-cord-cutting/.

Price, Joseph L. *Rounding the Bases: Baseball and Religion in America*. Macon, GA: Mercer University Press, 2006.

Przybylski, Andrew, and Netta Weinstein. "Can You Connect with Me Now? How the Presence of Mobile Communication Technology Influences Face-to-Face Conversation Quality." *Journal of Social and Personal Relationships* 30, no. 3 (May 2013): 237–46.

Putnam, Robert. *Bowling Alone: The Collapse and Revival of American Community*. New York: Simon & Schuster, 2000.

———. "Tuning In, Tuning Out: The Strange Disappearance of Social Capital in America." *PS: Political Science and Politics* 28, no. 4 (December 1995): 664–83.

Rahner, Karl. *Foundations of Christian Faith: An Introduction to the Idea of Christianity*. Translated by William V. Dych. New York: Seabury Press, 1978.

Rao, Mayuree, Ashkan Afshin, Gitanjali Singh, and Dariush Mozaffarian. "Do Healthier Foods and Diet Patterns Cost More than Less Healthy Options? A Systematic Review and Meta-Analysis." *BMJ Open* 3, no. 12 (December 5, 2013): doi:10.1136/bmjopen-2013-004277.

Rathbone, Eleanor F. *The Disinherited Family: A Plea for the Endowment of the Family*. London: Edward Arnold, 1924.
Ravishankar, Karthik. "The Establishment Clause's Hydra: The *Lemon* Test in the Circuit Courts." *University of Dayton Law Review* 41, no. 2 (2016): 261–301.
Rawls, John. "The Idea of an Overlapping Consensus." *Oxford Journal of Legal Studies* 7, no. 1 (Spring 1987): 1–25.
Ray, Rebecca, Milla Sanes, and John Schmitt. *No-Vacation Nation Revisited*. Washington, DC: Center for Economic and Policy Research, 2013.
Rieger, Joseph. *Faith on the Road: A Short Theology of Travel and Justice*. Rev. ed. Downers Grove, IL: InterVarsity Press, 2015.
Ripley, Amanda. "The Case against High-School Sports." *The Atlantic*, October 2013. www.theatlantic.com/magazine/archive/2013/10/the-case-against-high-school-sports/309447/.
Roberts, Paul. *The Impulse Society: America in the Age of Instant Gratification*. New York: Bloomsbury, 2014.
Robinson, John P., and Geoffrey Godbey. *Time for Life: The Surprising Ways Americans Use Their Time*. University Park: Pennsylvania State University Press, 1997.
Robinson, John P., and Steve Martin. "Of Time and Television," *Annals of the American Academy of Political and Social Science* 625 (September 2009): 74–86.
Rubio, Julie Hanlon. *A Christian Theology of Marriage and Family*. New York: Paulist Press, 2003.
———. *Family Ethics: Practices for Christians*. Washington, DC: Georgetown University Press, 2010.
Ruiz, Rebecca R., and Steve Lohr. "FCC Approves Net Neutrality Rules, Classifying Broadband Internet Service as a Utility." *New York Times*, February 27, 2015. www.nytimes.com/2015/02/27/technology/net-neutrality-fcc-vote-internet-utility.html.
Ryan, John A. *A Living Wage: Its Ethical and Economic Aspects*. New York: Macmillan, 1906.
Ryan, Tracii, and Sophia Xenos. "Who Uses Facebook? An Investigation into the Relationship between the Big Five, Shyness, Narcissism, Loneliness, and Facebook Usage." *Computers in Human Behavior* 27, no. 5 (September 2011): 1658–64.
Ryken, Leland. *Redeeming the Time: A Christian Approach to Work and Leisure*. Grand Rapids: Baker Books, 1995.
Sacrosanctum concilium (Constitution on the Sacred Liturgy). December 4, 1964. www.vatican.va/archive/hist_councils/ii_vatican_council/documents/vat-ii_const_19631204_sacrosanctum-concilium_en.html.
Saliers, Don E. *Worship as Theology: Foretaste of Glory Divine*. Nashville: Abingdon Press, 1994.
Sandel, Michael. *Democracy's Discontent: America in Search of a Public Philosophy*. Cambridge, MA: Harvard University Press, 1996.
———. "The Moral Economy of Speculation: Gambling, Finance, and the Common Good." *Tanner Lectures on Human Values* 33 (2014): 333–59.
———. "Sports and Civic Identity." In *Public Philosophy: Essays on Morality*, 81–84. Cambridge, MA: Harvard University Press, 2005.
Schlozman, Kay Lehman, Sidney Verba, and Henry E. Brady. *The Unheavenly Chorus: Unequal Political Participation and the Broken Promise of American Democracy*. Princeton, NJ: Princeton University Press, 2012.
Schneiders, Sandra. "A Vow of Poverty." In Himes and Kelly, *Poverty*, 41–48.

Schor, Juliet B. "The (Even More) Overworked American." In de Graaf, *Take Back Your Time*, 6–11.

———. *The Overworked American: The Unexpected Decline of Leisure*. New York: Basic Books, 1991.

Shadle, Matthew. "Where Is Structural Sin in *Laudato si'*?" *Catholic Moral Theology*, November 2, 2015. https://catholicmoraltheology.com/where-is-structural-sin-in-laudato-si/.

Shakhnov, Kirill. "How Wealth Inequality Entices Talent into Finance." *World Economic Forum*, January 19, 2015. www.weforum.org/agenda/2015/01/how-wealth-inequality-entices-talent-into-finance/.

Shaw, Susan M., Mark E. Havitz, and Fern M. Delemere. "'I Decided to Invest in My Kids' Memories': Family Vacations, Memories, and the Social Construction of the Family." *Tourism Culture and Communication* 8, no. 1 (2008): 13–26.

Sherry, John L. "Flow and Media Enjoyment." *Communication Theory* 14, no. 4 (November 2004): 328–47.

Shippen, Nichole Marie. "Review of *Idleness: A Philosophical Essay*, by Brian O'Connor." *Notre Dame Philosophical Review*, November 18, 2018. https://ndpr.nd.edu/news/idleness-a-philosophical-essay/.

Shirky, Clay. *Cognitive Surplus: Creativity and Generosity in a Connected Age*. New York: Penguin Books, 2010.

Sievernich, Michael. "Social Sin and Its Acknowledgment." In *The Fate of Confession*, edited by Mary Collins and David Power (*Concilium*, no. 190, 52–63). Edinburgh: T. and T. Clark, 1987.

Skinner, Daniel. "'Keep Your Government Hands Off My Medicare!' An Analysis of Media Effects on Tea Party Health Care Politics." *New Political Science* 34, no. 4 (December 2012): 605–19.

Slater, Thomas. *A Manual of Moral Theology for English-Speaking Countries*. 3rd ed. New York: Benziger Brothers, 1908.

Slaughter, Anne-Marie. "Why Women Still Can't Have It All." *The Atlantic*, July 2012. www.theatlantic.com/magazine/archive/2012/07/why-women-still-cant-have-it-all/309020/.

Smith, Christian, and Melinda Lundquist Denton. *Soul Searching: The Religious and Spiritual Lives of American Teenagers*. Oxford: Oxford University Press, 2005.

Smith, Paul. "Playing Under Pressure: Sport, Public Service Broadcasting, and the British Broadcasting Corporation." *International Communication Gazette* 27, no. 2 (March 2017): 203–16.

Snarr, C. Melissa. *All You That Labor: Religion and Ethics in the Living Wage Movement*. New York: New York University Press, 2011.

Sobrino, Jon. "Bearing with One Another in Faith." In *Theology of Christian Solidarity*. Edited by Jon Sobrino and Juan Hernández Pico. Translated by Phillip Berryman. Maryknoll, NY: Orbis Books, 1985.

———. "Communion, Conflict, and Ecclesial Solidarity." In Ellacuría and Sobrino, *Mysterium liberationis*, 615–35.

———. *Christ the Liberator: A View from the Victims*. Translated by Paul Burns. Maryknoll, NY: Orbis Books, 2001.

Soltis, Kathryn Getek. "*Gaudium et spes* and the Family: A Social Tradition with Room to Grow." *Journal of Catholic Social Thought* 12, no. 2 (2015): 245–58.

Song, Felicia Wu. *Virtual Communities: Bowling Alone, Online Together*. New York: Peter Lang, 2009.

Spohn, William. *Go and Do Likewise: Jesus and Ethics.* New York: Continuum, 1999.
Spracklen, Karl. *The Meaning and Purpose of Leisure: Habermas and Leisure at the End of Modernity.* New York: Palgrave Macmillan, 2009.
Stausberg, Michael. *Religion and Tourism: Crossroads, Destinations, and Encounters.* New York: Routledge, 2011.
Stebbins, Robert A. *The Idea of Leisure: First Principles.* New Brunswick, NJ: Transaction Publishers, 2012.
Steers, Mai-Ly N., Robert E. Wickham, and Linda K. Acitelli. "Seeing Everyone Else's Highlight Reels: How Facebook Usage Is Linked to Depressive Symptoms." *Journal of Social and Clinical Psychology* 33, no. 8 (October 2014): 701–31.
Stephens, Bret. "Alex Honnold, a Soul Freed in 'Free Solo.'" *New York Times*, October 25, 2018. www.nytimes.com/2018/10/25/opinion/alex-honnold-free-solo-movie.tml.
Stewart, Jack. "Stop Worrying about Buying Carbon Offsets for Your Flights." *Wired*, November 20, 2018. www.wired.com/story/airline-emissions-carbon-offsets-travel/.
Stewart, Walter F., et al. "Symptoms from Repeated Intentional and Unintentional Head Impact in Soccer Players." *Neurology* 88, no. 9 (February 28, 2017): 901–8.
Stewart-Kroeker, Sarah. "Resisting Idolatry and Instrumentalisation in Loving the Neighbour: The Significance of the Pilgrimage Motif for Augustine's *Usus-Fruitio* Distinction." *Studies in Christian Ethics* 27, no. 2 (2014): 202–21.
Stites, Adam. "How Does the NFL's Concussion Protocol Work?" SBNation, February 4, 2018. www.sbnation.com/nfl/2016/9/18/12940926/nfl-concussion-protocol-explained.
Strauss-Blasche, G., C. Ekmekcioglu, and W. Marktl. "Does Vacation Enable Recuperation? Changes in Well-Being Associated with Time Away from Work." *Occupational Medicine* 50, no. 3 (2000): 167–72.
Sullivan, Joseph T. "The Sunday Rest: The Negative Aspects of the Precept." STD dissertation, Pontifical University of Saint Thomas Aquinas, 1952.
Surdam, David George. *The Big Leagues Go to Washington: Congress and Sports Antitrust, 1951–1989.* Urbana: University of Illinois Press, 2015.
Sylvester, Charles D. "The Ethics of Play, Leisure, and Recreation in the Twentieth Century, 1900–1983." *Leisure Sciences* 9, no. 3 (1987): 173–88.
Taylor, Betsey. "Recapturing Childhood." In de Graaf, *Take Back Your Time*, 46–51.
Taylor, Charles. "Atomism." In *Philosophical Papers, Volume 2: Philosophy and the Human Sciences*, 187–210. Cambridge: Cambridge University Press, 1985.
Taylor, Gregory, and Barbara Thomass. "Sports Rights and Public Service Media / Public Broadcasting: Case Studies on Economic and Political Implications." *International Communication Gazette* 79, no. 2 (March 2017): 111–19.
Tessman, Lisa. *Burdened Virtues: Virtue Ethics for Liberatory Struggles.* Oxford: Oxford University Press, 2005.
Tillich, Paul. *Systematic Theology, Volume 1.* Chicago: Chicago University Press, 1951.
Tillman, Fritz. *The Master Calls: A Handbook of Morals for the Layman.* Translated by Gregory J. Roettger. Baltimore: Helicon Press, 1963.
Timothy, Dallen, and Daniel H. Olsen. *Tourism, Religion, and Spiritual Journeys.* New York: Routledge, 2006.
Towey, Cathleen A. "Flow: The Benefits of Pleasure Reading and Tapping Readers' Interests." *Acquisitions Librarian* 13, no. 25 (2000): 131–40.
Turkle, Sherry. *Alone Together: Why We Expect More from Technology and Less from Each Other.* New York: Basic Books, 2011.

———. *Reclaiming Conversation: The Power of Talk in a Digital Age.* New York: Penguin Press, 2015.

US Census Bureau. "Households and Families: 2010." Census.gov, April 2010. www.census.gov/prod/cen2010/briefs/c2010br-14.pdf.

US Conference of Catholic Bishops. *Economic Justice for All: Pastoral Letter on Catholic Social Teaching and the US Economy.* Washington, DC: US Conference of Catholic Bishops, 1986.

———. *Ethical and Religious Directives for Catholic Health Care Services.* 5th ed. Washington, DC: US Conference of Catholic Bishops, 2009.

———. *Forming Consciences for Faithful Citizenship.* Washington, DC: US Conference of Catholic Bishops, 2015.

US Department of Health and Human Services. "Poverty Guidelines." January 11, 2019. https://aspe.hhs.gov/poverty-guidelines.

US Environmental Protection Agency. "Sources of Greenhouse Gas Emissions." April 10, 2019. www.epa.gov/ghgemissions/sources-greenhouse-gas-emissions.

Valiante, Gio. *Golf Flow: Master Your Mind, Master the Course.* Champaign, IL: Human Kinetics, 2013.

Van Melsen, Andrew G. *From Atomos to Atom: The History of the Concept Atom.* Translated by Henry J. Koren. Mineola, NY: Dover, 2004.

Veblen, Thorstein. *The Theory of the Leisure Class: An Economic Study in the Evolution of Institutions.* New York: Macmillan, 1899.

Verduyn, Philippe, David Seungjae Lee, Jiyoung Park, Holly Shablack, Ariana Orvell, Joseph Bayer, Oscar Ybarra, John Jonides, and Ethan Kross. "Passive Facebook Use Undermines Affective Well-Being: Experimental and Longitudinal Evidence." *Journal of Experimental Psychology* 144, no. 2 (April 2015): 480–88.

Vereecke, Louis. "Repos du Dimanche et oeuvres serviles." *Lumière et Vie* 11, no. 58 (June–July 1962): 50–74.

Waldron, Travis. "The NBA's New TV Deal Includes Good News for the WNBA." *Think Progress*, October 7, 2014. https://thinkprogress.org/the-nbas-new-tv-deal-includes-good-news-for-the-wnba-425e99fad164/.

Walker, Charles J. "Experiencing Flow: Is Doing It Together Better than Doing It Alone?" *Journal of Positive Psychology* 5, no. 1 (January 2010): 3–11.

Walker, James R., and Robert V. Bellamy. *Center Field Shot: A History of Baseball and Television.* Lincoln: University of Nebraska Press, 2008.

Wallsten, Scott. *What Are We Not Doing When We're Online?* Cambridge, MA: National Bureau of Economic Research, 2013.

Wall Street Journal. "Data Point: How Many Hours Do Millennials Eat Up a Day?" March 13, 2014. http://blogs.wsj.com/digits/2014/03/13/data-point-how-many-hours-do-millennials-eat-up-a-day/.

Ward, Kate. "Toward a Christian Virtue Account of Moral Luck." *Journal of the Society of Christian Ethics* 38, no. 1 (Spring–Summer 2018): 131–45.

Webber, Jonathan. "Character, Attitude and Disposition." *European Journal of Philosophy* 23, no. 4 (December 2015): 1082–96.

Weber, René, Ron Tamborini, Amber Westcott-Baker, and Benjamin Kantor. "Theorizing Flow and Media Enjoyment as Cognitive Synchronization of Attentional Reward Networks." *Communication Theory* 19, no. 4 (November 2009): 397–422.

Wellman, Barry, Anabel Quan Haase, James Witte, and Keith Hampton. "Does the Internet Increase, Decrease, or Supplement Social Capital? Social Networks, Participation, and

Community Commitment." *American Behavioral Scientist* 45, no. 3 (November 2001): 436–55.
Wellman, Barry, and Bernie Hogan. "Connected Lives: The Project." With Kristen Berg, Jeffrey Boase, Juan-Antonio Carrasco, Rochelle Côté, Jennifer Kayahara, Tracy L. M. Kennedy, and Phuoc Tran. In *Networked Neighbourhoods: The Connected Community in Context*. Edited by Patrick Purcell. London: Springer-Verlag, 2006.
Wells, Samuel. "Rethinking Service." *The Cresset* 76, no. 4 (Easter 2013): 6–14.
Williams, Joan. *Unbending Gender: Why Family and Work Conflict and What to Do about It*. New York: Oxford University Press, 2000.
Williams, Raymond. *Keywords: A Vocabulary of Culture and Society*. 3rd ed. New York: Oxford University Press, 2015.
Williams, Tannis Macbeth, ed. *The Impact of Television: A Natural Experiment in Three Communities*. Orlando: Academic Press, 1986.
Williams, Tannis Macbeth, and A. Gordon Handford. "Television and Other Leisure Activities." In Williams, *Impact of Television*, 143–213.
Willoughby, Teena, Paul J. C. Adachi, and Marie Good. "A Longitudinal Study of the Association between Violent Video Game Play and Aggression among Adolescents." *Developmental Psychology* 48, no. 4 (July 2012): 1044–57.
Wilson, Timothy D., David A. Reinhard, Erin C. Westgate, Daniel T. Gilbert, Nicole Ellerbeck, Cheryl Hahn, Casey L. Brown, and Adi Shaked. "Just Think: The Challenges of the Disengaged Mind." *Science* 345, no. 6192 (July 4, 2014): 75–77.
Winn, Marie. *The Plug-In Drug: Television, Computers, and Family Life*. 25th annual ed. New York: Penguin Books, 2002.
Wise, Kevin, Saleem Alhaash, and Hyojung Park. "Emotional Responses during Social Information Seeking on Facebook." *Cyberpsychology, Behavior, and Social Networking* 13, no. 5 (2010): 555–62.
Witherington, Ben, III. *The Rest of Life: Rest, Play, Eating, Studying, Sex from a Kingdom Perspective*. Grand Rapids: Wm. B. Eerdmans, 2012.
———. *Work: A Kingdom Perspective on Labor*. Grand Rapids: Wm. B. Eerdmans, 2011.
Wojcicki, Susan. "Paid Maternity Leave Is Good for Business." *Wall Street Journal*, December 16, 2014. www.wsj.com/articles/susan-wojcicki-paid-maternity-leave-is-good-for-business-1418773756?mod=e2tw.
Wolfteich, Claire E. "Time Poverty, Women's Labor, and Catholic Social Teaching: A Practical Theological Exploration." *Journal of Moral Theology* 2, no. 2 (June 2013): 40–59.
World Travel and Tourism Council. "Economic Impact." No date. www.wttc.org/economic-impact/.
You, Sukkyung, Euikyung Kim, and Unkyung No. "Impact of Violent Video Games on the Social Behaviors of Adolescents: The Mediating Role of Emotional Competence." *School Psychology International* 36, no. 1 (February 2015): 94–111.
Zabriskie, Ramon B., and Bryan P. McCormick. "Parent and Child Perspectives of Family Leisure Involvement and Satisfaction with Family Life." *Journal of Leisure Research* 35, no. 2 (2003): 163–89.

INDEX

"absent presence," 143
American Time Use Survey, 129n1, 133, 135
Aquinas, Thomas: on goodness of creation, xiii; on humanity's last end, 20, 66, 80n6; and ordering of love, 69-70, 74-75, 77, 80n24, 185; on recreation, 23
Aristotle, 6, 14, 15, 17, 38, 206
Augustine of Hippo: on goodness of creation, xiii; on heavenly rest, 20, 28n68, 68; insights applied to leisure, 21-22, 64, 206; insights applied to recreation, 25, 206; on use and enjoyment, 4, 17-19, 28n61, 28n66, 206, 212

Bain-Selbo, Eric, 159-60, 161
Banner, Michael, xx
baseball, 125, 126, 127, 159, 169, 178n9
Beauchamp, Tom, 47-48
Bellah, Robert, 39, 58n30, 177n3
Benedict XVI, 37, 45, 195
"Big Sort," 39, 58n33
Bishop, Bill, 39
Bonhoeffer, Dietrich, 162

Caritas in veritate, 37, 195
Catechism of the Catholic Church, 68, 71
Cates, Diana Fritz, 65
Catholic social teaching, xxvi, 32, 33, 34, 37, 43, 44
Catholic theological anthropology, *see* theological anthropology
Centesimus annus, 37
charity, 33, 75, 127, 216; ordering of, 69, 70, 74, 80n24, 185; *see also* love of God; love of neighbor; love of self

chronic traumatic encephalopathy (CTE), 165
Clark, Meghan J., 37, 46,
Cloutier, David, 186
common good: Catholic account of, xix, 51-52, 126; and flourishing, 56, 126-27; guiding structural transformation, 53-54, 56, 83, 131, 192, 207; participation in, xix, 128, 129, 148; and preferential option for the poor, 42, 43, 93, 147, 215; responsibility for, 127, 161, 212, 214, 215; and solidarity, 41-42, 43, 83; and stadium subsidies, 173-76; and structural sin, 54, 56, 168-69, 171, 172, 173-76; *see also* theological anthropology, and the common good
communion, 24, 65, 69, 79, 206
communion of the saints, 80n18
Compendium of the Social Doctrine of the Church, 65
concussions, 165-66, 178n29
Connors, Russel, 51
conscience: formation of, 50-52, 216; judicial conscience, 50; process of conscience/2, 51-52, 54-55, 70, 128, 191, 207, 216; as site of discernment, xxiii
consumerism, 84, 190
conversion (personal), xxiv, 53; *see also* structural transformation
cooperation with evil, 50, 167, 179nn37-38, 198-99, 204n86
Copeland, M. Shawn, 46
Csikszentmihalyi, Mihaly: on finding flow, 75, 78; on flow, 9-12, 19, 67, 71, 206, 206; on television, 82n56, 82n58, 75, 78, 113-14

243

CTE (chronic traumatic encephalopathy), 165

DeCosse, David, 204n86
Dicastery for the Promotion of Human Development, 192
digital distraction, 80n17, 143
digital media use: access to, 147; defined, 133; displacing in-person connections, 142–43, 145, 150; eroding relational capacities, 143–44, 145, 151–52, 208; intentionality and, 145–46, 150, 153, 208; popularity of, 135, 146, 154n5, 208; video as, 135, 153; *see also* internet access; social media; video games
Doohan, Leonard, xxii
Doran, Kevin P., 47
Durkheim, Émile, 158, 160

economic ethics, 195–96
égoïsme à la famille, 187, 191
Elder-Vass, Dave, 42
Eliade, Mircea, xix, 159
Ellis, Joseph, 125
enjoyment and use, *see* use and enjoyment
environmental ethics, 59n92, 192, 193–95, 196–200, 209
ethical discernment, *see* moral discernment
Evans, Christopher, 159
everyday solidarity, 31–32, 44; orientation to relational flourishing, 51, 54, 64, 65, 206; principle of, 49–52, 63, 65, 206–7; virtue of, 53–55, 207; *see also* solidarity
examen, 70

Fagerberg, David, 81nn43–44
family: common human family, 34, 35, 37; digital media and, 139, 142, 143, 155n33; effects of television on, 118, 130n35; effects of travel on, 181, 182–87, 209; family friendly workplace policies, 101; household responsibilities, 16; leisure and, 67, 97; and ordering of love, 69, 77; qualifying moral responsibilities to, 187, 209, 210; *see also* living wage, family living wage

Federal Communications Commission (FCC), 149
feminist theology, 25, 46, 90
fidelity, 77, 187
finitude, *see* human finitude
Finn, Daniel, 42, 53
Florida, Richard, 58n33
flourishing, *see* human flourishing
flow: "co-active flow," 77; defined, 9–10; "interactive flow," 77; and liturgy, 73; motivations and, 10–11, 27n35; and prayer, 71–72; theological parallels, 19–21; *see also* Csikszentmihalyi, Mihaly; leisure, connected to flow; television, inimical to flow; video games, and flow
football, 159–60, 161, 165–166, 178n29, 178n32, 178n34
Forney, Craig, 159
Fowles, Jib, 114
Francis: on conscience, 217; on environmental concerns, 59n92, 193–94: on prayer, 72; on solidarity, 45, 56; on technology, 144–47, 153, 208; on travel, 192
Frankena, William, 49
free time: "core" and "balance" pursuits, 183, 202n7; insufficient theological attention to, xxi–xxv; moral significance of, xvi, xxiv–xxv, 205; negative view of, xiii–xiv, xv; paradox, 85, 103; structural obstacles to, xvi, xvii, xxv, xxviiin28, 84–86; technology affecting, 67, 80n14, 97; *see also* leisure; recreation
free time gap, 85, 86, 96, 102, 103
Fukuyama, Francis, 39

Gaudium et Spes, 35, 36–37, 57n10
Gergen, Kenneth, 143
Golden Rule, xxii
Goldstein, Valerie Saiving, 25
golf, 75
Graham, Mark, 194–95
Gula, Richard, 51

Hammerstein, Oscar, II, xiii, xiv, xv, xxviii
health care ethics, 203n73, 211, 214–16, 217n9

INDEX 245

Heintzman, Paul, xxii
Hinze, Christine Firer, 46, 90
Honnold, Alex, 163–64
hospitality, 188–92, 201, 209
human finitude, 23
human flourishing: as aim in discernment, 54–55, 65, 112, 116, 187, 210; Catholic vision for, xix, xxvi; digital media and, 134, 136, 138, 142, 143, 145–46, 151–153; economic well-being and, 195; for all, xxv, 25, 52, 55, 80, 101, 103, 191; free time and, 64, 78, 79, 92, 134, 146, 205, 207; realized in self gift, 35, 52, 54, 157; relational aspects, xxvii, 35, 63, 65, 76, 79–80, 187; spectator sports and, 162, 167, 176; structural constraints on, 55, 85, 91, 123, 151–52, 167; television and, 118, 119, 121, 128; travel and, 182, 185, 191, 200, 209; video games and, 139; in union with God, 65–66, 68, 79

idolatry, 21–22, 23
individualism: atomistic form of, 33, 38–40, 52, 57n26, 58n30; contrasts with theological anthropology, xix, 33, 36–37, 207; see also "networked individualism"
integral ecology, 194
internet access: as an ethical concern, 147–48, 208; as a public good, 149, 150–51; in public spaces, 151–52, 156n69; structural constraints on, 148–50, 151–52
intrinsic evil, 167, 179n37
Iso-Ahola, Seppo, 5–6

"job spill," 97; see also, time poverty
John Paul II: on rest, 96, 98; on solidarity, 37, 40–42, 44, 48, 53; on travel, 188, 190, 191, 192, 201
John XXIII, 35, 58n38, 96
Johnson, Elizabeth, 80n18
justice: liturgy and, 73, 81n43; living wage and, 87–88, 89, 92; as moral responsibility, xxvii, 77, 187; rest as demand of, 24; tension with love, 93, 106n52

Keenan, James, 50, 74, 77, 81n49, 202n26

Kraus, Richard, 15, 16
Kubey, Robert, 82n56, 113, 114, 131n36

Lamoureux, Patricia, 105n28
Laudato si', 194
leisure: commodification of, 87, 124, 125, 128; connected to flow, 10–13, 66–67, 72–78; definition of, 4, 5–13, 25; distinguished from recreation, 3, 19, 63, 64, 67–68; ethical discernment and, 63–64; ideal nature of, 7–8, 12, 67, 79; intrinsic motivation, 6, 12; intrinsic value of, 6, 10, 17, 19, 64– 67, 79, 206; ordering of, 68, 69–71, 74, 79; perceived freedom and, 6, 26n10, 26n13; prefiguring heavenly rest, 19, 21–22, 65–66, 73, 210; priority of, 64–68, 78, 79, 111; and relational flourishing, 64, 65–69, 71–78, 79, 207; rest and activity in, 11–12, 19, 20–21; serving relationship with God, 71–74; serving relationship with others, 76–78; serving relationship with self, 74–76; and spirituality, xxii; subjective accounts of, 5–6, 7; theological value of, 19, 21–22, 25–26, 65–66
Leo XIII, 87, 96, 105n28,
liberation theology, 40, 41, 45, 46
Lipset, Seymor Martin, 57n21
liturgy, 73–74
living wage: alternative to legal mandates, 94; benefitting leisure, 87, 88, 95; calculating, 92–93; Catholic activism for, 88–89; Catholic theology and, 87–88, 89, 105n28; family living wage, 89–92, 105n28; and "just price," 87; as legal minimum, 94, 207; qualitative v. quantitative determination, 88–89
love of God, 20, 33, 65, 69; see also, charity; love of neighbor; love of self
love of neighbor, 33, 65, 69, 74, 80n24; see also, charity; love of God; love of self
love of self, 74–75; see also charity; love of God, love of neighbor

MacIntyre, Alasdair, 27n35
Malesic, Jonathan, xxviiin6

Massingale, Bryan, 178n22
Mater et magistra, 35, 58n36, 96
"maternal wall," 101
McAuliffe, Patricia, 45
McCormick, Patrick, 51, 188, 190, 192
Mill, John Stuart, 87
Miller, Vincent, 45, 46
Moltmann, Jürgen, 59n90
moral discernment: necessity of, xvi, xix, 55; practice of, xx, 51–52, 211–12; strengthening, xx–xxi, 33, 42, 211–17
moral principles, 47–48, 49–50

National Council of Catholic Women (NCCW), 88–89
net neutrality, 149–50, 155n65
"networked individualism," 137
Neulinger, John, 6–7, 8, 13
Neumeyer, Martin and Esther, 15
Neville, Graham, xiv
Niebuhr, Reinhold, 23, 93, 106n52

O'Connell, Timothy, 51
O'Connor, Brian, xiv
OECD (Organization for Economic Cooperation and Development) countries, 98, 99, 101, 102
ordering of love, *see* charity, ordering of
ordinary life and theological ethics, xvi, xviii–xxi, 31–32, 210–17; framework for integrating, 42, 49–56, 216–17; free time's contributions to, xxii–xxiii, 31, 78–79, 205–206, 209–10; *see also* moral discernment
Organization for Economic Cooperation and Development (OECD) countries, 98, 99, 101, 102

panem et circenses, 161
parental leave, 100–102
Paul VI, 37, 195
Peters, Rebecca Todd, 46
Pieper, Josef, xiv, 7, 8, 11–12, 206
Pius XII, 34
Populorum progressio, 37, 44, 195
poverty guidelines, 92, 93, 105n46
prayer, 72, 81n38; *see also* flow and prayer

preferential option for the poor: in Catholic social teaching, 41–42; and digital media use, 147; lens for ethical analysis, 92, 93, 98, 126, 171, 215; and spectator sports, 171, 174; *see also* common good, and preferential option for the poor; solidarity, and preferential option for the poor
principle of cooperation, *see* cooperation with evil
principles, *see* moral principles
process of conscience/2, *see* conscience, process of conscience/2
proportionate reason, 179n37, 198–99, 209, 204n87
prudence, 106n79, 198, 200; *see also* proportionate reason
public goods, 126–27, 149, 150, 151, 171, 175
public libraries, 126
public service broadcasters, 171–72
Putnam, Robert, 40, 116–17, 120,

reading, 76, 114, 126
recreation: connected to work, 15–16, 23, 24; definition of, 4, 13–17, 25; distinguished from leisure, 3, 13, 15, 16–17, 19, 63; extrinsic motivation and, 13–14, 22; in Jesus's life, 24; as response to finitude, 23–24; theological value of, 22–25, 25–26
relational flourishing, *see* human flourishing
Rerum novarum, 23, 87, 90,
revelation, 72, 81n35, 188
Rubio, Julie Hanlon, xviii
running, 75
Ryan, John A., 88–89, 90, 92, 104n24
Ryken, Leland, xxii

Sabbath, xxii, 20, 65, 73, 81n43
Schor, Juliet, 84
Second Vatican Council, 16, 35, 37, 40
self-care, xxvii, 24, 74, 76 81n49, 201, 215; *see also* love of self
Sharma, Hemant, 125
sin, 23, 70, 50; *see also* structural sin
soccer, 125, 161, 164–65, 166, 179n40, 196

INDEX   247

social media: and envy, 137, 146; negative social effects of, 136–38, 144, 153; purported relational benefits of, 135–36, 138, 153; tendency toward passive use of, 136; time spent with, 135, 138

solidarity; as antidote to individualism, 36–38, 40, 43; Catholic account of, xiv, 32–43, 44–47; for collective agents, 44, 46; and conflict, 162, 178n22; deceptive forms of, 160–62; descriptive and prescriptive dimensions of, 34–35, 36, 57n8; incarnational, 46; for personal agents, 45–46; and preferential option for the poor, 41–42, 43, 52, 83; prescriptive ambiguity, 47; as a principle, 47, 49, 58n36; and structural sin, 40–43, 53, 54; theological anthropology and, 35–36, 43, 57n10; as a virtue, 41, 47, 48–49; *see also* common good, and solidarity; everyday solidarity; structural transformation, solidarity and; theological anthropology

spectator sports: antitrust laws and, 170, 175–76; broadcasting revenues, 169–72, 177, 179n44, 179n51, 179n56; as civil religion, 158–60, 162, 208; communal broadcast viewing, 172, 177, 209; free agency, 169; as an instrumental good, 162; intolerable sacrifices of participants, 165–67, 176–77, 178n29, 208–9; leagues and structural constraints, 164–65, 172; moral responsibilities to participants, 162–67, 208; perverse incentives and, 168–69, 171, 209; potential for cultivating solidarity, 157, 158, 160, 176, 177; semblance of solidarity in, 160–62; stadium subsidies, 173–76, 177; *see also* baseball; football; soccer; sports

sports: cultural influence of, 157; as leisure, 76, 78, 81n55, 124–25, 157; structural obstacles to enjoying, 125, 126, 127; *see also* spectator sports

Stewart-Kroeker, Sarah, 19

structural injustices, *see* structural sin

structural sin (structures of sin), xxiii–xxiv, 40–41, 53, 58n38, 194; causal power of, 42–43, 204n88; and spectator sports, 168, 174; *see also* structural transformation

structural transformation, xxiii–xxiv, 40; accompanying personal conversion, xxiv, xxviiin27, 33, 42–43, 53; solidarity and, 45–46, 53, 54–55, 83–84

structure of grace, 54

subsidiarity, 56, 150

Sunday rest, *see* work, and Sunday observance

Sylvester, Charles, 14

Taylor, Charles, 38, 39

technology, *see* free time, technology affecting

television (TV): effects on relational flourishing, 116–19, 120–21, 124, 128, 131n41; effects on social capital, 116–17, 118, 120, 130n24, 130n33; as free time default, 111, 112, 114–15, 123, 128, 129n2; goal of watching less, 115, 119, 129, 208; "golden age," 121; inimical to flow, 82n56, 82n58, 112, 113–14, 115–16; intentionality and, 114–15, 121; negative residual effects of, 115, 119–20, 128; passivity of, 113–14, 115; prioritizing recreation over leisure, 111, 112, 115–16; recreational potential of, 114, 119, 120, 122, 128, 134; reforming structural constraints affecting, 126–28, 129, 208; relative affordability, 87, 122–24, 127–28, 129, 131n43; and spectator sports, 169–72, 177; structural constraints affecting, 121, 122–25, 129

Tessman, Lisa, 55, 60n100

theological anthropology: basis for everyday solidarity, xxv, 32, 205, 206, 210, 214; and the common good, xix, 161, 214; and creatureliness, 23; and ethical discernment, xxii, xxvi, 43, 50, 85, 216; full realization of, 25, 54, 56, 185; and ordering of love, 69; relational emphases, xix, 33, 50, 55, 57n10, 153, 185; and solidarity, 35–36, 51, 57n10, 206; *see also* human flourishing; solidarity

time poverty, 95, 97, 98; distinguished from resource poverty, 83–84, 86; negative

effects on leisure, 95, 100, 102; rooted in work, 97, 98
tourism, *see* travel
travel: contributions to relational flourishing, 181–82, 183–92, 200, 209; economic impact, 192, 193, 197–98, 199–200, 201, 204n84; environmental impact, 192–93, 196–97, 198, 199–200, 201; ethical discernment and, 185–86, 193, 198–200, 201, 209; exploitative structures and, 190, 197, 200, 203n49; and family bonding, 184–87; luxury and, 186; responsibilities of hosts, 188, 189; responsibilities to hosts, 188–92, 201; theological significance, 182, 202n3
Turkle, Sherry, 67, 143–44, 152
TV, *see* television

US Conference of Catholic Bishops (USCCB), 179n38
use and enjoyment, 18–19, 21, 25, 28n61, 64, 206
US Women's national Team (soccer), 164–65
utilitarian assumptions, 6, 51, 67, 212

vacation time, 97–100

Veblen, Thorstein, 103
video games: and addictive behavior, 141; criticisms of, 138; effects of content, 138–39, 140, 153; effects on relationality, 138, 139, 141; and flow, 138, 139–40, 154n25; as leisure, 138, 139–40; recreational potential of, 141–2, 153; violent video games, 138–39, 140–41
virtue ethics, xviii, 48–49, 53, 54–55; and cardinal virtues, 74, 77, 202n26; *see also* charity; fidelity; hospitality; justice; prudence; self-care

watching television, *see* television
Wellman, Barry, 137
Wells, Samuel, 66, 131n55
Witherington III, Ben, xxii, xxiii–xxiv, xxixn32.
work: Catholic theology of, xiv, 16, 190, 213; effects on free time, 86, 95; and everyday solidarity, 213–14; and Sunday observance, 73, 96–97; working hours, 84–85, 95, 97, 104n7; *see also* parental leave; recreation, connected to work; time poverty, rooted in work; vacation time
work ethic, xiv, xv

ABOUT THE AUTHOR

CONOR M. KELLY is an assistant professor in the Department of Theology at Marquette University, where his teaching and research focus on the ways theology can provide resources for ethical discernment in ordinary life. His scholarly articles have appeared in a range of academic journals, including *Theological Studies*, the *Journal of Moral Theology*, *Horizons*, and the *Journal of Catholic Higher Education*. He coedited *Poverty: Responding Like Jesus*, with Kenneth R. Himes. During his free time, he enjoys running, cooking meals for friends and family, and outings with his wife and two young children.

www.ingramcontent.com/pod-product-compliance
Lightning Source LLC
Chambersburg PA
CBHW032034300426
44117CB00009B/1053